The History and Culture of
IROQUOIS DIPLOMACY

AN IROQUOIS BOOK

The History and Culture of
IROQUOIS DIPLOMACY

An Interdisciplinary Guide to the Treaties
of the Six Nations and Their League

FRANCIS JENNINGS, Editor
WILLIAM N. FENTON, Joint Editor
MARY A. DRUKE, Associate Editor
DAVID R. MILLER, Research Editor
for
The D'Arcy McNickle Center for the
History of the American Indian
The Newberry Library

SYRACUSE UNIVERSITY PRESS
1985

This work was made possible through the assistance of a research grant from the National Endowment for the Humanities and a publication grant from The Newberry Library.

Thanks are due to cartographer Judith Crawley Wojcik and General Editor William C. Sturtevant for the maps reproduced from *Handbook of North American Indians*, volume 15, *Northeast* (Smithsonian Institution, 1978). The editors are obliged also to the New York State Museum for courteous provision of the photograph of the Hiawatha Wampum Belt.

Library of Congress Cataloging in Publication Data
Main entry under title:

The History and culture of Iroquois diplomacy.

(An Iroquois book)
Bibliography: p.
Includes index.
1. Iroquois Indians—Government relations—To 1789—
Addresses, essays, lectures. 2. Indians of North America
—Government—Relations—To 1789—Addresses, essays,
lectures. 3. Iroquois Indians—Treaties—History—Address-
es, essays, lectures. 4. Indians of North America—
Treaties—History—Addresses, essays, lectures.
5. Iroquois Indians—History. I. Jennings, Francis,
1918- . II. Series.
E99.I7H63 1985   973'.0497   84-16234
ISBN 0-8156-2271-6

Manufactured in the United States of America

To the Iroquois People

"CONTRIBUTORS"

FRANCIS JENNINGS is Director Emeritus of the D'Arcy McNickle Center for the History of the American Indian at The Newberry Library. He holds the Ph.D. in American Civilization from the University of Pennsylvania, is a past president of the American Society for Ethnohistory and has served a term on the Executive Board of the Organization of American Historians. He is author of *The Invasion of America: Indians, Colonialism, and the Cant of Conquest* and *The Ambiguous Iroquois Empire: The Covenant Chain Confederation of Indian Tribes with English Colonies*, general editor of 29 volumes of The Newberry Library's bibliographical series on Indian history, and editor of the microfilm compilation *Iroquois Indians: A Documentary History*.

WILLIAM N. FENTON, Distinguished Professor of Anthropology Emeritus of the State University of New York at Albany, received the Ph.D. in Anthropology from Yale University. He is past president of the American Ethnological Society, the American Folklore Society, and the American Society for Ethnohistory; and he has presided for forty years over the interdisciplinary Conference on Iroquois Research which awarded him the honorary title of "Dean of Iroquois Studies." He has been awarded the Cornplanter Medal for Iroquois Research and the Peter Doctor Award of the Seneca Nation, and has recently been honored with a festschrift called *Extending the Rafters*. He has written more than 20 books and monographs, more than 80 articles, and is editor of *Parker on the Iroquois*.

MARY A. DRUKE has the Ph.D. in Anthropology from the University of Chicago. She has researched for the design of permanent exhibits at the Yager Museum of Hartwick College, and is revising her dissertation for publication.

MICHAEL K. FOSTER is Iroquoian Ethnologist at the Canadian National Museum of Man, Ottawa, an editor of *Extending the Rafters: Interdisciplinary Approaches to Iroquoian Studies*, and the author of articles on the ritual and semantics of Iroquois treaties. He is now doing field research on the meanings of symbols in wampum belts.

ROBERT J. SURTEES professes history at Nipissing University, Ontario. He is the author of *Canadian Indian Policy: A Critical Bibliography* and the textbook *The Original People* as well as research studies written for Indian and Northern Affairs Canada and the National Museum of Man, and he has been a consultant on *The Atlas of Great Lakes Indian History*.

DAVID R. MILLER currently serves as Associate Director of the D'Arcy McNickle Center for the History of the American Indian and is a Ph.D. candidate in cultural anthropology at Indiana University, Bloomington. Although a specialist in northern Plains Indians, he is responsible for the partial index completed by the project and for supervision of the microfilming and calendar creation stages.

CONTENTS

LIST OF MAPS

ACKNOWLEDGMENTS

W E ARE GRATEFUL to the many Indian persons who shared information and advice, especially Cayuga Chief Jacob E. Thomas; and to members of The Newberry Library staff, John Aubrey, Michael Kaplan, Steve Mandel, Terry Sullivan, and Michelene Fixico, who gave special attention to our project. We are indebted also to our colleagues, the editors of *The Atlas of Great Lakes Indian History* (University of Oklahoma Press, 1984) for their unstinting cooperation: Helen Hornbeck Tanner, Adele Hast, and Jacqueline Peterson.

Full acknowledgment to all the persons and institutions contributing to the general project that produced this book as one of its publications is set forth in *Iroquois Indians: A Documentary History* (Research Publications, 1984).

FJ

INTRODUCTION

THIS GUIDE is concerned with the political history of what Englishmen called the Five Nations (later Six Nations), Frenchmen called the Iroquois, and the people themselves called by a name that was rendered by Lewis Henry Morgan as Ho-dé-no-sau-nee and is currently spelled by the traditionalist Iroquois Grand Council as Houdenosaunee. The Iroquois were the aboriginal inhabitants of what is now upstate New York at the time of European invasion and colonization of America. In the records of the seventeenth and eighteenth centuries they never numbered more than about 20,000 people, all told, but they played an immensely important role as leaders of many Indian tribes and as intermediaries between the tribes and the English colonies.

Their importance has long been recognized by historians, but their activity ranged so widely, with so many complex developments, that no student has yet attempted to write a full history. The task of searching out all the relevant documents, scattered from California to Paris, has been daunting. Literally thousands of documents exist recording and concerning the treaties made by the Iroquois nations with the colonies of the Netherlands, France, and England, and subsequently with the United States, individual states, and Canada, as well as other Indian nations. Besides what these documents have to say about the Iroquois themselves, they are a mine of information about the struggles of colonies and empires to control North America. Yet they have been little used by historians of those struggles, and our understanding, especially of the colonial era, has consequently been impoverished.

The materials in this book have been written and compiled as part of a project to make available and accessible this vast "new" field of source materials for the professional historian and ethnologist; but the book is also intended for the lay reader as a readable introduction to the functioning of tribal government and diplomacy. It does not aspire to encyclopedic comprehensiveness of the vast literature on Iroquois history and culture; its purpose rather is to give direction to make those materials more accessible and understandable.

Though recorded treaties of the Iroquois have been preserved from as early as 1642, and there are references to even earlier negotiations, their significance has been obscured by European and Euramerican assumptions that Indians had no "real" governments and that the tribes were negligible in the conflicts of empires. These assumptions have been strengthened by the scattered and fragmented condition of the treaty documents which were invariably preserved as subordinate parts of the archives of colonies, states, and stateform nations. Nowhere, until this project was undertaken, has there existed an archive of Indian nations having a tribal form of government. Now such an archive has been assembled at the Newberry Library from texts copied in repositories throughout the United States and in the national archives of Canada, England, and France; but in order to grasp the full significance of the recorded events a reader needs to know how the treaty institution worked. Otherwise we might all be back at the stage of admiring the eloquence and drama displayed in these records without understanding what was really going on. Echoing Roger Williams' Key into the Language of America, the editors offer herein a key into the language and proceedings of Iroquois treaties. It will open the gate to a world of history and ethnology so little known as to deserve being called new despite its age.

Europeans entered ambivalently into treaty relationships with Indians. On the one hand, real relationships of power required negotiation rather than dictation. On the other hand, such negotiations flouted legal theories that assumed the sovereignty of European monarchs over the Indians; and in theory kings do not negotiate with their subjects. From the time of first contact between Europeans and Indians the ideology of Europeans has insisted that tribal Indians had no "true" government because Indians ordered their communities by kin relationships instead of the impersonal, bureaucratic European state form. Only Europeans, in this view, had "civil" government, so only Europeans were civilized. Because politics were assumed to be exclusively associated with the civil government that Indians supposedly lacked, Europeans assumed further that Indians had no political history.

Such assumptions have plagued scholars to the present day, but the kings' agents in America knew how to distinguish between theory and practice. They understood very well that Indians were organized in communities with functioning governments that exercised real powers of control over trade, territory, and military activity. These agents called the Indian governments "nations" and made treaties with them to take advantage of those nations' controls and powers.

The treaty documents refute the no-true-government myth on their face. These texts show colonial and imperial statesmen formally recognizing Indian chiefs as peers—"brethren"—with power and responsibility to act on behalf of their nations and to fulfill contracts. Recognition of, and purposeful interaction with, Indian political organizations is fully in evidence.

In focusing attention upon the political aspect of Iroquois history we have sought to overcome neglect and to show by overwhelming documentation that such a history did exist, contrary to the theories that Indian tribes had only "social" histories. In doing so, however, we have had to deal with some documents involved in legal disputes in current and anticipated court cases concerning rights to land and territory. We take no sides and pass no judgments on such litigation. The reference materials of our compilation at the Newberry Library will doubtless be useful to contending parties in various ways, but neither the documents nor our editorial comments have been made to help or disadvantage any party; nor has there been censorship from any source.

One purpose of this Guide is to help readers understand what is being said in the treaty texts. Like the diplomatic negotiations between European nation-states, these texts contain special formalities of protocol and conventions of phrase that the negotiating parties understood but that can be deciphered now only with careful scrutiny and an informed appreciation of cross-cultural interaction. It is possible to read the documents superficially and miss much of their significance because the treaty proceedings were conducted according to Iroquois ritual and in the phrasing of Iroquois metaphor. The passage of time has dimmed their meanings for a modern reader who needs to know that the metaphor was not childish babble—that its terms had meanings so precise that negotiators could quarrel harshly over whether *brother* or *father* was the proper term of address from an Indian chief to a colonial governor. When European officials tried to enforce their own terminology with their own meanings, resistance developed on the other side of the council fire, and the historical record became confused.

The ritualistic actions of the proceedings had symbolic significance also. If a negotiator accompanied his speech by passing a belt of wampum to the other side, he was making a serious proposition. If he failed to pass wampum, he was just talking. If the wampum was accepted, the proposition would be considered and a response given. If it was let drop to the ground or cast aside, the answer was instant rejection, with as much emphasis as the action indicated. To grasp a treaty's full meaning, therefore, one must note the actions taken as well as the words spoken.

This book includes background information about Iroquois political history and culture, a sample treaty with editorial commentary, and lists of reference data. Its essays are intended to be read straight through. They will be useful also for later reference because they provide in one place a concise summary of Iroquois political history in the broadest sense involving cultural change through time as well as a narrative of events. The range and evolution of Iroquois treaty events are itemized in detail in a Descriptive Treaty Calendar. Because many names of persons and places will be unfamiliar to a modern reader, major identifications are provided in a Gazetteer and a list of Persons Participating in Iroquois Treaties.

In general the editors have attempted to make the book self-contained and comprehensive enough to provide a basic reference tool, a good place to look first when information is needed. The vastness of the field, however, precludes any possibility of definitive coverage. All lists are selective, and a brief bibliography suggests where to look further.

As with matters of fact, so also with their significance. Issues viewed across cultural boundaries are seen by scholars through varied lenses. This has been true of this volume's contributors, and their differences have been allowed to stand instead of being molded to fit the editors' views. Although a remarkable degree of consensus will appear, and facts have been checked conscientiously against the most reliable sources, the book does not purport to lay down a final, unchallengeable Truth. Rather it is a guide to study, in which cooperating contributors have set forth their personal visions as acquired from their individual disciplines and researches.

The reader may like to know that this Guide is one of the products of a research and publication project for a Documentary History of the Iroquois initiated by the D'Arcy McNickle Center for the History of the American Indian at the Newberry Library in 1978 and funded by the National Endowment for the Humanities. The project has compiled copies of thousands of available documents relating to treaties negotiated by the Iroquois nations and their League, including pictures of the wampum belts that were the Indians' device to organize council procedures and to preserve accurate memories of the treaties' provisions. The whole archive, *Iroquois Indians: A Documentary History*, on 35mm microfilm, and its two-volume guide, is published by Research Publications, Inc., 12 Lunar Drive, Woodbridge, Connecticut 06525.

Project staff were happy to secure cooperation from Iroquois Indians of both traditionalist and modernist orientation. Of the traditionalists the most important contribution was made by Cayuga Chief Jacob E. Thomas, of the Grand River Reserve, who is one of the venerated repositories of traditional lore. As appears in the essay by Dr. Michael K. Foster, Chief Thomas has collaborated in the interpretation of treaty ritual and wampum reading. He also visited the Newberry where he led seminar sessions and talked extensively with project staff, and he answered queries by mail.

A Mohawk traditionalist and a modernist Mohawk retiree from the Bureau of Indian Affairs accepted fellowship grants and took up residence at the Newberry Center.

A delegation from the Union of Ontario Indians visited the project and continued cordial communication afterward.

There was much reciprocal visiting between project staff and the nearby Oneida Indians of Wisconsin, and several Oneidas took residence as fellows at the Newberry, including Ernest Stevens.

Dr. George Abrams, Director of the Seneca-Iroquois National Museum, accepted membership on the advisory committee of the Center and project.

Associate Editor Mary A. Druke made research tours of Iroquois communities.

All of the fellows and visitors met with members of the project's staff and had access to its files of documents.

Regrettably, some other Iroquois groups chose to rebuff our invitations to participate. Nevertheless, the staff maintained an open-door policy throughout the project's existence and continued their established rule of nonpartisan objective inquiry.

The Guide also demonstrates the editors' policy of preserving international and interdisciplinary cooperation. At three annual meetings of the Conference on Iroquois Research, one of which was held jointly with the American Society for Ethnohistory, we presented interim findings for criticism and advice by our colleagues. Criticism was given close attention and corrections were made, when necessary. Comments were generally favorable.

Three years were allowed for the project. In advance the time seemed ample, but the staff found more than double the quantity of documents than had been estimated, and its tasks increased proportionately though the available time remained constant. Regrettably some signs of haste could not be avoided. To eliminate these from future editions, readers are requested to notify the D'Arcy McNickle Center at the Newberry of oversights or errors.

That the project could be accomplished within any time limits was possible because it had been begun, in one sense, many years before its formal start. Anthropologist William N. Fenton brought to it the knowledge and notes accumulated in a life career of field and library research that has won his colleagues' accolade of "Dean of Iroquois Studies." Anthropologist Mary A. Druke was fresh from doctoral studies at the University of Chicago, including field work among the Iroquois and archival travel in England and Scotland during which she had immersed herself in manuscript sources. Historian Francis Jennings had been wrestling with the protean Iroquois Covenant Chain throughout his professional career. The Newberry Library Center for the History of the American Indian had been created for the purpose of encouraging such research, and the Newberry's collections of materials in American Indian history are unrivalled.

Finally, some notice must be given to Mary Druke's special contribution to the whole project. She has overseen the operations of the office and the complicated logistics of locating, copying, and acquiring the materials, and organizing them into an accessible archive. In the process she has traveled much, and her work day was not determined by the clock. The project could not have come within sight of completion without her dedication.

Chilmark, Massachusetts   FJ
Spring 1984

The History and Culture of
IROQUOIS DIPLOMACY

SECTION I

TREATY DIPLOMACY

1

Structure, Continuity, and Change in the Process of Iroquois Treaty Making

WILLIAM N. FENTON

M Y INTEREST in the treaty-making process stems from a long association with the descendants of the old Six Nations extending over a half-century. From the beginning of my field work as an anthropologist among the Senecas of western New York during the 1930s I have heard the old people and the younger "Indian lawyers" declaim about the treaties and our failure to observe their stipulations. Although at times these recitations of wrongs and assertions of rights grew tiresome, one could not but be impressed by the erudition and memories of the narrators and wonder about the possible merits of their claims. I never thought the prosecution of these claims was any of my business as a scientist, and I steadfastly refused to get involved in the cases. It was not until I became interested in tracing the roots of political institutions and rituals available for study during the 1940s—notably the Condolence Council for mourning and installing chiefs—that I began to search for earlier descriptions of these customs and discovered that the record of their prior existence is to be found in the crucible of Indian and White relations, particularly in the treaty negotiations spanning three centuries.[1]

My interest in the treaties is scholarly. In them I seek to trace the roots of customs that I have observed among the living Iroquois of this century, and with these observations I hope to illuminate the past. The quest is ethnological and historical. Litigation of treaty claims, or defense against such claims, is not my concern.

How then does one utilize the living tradition for interpreting the past? The answer requires some explanation of how an ethnohistorian approaches the sources. He presumably seeks historical depth for some cultural activity described to him by living informants and which perhaps he has observed at first hand himself in the field. He seeks earlier accounts of the same phenomena, proceeding from the known to the unknown and testing each

3

earlier source from his own knowledge as to its fullness and fidelity to native concepts and behavior. How close and how qualified was the observer? This approach, which proceeds from the present to the past, I have termed "upstreaming" because it runs against the flow of history. In each preceding generation or period, there was perhaps one good observer who had learned the language, understood the concepts, recorded what he saw and heard, and left an account of events in which he participated. Often he depended on interpreters. I have in mind such men as L. H. Morgan, the first Iroquoian ethnologist; Asher Wright, missionary to the Senecas during the nineteenth century; Samuel Kirkland, missionary to the Oneidas in the preceding century; Sir William Johnson, crown Superintendent of the Six Nations; Conrad Weiser, half Palatine German and half Mohawk in culture; Father J. F. Lafitau, Jesuit comparative ethnologist and some of his predecessors in the Iroquois missions going back to 1650; and others like Cadwallader Colden who were men of intellectual curiosity and regarded the Indian as worthy of philosophical scrutiny.

The method of upstreaming in Iroquois political history has entailed recording and then analysing the traditions of the founding of the Iroquois Confederacy;[2] it has been reinforced by the observations and analysis of the institution known as the Condolence Council[3] and the study and interpretation of its supporting props such as wampum strings and mnemonic systems, notably the cane for recalling the Roll Call of the Fifty Founders of the Confederacy,[4] so as to discover the patterns that govern these rituals. These patterns of sequence and reciprocity are invariably adhered to and are presumably old, and they constitute models of continuity that are traceable in earlier sources.[5] One looks for early enumerations of the Five Nations, contemporary estimates of the power and age of the Confederacy, the tradition of its founding, lists of chiefs to compare with the famous fifty of the Roll Call, recorded meetings of the League at Onondaga; but the discovery that the "Condolence business" permeates the protocol of treaty making is of greatest significance to the present inquiry. Not only are key parts of the paradigm of condolence performed in some of the earliest treaties, but the negotiations are embellished by the metaphors in which the later ritual is couched. In regarding the records of these early council and treaty proceedings in the light of my field studies of extant political myth and ritual, and then reappraising my own materials in the light of ancestral forms, I am reminded that ethnohistorical research is also governed by the principle of reciprocal illumination, which Father Lafitau first stated in comparing his Mohawks and their customs with the peoples of antiquity, and vice-versa.[6]

The search for historical depth and continuity of political institutions is limited by the perceptions of persons who wrote the early sources. Intellectually these Europeans, who often had the best opportunities to observe, were unprepared to cope with the institutions of another culture; and few of them, save the French Jesuits, bothered to learn an Iroquoian language. For the most part they depended on interpreters who were progeny of "bush-lopers" or coureurs de bois and were largely illiterate. Moreover, the interests of trade, land acquisition, and military affairs channeled their learning in practical directions. Only the necessity of treating with the Indians to secure their furs, to increase the land base of the expanding settlements, and to form alliances for peace and war required maintaining a running record of such negotiations and reporting them to the proprietors of the colonies and the crowned heads of Europe. Secretaries of Indian Commissioners became adept at keeping the record of these transactions, and even though they depended on interpreters from Mohawk to Dutch to English, or from Mohawk to French, several of these scribes penetrated beyond the buckskin curtain to an understanding of Iroquois polity. At the same time the metaphors of forest diplomacy came through the chain of interpreters to embellish the treaty literature.

The ethnohistorian in examining this literature is confronted by the paradox of change and stability. Iroquois culture was indeed radically affected by its growing dependency on the European trade. The most obvious changes occurred in material culture, while social organization and political institutions remained relatively unaffected. Learning a few Dutch, French, or English words did not alter their grammar; and, as in language, the underlying patterns of their rituals remained stable over long periods of time. Content changed but structure persisted. But in time the structure itself evolved so that when one compares the paradigm of the Condolence Council of today with the protocol of the earliest alliances and treaties, essential parts are recognizable and seemingly identical; but because some elements dropped out and others were inserted, the two patterns of sequence are not identical at both ends of the time span.[7]

THE INDIAN TREATY: A NATIVE LITERARY FORM

The discovery of the Indian treaty as a native American literary form is shared by Cadwallader Colden and Benjamin Franklin. In his *History of the Five Indian Nations*, Colden sketched a short view of their government, treated at length their affairs with the English colonies, including the texts of Indian speeches at treaty negotiations from the Indian Records.[8] He very much admired the style of their oratory and attempted to characterize it. His two London reprints of 1747 and 1750 are greatly reworked and include the complete texts of several important treaties, notably Lancaster (1744), and the treaty at Albany that Colden conducted himself two years later. Of the fifty small books, containing the transactions of some forty-five treaty conferences, that appeared in the century prior to the American Revolution,[9] Franklin printed thirteen in stately folios. These publications were undertaken largely at private risk by printers in the colonies, and later were printed in London. Franklin sensed in the ritual and rhetoric of the participants of the Six Nations a certain literary appeal that prompted him to print three hundred separates of the Lancaster Treaty of 1744, which he shipped to William Strahan in London, hoping that "the method of doing business with those barbarians" might amuse him.[10] Here was a new form of literature that was native American, as straightforward as a play, replete with home grown metaphors, and with a certain style that found immediate appeal. William Parks of Williamsburg, a discriminating publisher, reprinted the Lancaster Treaty with an explanatory account of the Six Nations Confederacy and the protocol of their conferences. The commentary appeared in London in December 1774.[11] His source was Conrad Weiser's famous letter to Col. Thomas Lee, a Virginia commissioner at the Treaty, written to satisfy the gentleman's queries after the event.[12] The balance of the account was written out of Colden, de la Potherie,[13] and other sources.

Modern scholarship on the Indian treaty as a native American literary form stems from an article which Lawrence C. Wroth, the noted bibliographer of the J. C. Brown Library, contributed to the Yale Review in 1928. In this exemplary piece, Wroth made most of the points that were afterward taken up by Carl Van Doren, in the Introduction, and Julian B. Boyd, in the history of Indian Affairs in Pennsylvania, that accompanied the folio reprinting of Indian Treaties Printed by Benjamin Franklin.[14] The purpose of the treaties was to make alliances and maintain them; but in performance, as Van Doren perceived, they were "diplomatic dramas in the form prescribed by Iroquois ritual," and, as we shall see, the ritual was the Condolence Council, which imparted its structure to treaty protocol.

In the crucible of Indian and White relations the patterns that had governed Iroquois life for centuries became compelling and forced the White people to approach the Indian in a highly ritualized way that was completely foreign to European ways and thinking. The Indian idea that alliances once made had to be constantly renewed was equally alien to European thought. The place of councils was established by tradition and practice, and in this the Iroquois were sticklers. On one occasion a governor was told "there is no road to Williamsburg," so he came to Albany where a fire had been kindled. For the Indian, time was ecological and affixed to the annual round of activities; particularly days and hours meant nothing. The way a conference was held, who spoke first, the attestation of formal speeches with strings and belts of wampum, and time to deliberate before replying, were of equal importance with the content of the agreements. Unless it was done properly, unless the ritual was fulfilled, and unless there were presents and mnemonics to remember agreements, it was a poor show. Indeed the Indians could never understand why American public officials, having done all this, and even having written down their words, had poor memories.

The present guide should remove the charge that the treaties are "a neglected literary type that arose without conscious artistic design from the conflict of two distinct civilizations on the same soil."[15] They were also a species of drama in which the Iroquois were the playwrights, the directors and teaching actors, and the joint producers with the colonial hosts. Although forest diplomacy began before Europeans tied their ships to the shore, the Indian treaty, like much of American culture, was the product of the interaction of the two cultures.

IROQUOIS SOCIETY AND POLITY

Iroquois settlements were typically a cluster of 30 to 150 longhouses, surrounded by a palisade and situated on a height of land accessible to drinking water and not too far removed from a waterway. The localized character of Iroquois culture has persisted from the time the League was formed out of autonomous village bands. The prevailing residential group was the lineage consisting of a core of mothers, sisters, and daughters who in native theory were a longhouse family. They were surrounded and supported by a fringe of spouses of other lineages. Together this conglomerate comprises what the political liturgy refers to as the "ongoing family." This group identifies with an eponymous animal—bird, mammal, or reptile—that serves as its crest, was anciently displayed on the gable ends of lodges, was tattooed on the chests of members, and, when predominant, became the name of the community. It was in this sense that the Mohawks had three clan towns—Bear, Wolf, and Turtle—named for the three clans that all members of the League shared, although the upper Iroquois had other clans as well. All persons of the same crest, in whatever nation, acted as if they were indeed siblings, and welcomed each other in their respective lodges. The same clan identity and hospitality holds today.[16]

The longhouse of the Iroquois Confederacy extended from the Schoharie Creek westward to the Genesee River at Rochester and sheltered under its extended roof poles the old Five Nations of New York—the Mohawk, Oneida, Onondaga, Cayuga and Seneca peoples—who were its founders. Early in the eighteenth century the Tuscarora of North Carolina came north as refu-

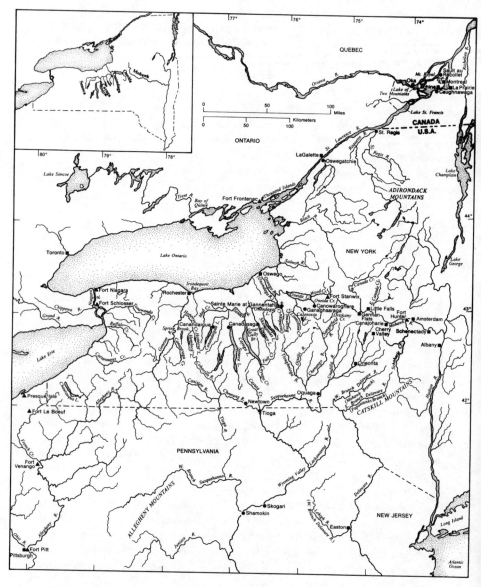

1. Iroquois territory in the 17th and 18th centuries. Core areas for each tribe in the 17th century are indicated by the placement of the tribal names in inset. Where river names have changed, earlier names are in parentheses.

gees and were taken in under the wing of the Oneida as the Sixth Nation, and the League was subsequently called The Six Nations.

It was, as Van Doren perceived, "a League of ragged villages," and each community had its local ways which it zealously maintained and defended. The relevance of this diversity for history, which continues to this day, is that differences between settlements and between nations composed of several settlements or village bands had to be composed and unified in the formation of the League. This was accomplished by allowing much local autonomy, accepting disparate delegations to the grand council, but limiting national delegations to a single voice or vote.

The settlement and its chief, who took his name from the place or gave his name to the settlement, is a recurring theme in Iroquois political literature.[17] It is apparent in the Deganawidah epic that the Five Nations were comprised of a disparate number of such settlements, which accounts in part for the unequal distribution of federal chiefs among them. An ambassador on arriving at a foreign town sought the lodge of the chief who then assembled the community to hear the message. The chief's lodge was built in proportion to accommodate such gatherings; it had extra apartments for guests, and it became in fact the council house. The council house or longhouse has been a separate building for nearly two hundred years.

Single towns frequently had multiple chiefships because chiefs were chosen from smaller residential segments, even from a single household. The three Mohawk towns were each identified with a clan, but each of these clans had three chiefships, each belonging to a segment, lineage or household. The Oneida had almost the same distribution of chiefships among the same three clans, but they all lived in a single town. Onondaga, with one main town and a satellite, had fourteen chiefships. The ten Cayuga chiefships were distributed among three towns, and the eight Seneca chiefships were arranged in a moiety division between two great towns and two small towns, each side having one of each. We shall have to look beyond locality to social organization for an explanation.

The basic patterns of Iroquois social structure have been known since the mid-nineteenth century. Colonial writers remarked the division of labor between the sexes, which is both functional and spatial. Although Iroquois towns were built and governed by men, and to all appearances the women were drudges, men owed their offices to female succession, and the village and its environs of cleared fields up to the wood's edge were the domain of women. Apart from councils, men's roles were carried out in the forest—hunting, the war path, embassies of peace and trade, treaties.

Each of the Five Nations was comprised of villages and longhouse families and it was divided into two moieties, or phratries. Each moiety comprised two or more clans, and the clans were again segmented into one or more maternal families or lineages. Every maternal family traced its home to some long-house of which it once formed the household, and so the terms for the two, in the Iroquois mind, are synonymous. These lineages, which later formed the segments of clans and with which they share their functions, are the building blocks of the social system.[18]

Viewed by the individual from within, tribal society rested on certain fundamental organic analogies, most important of which was a fundamental dualism that consisted in the symbolic recognition of the sexes. Starting from the fireside family of husband and wife, it extended to the clans, to the moieties, to the nation, and to the confederacy. In operation it embodied the principle of reciprocity, which governs the functions of the moieties, both tribal and confederate.[19]

The simplest unit of Iroquois society is the "fireside" or nuclear family of husband and wife and their children. Stemming from the fireside family and including any living siblings of the wife's mother, both male and female, the wife's brothers and sisters, the wife's children, and her daughter's children, and the descendants of any of the preceding women in the female line, is the household of fact and legal fiction, or the continuing maternal family. Ascending the matrilineal scale, the senior living woman is the matriarch and she presides over the household and makes ultimate decisions on social and political matters. This lineage of persons tracing descent from a common mother forms an exogamic incest group, members of which must take their spouses from other similar matrilineages. In time such a lineage might occupy several longhouses in several villages, giving rise to segments of a clan.

An Iroquois clan is composed of two or more maternal families who behave as if the members of each generation are indeed siblings, or as if they constitute a single maternal family. Historically, the two maternal families or segments may be derived from a single lineage, but long since the connecting links have been forgotten. This may have followed a village removal and a separation; or possibly some matron was adopted and the segment represents her descendants. The clan, therefore, is a legal fiction, while the maternal family is a physical reality and may become extinct—"its ashes grow cold"—while the clan continues.

One or more clans constituted a moiety and acted together, referring to one another as siblings. The typical Iroquois community and tribe had two such moieties, or ways of grouping and serving one another in crises. Moiety functions are mainly ceremonial: they act reciprocally to condole and bury each other's dead; they perform games like lacrosse, which drain internal tensions; and many ritual acts are conceived and acted as one side supporting the other. They are frequently referred to as the "sides." At the level of the League two similar moieties of tribes, the so-called nations, carry out symbolic functions derived from a lower level of integration. In the Condolence

Council for mourning dead chiefs and installing their successors, the Mohawk, Onondaga, and Seneca tribes comprise the "Three Brothers," or symbolically the Male principle, the "Sires"; and the second moiety comprised originally the Oneidas and Cayugas (but much later included the Tuscaroras and Delawares, and other adopted peoples) and is known as the "Four Brothers" who represent the Female principle in nature, or the "offspring" of the preceding. Whether this has any historical significance is unknown. The two halves of the League are sometimes referred to as Elder Brothers and Younger Brothers respectively, or uncles (sires)-Agado:ni—and nephews-Kheyáʔtaweñh. We shall see such symbolic kinship terms employed in treaties presently.

These terms derive from the fireside family, which in essence was bilateral and provided the individual with two lines of appeal, first to his mother's line, and second to his father's. It defined his duties and obligations, particularly to his mother's brother who might be the clan chief, but also to his father's kinsmen. Thus the agado:ni/kheyáʔtaweñh principle had an operating base in the bilateral family and a symbolic projection in the confederacy.

Europeans never appreciated the widespread network of kinship that encompassed the Eastern Woodlands, and they misunderstood the values that Indians gave to the terms "brothers," "cousins," "uncles/nephews," fathers/sons," assigning these terms the meanings conventional in Europe. The English and the Iroquois had little difficulty over the reciprocal term "Brethren," although they missed the nuances of "elder/younger" siblings that were important in Iroquois society;[20] but the French assumed that as "fathers" they had enjoyed seniority rights over their "children," which the Iroquois were never prepared to accept. The symbolic usage of kinship terms among the nations of the Iroquois League was extended to neighboring tribes, and by analogy similar terms were employed in forming treaty alliances during the colonial period, where their significance has been a source of confusion.

Neither did characteristic American Indian age grades accord with European usage. The Iroquois revere the dead and include them as the highest grade; they constantly appealed to wisdom of the Founders of the League, and the ways that they had established; and deprecated contemporary learning in contrast.[21] The next grade is the Elders, the "Old People"— the "Old Men" and the "Old Ladies." They next speak of "Young People." They invariably include children, "those still on the boards" or "crawling on the ground"; and there are the Unborn "whose faces are turned this way from beneath the ground." Indeed babies are barely separated from the spirit world: as the saying runs, "an infant's life is as the thinness of a maple leaf." There is an element of circular reincarnation in all this with a tendency of individuals to move up through the grades and statuses that pass in the continuing family, assuming the same names in alternate generations, as the cycle repeats itself and society continues.

Iroquois political organization extends the basic patterns of social structure and local organization to a wider context. This concept is important for understanding their view of alliances and treaties because they included colonial governments in the network of symbolic kinship by such devices as the "Chain", of which more later. It works this way: as one moves from the lineage to the clan, to the moiety, to the tribe or nation, and thence to the League, the projected use of kinship terms becomes more fictional and the expected behavior more symbolic. The principle that operates throughout this extension is duality or reciprocity. Even one's fictional or symbolic relatives were expected to respond in kind with set speeches of condolence, wampum string or belt or its like, present for present, word for word, and the host was to hang an ample kettle and provide a beverage to wash away the taste of smoking.

The village, its headman, and the council of elders is a theme that recurs throughout Iroquois culture history. The clans had their separate councils; but an ad hoc village council of ranking clan chiefs, elders, and wise men made local policy. In a sense the same thing happened at the national and League levels. The offices and titles of clan chiefs were ascribed in specific maternal families or households, which were segments of clans, and the ranking matron of that lineage presided over the caucus that nominated, censured, or recalled a clan chief. The holders of such titles were also tribal chiefs and they represented their village and nation in the General Council of the League. They enjoyed great prestige but had little power.[22]

The Reverend Asher Wright (1803–75), who spent the greater part of a lifetime among the Senecas, left us the best statement of Iroquois political procedures. Officers were known by the name of the office, and each clan had its own names and titles that descended matrilineally. These offices were graded. A vacancy, whether created by death, resignation, or deposition "was filled by raising all below a degree higher." The process of review was hierarchical and clear. "Hence at every occasion of filling vacancies, the character and merits of all the officers in the series and of all candidates, were liable to be passed upon: first, in the discussion of the families interested; secondly, in the convocation of the clans to which they belong; thirdly, in the meeting of the four clans, which occupied respectively the two ends of the council house; fourthly, by the assembled council of the particular nation; and fifthly, [by the] council at the Longhouse of the Six Nations."[23]

Likewise, there was a regular way to communicate concerns from the least fire to the great council fire, and for the great chiefs to enlist public opinion. Again in Wright's words:

If any individual desired to bring any proposition before the general council, he must first gain the assent of his family, then his clan, next of the four related clans in his end of the council house, then of his nation, and thus in

STRUCTURE, CONTINUITY, AND CHANGE

due course . . . the business would be brought up before the representatives of the confederacy. In the reverse order, the measures of the general council were sent down to the people for their approval. It was a standing rule that all action should be unanimous. Hence, the discussions were . . . continued until all opposition was reasoned down, or the proposed measure abandoned.

This process of attaining "one mind," and the ability to speak with "one voice, one mind, and one heart" is what, in Wright's opinion, contributed to the power of the confederacy; and it was not "until their councils were divided by bribery and Whiskey of the Whites," and they adopted majority rule that their power declined. This process reached its climax in the negotiations leading to the treaty at Buffalo Creek in 1838.[24]

The Eastern Indians distinguished between civil chiefs – the sachems (an Algonquian term), the *agoianders* of Lafitau's Mohawks, or the hotiyanéshǫ? of the Senecas – whose offices were descended in matrilineages or clan segments – and other chiefs who achieved their rank on the war path or for council oratory, and whose titles died with them and were not hereditary. The first group and their families constituted a class apart. The achieved statuses included the so-called Pine Tree Chiefs, honorary titles that carried no voting power, the Speaker for the Women, and the Speaker for the Warriors. This second group numbered the most famous names in Indian history. Brant was a war chief, and Red Jacket came up as Speaker for the Women, and later for the Council. Even the sachems employed a speaker to announce their decisions reached in committee, and very few of their titles appear in treaty negotiations. Speakers were chosen for their ability to grasp principle and fact, for rhetorical gifts, and for retentive memory in a society in which most men and women were walking archives. The speaker's presence had a powerful effect on history, since he is often identified by colonial recorders when the decision makers for whom he was the voice remain anonymous.

Civil chiefs were responsible for external affairs, which included trade, alliances, and treaties. An understanding of this responsibility lends credence to the statement of their speaker in 1735: "for the Trade & Peace we take to be one thing."[25]

One can summarize Iroquois society, in their terms, as a body of relatives, "my people," who are residents of a place – a village or settlement. The public includes everyone; therefore, any stranger must be adopted. They consider themselves a "nation," literally "a native land," a concept that is at once kindred and territorial; and the several bands, tribes, or nations are confederated on a model of the longhouse that implies both kin and territory.

Vertically, society is ranked into "grandfathers of old," the founders; chiefs (sachems or lords) who are metaphorically called "Trees;" Warriors or "Matbearers," sometimes called "Big Tobacco Pouches," otherwise "Tree Watchers" or "Props" to the chiefs; Women, our Mothers, who really count in main-taining the ongoing families; as well as age grades from the unborn to the re-vered dead. All of these persons and statuses were somehow involved in a treaty agreement and most of them usually managed to be represented on the ground.

The treaty presented a means of resolving tensions between alterna-tives that may be expressed in a series of dyads that characterize the life of Iroquois society. The solution to the dyad of relations (kinsmen) vs. outland-ers was adoption: everyone should have a name and a place in the kinship system; therefore, colonial governors and officials were adopted and given names. To achieve friendship and overcome feud (and even murder), there was a regular way to compound delicts with presents. To achieve peace vs. war, there was the "Chain," or alliance, reaffirmed by exchange of wampum belts. To overcome the inevitable conflict of life vs. death, there was the ritual of requickening, the heart of condolence, which sought to restore light vs. dark-ness of grief by dispelling the clouds and bringing back the sun. Persons, clans, and nations unaffected by grief were termed "clearminded" vs. the "down-minded" whose minds were lifted out of the depths of depression. Thus the treaty was a way of agreeing to restore normal relations between parties in disparate circumstances.[26]

"THE GREAT PEACE"

All of this was made explicit to the Iroquois in the charter myth of the found-ing of the Great Peace, or the League. The Deganawidah Epic in all of its ver-sions comprises one genre, which in the words of Lévi-Strauss "can be thought of as belonging together," and in this sense have a single identity over time.[27] But even in societies like the Iroquois who aspire to verbatim recall,[28] each narrator has his own version of the myth: he never tells it twice in precisely the same way, and there is bound to be substitution of content over time. Listeners, nevertheless, recognize the several versions as belonging to the one myth, even though the narrators are unable to agree on details or the precise order of incidents. One need not pursue the search for the one true version; it never existed. One can, however, reconstruct its main outlines and plot.

The Deganawidah epic is the story of an Iroquois prophet, who sup-posedly lived during the Stone Age of North America and who brought a message of peace—that all men should be kindred and should stop hunting, killing and scalping one another. He preached the principles of "righteous-ness, civil authority, and peace," which together constitute "The Great Law."

He persuaded the local chiefs of settlements scattered in the forests of what is now upstate New York to abandon their feuds, reform their minds, and unite. He formed the Iroquois Confederacy, endowed it with symbols, and supported it with ritual sanctions. Central to its plot are feuding factions which, one by one, grasp the message that is carried by a fatherless boy, the typical Iroquois culture hero. Deganawidah teams up with a disturbed chief (Hiawatha) —himself a recidivist cannibal and victim of witchcraft—to reform the Onondaga sorcerer (Thadodaho). They make Thadodaho prime minister of the League, they create symbols for its identity and unity, and establish rules and procedures for its governance and perpetuation. At the end the hero departs, promising to return—"call my name in the bushes"—whenever disaster threatens the system.

The Deganawidah epic as a discourse is a composite of myth and legend that approaches native history, having undergone transformation from myth toward historical tradition, a process that has affected Iroquois mythology generally since it was first collected. Seen as an historical discourse, it is comprised of three main parts: (1) the myth of Deganawidah and the conversion of the cannibal; (2) the legend of the conversion of local chiefs to the cause of peace; (3) the principles of the League—its internal structure and rituals. This last, in some versions, is virtually by-law stuff.[29]

This composite document serves as the charter for the League of the Five (later Six) Nations, and since the efforts by native annalists to codify it during the late nineteenth century, culminating in Parker's edition of two of these sources, has come to be regarded as a "Constitution of the Five Nations."[30] It contains the tradition of the founding; it names the fifty founders, the then village chiefs; it specifies the council arrangements as between moieties of nations in mourning and condoling, and a tripartite seating for business at the great council fire. Here the Mohawks and Senecas sit to the east, as one moiety; the Oneidas and Cayugas across the fire to the west, as the other moiety; and the Onondaga firekeepers to the north as arbiters of the two opinions. Clearly, in the versions extant, one can detect a process of projection and feedback of content, structure and ritual process that is yet evolving.[31] Some of the by-laws have a distinct nineteenth century tone; others hark back to aboriginal times.

A document of this full-blown magnitude should have some historical antecedents. The Deganawidah epic was not recorded until late in the nineteenth century, when Hale published on it, revealing its roots in the previous century.[32] Two recently discovered manuscripts—Joseph Brant's answers to a questionnaire by Rev. Elkanah Holmes in 1801, and the journal of Brant's protégé John Norton—transport the plot and characters into the eighteenth century, both of which accounts make the earlier sketch by Reverend Pyrlaeus (1743) the more plausible.[33] Beyond that the written record fails.

There is a hint that the League was in existence in 1635, when the Five Nations are denominated and their countries laid out with kernels of corn for the benefit of Dutch travelers at Oneida.[34] Contemporary estimates of its importance to the colonies and its antiquity abound from Colden's time onward.[35] The most impressive evidence of its operations is the continuous record of its meetings at Onondaga from 1641 to the present. The weakest link in the chain of evidence is the erratic appearance or absence of the famous fifty titles of the founders among the delegations to important conferences and as the acknowledged leaders of their respective nations. It is certain, however, that the League was founded before European settlement, probably about A.D. 1500, give or take twenty-five years, although arguments for earlier and later dates abound.[36] The important thing is that it was an evolving institution, the full-blown reality of which cannot be demonstrated at an early time, and that it has persisted as a symbolic system.

The enduring symbolism of the League is couched in a series of metaphors which are supported by mnemonic devices that are learned simultaneously. The metaphors fall into categories of structure, process, action, unity, continuity, and identity, although they are all aimed at strengthening and maintaining the system for which they are models or continuators. The "Whole House" is symbolically a household of one family; politically it is a confederation of autonomous tribal territories. The clearing to the woods-edge contrasts with the forest, as community and polity contrast with anarchy, as "talk in the bushes" vs. "deliberation in council." There is a strong sense of the "proper way": certain accepted procedures govern life and council, as well as treaties. Life follows a set path, and chiefs who stray from it are "lost in the woods." A path runs through the longhouse to the accepted place of treaties, and it must not be obstructed. "To throw a log in the path" is to impede proceedings. The path to peace through treaty negotiations contrasts with the war path. There are rules for kindling a council fire that its smoke may touch the sky and draw people to it, for the fire symbolized an ongoing government. Embassies traverse the woods to the clearing where they expect to be welcomed and exchange word for word and song for song and then enter the place of council in a procession. "Let me drive it into your mind with a song" expresses a belief in the magical power of song which is synonymous with power (orenda) itself. The hatchet of war which can be declined in varying aspects—to throw it in the sky, to withdraw it by a string, to remove it from someone's head, to bury it in a bottomless pit where an underground stream carries evil to oblivion—contrasts with the kettle which is hung and set down in hospitality, boiled with enemy heads of war, and overset when a campaign is cancelled. Metaphors of union and increase comprise a series of continuative models that apply equally to local society and to its political extensions. The ever-growing tree of the long leaves stands for the commonwealth. It shelters the council, and it should not be let topple. Chiefs, though, are metaphorically trees that do topple and have to be raised up again, just as the "Tree of Peace" is planted. From it "Four White Roots of Peace" extend in cardinal directions: they should be followed to the fire; but if chopped, they bleed, and the people of the loghouse feel it. Chiefs are marked with emblems of identity when crowned with a symbolic rack of antlers; just as deer shed their racks, the antlers are removed from a chief's head in illness, at death, if he goes on the warpath, or for malfeasance in office. Women provide corn, but venison is man's contribution to the larder. As hunters have observed buck deer rubbing antlers on brush during the rutting season and clashing in combat, so the great stomp dance following the installation of chiefs is called "rubbing antlers," when the chiefs socialize and diffuse their power.[37]

While Iroquois thought runs to metaphors, their speakers employed mnemonic devices to "prop up their minds." These devices for ordering memory and recalling oral passages verbatim were digital, spatial, and pictorial. Listeners kept track of items in a speech with short sticks which also served in enumerations of towns, populations, and the like, as did kernels of corn or beans that were readily arranged in piles and in patterns illustrating order and oppositions. The most famous examples are the attempt of Oneida hosts to map and enumerate Iroquois towns and tribes for Dutch visitors in 1635 and the now famous condolence canes carrying the roll call of the fifty founders of the League.[38]

Strings and belts of wampum served to affirm messages, to stress the import and truth of what was being said, and to convey the nature of the message. Before the Dutch introduced steel drills and grindstones to coastal Algonquians living at the source of clam and conch shells from which it was fabricated, there was virtually no wampum in Iroquoia; but as it became more plentiful during the fur trade, emphasis shifted from strings to broad and elaborate belts carrying pictorial designs of villages, paths between nations and parties to contracts, and slanting lines, sometimes called "props" to the leaning longhouse. An urgent message sent with seven strings early on might be parlayed later to a belt of seven to twelve rows deep. Strings were measured in fathoms, and sometimes unstrung wampum by the scheppel or bushel was available at Albany, where "River Indian" women were employed to make up belts for a treaty. Fifteen strings of variegated beads, purple and white, are still used in the Condolence Council.[39]

Each of the belts exchanged at treaties and important conferences related to a particular item of business that some member of the Iroquois delegation was designated to commit to memory. Although each nation had some belts of its own, the more important records of transactions were taken to Onondaga, racked up in the Council House, and later kept in a hemp bag by a designated wampum keeper. Periodically they were brought out and rehearsed. This "reading" of the wampum belts was possible so long as the mem-

ory of the particular verbal stream could be recalled and taught by association with the character and design of the particular belt. When the belt and
the verbal stream became separated from the written transactions at treaties
which repose in archives, as happened with belts kept in museums, a reading
became less probable and in time virtually impossible. Together, belt and verbal stream supported each other in learning and in remembering, two centuries before anyone thought of the split-brain theory of learning and recall.
Whether a grammar of wampum belt symbols can still be recovered remains
an open question.[40]

THE CONDOLENCE COUNCIL

Acting out in ritual the paradigm for maintaining the system evoked the
thought: "And this will strengthen the house." Underlying protocol of treaties and the drama of forest diplomacy was an Indian ceremony for renewing
their political forms and restoring society known as the Condolence Council. This developed into a drama in which the actors were Indian sachems
and colonial governors. With different casts and slight changes in the script
it ran for more than a century, principally at Albany, occasionally at Philadelphia, Lancaster, and Easton, later at Johnson Hall, Fort Stanwix, and
Canandaigua. There were French actors when the play was staged at Montreal. But in its purest form it was celebrated at the great drama festivals held
each fall at Onondaga where it is said the ceremony originated with the founding of the League of the Five Nations before the Dutch came to America.
Deganawidah was the playwright and Hiawatha its leading actor.[41]

  The program of the Condolence Council comprises now some sixteen
events arranged in a pattern of sequence that has governed its performance
since early times. Its content has changed and only some of the sixteen events
are mentioned in historical accounts. To understand the pattern one must
recall that one side, called the Clearminded (C), condoles or performs the
ceremony to lift up the minds of the Mourners (M) who have suffered a loss
by the death of a chief or some colonial official or relation.

Program of the Condolence Council

1. Procession: taking the ceremony over the path to the house of the
   Mourners, calling out the roll of the Founders (C).
2. Welcome at the fire by the woods (M).

3. The three bare words of requickening: tears, ears, and throat (C&M).
4. Taking them by the arm to the council place (M).
5. The Roll Call or Eulogy: "Putting their house in order" (C).
6. Farewell chant to the Dead Chief: the Six Songs (less one). (C behind blanket partition.) (The sixth song is withheld until 8.)
7. Over the Forest (Part one): recitation of laws (C blanket removed).
8. The Sixth Song to the Founders (C partitioned).
9. Over the Forest (Part two). (C blanket removed)
10. Remainder of Requickening Address with wampum strings 4–15: Clear-minded threaten to withdraw but are asked to stay until Mourners can compose a reply.
11. The reply of the Mourners: Six Songs (M).
12. Return of condolences and wampum strings 4–15 (M).
13. Showing the face of the new chief (M).
14. Charge to the new chief and to the public (C).
15. Feast to wash away the tobacco (M). Cries of approbation: Yuhhenh: *Hii yah!* (C).
16. Rubbing Antlers: the celebration dance, in which the hosts (M) release their women folk to the visiting party (C) and society is restored.

Fulfilling this ritual pattern illustrates certain theoretical principles that are a consequence of one half of the society (who are unaffected) condoling the other half (whose minds are depressed with grief) so that they can discharge their normal obligations to society. This is called "lifting up their minds." The ritual process is a beautiful illustration of Radcliffe-Brown's concepts of dysphoria transformed to euphoria.[42] The transformation is accomplished by the interaction of the Clearminded and the Downminded in a series of mutual acts, which Malinowski termed reciprocity.[43] In the discharge of this paradigm it is important not to use too much power. So in lifting up the minds of the grieving party (M) the two sides employ four principles in mutual segments: (1) separation vs. approach, (2) alternation and reciprocation of acts (C & M), (3) interdigitation of rites (C), (4) threat of withdrawal (C) vs. appeal to stay (M) to hear the rapid return of condolences, wampums, and songs without hitch (M).

Having traversed the first twelve items of the agenda, which achieved the restoration of society, the ceremony reaches a climax of intensity in raising the new chief in the title of his predecessor (M), charging him with his duties (C), and in a friendly exchange of news, referred to as "dreams," which might call for a recitation from the origin myth. Finally, the terminal feast, always by the host (M), followed by the great social dance of the chiefs, discharges any tensions or social distance. When the visitors are asked not to be too hard on the women whom the hosts (M) "let slip through their fingers," the standard reply is: "We are but old men" (C).

Naturally all of these amenities were not expected or exchanged when colonial powers were hosts and in the process of learning what was expected of them. The paradigm was flexible enough to be truncated and altered accordingly. The Iroquois were naturally pleased when attempts were made to fulfill it.

We are now prepared to identify some features to be found in earlier performances. The procession of chiefs to the council fire, headed by a singer, opened at least three treaty councils at Albany 1694, at Lancaster 1744, and Sir William Johnson's celebrated entrance into Onondaga in 1756. The chanting of the Eulogy to the Founders is implied on several of these occasions. Pausing at the woodsedge to await a welcoming party occurs frequently. Singing for power occurs quite early, and is noted as the manner of establishing a new covenant in 1677.[44] And eight years later, *Canondondawe*, the Mohawk speaker at Albany, "sang completely the covenant song," which suggests the Sixth Song (above) in the modern Condolence ceremony, and then admonished his listeners: "Let me drive it into you with a song. Open now your ears."[45] The French heard the Song of Peace rendered by *Kiotseaeton*, "The Hook" even earlier at Three Rivers in 1645.[46]

The cries of approbation: the *Yuh henh:* or (*jo-hah*), which were new to Maryland and Virginia ears at Lancaster (1744), had greeted a round of drinks, saluted an agreement nation by nation, and hailed a feast at Albany and in Canada for a century.[47] A leader sounded the cry, and his constituents replied in unison "from the depths of their chests."

The use of condolence messages attested by strings and belts of wampum was the generally accepted way of firming an alliance between Iroquois and their neighbors and is abundantly documented. Negotiations at Three Rivers for the Peace of 1645 witnessed the first recorded performance of the condolence ritual by an Iroquois performer.[48] *Kiotseaeton*, heading a Mohawk delegation of three, stood offshore in a canoe draped in beads. There was a welcome at the water's edge, the planting of two poles and stretching a line to arrange and tie strings and five belts attesting the seventeen "words" of his countrymen, and the singing between gifts as he acted out their import pacing to and fro. While the order and content are not precisely the modern paradigm, there is sufficient overlap to relate the two, including clearing river, rapids, and road; perpetual fire "to bind us close;" eating together; dispelling clouds; and restoring the Sun. A great social dance of all parties followed.

The most poignant example in the English records came forty-five years later, when eight Mohawk sachems from three "Castles" came to Albany in February to condole the dead in the Schenectady massacre. Their first belt spoke with tears for all in the same covenant chain. The second spoke for the "Whole House," now broken in at both ends. The third remarked, "We come with tears in our eyes," a familiar phrase in the modern ritual. Their fourth belt stated condolence law: namely, that they were taught by their "forefathers that when any sad accident befalls any of the Covenant, go and bemoan the death." Here was "eye-water" for vigilance. A fifth belt was to wipe away blood from the defiled house and keep it clean henceforth: this was the Covenant Belt. A sixth spoke of the "Silver Chain" and courage, "for we are the race of the Bear which does not yield." A seventh, a bearskin, dispelled clouds and restored the Sun: the dyad of healing. And so it went.

The English reply equated the "Whole House" metaphor with the "Chain." They proposed an executive committee to act for the League composed of a sachem and warchief of each nation. When the English returned six belts, and promised duffels, tobacco and provisions, came the cry of approbation.

In acknowledging the speech of the Governor, the Mohawk speaker stated it was their custom to consult the other nations when they come to condole. In May Diadorus expressed their gratitude that the English had learned the proper metaphors: the evergrowing tree, the bundle of arrows, silver chain, "our House," to hang the kettle, and to take up the hatchet. Thus the recitation of laws and the admonition to observe customs, that descends in the tradition of the founders, became a regular part of treaty conferences. The Five Nations produced some able teachers by example. And those colonials responsible for Indian Affairs learned to handle wampum properly, to pass strings and belts, to reject them on occasion, and above all to give presents.[49]

ALLIANCE MECHANISMS

It was inherent in the system that the Great Law be extended and renewed. This was accomplished through a network of alliance mechanisms, which again were modelled on usages at lower levels of society. There was first the kinship system and its extension by adopting individuals who were taken into families and clans and given names of deceased relatives. Indeed one became that person, assuming his rights and obligations. This was the lot of captives who were not burned, and Iroquois speakers at treaties were often at pains to explain to colonial officials that the chiefs in council did not have the power to return captives who had already been given to families and clans who possessed the right. Ceremonial friendships were another way of supplementing the kinship system. Friendship entailed an exchange of gifts and a lifetime obligation to renew the bond.

Kinship terms of address permeate the treaty literature. The English were "Brethren," the French governors and Kings "Father." The former caused relatively less confusion, except for the Iroquois distinction between elder and younger siblings; but the latter implied different obligations and expectations in the two cultures. The strong European bias toward patrilineal institutions and primogeniture had no meaning for the Iroquois who were matrilineal and avuncular.[50]

Such ties of symbolic kinship were supported by ritual sanctions. Between persons at the tribal or local level the particular rite was established by the ceremony that was celebrated when the bond was made. Among the Five Nations it was the Condolence Council that replenished their confederacy. By extension this ceremony became the model for treaty protocol.

Just how much store the Iroquois attached to renewing treaty ties with the New York colonial government is best expressed in the words of an Oneida speaker to the Governor's agent after a three-year lapse of conferences due to smallpox: "You may say that Love & Affection may be strong in Absence as when present but we say not. . . . Nothing more revives & enlivens affection than frequent Conferences."[51]

A number of metaphors express the ideas of maintenance and extension. There was first the idea of "keeping the path open" by removing any obstacles. Second, the necessity of kindling and maintaining the council fire is frequently expressed. Third, the sign of a well-established relationship was couched as "Planting the Tree of Peace" and nourishing it so that its roots and branches extended and its top touched the sky; alien peoples might follow the roots to the trunk and even perceive the tree beneath which they could be sheltered. Since each of these metaphors of growth and extension has an antithesis, in time of trouble, or following a breach between the parties, the Clearminded one could "uproot a tree and cast down weapons into a bottomless pit" where they would be carried away by an underground stream, and then the tree was replanted. And fifth, perhaps the most famous metaphor of the treaty literature was the "Chain." Keeping the Chain of Friendship bright and free of rust required frequent meetings well-oiled with food and presents and laced with rum. The Chain concept was indeed the umbilical cord of the Five Nations, as Sadeganaktie impressed on Governor Fletcher at Albany in 1694 the importance of "Keeping [the] Chain firm and inviolable [and] all that are linked therein." And he went on, "The least Member cannot be touched, but the whole Body must feel and be sensible; if therefore an Enemy hurt the least part of the Convenant Chain, we will join to destroy that Enemy, for we are one Head, one Flesh, and one Blood."[52]

Brightening the Chain was accomplished by renewing the Covenant. This was a sophisticated business with its own rules to be learned by all who participated in it. No one has described the strategy and tactics of concluding a peace alliance as well as Father Lafitau during the second decade of the Eighteenth Century.[53] Negotiations began even during hostilities, usually through a neutral party. Prisoners might be sent home with presents, including wampum from the public treasury. An old man of reputation might accept the risk of "going with wampum belts to clear the road" and thus "take away the thorns and thistles" to smooth the way for ambassadors who take the path when their welcome is ascertained. Invariably the council chose for this role old men of known competence. The council then charged the ambassadors with public and secret propositions and rehearsed them. "As if the words were written, they are given instructions by their wampum belts or with little sticks of different designs which have different meanings," so that they might forget nothing and not exceed their instructions. Presents were provided from the public treasury. An escort of warriors was appointed to hunt and scout their flanks, and one of them was dispatched to give advance notice of their approach. This enabled the host nation to prepare. Arriving at the woodsedge, a mile or so from the village, the embassy halted and sent word in of their presence.

Then the host council sent some elders to greet them properly and some young men to carry their packs. "The word-bearer among the host elders, seating himself for a moment near them, after lighting his pipe, coughing and spitting, tells them very eloquently that they are very welcome; that his nation is much obliged to them for having undertaken such a difficult journey; that they must, doubtless, have suffered very much from the length of the journey through heat and cold, etc." These are familiar passages of the Welcome beside the fire at the Woodsedge.[54] Then he tells them that a cabin has been made ready for the entire party during their visit. Lafitau says that their entrance into the village is without fanfare.

At the appointed lodge the kettle has been hung high for them, and young men of the village serve as cooks and servants to the visitors. It is all done at the public expense and the hosts touch nothing of the feast.

The ambassadors are allowed to rest one or two days before making their propositions with belts in a public council held to hear them. No reply is made on the same day. The real negotiations go on in private—"talk in the bushes"—conferences, which are not binding until formally stated in public council by a speaker with belts. The formal reply may come in a matter of days, or the ambassadors may be allowed to return home to await a return embassy with the word. In either case the number of belts must equal the number of original propositions.

If the sentiment is for continuing warfare, Lafitau says the visiting ambassadors run the risk of having their heads broken then and there on the mat. If they are spared that, a party may ambush them on the road home.

Lafitau's account of a typical embassy throws light on one thing that recurs in the New York Indian Records, namely, the frequent visits to Albany of one or two chiefs or warriors to take the pulse of the Indian Commissioners preliminary to a more formal approach resulting in a conference or treaty. It also helps us to understand the exploratory visits to Canada of two or three chiefs which the English governors invariably misinterpreted as violations of the Covenant Chain and which the old men of Onondaga tried to explain.

Toward the close of the seventeenth century colonial agents had learned the essential lessons in forest diplomacy. First, that there is a proper way to join in and maintain an alliance. This means that after the approach over the path to the council fire, should there be a death on either side, condolence law must be observed before any business is taken up. Council procedure was fairly established with definite rules as to who spoke first and who responded, as between petitioner and respondent.[55] In general, the party that kindles the fire (calls the meeting) must open and cover it, if only to open the council so as to hear the message of the petitioners, and later to reply and send them on their way. Moreover, a council called for one purpose such as peace, and so stated in the invitation belts, may not be diverted midstream to another purpose, such as war. The Indians were very particular about this. And a council called for a particular place might not be moved to a second place without the permission of the party invited.

An appointed speaker is the voice of the nation, or of nations. He is prompted by those principals who are responsible for the decisions and positions of their nation, or of the Five Nations. The principals themselves are frequently nameless in the treaty proceedings. A second or third speaker may be employed for a different range of issues, or to perform some special function for which his eloquence commends him.

Propositions must be stated clearly and they must be heard without interruption. At the end, listeners may raise questions in acknowledging the speech, which may be answered then and there or postponed to another day. Dramatic action is desirable in presenting an issue; there was a special council style of intoning and modulating the voice as subject matter shifted and to gain attention. Pacing was customary or habitual with some speakers; others stood in place.

Shouts of approval—Yu henh; Hi: yah—greeted a felicitous issue, acknowledged food and drinks, and were rendered in antiphony, nation by nation. Someone raised the cry and the others joined in.

It was customary, and almost a rule, to acknowledge a message, but not to answer the same day. The proper way was to sleep on it over night, counsel together the next day until they attained unanimity—"One Mind"—and then speak with one voice.

Just as it was customary to document each "word" or item with a gift, string of wampum, or belt symbolic of it; so each word must be returned and attested by comparable gift, string or belt. A temporary substitute might be invoked and the belts delivered later. The host was expected to provide to-bacco for the councillors' pipes, for it was said that "from smoking comes good thoughts," and he was also expected to provide "something to wash away the tobacco taste," be it berry water, wine, rum, or brandy. And fulfilling this de-mand led to abuse. Finally, there was the requisite feast—a beef and kettles of soup. The Indians were great eaters and persons of all ages attended both as witnesses and to share in the great event. Small wonder the colonials com-plained bitterly over the increasing costs of food, liquor, and presents to In-dians during the eighteenth century, but they tolerated the expense at treaty councils so long as the crown subsidized it. However, part of the American backlash against British treaty practices was to try to eliminate or cut down on such outlays following the Revolution.

Communication between the principals or actors on both sides of the fire encountered formidable obstacles, which were at once verbal and non-verbal. First, there was the language barrier; second, literacy as opposed to an oral tradition; and third, interpretation. The native American participants had already confronted the radical differences between Iroquoian and Algon-quian language families that were certainly as great as those between Dutch and English, and between these languages and French. Indeed more than an isogloss separated the Mohawk Iroquois from Algonquian-speaking River In-dians at Albany, and yet individuals on both sides learned the other language, and developed a trade jargon.[56] And the same was true of Iroquois relations with northern members of the Algonquian family and with the Delaware to the south. There are terms in both language families—notably geographical names—that have the same meaning. Of the Europeans who had to do busi-ness with the Indians, very few of the Dutch settlers, and virtually no English-men bothered to learn an Iroquoian language; but in New France the Jesuit missionaries, who were the scholars of the day, studied, wrote grammars and learned to speak both Algonquian and Iroquoian dialects; and the *coureurs de bois* frequently took Indian wives and were equally at home in the dialects of their Indian trading partners. Between the learned fathers and the traders there was no shortage of good interpreters at Montreal or Quebec. The situa-tion at Fort Orange was gradually accommodated by the offspring of *Buschlopers* —the Dutch equivalent to French *coureurs de bois*—and Mahican and Mohawk women. Formal efforts to teach the Mohawks Dutch ended in failure. Of the mixed blood progeny who learned both languages the most interesting is the "Flemish Bastard," Smith's John, Smits Jan, or Canaqueese who, at a peace treaty with the French in 1654, apprised the French of the nature of the Iro-quois Longhouse, and that the proper approach was through its eastern door, and not through the smoke hole at Onondaga.[57] The Dutch and afterward English interpreters were field representatives of the Albany magistrates. None of them ranked high in the social scale, and it is a pity they were not educated men and women because they played a vital role in making the record of Indian affairs. In the next century, Weiser, despite his acceptance in both cultures, spoke Pennsylvania German and was barely literate in English. And after a lifetime of learning Oneida, Samuel Kirkland, though educated at Princeton, seemed "incompetent to infuse the fire of Indian Oratory into his expressions" when he acted as a treaty interpreter, in the estimation of Dewitt Clinton and contemporary observers.[58]

The Kinesics of handling wampum, the gestures that accompanied oratory, and the maintenance of ostensible imperturbability while listening to unwelcome words or in expressing a position were behaviors beyond the ken of most Europeans and learned by few colonials. The Indian participants at treaties were equally uncomfortable at the sight of constant scribbling by clerks and occasionally protested that they were "being impoverished by all of that pen and ink work."

Just as the speakers who were the voices of their nations were the prime agents in communicating the decisions of their sachems, so the recorders, or secretaries for Indian Affairs at Albany, such as Robert Livingston (1654–1728)[59] and his successors, created the Indian Records as they made their own versions of what they heard from the mouths of the interpreters. The amazing thing in all of this literature of forest diplomacy is the degree to which the Indian flavor comes through the faulty chain of communication. As these scribes came to understand the native customs, they often just refer to them without describing them, which is a source of frustration to the ethnohistorian. One would like to know what the "ancient laws" were that they rehearsed before formally opening the council.

Once the nature of the Iroquois Confederacy dawned on the consciousness of colonial governors they began to magnify its importance and improve its efficiency for colonial purposes. Frontenac at Quebec learned of the "Whole House" and attempted to dominate its policies for the advantage of New France. Failing that he twice invaded Iroquoia. Governor Dongan of New York, himself educated by Jesuits, countered French actions against the New York colony, in which he included the Iroquois, by persuading them to post the arms of the Duke of York on the "Castles" of the Five Nations. And to make their League more responsive, he urged them to appoint an executive committee of chiefs and warriors from each nation to confer with the commissioners in Albany. Later, Logan and Peters in Pennsylvania, sensing the importance of the Six Nations to the expansion of the Quaker colony, sought through Conrad Weiser and Shikellamy, the Oneida overseer on the Susquehanna, to harness the Onondaga council in displacing the Delaware. The Mohawks, who had no part in these affairs, became the creatures of Sir William Johnson who dealt through them to manipulate the Six Nations in the British interest. Despite his intimacy in Mohawk affairs, his familiarity with Condolence Law, and the fact that he once led a Eulogy Procession into Onondaga, Johnson left no record of the structure of the League or indication that he really understood it, if it then existed as we later came to know it. He was a participant rather than an observer. Finally, Timothy Pickering of Salem, the arch-Federalist who stood as the U.S. Commissioner to the Six Nations against the New York Commissioners at Canandaigua in 1794, had learned treaty protocol from Red Jacket, the Seneca orator, during a series of preliminary conferences at Newton and Painted Post, as the sole agent of the General Government vs. the State of New York.

At this point it may be helpful to distinguish a conference from a treaty. The Indians distinguished "talk in the bushes" when an issue might be explored or an agenda formulated from more formal meetings or conferences preliminary to a treaty. A large part of the Indian Records is comprised of such sessions. Then there were frequent councils for condoling someone, for showing new chiefs, for communication of "news," and polishing the Chain. The large conferences leading to a definite result—extending the Chain, fixing boundaries, land cessions, and formal alliances for peace and war—which are documented by deed or written proceedings afterward published—are what we know as Indian treaties. The latter were usually initiated by colonial officials and held at colonial or Crown expense. They form the body of the Indian treaty literature surviving today.

TREATY PROTOCOL

An analysis of four or more treaties produces an evolving pattern. Starting with the Mohawks condoling the Albanians for the deaths in the Schenectady massacre of 1690, wherein they congratulate the English on the mastery of the forms, one may note two conferences held by Governor Fletcher, "Swift Arrow," in 1694 and 1696, to brighten the Chain. These were marked by a procession of the Mohawk delegation who spoke first as respondents, and by the Governor's reply in Five Nations' metaphors. Then one may observe how Canasatego, the Onondaga orator, succeeded fifty years later at Lancaster in manipulating the forms to the advantage of the Six Nations and then lectured the Colonials on the advantages of union. And finally, a half-century later, when Timothy Pickering treated with the Six Nations at Canandaigua, the proceedings witness the final American respect for the ancient forms. After that the Americans were unwilling to observe native protocol.

The Iroquois themselves learned to accommodate the forms to the circumstances. Delegations were not always composed of the persons holding prestigious symbolic offices: they simply sent the best people available. When ascribed offices were held by persons of indifferent ability, those who had achieved stature by wisdom and the power of oratory were selected. Moreover, war chiefs were in the ascendancy during much of the eighteenth century. Hence few sachem names appear on treaties, and of these but few are of the famous fifty founders.

Native theory is frequently at odds with native practice. Except in recent times when the program of the Condolence Council has become fixed and there is fanatical insistence on adhering to its forms, the evidence from the treaty documents demonstrates how facile the Iroquois were in accommodating its forms to the particular circumstances. They could improvise "props to strengthen the longhouse," after the rude imagery of placing a pole to shore up a leaning bark building, but the elegant metaphor recalls the flying buttresses of Chartres. An omission could be remedied out of humility toward the founders, or a speech amended by applying a patch. Moreover, when a ceremonial role required a person of particular status with a title name to perform in reciprocal relation to another such specified status, and either of the persons was not available or capable of fulfilling the role, substitutes were readily found by the mechanism of borrowing a capable person from either side. This is a practice that still operates in Longhouse ceremonies.

Taking all of these things into consideration and accommodating the variants found in the treaty literature, one can reconstruct an ideal pattern of treaty protocol.[60] This may help explain how a symbolic system endures even when the fulfillment of the forms cannot be accomplished.

A Paradigm

1. Invitation by string or belt of wampum to open the road to the fire (clear river)
2. Approach
   a. procession singing on road
   b. by canoe to landing
3. 'Welcome at the Woodsedge' or landing
   a. messenger stands in canoe draped in beads
   b. embassy pauses at edge of clearing
   c. Welcome address (host)
   d. Exchange of condolence: "We came with tears in our eyes"
      (1) 'Three Bare Words': Eyes, Ears, Throat
      (2) Host takes embassy by arm to main fire

4. Seating across the council fire
   a. Indians on sheets of bark or mats
   b. governors and commissioners and gents on chairs
   c. rack or line for displaying wampums
   d. Indians enter singing songs of peace before sitting: "Let me drive it into your mind with a song"
   e. Indians withdraw to encampment: lodged by national delegations, hold separate councils, prepare replies, hold social dances
   f. at Onondaga, Indians prepare room for guests in chief's lodge or Council House (contrast inhospitable Christians)
5. Condolence law: "Our forefathers taught us: when any sad accident befalls any of the Covenant Chain, go and bemoan the death"
   a. eye-water
   b. a cordial to restore facilities: purge mind, heart, vomit bile of revenge
   c. wipe blood from defiled house, mat, seat, bed, etc.
   d. cover grave
   e. the chain (link) that binds us
   f. to gather up the bones of one who falls afield
   g. to dispel the clouds and restore the sun
   h. to rekindle the fire
   i. to return the summons (invitation string or belt) (sometimes returned at woodsedge)
6. Recitation of the law ways (customs)
   a. "We are diminished: may the Founders forgive omissions; we are being impoverished by pen and ink work" (the drafting of deeds)
   b. the party that kindles the fire (calls meeting) uncovers (opens) and covers (closes) it.
   c. one may not shift place of meeting once invitations are issued and accepted.
   d. at a peace treaty one may not speak of war
   e. the proper way is reciprocal action
7. "Our words are on the way to thee":
   a. a belt drawn from a pouch is held by the speaker, passed over the fire, and racked up; to touch is to accept
   b. a belt held by the middle blocks the path
   c. custom: return string for string; belt for belt
   d. custom: listen without interrupting, acknowledge, retire and consider, reply next day (or when ready).
   e. cries of approbation: Yo—henh: hi-yen (first party)
      waʔ wa: (second party)
   f. war belts are thrown

    g. to kick aside is to reject
    h. no wampum = no word
8. Signing the deed or treaty
9. The feast and presents

PERSISTENT SYMBOLIC SYSTEMS

Symbolic systems endure even when the fulfillment of the forms cannot be accomplished. They can tolerate changes in their content so long as the main outlines are adhered to. They can suffer changes in purpose or function without great changes in structure. This should become apparent by comparing the pattern of treaty protocol with the program of the Condolence Council of modern times. It would seem that a condolence mechanism at the local level was projected and applied for making alliances at the intertribal and international levels. In process of becoming treaty protocol it underwent some early innovations. Among these was the substitution of rum for berry water and the lavish laying on of presents. Where hunters once went out to bring in deer and bear for the feast, the English introduced beef, and that has remained a requisite for the Condolence Council. Early on, strings of wampum sufficed; but as the seventeenth century wore on, wampum belts with woven symbolic figures became necessary for proper treaty documentation. These were fabricated for the occasion and later racked up and bagged at Onondaga. Wampum was itself an innovation. Once common, now it is scarce, no longer secular and political, but sacred.

    When in 1777 the Five Nations could not agree on participation in the American Revolution, the League covered its fire, which had burned since the founding at Onondaga; for all viable historical purposes, it suspended functioning as a general government for the Six Nations. The Oneida and the Sixth Nation, the Tuscarora, withdrew and espoused the patriot cause.[61] The Onondaga moved their fire to Buffalo Creek among the Seneca, where they were joined in council by Cayugas and Mohawks. Here the fire burned during the war out of Niagara, and here the wampum belts were concentrated for nearly a decade. After 1785 Joseph Brant's Loyalist Mohawks were joined on the Grand River in Canada by a band of Onondagas and two bands of the Cayugas, afterward known as the Upper and Lower Cayugas from their position on the river. But few of the Senecas followed them. The nearest Oneidas would settle on the Thames river near modern London, Ontario. Finding that a substantial number of chiefly families had removed to Canada, the extant resident chiefs re-kindled the fire of the League which became the model for local government of the Six Nations Reserve on Grand River. As such it was the legitimate government of the reserve until 1924, when it was abolished by the Canadian Indian Act, and a government of elected councillors was substituted. At Buffalo Creek the old chiefs had divided the treasury of wampum belts and half were carried to Canada. There the institutions of the League were best preserved for later study, including the "reading of the wampum belts" and the Condolence Council. Following Horatio Hale, Six Nations Reserve became the Mecca for Iroquianists, for here the traditions and the grand style of council and ritual oratory flourish even now. The adherents of the League today are mainly Longhouse people who maintain a second government in opposition to the elected chiefs.

Meanwhile during the diaspora at Buffalo Creek, Onondagas drifted back to Old Onondaga, and the then wampum keeper shouldered the bag containing the remaining half of the wampum belts and carried it back to the valley south of modern Syracuse. After the years of trouble that preceded and followed the disastrous treaties at Buffalo Creek and the sale of the Seneca reservation, the two main divisions of the Senecas at Cattaraugus and Allegany formed the Seneca Nation of Indians with a written constitution and by-laws, which provided for an elected council.[62] It is a viable government today, and comprises most of the Seneca descendants. The Tonawanda Band of Senecas, however, adheres to the old system with eight sachems, just as Onondaga has retained the fourteen chiefs of its League delegation. Both of these councils of life chiefs are the local governments of a reserve. The Tuscaroras have a similar system, and have joined with the preceding two to form the League east of Niagara that now includes some Mohawks at Akwesasne and Caughnawaga. Retaining and reviving the ancient forms, the ritual and the symbolism are compelling. Today the symbols are the supports of national identity. Small wonder that its adherents have aspirations to grandeur, for theirs is a glorious tradition.

NOTES

1. W. N. Fenton, "An Iroquois Condolence Council for Installing Cayuga Chiefs in 1945," *Journal of the Washington Academy of Sciences* 36(1946):110–27; idem, "Collecting Materials for a Political History of the Six Nations," *Proceedings of the American Philosophical Society* 93 (1949): 233–38.

2. W. N. Fenton, "The Lore of the Longhouse: Myth, Ritual, and Red Power," *Anthropological Quarterly* 48(1975): 131–47.

3. Fenton, "Iroquois Condolence Council."

4. W. N. Fenton, "The Roll Call of the Iroquois Chiefs: A Study of a Mnemonic Cane from the Six Nations Reserve," *Smithsonian Miscellaneous Collections* 111:15(1950): 1–73.

5. W. N. Fenton, "Northern Iroquoian Culture Patterns," in *Northeast*, ed. Bruce C. Trigger, vol. 15 of *Handbook of North American Indians*, gen. ed. Wm. C. Sturtevant (Washington, D.C.: Smithsonian Institution 1978), pp. 296–321.

6. Joseph-Francois Lafitau, *Customs of the American Indians Compared with the Customs of Primitive Times*, trans. and ed. William N. Fenton and Elizabeth L. Moore, 2 vols. Publications of the Champlain Society 48–49 (Toronto, 1974, 1975), 1:li, 72.

7. But the historical descent of the condolence paradigm may not be quite this direct. Since the writing of this essay, Dr. Michael K. Foster's research with Chief Jacob Thomas of Six Nations Reserve on a secular form of council, as distinct from the "mixed religious-political event that was the Condolence," discloses features shared by both, particularly in the preliminary phase when the two moieties or "sides" lift the burden of grief from each other's minds by exchanging what Hewitt termed "The Three Rare (or Bare) Words." Foster finds important differences in the format of the two types of councils. Until it can be demonstrated that the distinction between two types of councils extends back to the earliest historical records, and they have separate histories, one cannot know whether the differences are greater than the similarities. One thing is clear. The historical antecedents of the Codolence protocol go back to 1645; it frequently precedes secular councils and occupies the first day before the business can be put on the mat; and the two are scarcely distinguishable. The roots of the secular council protocol as such await recovery (M. K. Foster to Francis Jennings, letter dated 31 October 1980).

8. Cadwallader Colden, *The History of the Five Indian Nations Depending on the Province of New York* (1727), ed. John Gilmary Shea (New York, 1866). There are augmented London editions of 1747 and 1750.

9. Lawrence C. Wroth, "The Indian Treaty as Literature," *Yale Review* 17(1928): 749–66.

10. Carl Van Doren, "Introduction," in *Indian Treaties Printed by Benjamin Franklin, 1736–1762*, ed. Julian P. Boyd (Philadelphia: Historical Society of Pennsylvania, 1938), p. vii.

11. "An Account of the First Confederacy of the Six Nations . . . ," *The American Magazine* (December 1744): 665–69. (London)

12. Paul A. W. Wallace, *Conrad Weiser (1696–1760) Friend of Colonist and Mohawk* (Philadelphia: University of Pennsylvania Press, 1945), pp. 198ff.

13. Claude-Charles Le Roy de Bacqueville de La Potherie, *Histoire de l'Amérique Septentrionale*, 4 vols. (Paris, 1722).

14. Wroth, "Indian Treaty as Literature"; Van Doren, "Introduction," in *Indian Treaties*, ed. Boyd.

15. Wroth, "Indian Treaty as Literature," p. 766.

16. This entire section depends heavily on Fenton's "Northern Iroquoian Culture Patterns," in *Northeast*, ed. Trigger.

17. This reciprocal relationship between the chief's title and the name of the town applies to but two or three of the fifty Founders—notably the first two titles on the Seneca roster: Skanyada:yoʔ, "Handsome Lake" and Shaʔdagaenhyeːs, "Skies of equal height or length"; but in later times the towns were known after the title of the principal chief resident there.

18. A. A. Goldenweiser, "On Iroquois Work 1912," pp. 464–75, in *Summary Report of the Geological Survey Branch of the Canadian Department of Mines for the Calendar Year 1912* (Ottawa, 1914), p. 473; Fenton, *Patterns*, 309.

19. J. N. B. Hewitt and W. N. Fenton, ed., "The Requickening Address of the Iroquois Condolence Council," *Journal of the Washington Academy of Sciences* 34, no. 3 (1944): 65–85, 82. In editing Hewitt's posthumous manuscript, I adhered to his "organic analogy" for interpreting Iroquois kinship and moiety reciprocity. Other explanations may have equal validity. My colleague, Dr. Mary Druke, has questioned the concept of extension of kinship terms from "real" (biological) kinship relations to political relations as being the most useful way of viewing use of kinship terms in political rhetoric. She suggests rather that the use of kinship terms in political contexts may exert a feedback effect into the usage of such terms in reference to biological relationships. (Druke to Fenton, p.c. 7 January 1981). Both Hewitt and Goldenweiser made a case for the biological reality of the uterine or maternal family (a lineage) as distinguished from the fictional clan. This whole problem of the use of kin terms in political relations awaits further study. My own view is that the political liturgy carries the baggage of former usage, long since obsolete in social relations. This is certainly true of the Agadoni-Kheyahdawenh relationship of the two moieties in the Confederacy. These terms count for much less in contemporary social relations.

20. In Chief Thomas' reading of the Friendship Belt, according to Dr. Foster, there is a passage bearing on the relationship of Whites and Indians. The White man at first proposes to address the Iroquois as "son", but on the Indian's refusing this term, he suggests "brother." The term in this text is the relatively neutral sibling term, which translates "we two are as siblings." After they had joined hands, in ritual contexts the term shifted to the customary elder and younger sibling relationship, with the Iroquois in the senior position (Chafe, *Seneca Dictionary*, 42; Foster, p.c.).

21. In the "readings" of the wampum belts by Chief Thomas, Dr. Foster reminds us that "there are indeed constant references to the Founders of the League. The fact that the 'ancestors' did something is sufficient sanction for doing that thing today" (M. K. Foster to Francis Jennings, p.c., 31 October 1980).

22. I use "power" here in the sense of prestige translated into action. In Iroquois polity no one ordered anyone else around. Issues were argued to consensus, and if agreement was not reached, the matter was dropped. Even when the chiefs had attained "one mind," an appeal was made to the people, hoping they would agree.

23. The Reverend Asher Wright, "Seneca Indians" (1859), W. N. Fenton, ed., *Ethnohistory* 4, no. 3 (1957): 302–21, p. 310. Goldenweiser took extensive genealogies at Six Nations Reserve ca. 1912 and discovered rules as to how offices descended within maternal lineages. I repeated this among the Seneca during the nineteen thirties to get at the nature of clanship, the function of moieties, and to collect sets of clan personal names. The old ladies who were my sources were often keepers of the names in their respective clans, and they frequently commented that a certain person, having been given a particular name, was "following" another person and would be expected to succeed to that person's offices and duties. This lends credence to Asher Wright's statement.

24. Wright, "Seneca Indians," 310–11; Fenton, "Toward the Gradual Civilization of the Indian Natives: the Missionary and Linguistic Work of Asher Wright (1803–1875) Among the Senecas of Western New York," *Proceedings of the American Philosophical Society* 100, no. 6 (1956): 567–581. Philadelphia.

25. Peter Wraxall, *An Abridgement of the Indian Affairs . . . Transacted in the Colony of New York, from the Year 1678 to the Year 1751*, ed. Chárles H. McIlwain (Cambridge, Mass., 1915), p. 195.

26. For more detailed information of Iroquois local society see Fenton, "Northern Iroquois Culture Patterns," in *Northeast*, ed. Trigger.

27. Claude Lévi-Strauss, *Structural Anthropology* (New York: Basic Books, 1963), p. 217.

28. Dr. Foster objects to my use of the term "verbatim recall," which is certainly true of songs and ritual texts, such as the "Eulogy to the Founders." But with what I have said about myth recall and recitation, which agrees with his own findings, he rather prefers "formulaic composition," which he has demonstrated is the way in which tradition works today. Rather than "memorizing" speeches, good memories depended on recalling the structure of what was said and filling in with expected phrases and figures of speech. The speakers were relaying what the chiefs prompted them to say, but in their own words. They were accomplished and recognized virtuosos. This is what impressed colonial observers who were struck with the good memories of the speakers. "Verbatim recall" applies then to the structure if not to the identical words of the original.

29. Ursula Chodowiecz first pointed out to me in an analysis of the Deganawidah myth that the epic had shifted from myth to historical tradition. Fenton, "The Lore of the Longhouse," 139. The term "by-law stuff" derives from the writings of E. A. Hoebel on Primitive Law, E. A. Hoebel, *The Law of Primitive Man: A Study in Comparative Legal Dynamics:* (Cambridge, Mass.: Harvard University Press, 1954).

30. Arthur C. Parker, "The Constitution of the Five Nations," *New York State Museum Bulletin* 184 (Albany, 1916; rpt. Syracuse University Press 1968). The history of the transformation of the several versions of an oral tradition into a chapter and then a constitution is traced in Fenton's Introduction to *Parker on the Iroquois* (Syracuse: Syracuse University Press, 1968), pp. 38–46; and in Fenton, "The Lore of the Longhouse," pp. 134–35, 144. A. A. Goldenweiser, who had recorded from Chief John Arthur Gibson in 1912 the longest version of the Deganawidah epic, concluded his review of Parker's monograph with the comment: "The Constitution of the Five Nations is a figment. It does not exist. For, apart from the legend of Dekanawidah, the Indians of the Iroquois League had no constitution, either written or unwritten." *American Anthropologist* 18(1916): 431–36. J. N. B. Hewitt was equally critical of Parker's failure to acknowledge already published material, technical errors, arbitrary editing, and insertions that he himself had provided to Seth Newhouse, its native author. Hewitt's review in *American Anthropologist* 19(1917): 429–38. My own views are expressed in "The Lore of the Longhouse," pp. 134–35, 144. These arguments aside, there is no doubt that since 1916 their "constitution" has had validity for the traditional Longhouse people.

31. Later versions are certainly more complex and longer. They often elaborate on earlier versions as selected material is fed back into them by narrators and ritualists.

32. Horatio Hale, *The Iroquois Book of Rites* (Philadelphia: D.G. Brinton, 1883), pp. 13–18; facsimile rp. with intro. by W. N. Fenton (Toronto: University of Toronto Press, 1963); J. N. B. Hewitt, "Legend of the Founding of the Iroquois League," *American Anthropologist* 5:2(1892): 131–48.

33. Douglas W. Boyce, "A Glimpse of Iroquois Culture History Through the Eyes of Joseph Brant and John Norton," *Proceedings of the American Philosophical Society* 117 no. 4 (1973): 286–94; John Norton, *The Journal of Major John Norton, 1816,* eds. Carl F. Klinck and James J. Talman, *Publications of the Champlain Society* (Toronto) 46 (1970): 98–106; John Heckewelder, *An Account of the History, Manners, and Customs of the Indian Nations Who Once Inhabited Pennsylvania and the Neighboring States* (1819), rev. ed. ed. William C. Reichel, Memoirs of the Historical Society of Pennsylvania 12 (Philadelphia, 1876): xxviii, 56, 96; Fenton, "Iroquoian Culture History: A General Evaluation," in *Symposium on Cherokee and Iroquois Culture,* eds. William N. Fenton and John Gulick, *Bureau of American Ethnology Bulletin* 180 (Washington, D.C., 1961): 270–71.

34. H. M. van den Bogaert, ". . . . Journey to the 'Maques' and 'Sinnekins' Indians, 1634–35," Ms. 819, Henry E. Huntington Library, San Marino, California. This journal was once attributed to Arendt van Corlaer (or Curler). Published in *Narratives of New Netherland, 1609–1664,* original narratives of early American history series (New York: Charles Scribner's Sons, 1909). A new translation from the Dutch is in preparation by Dr. Charles Gehring of the New York State Library.

35. Colden, *History of the Five Indian Nations*, p. xiv.

36. Elisabeth Tooker, "The League of the Iroquois: Its History, Politics, and Ritual," in *Northeast*, ed. Trigger, pp. 418–22.

37. Cf. Glossary of Figures of Speech, Section III.

38. Fenton, *The Roll Call of the Iroquois Chiefs*; Tooker, "League of the Iroquois," p. 427.

39. Tooker, "League of the Iroquois," p. 439; W. N. Fenton, "The New York State Wampum Collection: the Case for the Preservation of Cultural Treasures," *Proceedings of the American Philosophical Society* 115, no. 6(1971): 437–61.

40. Fenton, "Wampum Collection," p. 455. As for recalling what particular belts mean, Dr. Michael Foster makes a distinction between the hundreds of belts and strings that were exchanged at treaty sessions during the colonial period, for which the specific provisions and terms reached have been lost for the most part, and those belts and strings which are thought to be the validating instruments for the League – Hiawatha, Thadodaho, League circlet of fifty strings, etc. – the ceremonial instruments of the Handsome Lake religion, the fifteen strings of the present Requickening ritual of the Condolence Council, and such other belts as are now in the possession of the traditionalists. For the latter category Dr. Foster is in the process of recovering lengthy speeches from the present ritual custodians. It is already apparent that some of the ideas contained in the ritual speeches are quite old, and may even antedate the symbolism in extant belts.

41. Hale, *Iroquois Book of Rites*; W. N. Fenton, *American Indian and White Relations to 1830* (Chapel Hill: University of North Carolina Press, 1957), pp. 22–24.

42. Alfred R. Radcliffe-Brown, *Method in Social Anthropology; Selected Essays*, ed. Srinivas (Chicago: University of Chicago Press, 1958).

43. The operation of the concept of reciprocity comes through in most of Malinowski's writings, from *Argonauts of the Western Pacific* (1922) onward, and particularly in *Crime and Customs in Savage Society* (1926).

44. *The Livingston Indian Records, 1666–1723*, ed. Lawrence H. Leder (Gettysburg, Pa.: Pennsylvania Historical Association, 1956), p. 46.

45. Ibid., pp. 88–89.

46. *The Jesuit Relations and Allied Documents: Travels and Explorations of the Jesuit Missionaries in New France, 1610–1791*, ed. Reuben Gold Thwaites, 73 vols. (Cleveland, Ohio: Burrows Brothers Co., 1896–1902), 27:246 ff. See Section II, below.

47. *Jesuit Relations* 27:267.

48. *Jesuit Relations* 27:251–65; Bruce G. Trigger, *The Children of Aataentsic: A History of the Huron People to 1660*, 2 vols. (Montreal and London: McGill-Queen's University Press, 1976), 2:648.

49. *Propositions Made by the Sachems of the three Maquas Castles, to the Mayor, Aldermen, and Commonalty of the City of Albany, and Military Officers of the said City, and County in the City-Hall, February 25th, 1689/90* (Boston, 1690); Colden, *History*, p. 116–20; *Documentary History of the State of New York*, ed. E. B. O'Callaghan, 4 vols. (Albany, N.Y.: Weed, Parsons and Co., 1849–51), 2:164–70; *Collections of the New York Historical Society for the Year 1869*, Publication Fund Series, No. 2 (New York, 1870), pp. 165–72. New York Colonial Documents 3:712–14.

50. No one, to my knowledge, has worked out completely the network of kinship terms that the Iroquois projected symbolically to their neighbors, although these terms occur frequently in the literature.

51. Wraxall, *Abridgement of the Indian Affairs*, p. 217.

52. *An Account of the Treaty Between His Excellency Benjamin Fletcher . . . And the Indians*

of the Five Nations . . . at Albany, beginning the 15th of August, 1694 (New York: William Bradford, 1694).

53. Lafitau, *Customs of the American Indians* 2:173–75.

54. Hale, *Book of Rites,* p. 117; Lafitau, *Customs,* p. 174.

55. Michael K. Foster and Chief Jacob Thomas, "Kindling the Fire at Iroquois-White Councils: an Exercise in Upstreaming," ms. in author's possession.

56. Lois M. Feister, "Linguistic Communication between the Dutch and Indians in New Netherland, 1609–1664," *Ethnohistory* 20, no. 1 (1973): 25–38.

57. *Jesuit Relations* 41:87–91.

58. Dewitt Clinton, *Discourse* [on the Six Nations] *Delivered Before the New-York Historical Society, 1811* (New York, 1812), p. 36.

59. Lawrence H. Leder, *Robert Livingston, 1654–1728, and the Politics of Colonial New York* (Chapel Hill: University of North Carolina Press, 1961), see index entry "Livingston, Robert . . . Indian Affairs."

60. The reconstructed ideal paradigm is much too elaborate as a guide to actual practice. Rather, it simply incorporates a wide range of possibilities suggested by the practices found in the documents, and in that respect is a "reconstructed form" in the manner of linguistics.

61. Barbara Graymont, *The Iroquois in the American Revolution* (Syracuse: Syracuse University Press, 1972), p. 113; Samuel Kirkland, *The Journals of Samuel Kirkland, 18th-century Missionary to the Iroquois, Government Agent, Father of Hamilton College,* ed. Walter Pilkington (Clinton, N.Y.: Hamilton College, 1980), p. 120.

62. *Constitution of the Seneca Nation of Indians* (Baltimore: William Wooddy and Sons, 1848); Lester Hargrett, *A Bibliography of the Constitutions and Laws of the American Indians* (Cambridge, Mass.: Harvard University Press, 1947), 106–107; Tooker, "League of the Iroquois," pp. 435–37.

2

Iroquois Alliances in American History

FRANCIS JENNINGS

THE IROQUOIS played a special role in the history of North America during the era when European empires contested with each other for su-
premacy there. It was a complex role, not to be disposed of in a single sentence. From the point of view of the English Lords of Trade and Plantations
the Iroquois were a "barrier between his Majesty's plantations and Canada."[1]
The French of Canada saw them alternatively as a barrier or as an intrusive
threat because the Iroquois strove constantly to conquer French-allied Indians
or win them over to alliance with Great Britain. In one aspect, therefore, the
Iroquois role was active political intervention in the imperial struggles of France
and Britain.

In another aspect the Iroquois had objectives of their own that include winning a position of leadership and ascendancy over other Indian
peoples. This ascendancy has often been mentioned as a vast Indian "empire,"
but it was something peculiar to Indian cultures rather than an imitation of
European-style empires. Iroquois tributary allies came and went according to
circumstances, and the Five Nations never acquired the impersonal institutions of the bureaucratic state that were required to control and stabilize an
empire.

The Iroquois Five Nations were linked in a loose confederation rather
than a unitary state. Each of these Five Nations retained full sovereignty over
its own affairs in its own hands, and their internal structures were bound
together by kinship ties rather than relationships of estates in real property.
With this form of political organization, it was simply impossible for the Five
Nations to maintain an empire, and when the tradition of empires is examined closely it falls to pieces.

Nevertheless, the Iroquois did exert great influence over other Indians.
Sometimes they were able to conquer other tribes, and sometimes they were

able to mobilize other tribes behind a common policy. How they managed these feats depended on time, place, and circumstance.

TRADE AND ALLIANCE

The dominant factor in all diplomatic relationships after Europeans colonized the American Northeast was trade between tribes and colonies. Prerequisite for trading was a treaty relationship that might vary from a simple pact of nonbelligerence to a full alliance for mutual military aid. European powers made a point of collecting client tribes for the sake of the wealth to be gained from their trade and the power to be acquired with their manpower. By the latter part of the seventeenth century two great systems of colonial-tribal alliance had come into being—the French and the English—and the Iroquois were involved in both, but in different ways. Though they treated constantly with the French, they were always kept at arm's length because the French wanted to keep them as barriers between Canada's Indians and the English markets that offered better bargains than the French could match. With the English, however, the Iroquois became close partners in trade and war, especially after 1677 when two peace treaties were negotiated in Albany to end Indian wars in New England and on the Chesapeake Bay.[2]

THE COVENANT CHAIN

Out of the peacemaking a new organization emerged which was to maintain English-Indian peace and trade among its members for three-quarters of a century. Called the Covenant Chain, it was a multiparty alliance of two groupings of members: tribes, under the general leadership of the Iroquois, and English colonies, under the general supervision of New York. As in the modern United Nations, no member gave up its sovereignty. All decisions were made by consultation and treaty, and all were implemented by each member individually. Though seemingly amorphous, the Covenant Chain performed its functions well. These functions changed, however, as Iroquois history evolved.[3]

    During the remainder of the seventeenth century the Covenant Chain functioned primarily as an aggressive partnership of the Five Nations and New

York to penetrate the French trading and alliance systems that spread over the Great Lakes and Mississippi valley regions. For most of this period the Five Nations were at war with the French. They lost. Though the Iroquois ravaged Canada with guerrilla attacks, they failed to take any fortified town. The French, on the other hand, sent armies into Iroquoia to burn and destroy the towns of Mohawks, Onondagas, and Senecas; and French-allied Indians forced the Iroquois to withdraw from the territories in Ontario that they had conquered during the Beaver Wars.[4] Few Covenant Chain allies of the Iroquois would help. New York's governors appealed plaintively for aid from other colonies, but got little.[5] Iroquois tributaries refused to contribute warriors to the slaughter.[6] Tribesmen of the Five Nations themselves abandoned Iroquoia to seek refuge elsewhere: Onondaga chief Sadeganaktie complained in 1701 that the French "have drain'd us of our people. They all goe to Canada and that upon pretence of Religion and to be converted. Wee see itt is only to enslave us."[7] Susquehannocks who had been adopted into Iroquois tribes returned to the Susquehanna valley to renew their tribal existence at Conestoga, and some Senecas went with them.[8] By 1700 the Iroquois were beaten and battered. Defying New York's prohibition, they made peace with the French in a historic series of treaty negotiations.[9]

Again a myth obtrudes; to wit, that the Five Nations cleverly decided upon a policy of neutrality for themselves between the French and English colonies, and persuaded the French to agree to it. It has to be said plainly that the Iroquois were in such a condition that they had to take what terms the French would offer. They dared not risk resumption of war. Facing the French and the Indian allies of the French, who far outnumbered them and now had firearms, the Five Nations capitulated to a policy of neutrality imposed upon them by the French.

It is not hard to understand the reasoning behind the French terms. Since Champlain's era, the French had desired to keep the Iroquois as a barrier between English traders and New France's allied tribes. For that purpose, it was necessary to keep the Five Nations independent and at odds with the French allies. Divide and conquer. If the great treaty ratified in 1701 had stipulated that the Iroquois were to be conquered subjects of the French, then the French allies would have had free passage through Iroquoia to Albany, and Montreal's trade would have been ruined.[10] The alternative was to let the Iroquois keep their independence as a barrier to free trade and a buffer between the empires. For the Iroquois it was far preferable to outright subjection, and they accepted.

Neutrality to them did not mean passivity. In the peace that followed the great treaty, they used diplomacy to slowly regain their former position of importance. Source records are very scant for the early part of the eighteenth century, but such as exist show a gradual resurgence of Iroquois leadership among the tribes. They succeeded poorly in the west and north, where French agents acted alertly to counter their influence, but they made headway among the Indians to the southward of Iroquoia, along the lower Susquehanna valley.

This was awkward territory. While at their height of prowess, the Iroquois had claimed ownership of the whole Susquehanna valley on grounds of a spurious "conquest" of its Susquehannock inhabitants who had, in fact, been given sanctuary and adoption within the Five Nations.[11] When William Penn proposed to purchase the valley from them, they rejected his offer and gave a deed of trust to New York's governor instead; but Penn's royal charter ultimately withstood the Yorkers' attempts to take the valley away from him.[12] Then came the disasters of the French wars and the re-establishment of the Susquehannock tribe at Conestoga. William Penn came to America a second time and made a second offer to purchase the Susquehanna valley in 1701; but this time he had made his offer to the tribe at Conestoga instead of the Five Nations, and the Conestogas sold happily. Onondaga chief Ahookasoongh witnessed the transaction without protest and signed the deed of cession. So low had Iroquois fortunes sunk that he signed below the names of the Conestoga chiefs although the Five Nations claimed the Conestogas as tributaries.[13]

After 1701 the Susquehanna River and its valley became an arena for much intertribal and intercolonial contention. The river was the "warriors' path" from Iroquoia to the back country of Maryland, Virginia, and the Carolinas, and was much used by the Five Nations in their raids upon southern tribes. In the reverse direction it served two kinds of traffic: vengeance-bent Catawbas, and a variety of other tribes fleeing from conquest by the southern colonies. With a keen eye to strategy, the Iroquois allowed the refugees to settle undisturbed on the Susquehanna where they became buffers against Catawba retaliation and victuallers for Iroquois warriors heading south. The strategy worked perfectly to secure Iroquoia's southern flank, but it exposed the Indians of the Susquehanna to casualties from the wrathful Catawbas.

Pennsylvania turned a blind eye to the violence and cooperated gladly in these arrangements because the refugees built up a busy center of trade around Conestoga. However, the merchants and governments of New York were distressed.[14] In their understanding the Conestoga trade could grow only at the expense of Albany's. But the refugee Indians on the Susquehanna were only too glad to enjoy the combined hospitality of Pennsylvania's Quaker pacifists and the Five Nations' militarists, and the refugees willingly accepted simultaneous statuses as clients of the colony and tributaries of the Iroquois. Thus the Five Nations rebuilt their strength. In all likelihood the strategy was worked out by careful counselling of many leaders, but one Onondaga chief stands out as a guiding spirit. He was Decanisora (spelled *Teganissorens* by the French).[15] Under his leadership, and following his policies, the Onondagas led the Oneidas, Cayugas, and Senecas in a political course effectively independent of the Mohawks. The western Iroquois developed southern and western strategies, but the Mohawks clung to their partnership with Albany and conducted their individual diplomacy with Massachusetts and Connecticut.

In effect the Iroquois League became two confederations bound only by the rituals of the Five Nations' Great Law. The Mohawks drew into the Covenant Chain the tribes of the Hudson River and New England's back country. The other Iroquois nations, under Onondaga leadership, collected tributaries along the Susquehanna and labored incessantly to gather more from the French alliance system in the west. Mohawk tributaries seem to have come and gone in transitory fashion except for the Schaghticokes of the upper Hudson; this inconstancy was caused, as in the west, by French influence. But the tribes along the Susquehanna were mostly shielded from French intrigues and pressures (with the exception of some Shawnees), and they became the "props" of the Five Nations. The Conestogas were joined there by Brandywine Delawares, Shawnees from scattered regions of the west and south, Piscataway-Conoys from Maryland, and Tuscaroras from North Carolina. After 1722, the Iroquois village of Shamokin, at the forks of the Susquehanna's West and North branches, became home for Tutelos and Saponis from Virginia and the Carolinas, and Nanticokes from Delaware and Maryland; and after 1724 these were joined by a number of Schuylkill Delawares. By 1730 the Susquehanna valley held a veritable united nations of Indians speaking Iroquoian, Algonquian, and Siouan languages. They were all tributary to the Five Nations, and some moved northward to live in Iroquoia after a short stay on the Susquehanna.[16]

The myth of Iroquois conquest has been supported by this tributary network, but the source records show that almost all of these Indians were refugees from colonial mistreatment who took advantage of the welcome extended conjointly by the Five Nations and Pennsylvania. The true strength of the Five Nations arose less from bellicosity than from hospitality. Their losses from war were incalculably great. Their gains by negotiation and agreement offset the losses.

It must be stressed, however, that the bases from which they negotiated were their alliances with the British colonies to whom they made themselves useful in a variety of ways. Until 1700 they had fought New York's wars, as well as their own, against French Canada. Then and later they channeled vast quantities of furs to Albany. Mohawk tribal wars in New England reduced the damage of French-allied Indians to back country colonial settlements. The Iroquois tributaries on the Susquehanna supplied the hunting manpower with which Pennsylvania's trading system was built. For all the British colonies the

Iroquois acted as a barrier against incursions by the French and their tribal allies, and as a vanguard penetrating the vast French trading system.

At a multilateral treaty in Albany in 1722, the Five Nations began, rather reluctantly, to assume responsibility for policing certain other Indians at the request of the governors of Virginia, Pennsylvania, and New York. The single issue involved was the incessant raiding by Iroquois raiding parties (bolstered with tributary recruits) in Virginia's frontier regions. The treaty participants agreed on a limit line along the Blue Ridge mountains which the Iroquois promised not to cross, and they undertook also the responsibility to prevent five tributary groups from crossing it: the Tuscaroras in Iroquoia (who shortly became the Sixth nation of the League), the Conestogas, the Shawnee bands in the Covenant Chain, the Iroquois Ochtaghquanawicroones, and a mixed village called the Ostanghaes. All except the Tuscaroras dwelt on the Susquehanna main trunk or one of its branches. The special significance of this treaty is that the Iroquois assumption of authority had the implied backing of the colonies that were demanding Iroquois performance of a policing function. One might almost say that the authority was imposed by the colonies upon the Five Nations. The Iroquois were careful to limit their responsibility. They evaded assumption of authority over the still powerful Delawares. They had not the means to control the Delawares, and had no inclination to presume beyond their real power.[17] Even some of the fragmented Shawnees resisted Iroquois discipline—not by confrontation and battle, but by drifting off to the Ohio region where they made terms with the French and defied all efforts to draw them eastward again.

During the 1720s the Iroquois gave little attention to domineering over other tribes to serve the purposes of colonials because the Six Nations were deeply discontent with their Covenant Chain alliance. The Mohawks had been squeezed out of much of their participation in the fur trade by the growth of direct, though illegal, trade between merchants of Montreal and those of Albany.[18] Land speculators seized Mohawk lands to sell to a gradually increasing colonial population; even the town of Albany itself attempted a fraudulent, large-scale seizure.[19] Although there is no record of internal discussion of the Six Nations, it cannot be doubted that refugee Tuscaroras had much to say about their brutally harsh treatment by southern British colonies, including Virginia which was a member (by repeated treaties) of the Covenant Chain.[20] The Senecas were much disturbed by forts built in their territory by both New York and New France. The Cayugas and Oneidas, who had special claims to the Susquehanna valley, observed with dismay how the land east of the river was filling up with European immigrants, to the great disturbance of the tributary Indians resident in the valley. All signs pointed to dispossession and displacement of Covenant Chain Indians.

For the first and only time in their history, the Iroquois proposed to fight a war of race against race. In 1726 they summoned all Indians to take up the hatchet against all colonials. This was to be a war of surprise, so plans and preparations were kept deeply secret, but Shawnee chief Newcheconner disclosed years later that "the five nations Came and Said, our Land is goeing to be taken from us. Come, brothers, assisstt us. Lett us fall upon and fightt with the English." Simultaneously the Senecas had issued an "order" to all the Canadian tribes as far west as Lake Superior to attack all French posts. But the other tribes failed to respond favorably, and the Delawares and Shawnees rejected the Iroquois proposal categorically. The race war was aborted.[21]

In a cold fury the Iroquois decided to "let the English have all this land," and they "made women" of the Delawares and Shawnees—or more accurately, of those eastern bands living as guests on Iroquois territory. The significance of this rhetorical act is not clear. At first, it does not seem to have affected the Delawares much, one way or another; old chief Sassoonan continued to treat with Pennsylvania directly, without Iroquois intervention. Shawnee experience was different: in 1727 the Iroquois offered to cede the lower Susquehanna valley to Pennsylvania,[22] and they ordered the Shawnee villages to relocate north of the proposed cession. As even the village on the upper Delaware was moved, it seems clear that the relocation process was a deployment along a new Iroquois warriors' path to the west.[23] But not all the Shawnees obeyed. One band migrated to the vicinity of Lake Erie where it escaped Iroquois domination by obtaining French protection.[24]

Pennsylvanians were baffled by these mysterious happenings among the Indians. They turned aside the Iroquois offer to sell the Susquehanna valley because of belief that William Penn had already bought it from the occupying Conestogas. Baffled, the Iroquois sent Oneida chief Shikellamy to Shamokin to supervise the intransigent remaining Shawnees and to promote warmer friendship with Pennsylvania (Shikellamy was son of a French father and Cayuga mother, who had been adopted by the Oneidas when young).[25]

The Six Nations had become disillusioned with their special partnership with New York, and they were carefully exploring for alternatives. In the founding years of the Covenant Chain, the Mohawks had proclaimed that Albany was "the prefixed place" for all treaty negotiations with British colonies, and as late as 1722 the governors of Virginia and Pennsylvania had had to journey to Albany to do business with the Iroquois; but the Indians had become restless under New York's supervision of such meetings. In 1723, Albany's monopoly ended. Delegates from the Six Iroquois Nations, the Hudson River Schaghticokes, and the Mohegans took a "coal from the fire" at Albany to treat with the Great and General Court of Massachusetts at Boston. Accompanied though they were by New York's Colonel Schuyler, they agreed to negotiate "particular treaties" thereafter at Deerfield, Massachusetts.[26] (I do not know the history of subsequent negotiations there. The fire at Albany continued to burn, but issues concerning Massachusetts exclusively would be discussed over the new fire at Deerfield.)

As Keepers of the Eastern Door, the Mohawks were primarily responsible for relations with the New England colonies, and they relinquished to the western Iroquois under Onondaga leadership the conduct of negotiations with colonies south of New York. When the western four nations also looked for an alternative to New York's monopoly, they turned first to Pennsylvania. Their agent was Shikellamy, the Oneida/Cayuga chief at Shamokin. The records are a little murky; they do not disclose clearly who took the initiative. They do show quite clearly, however, that both sides were ready for close alliance. Only the terms were at issue. In 1731 Pennsylvania's council was distressed by one Shawnee band's departure from the colony because the Shawnees had become pawns in imperial competition. Traders reported from the Ohio country that the French claimed a protectorate over the western Shawnee bands, and on that basis claimed sovereignty over the chartered territory of western Pennsylvania. To nullify the French claim, the colony wanted the Indians safely back east, but lacked the power to enforce its desire. Though Pennsylvania's traders had pursued the Shawnees to their western villages, traders' exhortations fell on deaf ears; the western Shawnees continued to do business but maintained their independence and their distance. Pennsylvania's government turned to the Iroquois, all unaware that Iroquois domination was one reason for Shawnee behavior.[27]

ALLIANCE WITH PENNSYLVANIA

In 1732 the western four Iroquois nations journeyed to Philadelphia for a treaty at which William Penn's son Thomas proposed to light a new fire for them in his province; i.e., to establish Philadelphia as a regular site for future treaties, on a par with Albany. He asked them further to bring the Shawnees back, and offered help for the task. Since persuasion had failed with the Shawnees, it is clear that Penn was proposing coercion. In short, he asked the Iroquois to play policeman for him, in return for which he would support their authority. The Iroquois were interested but wary.[28] Penn's offers remained in limbo for four years. Tentatively, the Iroquois sent "orders" to the Shawnees, who ignored them, and the Iroquois let the rejection stand. They did not wish to take up the hatchet against Indians whom they still claimed as tributaries, however recalcitrant.[29]

Iroquois relations with New York did not improve, and other problems besides the Shawnees beset both the Iroquois and the Pennsylvanians.

In 1736 the western four Iroquois nations came once more to Philadelphia, prepared to come to terms. They lit a new fire, as Thomas Penn had suggested, and for the next couple of decades Pennsylvania became at least as important as New York in the Iroquois universe. Thomas Penn set aside all previous claims to the Susquehanna valley and purchased it once again, finally this time.[30] On the formal record all was love and good will, but secret negotiations followed the formal meetings. Initiating these, Pennsylvania's James Logan instructed provincial interpreter Conrad Weiser at Shamokin to strike a bargain well out of sight of Quaker moralists. Logan wanted the Iroquois to abandon the Delawares whose remaining lands on the upper Delaware River were being encroached upon by colonial immigrants and in which Logan personally had a large financial stake. He offered in return to revolutionize tribal relationships in Pennsylvania. For the future, if the Iroquois would comply, the colony would no longer treat directly with the Delawares and other tribes, but would recognize only the Iroquois as spokesmen for them all. Among other things, Pennsylvania would recognize no Indian right to cede land, except that of the Iroquois. In abstract terms of analysis, a number of individual tribal clients of the colony would be replaced by a client system under Iroquois governance with Pennsylvania's support. More bluntly, the Iroquois were to become the colony's "keepers" of its client tribes, and to get paid for their services.[31]

The bargaining "went hard" as Weiser reported, but the four western nations' chiefs consented after being plied with much rum and many presents. (The Mohawks were not represented.) In the long run the participants' acquiescence was to prove a serious mistake in high policy as the resentment resulting from Iroquois policing gradually disintegrated the Covenant Chain tributary system in Pennsylvania. Not foreseeing this, the Iroquois sensed only opportunity. They raised their price for disciplining Pennsylvania's tribes. More than a little money and a spree or two would be required. Pennsylvania must prevail on the governments of Maryland and Virginia to purchase territories within those colonies that the Iroquois claimed by "right of conquest." The demand was awkward, because Pennsylvania had border quarrels with the other colonies, but governor George Thomas promptly initiated correspondence with his counterparts.[32]

For various reasons, agreement was slow in forthcoming, and the Iroquois had to wait eight years for their southern treaty. They were patient. The Pennsylvanians, however, were in a hurry to accomplish their own purposes. In 1737 they consummated the infamous Walking Purchase by means of which they dispossessed the Delawares of their remaining territory without paying a penny.[33] Naturally enough, the Delawares reacted angrily, and the colony's governor threatened them toughly. The Delawares appealed to their "uncles," the Iroquois, for the help which was their due as tributary allies, and the western nations of the League came once more into the colony in 1742. But they came to help the colonists rather than the Indians. Onondaga speaker Canasatego reached heights of oratorical wrath as he metaphorically seized the Delawares by their hair and flung them off their lands. "You are women," he told them, and castigated them for asserting right to their lands. Though the Iroquois had explicitly recognized this right in 1736, Canasatego now vehemently denied it in 1742. The Delawares departed from the treaty, conquered without a shot.[34]

It was an easy victory for the western Iroquois. At last they were able to subdue the tribe whose independence and competitive spirit had been a source of repeated friction. At last they had an absolutely exclusive alliance with a colony by means of which they could strengthen their hold on their tributaries. And their patience with Pennsylvania was rewarded, after all. In 1744 arrangements were completed with Maryland and Virginia, and a grand multicolonial treaty was held in the frontier town of Lancaster, Pennsylvania. In high spirits, Canasatego strode into town at the head of his people. He ran the show. He insisted that Conrad Weiser should be the official interpreter, he managed all the proceedings according to Iroquois protocol, he dined and drank and joked with the colonial gentlemen, and he collected a quite satisfactory payment for the lands in their colonies to which the Iroquois claimed a right of conquest.[35]

But if Canasatego ran the show, the Virginians walked off with the proceeds of admission. When Canasatego signed the deed of cession, he failed to get its full meaning explained, and what he signed gave away half a continent. The deed was so phrased that the Iroquois renounced claim to all lands within Virginia's chartered territory, and the charter's sea-to-sea boundaries donated to the colony most of Ohio and all the rest of the future United States north of Virginia's southern boundary line, extending to the Pacific coast.[36]

That was not all that Canasatego gave away; indeed it was the least of his dispositions because, fortunately for the Iroquois, other Englishmen would never let Virginia get away with gobbling so much territory that they coveted themselves. The greatest loss to the Iroquois had come from forfeiting the respect and trust formerly accorded by their tributaries. The Walking Purchase fraud had ruptured the Convenant Chain. By it, the Iroquois had gained control over the fragments of Delawares on the Susquehanna and Delaware rivers, but the great bulk of the tribe had long since departed to the valleys of the Ohio River and its tributary streams, and they were in no mood to accept Iroquois domination. In the west, the Iroquois were on their own; Pennsylvania could not help them there. The western Delawares, on the other hand, were strengthened by their Shawnee friends and even by Mingo secessionists from Iroquoia who had no intention of letting the distant Grand

Council of the League dictate their affairs. It is not possible to second guess history, but it seems reasonable to assume that, if the Iroquois had befriended the eastern Delawares against Pennsylvania, the western Delawares would have retained some affection for their Iroquois "uncles." Instead they maintained a suspicious and latently hostile attitude that eventually led to a complete breakaway.

The 1744 treaty at Lancaster ended an era in more than one sense. For over thirty years the Iroquois and all other Eastern Indians had enjoyed the boon of a peace between the empires of Britain and France. This peace was far from being absolute and all-embracing because colonials often plunged into conflict on their own account and did not hesitate to involve client tribes; but at least there was no constant, widespread egging on by crown officials. For the Six Nations the benefit of the peace could be expressed very simply: Iroquoia remained free from invasion by armed forces though encroachment by settlers and land speculators never ceased. In 1744, however, the royal crowns of Great Britain and France declared war against each other, and the first worldwide war loomed on the horizon. Until France was expelled from Canada in 1763, all eastern Indians would live under threat of being crushed between the jaws of the imperial vise.

The war of 1744–48—called in America "King George's War"—did not see massive action in America; but, under the influence of New York's William Johnson, the Mohawks took the warpath, and the French retaliated with raids on Saratoga and Albany. These were signals of the showdown to come. Tension increased everywhere as the colonies prepared themselves. One British colony, in particular, had a master plan. A group of Virginians, under the leadership of Thomas Lee, intended to expand westward beyond the Appalachians into territory long claimed by France. Lee's Virginians had been deadly serious at Lancaster when they wrote the tricky language of their deed of cession from the Iroquois. They aimed determinedly at realizing the full potential of their charter by extending Virginia from the Atlantic to the Pacific. They petitioned to the government of Virginia in the following words: "It was generally reputed that, by the treaty of Lancaster, as well as by deed, bearing date July 2, 1744, the northern Indians, by the name of the Six Nations (who claimed all the lands west of Virginia, and also to, and on the waters of the Mississippi and the lakes, by right of conquest from the several nations of Indians who formerly inhabited that country, and had been extirpated by the said Six Nations) did yield up, make over, and for ever quit claim to his majesty, and his successors, all the said lands west of Virginia, with all their right thereto, as far as his majesty should at any time thereafter be pleased to extend the said colony. . . . In consequence thereof, at a council held April 26, 1745, several persons were allowed to take up and survey 300,000 acres thereof."[37]

THE CHAIN IN THE OHIO COUNTRY

In 1747 the Virginians organized the Ohio Company of Virginia, and in 1749 the crown granted the company 200,000 acres in the area bounded by the Ohio and Great Kanawha rivers and the Allegheny mountains on condition that the company build a fort and found a settlement. 300,000 acres more would be granted after the conditions had been met. Despite the earlier language about the Iroquois having "extirpated" the Indians who "formerly inhabited that country," it was well recognized that plenty of Indians were in residence at the time, and that they were unlikely to look kindly on colonial intrusion into their sanctuary. Most of the Ohio Indians had retreated to that region from colonial encroachment farther east. To soften their resentment, the crown provided £1000 for presents in goods, and Virginia invited them to a treaty.[38]

The Ohio Indians were divided among themselves. The Shawnees had left the Covenant Chain though they remained on amicable terms with the English and the Iroquois. The Delawares were restive though formally attached to the Chain. The "Mingo" Senecas did what they pleased regardless of strictures from Onondaga. Seneca "half king" Tanaghrisson, aided by Oneida chief Scarouady, represented the Onondaga grand council at the Ohio as Shikellamy did at Shamokin. They had increasing difficulty in keeping their charges in line as French pressure increased. Conrad Weiser had noticed the distinction between the claims to power and the realities of the situation when he traveled to the Ohio in 1748, and he recommended that Pennsylvania reverse the policy in effect since the Walking Purchase in order to treat directly once more with the Delawares.[39] In 1751, Pennsylvania's governor sent a message to the Ohio Delawares to "choose amongst Yourselves one of your wisest Counsellors and present to your Brethren the Six Nations and me for a Chief, and he so chosen by you shall be looked upon by us as your King, with whom Publick Business shall be transacted."[40] This was a grave blow to the Iroquois prestige because, since 1742, Pennsylvania's business with the Delawares had been transacted through the Iroquois. Thus, when Virginia sent commissioners in 1752 to treat with the Ohio Indians at Logstown, Tanaghrisson was at his wits' end. He knew that if commissioners from both Virginia and Pennsylvania treated directly with the Delawares, as they had every intention of doing, Iroquois pre-eminence in the west country would be irretrievably lost.

He resorted to a device as clever as anything ever schemed in the foreign ministries of Europe or Asia. In the presence of the colonial commissioners, Tanaghrisson asserted the right to the Iroquois to appoint a chief over the Delawares. Then he "gave" them, as "king," chief Shingas, who just happened to be the chief chosen by the Delawares themselves. In the same breath Tanaghrisson "ordered" the Delawares to conduct all their public business with the English through Shingas which was exactly what the Delawares had intended to do. Probably rather amused, they went along with the charade. Saving face with grace, Tanaghrisson preserved the form of command by pretending to deputize its substance, and the Delawares resumed their part in treaty making that they had lost in 1742 when Canasatego demoted them to "women."[41]

Tensions remained. The Indians desired protection against the advancing French. The Virginians wanted freedom to colonize and sell land, and were not at all enthusiastic about incurring the expense of building and garrisoning a fort. The Delawares were dead set against the introduction of settlers into their second homeland; that was what they had fled from in the east. The Iroquois were intent on re-establishing their former special partnerships with English colonies and their former ascendancy over other Indian nations. The formal result, in Randolph C. Downes's words, was that "in return for a half hearted consent to the reaffirmation of the Lancaster Treaty of 1744, the Indians obtained of the Virginians an equally half-hearted promise to build a 'strong house' at the forks of the Ohio."[42] But the Virginians got more: by judicious bribery of Pennsylvania's agents at Logstown—George Croghan and Andrew Montour—they arranged to get an agreement from Tanaghrisson and other Iroquois to permit a settlement at the forks of the Ohio. This was done in a back room, without Delaware knowledge.[43] The Virginians departed with what they had come for, the Delawares were befuddled, and Tanaghrisson had managed to save his position. What muddied these murky waters even more was the reaction of the grand council at Onondaga whose chiefs complained bitterly that they had neither been represented at Logstown, nor been properly informed of what transpired there, nor received any of the presents so lavishly distributed by the Virginians. On the other hand, the Ohio Indians complained of neglect by Onondaga.[44] The value of Tanaghrisson's secret deed to Virginia diminishes as one reads his statement in open council that nothing done at Logstown could be final without approval of the Onondaga council.[45] It appears that he covered himself both ways: If Onondaga should approve, the Virginians would love him for helping out, while if Onondaga disapproved, the secret "deed" was worthless in the eyes of the Iroquois.

The French made it worthless in any case. While Virginians wheedled at Logstown, a French party raided farther down the Ohio where a band of Miami (or Twightwee) Indians had become so attracted to George Croghan's bargains in trade, and so disenchanted with French constraints, that it had made a treaty of alliance with Pennsylvania and moved bodily to Croghan's stronghold of Pickawillany. Their chief was dubbed variously La Demoiselle by the French and Old Britain by the English. His representatives at Logstown were consternated in the midst of the treaty to learn that a French officer and allied western Indians had descended upon Pickawillany while most of its men were out hunting, and wiped out the village, not forgetting to cook Old Britain and eat his heart.[46] It was but the beginning of a general campaign by the French to sweep all the Pennsylvania traders out of the region. Indian desires for protection from the French became frantic demands.

New France began building a chain of forts down the west side of the Alleghenies, moving from one strategic waterway to another with the obvious objective of bringing the whole Ohio valley under tight control. These forts spelled deep trouble for all Indians. Unlike French forts along the Mississippi, which were designed primarily to protect and control trade and thus secure tribal loyalties, the new forts formed a line aimed directly at the region where the Ohio Company professed to build its own fort and found its own colony.

Virginia's Governor Dinwiddie commissioned the stalwart, though inexperienced, relative of a principal partner in the Ohio Company to journey to the commander of the foremost French post and tell him to go away. This young George Washington made his way to French Fort Le Boeuf, picking up Tanaghrisson along the way. They were received politely by the French commander and sent back with no satisfaction at all.

While Washington and Tanaghrisson failed at Fort Le Boeuf, a party of Delawares, Shawnees, Twightwees, and Wyandots rushed eastward to beg for help from Virginia and Pennsylvania. They were led by Tanaghrisson's partner Scarouady who was as anxious as Tanaghrisson himself to maintain authority over the unruly tributaries. Scarouady had difficulty at Winchester, Virginia, where the Delawares and Shawnees insisted on speaking for themselves—a grave breach of what the Iroquois held to be their privilege. Scarouady conferred privately with the Virginians to admonish them that the Shawnees had no right "to transact any publick business."[47] At Carlisle, Pennsylvania, he became the sole speaker for all the tribes by agreeing to speak the words they gave him. Again the form of leadership became an empty shell.[48]

Tanaghrisson and Scarouady used certain diplomatic amenities adapted to their different audiences, but they said essentially the same thing to both the French and the English: Keep us supplied with necessary goods, and stay off our land.

While the "upper" Iroquois struggled to stall off invasion of the Ohio region, the Mohawks were contending with another invasion of their own territory proper. Speculators had contrived over the years to get deeds of varying authenticity, but mostly fraudulent, to large tracts of Iroquois land, the most notorious of which was the Kayaderosseras patent embracing 800,000 acres of Mohawk territory.[49] As the speculators pushed settlers into these vast tracts, Mohawk patience with New York snapped. In June 1753 chief Hendrick declared an end to their ancient alliance: "As soon as we come home we will send up a Belt of Wampum to our Brothers the [other] 5 Nations to acquaint them the Covenant Chain is broken between you and us."[50]

When this news reached England, the crown's Board of Trade and Plantations instantly recognized its significance. The Board knew and stated that "the steady adherence of these Indians to the British interest" was needed to secure its colonies "from the fatal effects of the encroachment of a foreign power."[51] The issues at stake required intervention by the crown, so the Board instructed colonial governments to treat with the Iroquois in behalf of the crown.[52] But the Virginia gentlemen were determined to have the west for themselves. In a display of confident independence that foreshadowed events to come, they "excused" themselves from attendance at Albany and pursued their own strategy.[53]

In Virginia powerful men had invested heavily in the Ohio Company, including Governor Dinwiddie, so a company of soldiers was sent off to confront the French. In a serious mistake of judgment, Dinwiddie entrusted their command to young George Washington, newly commissioned as a colonel, whose rashness brought the expedition to grief. Washington marched to the forks of the Ohio, picked up Tanaghrisson again, and tried to inveigle the Delawares into joining his forces. He had not the gift to foresee the legends that were to be manufactured about his obsessive truthfulness, so he reported candidly that he told those Indians that the only motive of his conduct was "to put you again in possession of your lands, and to take care of your wives and children, to dispossess the French, to maintain your rights and to secure the whole country for you." The Delawares remained unconvinced. They criticized Washington's way of dealing with them through Tanaghrisson. They reminded him that Virginia had recognized their chief Shingas at Logstown "and told us he should transact all public Business between you and us." They added that they had notice from Onondaga of English and French intentions to fight each other, "and exhorted us to do nothing in that matter, but what was reasonable."[54] And they reasonably avoided getting involved.

The French continued to build forts, climaxing with Fort Duquesne precisely at the strategic forks of the Ohio where Virginia had proposed to build (now "the Point" of Pittsburgh). Their forts gave them full control over the Ohio Indians. Pennsylvania's traders were driven out and Virginia's militia defeated and driven from the field. To obtain the necessities of life, the Ohio Indians had to deal with French traders, however expensive; and to live without punishment they had to obey French commands, however harsh. They had become an occupied people paying what amounted to extra taxes to their occupiers. Neither English colonials nor the Iroquois League could help them. The British crown, however, had begun to move its own power.

While Washington was futilely tramping about, the grand multi-party treaty ordered by the Board of Trade convened in Albany. Its purpose, so far as the crown was concerned, was to unite the colonies and allied Indians in a concerted plan to stop French advance, but all the Albany Congress actually did was to display beyond doubt that the colonies could not and would not unite and that the allied Indians had lost faith in them. The famous plan of unity concocted at Albany by Benjamin Franklin was not confirmed by a single colony, including Franklin's Pennsylvania.[55] As noted above, Virginia boycotted the Congress. To counteract Virginia's schemes, Pennsylvania's Conrad Weiser came to Albany looking for Iroquois "greedy fellows for money" from whom to get a new cession of lands—and found some. The new deed's bounds overlapped those of Virginia's deed from the Lancaster treaty.[56] Undermining Pennsylvania from another direction, an agent for Connecticut adventurers got some Iroquois drunk "in the bushes" and had them sign a deed to the Wyoming valley of Pennsylvania (the valley of the north branch of the Susquehanna River).[57] Preoccupied already with the west, Pennsylvania and the Six Nations soon faced a new threat of invasion from the east by Connecticut in the valley claimed by both the Iroquois and Pennsylvania.

It is conceivable that the Iroquois individuals who signed such deeds acted in the full knowledge that no agreement could be valid unless made by a council with legitimate jurisdiction. By this interpretation the signatories simply accepted money thrust upon them knowing that their signatures were worthless, without any consciousness of doing wrong to their own people. Even on that assumption, however, a student cannot ignore the serious consequences of those deeds which, however valueless in Indian eyes, were used in colonial courts to justify seizure of Indian lands.

As the French destruction of Pickawillany had thrown the Logstown treaty into confusion, so the news of Washington's surrender at Great Meadows, July 4, 1754, arrived to frighten the conferees at the Albany Congress. It scared the statesmen in London even more when it arrived there. Their choices seemed to be three: to accept France's sovereignty over the entire Mississippi valley (which was unthinkable), to declare war (which was impractical at the moment), or to try to gain control of the Ohio region by localized combat. They chose the last and sent an expeditionary force under Major General Edward Braddock.

THE ROYAL CHAIN

As for the intercolonial cooperation supposed to have been produced by the Albany Congress, the rulers of the British Empire were not innocents; they saw at once that nothing useful had happened at Albany and that the colonies could no longer be trusted to handle Indian affairs. The crown created its own agency for treating with Indian nations. It set up two new "districts"

—northern and southern—and arranged for its own representative to act in each. These representatives, who were soon dubbed officially Superintendents of Indian Affairs, were experienced merchants in the Indian trade, and both knew Indian custom. We are concerned with the northern district's William Johnson.[58]

Johnson's base was among the Mohawks where his estate lay and where he traded. He knew them well—well enough for his purposes at any rate. He had dealt with the Mohawks politely as New York's Commissioner of Indian Affairs, and in due course he would follow the time-honored custom of Indian traders by taking a mistress from one of the most prestigious chiefly families (by Indian custom he had married her).[59] His expert management would revive the Covenant Chain and once more raise the Mohawks to pre-eminence in the Iroquois League, but his status was unclear at first. His first royal commission from General Braddock authorized "sole management and direction of the Affairs of the Six Nations of Indians and their Allies." His first task was to lead troops against the French, and his function as Indian superintendent was to recruit Indian auxiliaries.[60] It was not a promising beginning. It became less promising after the French defeated Braddock near Fort Duquesne, and as Massachusetts's William Shirley tried to wrest control of Indian affairs away from Johnson.[61] To complete the picture, Braddock's defeat left those affairs in a shambles. The Ohio Indians, with French officers, raided Pennsylvania and Virginia, and it was suspected that Iroquois were among them. The Grand Council at Onondaga had resolved to let the English and French fight this war by themselves.[62]

The Grand Council completely lost control of the Ohio Indians. Widespread and interlocked confederates of Delawares, Shawnees, Ojibwas, Mississaugas, Ottawas, Hurons, Potawatomies, and Kickapoos far outnumbered the dwindling membership of the Six Nations in Iroquoia, and French support gave the new confederates confidence to handle their own diplomacy. They ignored Onondaga's advice, and the Iroquois did not try to enforce it against such odds. Even after the tide began to turn in favor of the English, Colonel Hugh Mercer warned from Pittsburgh that the Six Nations lived in dread of the western Indians because the Iroquois were "by no means that powerful and Warlike People they were on our first Settling America: and should the Shawanese and Delawares join in the Confederacy against them, their ruin would soon be completed, unless a very powerful aid is afforded them by the English. This Support from us they come now to Supplicate.[63]

Within the western confederacy, the Delawares emerged to leadership during the war. Sharp distinction must be drawn between the Ohio Delawares who, by this time, included the majority of the nation, and the eastern remnants living along the north branch of the Susquehanna River. The Ohioans gloried in new independence from the Iroquois. The easterners were caught between the Iroquois hammer and Pennsylvania's anvil; though many of their young men avenged past wrongs by raiding the province's isolated back settlers, the chiefs equivocated. When Sir William Johnson summoned them to treaty in 1756, he found it best to mollify them by "taking off their skirts" to make them "men" like their Western brethren once more, i.e., by recognizing their right to speak in council for themselves rather than through an Iroquois spokesman. The Iroquois grudgingly accepted the rearrangement.[64]

Between 1756 and 1758, Johnson and the Pennsylvanians tried several approaches to pacify the eastern Delawares. (the Ohioans were beyond reach.) In the process, Philadelphia's Quakers, allied with the German "plain people" of the province, thrust themselves forward as a new force in Indian diplomacy, and they gained support in the assembly from the non-pacifist Anglicans led by Benjamin Franklin. The Quakers disturbed Johnson profoundly because they challenged his exclusive jurisdiction and because their aims and policies conflicted with his. The Quakers wanted only to restore peace with all Indians; Johnson wanted to draw them away from the French in order to recruit them for war against the French. The Quakers relied upon chief Teedyuscung and the eastern Delawares as their instrument for approaching hostile Indians with peace proposals, and this reliance implied backing the Delawares against Iroquois presumptions of hegemony; whereas Johnson's whole policy consisted of reliance primarily upon the Mohawks, through them the Iroquois League, and through them the tributaries of the old Covenant Chain. The tension between Delawares and Iroquois manifesting itself overtly during these years continued through the war of the American Revolution, sometimes masked by return of the Delawares to "women" status, sometimes breaking out in open violence. The Delawares donned and doffed their "skirts" in bewildering sequences.

After some tentative preliminary approaches, climax was reached in 1758. A new British army, under General John Forbes, passed through Philadelphia and hacked a laborious new road through the woods, only to become bogged down a short distance from Fort Duquesne. A couple of western Delawares came eastward to test the Pennsylvanians' mood. These two, Pisquetomen and Keekyuscung, took Moravian missionary Christian Frederick Post back to their tribal council near Fort Duquesne. Frenchmen from the fort tried unsuccessfully to get Post killed. Making up their minds to seek peace with the British, the Delawares protected Post and once more sent delegates eastward to participate in another great treaty council at Easton, Pennsylvania. Eastern and western Delawares sat down with chiefs from smaller fragmented tribes and other chiefs from the Six Nations (including Mohawks this time). Facing them across the fire, the governors of Pennsylvania and New Jersey negotiated within the limits of different sets of instructions from England. Superintendent Johnson's delegate George Croghan took part, but in a minor conspiratorial capacity. And a number of prominent Quakers showed up to advise the Delawares and to challenge officialdom's efforts to deceive.

The wrangling was long and intense. For present purposes we need notice only that the Iroquois reasserted authority over the other Indians, and the Delawares accepted it. In recompense, the colonials agreed to recommend to the crown that Indian territory in the west be preserved from colonial encroachment. (Johnson was already helping the Mohawks keep their lands.) Thus originated the policy that eventuated in the Royal Proclamation of 1763. The western Delawares returned to their home accompanied by Iroquois chiefs who "instructed" all the Ohio Indians to withdraw from French alliance. Much hurried counseling produced agreement. The French commander at Fort Duquesne, whose skeleton garrison depended heavily on Indian support, realized that his position had become untenable and abandoned it. And General Forbes's army marched forward without opposition to occupy the fort's smoldering ruins. Thus, negotiations with the Indians in 1758 recovered the ground that had been lost by simplistic reliance on military force.[65]

It was the war's turnaround point inland. In 1759 French Fort Niagara capitulated after British and Iroquois troops defeated a relief expedition decisively; and Brigadier General John Wolfe's expedition took Quebec city though he, as well as French commander Montcalm, was killed in battle. Serious French resistance in America disappeared thereafter. Military action became a series of British "mopping-up" operations. Political and diplomatic action heated up more than ever.

The British built Fort Pitt to replace Fort Duquesne. Traders rushed to it, but commander-in-chief Lord Amherst banned trade in the arms and ammunition necessary for the Indians to hunt successfully and thus to survive. Resentment grew, and grew more as Fort Pitt increased in size and British troops enforted themselves throughout the west. The Indians watched sullenly as French occupation gave way to British occupation instead of the promised liberation of their country to their own governments. Superintendent Johnson tried to keep a measure of stability from his base among the Mohawks, but many Senecas disregarded him and the Onondaga council. Resentment among all Indians became fierce when they were told that France had given *their* lands to Britain in the Treaty of Paris (1763) by which France gained peace at the price of ceding Canada. At last the west exploded in Pontiac's War with its Indian sieges of British forts.[66]

The major forts held out, and the fighting was brief though intense. The Indians subsided, but the crown's ministers recognized that the Indians were only taking time out. Until political measures resolved the conflict, the military stalemate would be succeeded by more eruptions. To pacify the Indians and stabilize the back country, the crown issued its Royal Proclamation of 7 October 1763 which decreed a vast reservation of crown lands to be reserved for Indian use and forbidden to colonial settlement. A line was to be drawn along Pennsylvania's western boundary and from there southwesterly along the Appalachian ridges, and only the military and licensed traders would be allowed beyond the line. The Proclamation was translated to the Indians with a small twist. They were told that the crown was saving *their* land instead of crown land, and saving it for them instead of the crown. But the Proclamation served its purpose, and the west subsided for a decade during which negotiations were pursued intensely for agreement as to the precise location where the proclamation line should be surveyed.[67]

Johnson, newly ennobled as a baronet, understood his role clearly, and there can be no doubt about his priorities. He was, above all else, a British lord. While he lived, the Iroquois were his instrument to control the other tribes, but when their controls faltered he did not hesitate to deal directly with the recalcitrants as he did with the rebellious Delawares when he "took off their petticoats" in 1756. Whether the Iroquois liked it or not, they had no choice but to follow Johnson's lead if they wished to keep any semblance of authority over other tribes. British garrisons occupied the Ohio country, and the Iroquois had long lost the capacity to wage war exclusively with their own resources. Their options consisted simply of supporting Johnson or having him turn to other tribes to achieve his ends.

Some of them, especially among the distant Senecas, were none too happy with the situation, at least partly because of Johnson's special favor for the Mohawks whose kinsman he became through his mistress/wife Molly Brant; but he held the Covenant Chain together as he reshaped it. In the process, Iroquois government underwent subtle change. Though old forms of tribal government were maintained, the authority of sachems diminished and war chiefs gained prestige as they were cossetted and supported by Johnson to raise the levies of warriors he needed. Outside the Iroquois League proper, the tributary Indians of the Covenant Chain perceived the Iroquois less and less as intermediaries between them and the English, and more and more as agents of English policy. When the Iroquois negotiated with Johnson, ostensibly in behalf of the Chain tribes, they frequently gave away what their clients wanted to keep.

Much of the process of treaty negotiations between Johnson and the Iroquois consisted in bending the Proclamation Line farther westward under pressure. Uncontrollable back country settlers paid no attention to the Proclamation and set up homesteads at will. Companies of speculators used ancient methods of persuasion on Johnson, and he grew richer as he pressed the Iroquois to agree to more expansion. The retreating western Indians, however, grew restless as they perceived how powerless the crown was to keep its promises to them. Only the form of a barrier line was maintained. In substance the line became a series of salients ever advancing and pushing the

Indians back.[68] Disillusioned, the western tribes counselled among themselves to forge a confederation independent of the Six Nations.[69]

The Iroquois were having their own troubles with those aggressive colonials. In the east, the Susquehannah Company of Connecticut thrust settlers into the Wyoming valley on the Susquehanna River's North Branch, heedless of Iroquois and Pennsylvania admonitions to stay out. By the Treaty of Fort Stanwix, 1768, the Six Nations ceded the Wyoming Valley to Pennsylvania, but the Susquehannah company continued operations and proclaimed Connecticut's jurisdiction. Pennsylvania speculators organized competitive settlement resulting in the "Yankee-Pennamite Wars" of 1769–84.[70] These are not our concern. For the Iroquois the main point was that their front line at the Susquehanna had been breached. Strategically speaking, the Yankees could thrust from a base in the Wyoming valley northward along the Susquehanna, eventually into Iroquoia proper. Only the new settlers' preoccupation with Pennsylvania and the restoration of Pennsylvania's controls could stop them.

Indian resentment everywhere came to a head in 1774 when a gang of Virginians, with governmental sanction, massacred Shawnees in what is called Lord Dunmore's War. The Same Virginians seized Fort Pitt, which had been evacuated by royal troops,and proclaimed another bite out of Pennsylvania's territory.[71] Six Nations chiefs protested vigorously to William Johnson. "Your people are as ungovernable, or rather more so, than ours," they charged. If the crown could not control the encroachers, "we must look upon every agreement you made with us as void and of no effect." How Johnson might have responded can only be guessed; he certainly could not bring the settlers under control, and he died in the midst of the treaty.[72]

The British government had plenty of other reasons to be annoyed by its fractious colonists. To reassert its badly deteriorated authority, Parliament enacted a series of Coercive Acts, promptly dubbed by the colonists the Intolerable Acts, that instituted forceful measures of control. With the separate enactment of the Quebec Act, Parliament finally set up a civil government for the conquered province of Canada. The Quebec Act made permanent the barrier line of the Royal Proclamation of 1763 and established Quebec's government over the "crown lands" of Indian territory north of the Ohio River and west of Pennsylvania.[73] It thus destroyed all hope of expansion into those territories by Virginia, Massachusetts, and Connecticut, and added yet another to their list of grievances. Angered speculators promptly dubbed the Quebec Act also "Intolerable."

No matter the justice of either side's behavior, "intolerable" government led to revolution. The colonists declared independence, and war began. The American Revolution was the greatest crisis ever to confront the Iroquois League, and the League broke under the strain. Though the chiefs tried to maintain hands-off neutrality, agents of both the warring powers worked upon the leaders of the individual Iroquois nations with such success that League consensus became impossible. The chiefs "covered the fire" at Onondaga to suspend League councils for an indefinite period.[74] Councils and individuals of each nation made independent decisions. Many of each nation continued to take a neutral stance. Of those who decided to fight, most Mohawks, Caughnawagas, Onondagas, Cayugas, and Senecas joined the British. Most Oneidas and Tuscaroras joined the Americans.

The suspension of the League ended de facto its supervision over the formerly tributary Indians. Sensing opportunity, the ever-restless Delawares negotiated a treaty with American General Lachlan MacIntosh in 1778 to set up an Indian fourteenth state, with the Delawares instead of the Iroquois at its head—but Congress refused to consider the treaty.[75]

In 1779 the British-allied Iroquois were unable to preserve their own homeland from devastation by troops of General John Sullivan. Though they fought bravely and ably till the war's end, they had no influence over the peace treaty that followed. The Iroquois were thunderstuck by the revelation that no provision had been made for them in the Treaty of Paris. So far as Britain was concerned, the Iroquois lands in New York were gone; the best that could be done by guilt-smitten British officials was to provide substitute territory in Canada.[76] So far as the United States was concerned, the Iroquois were a conquered people, and their lands in America were forfeit. "The King of Great Britain ceded to the United States *the whole*," according to Congress's commissioners at the treaty of Fort Stanwix in 1784. "By the right of conquest they might claim *the whole*," but they chose instead to require the Iroquois to renounce all claims to land beyond a specified boundary.[77]

Under pressure, division appeared in the Iroquois ranks. Mohawk Captain Aaron Hill professed to speak "not only on the part of the Six Nations, but also on that of the Ottawa, Chippewa, Hurons, Potawatamas, Messasaugas, Delawares, Cherokees, Shawnees, Chickasaws, Choctaws, and Creeks;" but Seneca Captain O'Bail (Cornplanter) disavowed Hill's position. "As to the territory westward," said O'Bail, "you must talk respecting it with the Western Nations toward the setting of the Sun—They must consult of what part they must cede to the United States."[78]

The commissioners had already made up their minds. They rejected the Mohawk effort to re-establish the Iroquois as spokesmen and intermediaries for the western nations: "your words will pass away like the winds of yesterday that are heard no more."[79] This was the de jure final ending to the great Iroquois Covenant Chain that had fallen apart de facto at the outbreak of the Revolution. No longer was the Chain anchored at Onondaga. No longer did it consist of a plural alliance in which the Iroquois spoke to Yorkers or the British or the Americans for all the other Indians.

Iroquois chiefs continued to meet in solemn council with the chiefs and warriors of the western Indians. They gave advice. They were addressed deferentially as Elder Brothers and Uncles. But even as the respectful forms were preserved, the substance of the western chiefs' remarks made the Iroquois complain of being addressed "roughly." Little attention was given to their advice. The western nations fought their own battles and finally negotiated their own peace at Fort Greenville in 1795 without the presence of a single Iroquois. When the Iroquois chiefs heard about it, they could only say that "it hurts the feelings of the Six Nations."[80]

Among the reasons for hurt feelings was the decision by Secretary of War Timothy Pickering, embodied in his instructions to the Greenville Treaty negotiator, that the Iroquois had no valid claim to "the lands Westward of the Allegany," thus confirming an end to Six Nations claims of empire that had been so bloodily disproved by western tribes for more than a century. There was, however, a consolation prize. Pickering went on to say that the conquest assumptions of the United States commissioners in 1784 at Fort Stanwix had constituted "a construction as unfounded in itself as it was unintelligible and mysterious to the Indians." The United States had no right of conquest; it had only a pre-emptive right to purchase Indian lands to the exclusion of all other "white nations." As for the Indians, "the land is theirs (and this we acknowledge)."[81] If Greenville marked the definitive end of Iroquois dreams of empire, it confirmed at the same time American official recognition of the "Indian title" territorial rights of individual tribes—including those of the Six Nations—recognition that has continued to the present day.

AFTER THE CHAIN

From the disintegration of the Revolution until today, Iroquois history is that of a people in a diaspora, and it parallels the histories of other Indian peoples of Canada and the United States. It is a history of encroachment by speculators and land companies; of quarrels and manipulation by the United States and component states, often in competition; of despair, demoralization, and revitalization; of necessary cultural adjustment and stubborn cultural preservation. There are too many strands for this essay to follow through the nineteenth century. The Iroquois in the United States, after much retreat and repression, were deprived by Congress in 1871 of recognition as independent nations with whom treaties might be negotiated. Some traditional chiefs have attempted in recent years to regain such recognition through appeals to international agencies. The Iroquois in Canada are discussed in this volume by Robert Surtees in a separate essay.

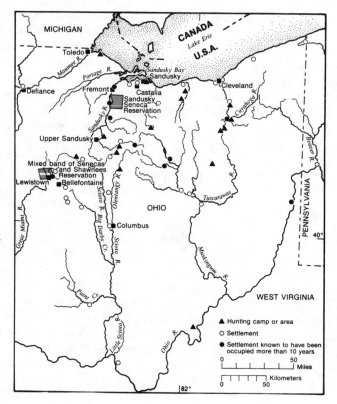

2. Approximate locations of Iroquois settlements and hunting areas in the Ohio country, 1742–1831.

According to Seneca scholar Arthur C. Parker, grandnephew of great sachem Ely S. Parker, the Iroquois in Canada revived "a closely knit and centralized government patterned upon the laws of Hiawatha and Deganawideh." But, "in a pitiful contrast stood the broken, dissipated tribes in New York whose government had been wrested from the civil sachems and seized by the war chiefs. Their attempt to maintain the ancient League seemed only a pretense."[82] There are two League councils today, one based at Grand River Reserve in Canada, the other at Onondaga, New York. Besides these traditionalist organizations, there are independent Seneca, Oneida, and Mohawk governments recognized by the United States and an Iroquois government recognized by Canada in which officers are elected under written constitutions instead of inheriting office by ancient custom.

Many Iroquois persons have scattered individually to live under the government of tribes other than their own, and many of the old tributary Indians live as guests under one or another Iroquois government; hospitality is still a potent sanction in Iroquois culture. Some Cayugas and Senecas migrated to Oklahoma in the nineteenth century where a reservation was temporarily set aside for them. Other Iroquois have followed job markets outside the jurisdiction of any tribal government. Some went west with the fur trade; some became lumberjacks in the timber industry on the northwest coast; some became high steel workers building skyscrapers and suspension bridges. The variety of such occupations offers startling contrast.[83]

While there can be small doubt that an uncertain number of Iroquois have assimilated without trace in the dominant large society of the United States, there can be no doubt whatever that the bulk of Iroquois people still proudly hold to their cultural heritage and proclaim their identity. Fragmented though they are—and I have not attempted to discuss the serious divisions between their competing religions—their disputes are "in the family." In one aspect, Iroquois history is a success story: far from from joining the ranks of vanishing Indians, many more Iroquois walk the earth today than were ever recorded before. If the policies of the United States and Canada ever wholeheartedly embrace the principle of cultural pluralism toward which these nations seem to be groping, it is not inconceivable that the Iroquois may emerge as a strong, united people once more.

NOTES

1. *Proceedings and Debates of the British Parliaments Respecting North America*, ed. Leo Francis Stock, 5 vols. (Washington, D.C.: Carnegie Institution, 1924–), 2:368.

2. Francis Jennings, *The Invasion of America: Indians, Colonialism, and the Cant of Conquest* (Chapel Hill: University of North Carolina Press, for the Institute of Early American History and Culture, 1975), ch. 18; idem., *The Ambiguous Iroquois Empire* (New York: 1984), ch. 8.

3. See Francis Jennings, "The Constitutional Evolution of the Covenant Chain," *Proceedings of the American Philosophical Society* 115, no. 2 (April 1971):88–96.

4. W. J. Eccles, *Canadian Frontier*, pp. 122–25; Leroy V. Eid, "The Ojibwa-Iroquois War: The War the Five Nations Did Not Win," *Ethnohistory* 26, no. 4 (Fall 1979):297–324; Donald B. Smith, "Who Are the Mississauga?" *Ontario History* 17, no. 4 (December 1975):211–22.

5. *Calendar of State Papers, Colonial Series, America and West Indies*, eds. W. Noel Sainsbury et al. (London: Her Majesty's Stationery Office, 1860–), Vol. 1693–1696, #500 #2054; treaty minutes, 15 August 1694, mss., Penn Mss., Indian Affairs 1:14, Historical Society of Pennsylvania, Philadelphia.

62

TREATY DIPLOMACY

6. *Minutes of the Provincial Council of Pennsylvania*, ed. Samuel Hazard, 16 vols. (Harrisburg and Philadelphia, Pa., 1838–1853), 6 July 1694, 1:447. Vols. 1–3 were reprinted in Philadelphia with different pagination from the original Harrisburg edition.

7. Treaty minutes, 21 July 1701, N.Y. Col. Docs. 4:907.

8. *Archives of Maryland*, eds. William Hand Browne, et al. (Baltimore, Md., 1883–), 8:518.

9. Various treaty minutes, 1770 and 1701, in N.Y. Col. Docs. 9:715–20, 722–25; 4:693–96, 798–807, 889–908, 917–20; treaty documents mss., Archives Nationales, Colonies, Series C¹¹A, Vol. 384, ff. 230–33, 262–72, 278–79; Vol. 19, ff. 41–44.

10. See the comments in Louis Armand de Lom D'Arce de Lahontan, *New Voyages to North-America* (1703), ed. Reuben Gold Thwaites, 2 vols. (Chicago: A.C. McClurg and Co., 1905), 1:394, 395.

11. Jennings, *Ambiguous Iroquois Empire*, chs. 8, 12.

12. Gary B. Nash, "The Quest for the Susquehanna Valley: New York, Pennsylvania, and the Seventeenth-Century Fur Trade," *New York History* 48 (1967):3–27.

13. *Pennsylvania Archives*, 9 series, 138 vols. (Philadelphia and Harrisburg, 1852–1949), 1st ser., 1:144–47; *Pennsylvania Council Minutes*, 23 April 1701, 2:15.

14. N.Y. Indian commissioners' minutes, 23 August 1699, in Peter Wraxall, *An Abridgement of the Indian Affairs . . . from the Year 1678 to the Year 1751*, ed. Charles Howard McIlwain, Harvard Historical Studies 21 (Cambridge, Mass: Harvard University Press, 1915), p. 33; New York Council Minutes, 30 August 1699, mss., 8:131, New York State Archives, Albany.

15. See W. J. Eccles, "Teganissorens (Decanesora)," in *Dictionary of Canadian Biography*, eds. George W. Brown, et al. (Toronto: University of Toronto Press, 1966–), 2:619–23. Because of the nasal quality of Iroquois speech, the French spelling when pronounced with French values is probably closer to correct.

16. A good, popularly written summary of the Indians who gathered on the Susquehanna is Paul A. W. Wallace, *Indians in Pennsylvania* (Harrisburg: Pennsylvania Historical and Museum Commission, 1964).

17. Treaty minutes, Aug.–Sept. 1722, N.Y. Col. Docs. 5:669–77.

18. Thomas Elliott Norton, *The Fur Trade in Colonial New York* (Madison: University of Wisconsin Press, 1974), ch. 8.

19. See Georgiana C. Nammack, *Fraud, Politics, and the Dispossession of the Indians: The Iroquois Land Frontier in the Colonial Period* (Norman: University of Oklahoma Press, 1969).

20. David Landy, "Tuscarora Among the Iroquois," in *Northeast*, ed. Bruce G. Trigger, vol. 15 (1978) of *Handbook of North American Indians*, gen. ed. Wm. C. Sturtevant, 20 vols. (Washington, D.C.: Smithsonian Institution, 1978–), p. 518.

21. *Pa. Archives*, 1st ser., 1:329; *Wilderness Chronicles of Northwestern Pennsylvania*, eds. Sylvester K. Stevens and Donald H. Kent (Harrisburg: Pennsylvania Historical Commission, 1941), pp. 6–7.

22. *Pa. Council Minutes*, 3–5 July 1727, 3:271–76.

23. *Pa. Archives*, 1st ser., 1:329–30.

24. *Pa. Archives*, 1st ser., 1:300–306; abstracts of dispatches, 1729–1732, N.Y. Col. Docs., 9:106, 1027, 1033, 1035.

25. Identification: John Bartram, *Observations on the Inhabitants, Climate, Soil, Rivers, Productions, Animals, and Other Matters Worthy of Notice* (London: J. Whiston and B. White, 1751), p. 17. According to Pennsylvania's official records and James Logan's private correspondence, only

the Shawnees were under Shikellamy's supervision; other tribes, notably the Delawares, are not mentioned. *Pa. Council Minutes*, 1 Sept and 11 Oct 1728, 3:330, 337; *Pa. Archives*, 1st ser., 1:228.

26. Treaty minutes, 23 May 1723, mss., Massachusetts Archives 29:105–30, Boston; treaty minutes, 20 September 1723, mss., Mass. Arch. 29:131–47; treaty minutes, 22 August–20 September 1723, mss., Thomas Gilcrease Institute of American History and Art, G329, Tulsa, Oklahoma. Photocopies at Newberry Library.

27. *Pa. Archives*, 1st ser., 1:305–306; *Pa. Council Minutes*, 4 Aug 1731, 3:402–403.

28. *Pa. Council Minutes*, 26 Aug 1732, 3:442.

29. Ibid., 10 Sep 1735, 3:608.

30. Ibid., 12 Oct 1736, 4:87–88; mss. deed; 11 Oct. 1736, Philadelphia Deed Book G-1:277ff., City Hall.

31. Paul A. W. Wallace, *Conrad Weiser, 1696–1760, Friend of Colonist and Mohawk* (Philadelphia: University of Pennyslvania Press, 1945), chs. 6, 9.

32. Indian request . . . , 19 Nov 1736, mss., Penn Mss., Indian Affairs 1:39, Hist. Soc. of Pa.; *Pa. Council Minutes*, 12 May 1737, 4:203–204.

33. Anthony F. C. Wallace, *King of the Delawares: Teedyuscung, 1700–1763* (Philadelphia: University of Pennsylvania Press, 1949), pp. 18–30; Francis Jennings, "The Scandalous Indian Policy of William Penn's Sons: Deeds and Documents of the Walking Purchase," *Pennsylvania History* 37:1 (Jan. 1970):19–39.

34. *Pa. Council Minutes*, July 1742, 4:560–86; Canasatego's speech on p. 579; Jennings, "Delaware Interregnum," pp. 190–92.

35. Witham Marshe, "Journal of the Treaty . . . at Lancaster in Pennsylvania, June, 1744," *Collections of the Massachusetts Historical Society*, 1st ser., 7:178–81; P. Wallace, *Conrad Weiser*, p. 184; *Pa. Council Minutes* 4:715–16, 726, 729.

36. Deed, 2 July 1744, mss. original in Virginia State Library, Richmond, Colonial Papers, Folder 41, Item 10. Photocopy in Newberry Library.

37. *George Mercer Papers Relating to the Ohio Company of Virginia*, ed. Lois Mulkearn (Pittsburgh: University of Pittsburgh Press, 1954), p. 331.

38. Ibid., pp. 2, 332–34, 14; *Acts of the Privy Council of England, Colonial Series, 1613–1783*, eds. W. L. Grant and James Munro, 6 vols. (London, 1908–12), 4:55–57, 200–203.

39. P. Wallace, *Weiser*, pp. 258–71.

40. Logstown Treaty minutes, 28 May 1751, in *Pa. Council Minutes* 5:553.

41. Journal of the Virginia commissioners, *Virginia Magazine of History and Biography* 13 (1905), p. 167; Jennings, "Interregnum," p. 197.

42. Randolph C. Downes, *Council Fires on the Upper Ohio: A Narrative of Indian Affairs in the Upper Ohio Valley until 1795* (Pittsburgh: University of Pittsburgh Press, 1940), p. 60.

43. The trick is described and documented in Francis Jennings, "Miquon's Passing: Indian-European Relations in Colonial Pennsylvania, 1674 to 1755," Ph.D. diss., University of Pennsylvania, 1965, pp. 424–28.

44. Penn Mss., Official Correspondence 6:47, 55, 73, Hist. Soc. of Pa.; conference memorandum, 27 Sep 1753, in *The Papers of Benjamin Franklin*, eds. Leonard W. Labaree, et al. (New Haven, Ct.: Yale University Press, 1959–), 5:66.

45. *Va. Mag. of Hist. and Biog.* 13:171; *Mercer Papers*, p. 63.

46. *Va. Mag. of Hist. and Biog.* 13:154; Paul Trap, "Mouet de Langlade, Charles-Michel," *Dict. Can. Biog.* 4:563.

47. Treaty minutes, mss., C.O.5/1328, esp. 16 Sep 1753, f. 29, Public Record Office, Great Britain, Kew, England. Scarouady is another name for the Monacatoocha of the minutes.

48. Carlisle treaty minutes, Sep.–Oct. 1753, in *Pa. Council Minutes* 5:665–85, esp. p. 679.

49. See Nammack, *Fraud, Politics*, passim.

50. Treaty minutes, 16 June 1753, N.Y. *Col. Docs.* 6:788.

51. Lords of Trade to Holdernesse, 18 Sep 1753, and to DeLancey, 5 July 1754, N.Y. *Col. Docs.* 6:799, 845–46.

52. Lords of Trade to Osborn, 18 Sep 1753, N.Y. *Col. Docs.* 6:855–56.

53. Treaty minutes, 27 June 1754, N.Y. *Col. Docs.* 6:861.

54. *The Diaries of George Washington, 1748–1799*, ed. John C. Fitzpatrick, 4 vols. (Boston: Houghton Mifflin, 1925) 1:94–97.

55. Lawrence Henry Gipson, *The British Empire Before the American Revolution*, 15 vols. (New York: Alfred A. Knopf, 1939–70), 5, ch. 5.

56. P. Wallace, *Weiser*, p. 353; Gipson, *British Empire* 5:121–22; Johnson to Lords of Trade, 11 Sep 1756, in *Doc. Hist. N.Y.* 2:736–37.

57. P. Wallace, *Weiser*, pp. 361–63; C. A. Weslager, *The Delaware Indians: A History* (New Brunswick, N.J.: Rutgers University Press, 1972) pp. 211–16; Oneida sachem Conochquiesie, 3 July 1755, in *N.Y. Col. Docs.* 6:984.

58. Commission, 17 April 1756, *The Papers of Sir William Johnson*, eds. James Sullivan, et al., 14 vols. (Albany: SUNY, 1921–65), 2:434–35 (*Johnson Papers*).

59. Milton W. Hamilton, *Sir William Johnson: Colonial American, 1715–1763* (Port Washington, N.Y.: Kennikat Press, 1976), pp. 44, 52, 58, 242, 338.

60. Commissions, 15 and 16 April 1755, *Johnson Papers* 1:465–68; *Doc. Hist. N.Y.* 2:651–54.

61. Memorandum, Sep.–Oct. 1755, *Johnson Papers* 2:2–3.

62. *Diaries of Washington* 1:97.

63. Mercer to Forbes, 8 Jan 1759, in *The Papers of Henry Bouquet*, eds. S. K. Stevens, et al. (Harrisburg: Pennsylvania Historical and Museum Commission, 1951–), 3:25.

64. N.Y. *Col. Docs.* 7:160.

65. Francis Jennings, "A Vanishing Indian: Francis Parkman Versus His Sources," *Pa. Mag. of Hist. and Biog.* 87, no. 3 (July 1963):306–23; Thayer, *Israel Pemberton*, ch. 12; *Pa. Council Minutes*, Oct. 1758, 8:173–223.

66. Howard H. Peckham, *Pontiac and the Indian Uprising* (Chicago: University of Chicago Press, 1947; Phoenix reprint 1961), chs. 7–9; Downes, *Council Fires*, ch. 5.

67. *Documents Relating to the Constitutional History of Canada, 1759–1791*, eds. Adam Shortt and Arthur G. Doughty (Ottawa, 1907), pp. 119–23, 433–437; Downes, *Council Fires*, ch. 6; N.Y. *Col. Docs.* 7:602–605, 641, 665, 725.

68. Jack M. Sosin, *Whitehall and the Wilderness: The Middle West in British Colonial Policy, 1760–1775* (Lincoln: University of Nebraska Press, 1961), ch. 5; idem, *The Revolutionary Frontier, 1763–1783* (New York: Holt, Rinehart and Winston, 1967), chs. 1–3.

69. Anthony F. C. Wallace, *The Death and Rebirth of the Seneca* (New York: Alfred A. Knopf, 1970), p. 154.

70. Sosin, *Revolutionary Frontier*, pp. 52–55.

71. Jack M. Sosin, The British Indian Department and Dunmore's War," *Virginia Magazine of History and Biography* 74 (1966):34–50; Thomas Perkins Abernethy, *Western Lands and the American Revolution* (1937; rpt. New York: Russell and Russell, 1959), ch. 6.

72. Treaty minutes, July 1774, N.Y. Col. Docs. 8:476, 479.

73. Sosin, Whitehall and the Wilderness, ch. 10; Documents Relating to Constitutional History of Canada, pp. 401–405.

74. Elisabeth Tooker, "The League of the Iroquois: Its History, Politics, and Ritual," in Northeast, ed. Trigger, p. 435; Barbara Graymont, The Iroquois in the American Revolution (Syracuse, N.Y.; Syracuse University Press, 1972), p. 133.

75. Indian Affairs. Laws and Treaties, comp. and ed. Charles J. Kappler, 2 vols. (Washington, D.C.: USGPO, 1903–1904), 2:3–5.

76. Reserve patent, 1, April 1793, in Canada. Indian Treaties and Surrenders. From 1680 to 1890, 2 vols. (Ottawa: Queen's Printer, 1891), 1:7–8; Graymont, Iroquois in Revolution, p. 342.

77. The minutes of the Treaty of Fort Stanwix, 1784, are hard to get. A manuscript copy of the Journal of the Commissioners of Indian Affairs for the Northern and Middle Departments of the United States, containing the minutes, is in the Wayne Mss., Indian Treaties, 1778–95, B, Historical Society of Pennsylvania. A photocopy of this is in the Iroquois Treaty Archive of the Newberry Library. The journal appears in print in The Olden Times, ed. Neville B. Craig, 2 vols. (1846–48; rpt. Cincinnati: Robert Clarke and Co., 1876), 2:404–432. Olden Times 2:414, 424, 426.

78. Ibid., 1:419–20, 423.

79. Ibid., 1:423–24.

80. The Correspondence of Lieut. Governor John Graves Simcoe, with Allied Documents Relating to His Administration of the Government of Upper Canada, comp. and ed. E. A. Cruickshank, 5 vols. (Toronto: Ontario History Society, 1923–31), 1:218–29; 4:88.

81. Pickering to Wayne, 8 April 1795, in Anthony Wayne, A Name in Arms: Soldier, Diplomat, Defender of Expansion Westward of a Nation, comp. and ed. Richard C. Knopf (Pittsburgh: University of Pittsburgh Press, 1960), pp. 397–98.

82. Arthur C. Parker, The Life of General Ely S. Parker, Last Grand Sachem of the Iroquois and General Grant's Military Secretary, Buffalo Historical Society Publications 23 (Buffalo, N.Y., 1919):71–72.

83. See the Iroquois group of articles in Northeast, ed. Trigger. For appeals to the United Nations for recognition of tribal sovereignty, see Treaty Council News, Official Bulletin of the International Indian Treaty Council.

3

The Iroquois in Canada

ROBERT J. SURTEES

THE IROQUOIS PRESENCE has been persistent in Canada since the days of first contact. It was with an Iroquoian people that Cartier had dealings during his voyages of 1534–36 and 1541–42. These "Laurentian Iroquois"[1] had vacated the St. Lawrence region by the time Champlain established the first permanent French base at Quebec in 1608, but relations with the Iroquois League began shortly afterwards. For the most part these dealings were hostile throughout the tenure of the French crown in Canada. The story of the French-Iroquois rivalry has been told many times and forms a truly vital and exciting chapter in Canadian history.[2] Within that larger story, however, lies a secondary development which has received less attention, but which also is vital, for it saw the evolution within Canada of permanent enclaves of Iroquois peoples during the period of the French regime and indeed during the era of Franco-Iroquois hostility. Ultimately, this resulted in the establishment of three permanent Iroquois settlements at Oka, Caughnawaga and St. Regis and a temporary one at Oswegatchie. And these villages, in turn, formed the basis of a new tribal grouping known as the Seven Nations of Canada.

The long era of hostility between the French and the Iroquois League was punctuated with periods of truce during which the French missionaries leapt eagerly at the opportunity to seek converts within the Iroquois cantons. It was a dangerous enterprise that could end in martyrdom, as in the case of Father Jogues in 1646;[3] but it also could produce some success, as was the case with the missions of Fathers Dablon, Chaumont and LeMoyne in the Onondaga villages in 1654–58 or of Fathers Fremin, Bruyas, and Pierron in the Mohawk country in 1667–87.[4]

Converted Iroquois, however, often found themselves the objects of scorn at the hands of their non-Christian brethren. This factor inclined the missionaries to encourage their converts to take up residence near the French settlements where they could feel more secure in their faith. There the priests could supervise their charges more closely and the Indian converts could be drawn more completely within the French sphere of influence, a consideration which had military as well as religious advantages.

Among the first to move into French territory were a half dozen Oneidas who visited Montreal in 1667; they also visited the mission of Notre Dame de Foye, where the remnants of the Huronia colony had taken refuge after the dispersals of 1649–50.[5] Apparently the example of the Huron village convinced them to accept baptism and settle near the St. Francois Xavier chapel, a recently built Jesuit chapel at La Prairie on a tract of land granted to the Order in 1647.[6] It was situated on the south shore of the St. Lawrence River, opposite the island of Montreal, and was just beginning to receive White settlers at this time. Though it was not designed as an Indian village, the French who moved to the area soon found themselves in the company of a growing Indian population which numbered 180 in 1674.[7] After the Oneidas' arrival, other migrants and converts swelled the number in the settlement which soon took on a predominently Mohawk temperament. Among the new arrivals was Chief Kryn who led forty Mohawks to La Prairie from the Mohawk Valley in 1673.[8] Perhaps the most famous of the Indian residents of La Prairie was the pious Catherine Tekakwitha who died in 1680 and has since been canonized by the Roman Catholic Church. Despite its Mohawk overtones, the village was widely mixed, and contemporary observers said that as many as 20 tribes were represented.[9]

For several reasons, including the flourishing brandy trade, the growing number of White settlers and the inadequacy of the soil for growing Indian corn, many of the Iroquois of La Prairie moved upstream in 1676 to Sault St. Louis,[10] near the rapids. The move was made at the urging of the Jesuits who were given a second grant, confirmed in 1680, in order to operate their mission. This peripatetic village, which became known as Caughnawaga, was moved short distances on four occasions, although it remained always within the confines of the tract given to the Order.[11] The Caughnawaga Indians also spent one year at Montreal following the massacre at Lachine in 1689.[12]

At about the time that the Sault St. Louis settlement was begun, other Iroquois and a mixture from other tribes, established themselves on the mountain on the island of Montreal, where they came under the tutelage of the Sulpician Order. Twenty years later, in 1696, this mission was moved to Riviére des Prairies near Sault au Recollect, although some Indians remained at the site of the mountain mission until 1704. In 1721, in order to move their Iroquois away from the temptations of the brandy trade, the Sulpicians moved the Sault au Recollect village from Montreal to the site of Oka, at the Lake of Two Mountains.[13] Shortly afterwards some Nipissings and Algonquins joined the village. As at Caughnawaga the tribal makeup was mixed, but the Iroquois portion, which remained quite distinct from the Nipissings and Algonquins, was largely Mohawk.[14]

About 1750 a faction of the Caughnawaga village broke away and moved upstream to form yet another village on the south shore of the St. Lawrence River at the mouth of the St. Regis River. This move, inspired partly by internal disputes and partly by soil depletion, was agreeable to the French who viewed the new village, called St. Regis, as a means of shoring up the defenses of the colony in the direction of Oswego.[15] Similar considerations caused the French to promote another Iroquois settlement even further upstream. In 1749 a Sulpician missionary named Fr. Francois Picquet began a mission at La Presentation at the present site of Ogdensburg, New York. The French also built a fort there, and to this fort-mission a substantial number of Onondagas as well as some Oneidas and Cayugas migrated in the 1750s. It was highly successful, for by the middle of the decade more than 500 families[16] had settled in several villages in the area, mainly on the north shore of the river. Located as it was at the mouth of the Oswegatchie River at a narrowing of the St. Lawrence, La Presentation was intended to protect the west against the British and to regulate the fur trade. In the process a large colony of Iroquois, who became known as the Oswegatchies, was drawn into the French sphere of influence.

As the Iroquois settlements evolved in New France they maintained some contacts with their former villages. The priests condoned this contact, including an illicit trade in furs through the Caughnawagas, for they saw it was a communications link for securing future converts. Civil authorities were less tolerant. They condemned the trade, but they could not prevent it, and they were generally leery of the effects of other contacts. Indeed the loyalty of the Canadian Iroquois was never totally above suspicion. While the Mohawk warriors from Oka and Caughnawaga did participate with the French in raids against English settlements and the territory of the League, and although the Canadian Iroquois were themselves the objects of attacks by Confederacy war parties, the French noted that the Canadian Iroquois were reluctant to wage war against their Iroquois brethren.[17] They also were aware of a continuing effort, by the Caughnawaga especially, to observe neutrality when possible.[18] Even the St. Regis settlement, which the French viewed as a military outpost, delivered only lukewarm assistance during the Seven Years War; and some of them actually joined General Amherst[19] after he secured the western flank for the British in 1760.

After the British conquered Canada, they too observed that the Canadian Iroquois were inclined to act in an independent fashion. As the governing power in Canada the British naturally wished to have Iroquois support against any enemy. It was disconcerting and worrisome when that support was not readily given. Although a majority of the St. Regis village supported Britain during the American Revolution, a portion of the inhabitants did sympathize with the Americans. The Caughnawagas tended to support the British during the Revolution, but they also stopped short of total and immediate commitment. Indeed, at the beginning of the war one Caughnawaga chief offered to support George Washington with five-hundred warriors,[20] and for a time afterward the Caughnawagas attempted to remain neutral.[21] Only later did they swing in behind the British; and throughout the war they were a source of consternation since the British were never certain of their support and often feared the influence of Washington's French allies under Lafayette might cause the Caughnawagas to change sides.

The fact is that the Iroquois in Canada, like Indians everywhere, considered themselves to be a distinct entity, separate from their White neighbors and allies; and they conducted themselves as best they could in an autonomous fashion. Also, the several groups of Indians who had established themselves in reasonably permanent villages in Canada came in time to view themselves—and to be viewed by others—as a new tribal grouping. In this fashion there was formed that loose alliance known as the Seven Nations of Canada, a unit that has been described by two recent scholars as "a confederacy of French mission Indians."[22] The precise composition and nature of this grouping, which appears to have taken form in the middle of the eighteenth century, is uncertain, but its importance then and in the early years of the nineteenth century is clear.

In 1786 the Seven Nations of Canada numbered more than two thousand people.[23] Included in that number were the Oswegatchies, whose villages in time were dispersed, and who by 1810 had either moved back into the tribal territories in the U.S. or joined with the St. Regis band. Delegates of the Seven Nations were involved in the western boundary disputes of the 1790s leading up to the invasion of the Indian country by General Wayne in 1793-94; and Lord Dorchester addressed the "Sept Villages du Bas Canada"[24] on February 10, 1794, in response to their address of a few days earlier. In that speech Dorchester indicated that he expected the Seven Nations would soon be involved, on the British side, in a general war with the United States. War did not come in 1794, but it did come in 1812. During that conflict the Iroquois of Lower Canada were active in the eastern theatre of operations and also were responsible, in collaboration with the Six Nations of the Grand River, for the British victory at Beaver Dams in Upper Canada in 1813.[25] In an 1842 official report the Seven Nations were described as containing 3,301 persons in the seven villages of Lower Canada, as follows: Caughnawaga (Iroquois); St. Regis (Iroquois); Lake of Two Mountains (Iroquois, Algonquins, and Nipissings); St. Francis (Abenaquis); Becancour (Abenaquis); Le Jeune Lorette (Hurons); and Restigouche (Micmacs).[26]

By the time of the 1842 report the Iroquois of the St. Lawrence River had been isolated from activities beyond the bounds of their community locations. As late as the 1837–38 rebellion in Lower Canada, the British Indian Department had sought to rally them to the side of government, but in general the activity of warfare was no longer a serious consideration. The rapid growth of the White population of Canada in the 1820s and 1830s had devalued the importance of the Iroquois as warriors; the three decades of peace with the United States further reduced the need to seek military help from the Indians; and the political and military contacts between the St. Lawrence Iroquois and the western Indians had also been rendered inconsequential. Likewise, the end of the Montreal fur trade occasioned by the 1821 amalgamation of the North West Company and the Hudson's Bay Company had closed off another enterprise for the Iroquois of Lower Canada. No doubt, a few individuals still moved beyond the confines of their reserves to engage in the trade, but after 1821 that once great enterprise no longer reached to its former horizons.

It should be observed, however, that the western trade had been a major field of employment for the Indians until 1821. Substantial numbers of Iroquois from Caughnawaga, Oka, and St. Regis had journeyed into the Canadian west in the employment of the North West Company and the Hudson's Bay Company as traders, trappers, and voyageurs. Some remained in the west. One group that did so was the Michel Band which was granted a reserve in the Saint Albert region of Alberta. The original grant was 25,600 acres, but by 1913 this had been reduced to 10,006.[27] The Michel Band enfranchised in 1958, thereby ceasing to exist legally as an Indian band, but its members still reside in the Edmonton region. Another band of Canadian Iroquois settled in the nearby Jasper National Park in the Alberta-British Columbia border region.[28] After the amalgamation of the two major fur companies in 1821, however, the opportunities in the western trade were reduced considerably. In short, a variety of circumstances forced the three Iroquois bands in Lower Canada back onto the resources of their village lands, thus rendering those lands, and the title to them, significantly more important.

In this connection it should be noted that the French never recognized Indian title to land, but rather claimed total sovereignty through discovery and conquest. Except for the lands granted to the Indians at Sillery in 1651 (under the direction of the Jesuits),[29] the Indian village and mission locations were held, through grants from the French Crown, by religious orders who were then charged with the task of converting and civilizing the Indians who lived within those tracts. The beneficiaries were intended to be the Indians, but the land was still held by the orders. The British would later recognize Indians' right to the occupation of lands and hunting territories through the Royal Proclamation of 1763, but because the area of the colony of Quebec was excluded from the workings of that principle the three Iroquois settlements there had to rely on the original French grants to protect their tenure.

The position of the St. Regis Iroquois was potentially the most insecure. They had moved to their new location with the approval of the French authorities, but before the move could be confirmed with land grants the Seven Years War ended the French regime in Canada.[30] There were few consequences for twenty years, but after 1783 British settlement whittled away at the lands of the St. Regis Iroquois. Their protests and occasional threats were of little consequence because they had no land titles or deeds to document their holdings or to define the boundaries of their claims. By virtue of long occupation and persistant claims, however, they did manage to secure recognition by 1842 of a triangular tract of 21,000 acres along the south shore of the St. Lawrence River at Lake St. Francis at the mouth of the St. Regis River. They also were credited with a reserve, called the Nutfield tract, opposite their village, but situated in Upper Canada, as well as nine islands in the St. Lawrence River.[31] The Nutfield Reserve was sold by treaty in 1847,[32] but the remaining lands form the Akwesasne Indian reserve which currently includes land in both Ontario and Quebec. It borders on the St. Regis Reserve in New York State.

The Caughnawaga lived on lands granted to the Jesuit Order which had received the Seigniory of La Prairie in 1647 and the Seigniory of Sault St. Louis in 1680. The latter, on which the Caughnawaga village was located, passed into the hands of the government in 1762 when the British appointed a Commissioner of Indian Affairs to see to its administration. The La Prairie Seigniory remained in the possession of the Jesuits. Regrettably the line between the two was ill defined, and thus a tract measuring "thirty seven acres wide by four leagues in depth from the river to the rear of the Seigniory of La Prairie"[33] was claimed by both the Order and the Indians. In 1762 a military court conducted by General Gage declared in favor of the Indians, but Gage later reversed his decision.[34] Over the years the Indians continued to press their case with Indian Department and Colonial Office officials in Canada and England, but by 1844, when the matter was declared to be closed, they were unable to secure another reversal. The present Caughnawaga reserve contains 12,477 acres.[35]

At Oka the Sulpician Order had been given grants, made and confirmed in 1718 and 1735, which constituted the Seigniory of the Lake of Two Mountains, "for the purpose of protecting, maintaining and giving religious instructions to the Indian and French inhabitants who placed themselves under their care."[36] This grant was confirmed again by government statute in 1841. In the middle of the nineteenth century the Iroquois of Oka expressed displeasure at the manner in which the Order was administering the Seigniory. They also claimed that they, the Iroquois, were the rightful proprietors of the

land. This claim was denied by H.C. Langevin, Secretary of State and Superintendent General of Indian Affairs.[37] The Iroquois remained adamant in their
claim, however, and persisted in their efforts to secure the lands for themselves for almost a century. In 1945, the Canadian government resolved the
issue somewhat by purchasing the land from the Sulpician Order.[38] It did so
in order to protect the Indians by preventing the Order from selling portions
of the tract which no longer were being used by Indians. In the course of this
long dispute the Oka band did receive lands elsewhere. Some 16,000 acres
in Duncaster, in the rear of the township of Wexford, were set apart in 1853
for the Iroquois of Oka and Caughnawaga. And in 1881 a tract of 25,000 acres
was provided for Oka Iroquois who were dissatisfied with the situation at the
Lake of Two Mountains and who wished to move to a new reserve in the
township of Gibson in Ontario.[39] The Gibson reserve presently contains 14,058
acres in the Muskoka district.[40]

The process by which an Iroquois presence was established in the province of Quebec was therefore a long one. It required several generations during which the first early communities were augmented by natural increase and
by new arrivals, in small numbers, from a variety of Iroquois and Algonquin
tribes. In Ontario,[41] however, the Iroquois established their presence suddenly
and effectively. In the course of a few months in 1784 and 1785 almost 2000
Iroquois loyalists moved from their wartime refuges to occupy new lands at
two locations set apart for them by Governor Haldimand in the western reaches
of the province. Their presence profoundly affected the development of the
region over the course of the next half century.

In 1783 the Iroquois were angry. Despite promises made in 1781 and
1782, the British had agreed to an international boundary which placed the
traditional Iroquois lands within the territory of the newly created American
republic. This was a particularly harsh blow to the Iroquois who had faithfully supported the British during the American Revolution, and who had
actually moved into Canada to provide that support. They felt betrayed. To
defuse that anger, which he feared might be re-directed against the British
and the refugee loyalists, Haldimand offered lands and asylum in Canada to
the Iroquois who wished to accept them. Two principal chiefs, Joseph Brant
and John Deseronto, accepted the offer. The Deseronto band selected land
on the north shore of Lake Ontario at the Bay of Quinte, apparently on the
grounds that this location would afford them security from the encroaching
Americans.[42] Brant also inspected the Quinte region but chose instead to occupy the valley of the Grand River. He did so because it placed him closer
to the Senecas who had asked that he not leave them totally isolated to cope
with the Americans, and because the Grand River afforded easier access to
the Indians of the Ohio Valley.[43] In addition the Grand River lands were more
fertile than those of the eastern end of Lake Ontario, although some of the

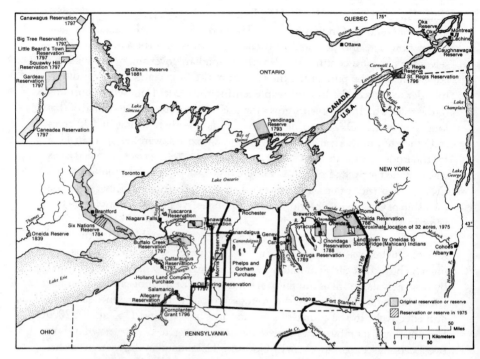

3. Iroquois reservations and reserves (except those in Wisconsin and Oklahoma). Dates
are given for those established after the American Revolution. Tyendinaga Reserve
was established in 1783; tone shows it as enlarged in 1793. Tuscarora Reservation was
established in 1797; tone shows area as enlarged in 1804.

Mohawks suggested that they were inferior to those they had abandoned in
the Mohawk Valley.[44]

Although these groups both had come to Canada to support Britain,
they did not co-operate with each other to any degree and followed quite different paths after 1784. Personal animosity between the two leaders and to
a high degree of stubbornness on the part of Captain John Deseronto[45] do
not adequately explain the split.

Captain John's Mohawks came from the Fort Hunter region of the Mohawk Valley. During the Revolution they had operated from Lachine, near
Montreal. Brant's followers moved to Niagara from Canajoharie and spent
the revolutionary years conducting raids from that western location.[46] The
division, therefore, had antecedents which were deepened during the critical
years 1777–1783. The Deseronto group became a somewhat isolated enclave

similar to the unique villages that already had evolved at St. Regis, Oka and Caughnawaga. They tried to join the Caughnawagas, but Haldimand resisted, possibly because the Caughnawagas were suspect during the war. Haldimand, however, could not overcome the Mohawks' determination to locate at the Bay of Quinte. Despite his preference that they join Brant's forces, Haldimand did provide the land for them at the Quinte region, and in May 1784 about a hundred Mohawks moved to what would become known as the Tyendinaga tract.[47]

The land had been purchased a year earlier from the Mississaugas of the region. Because the Mississaugas feared that the large numbers of the Six Nations might overwhelm their hunting grounds, they were at first reluctant to cede their land. The British were able to overcome this fear and also to allay the traditional friction between the Mississaugas and the Six Nations. Thus Captain John Deseronto reported in 1784 that when his party arrived at the Bay of Quinte they were greeted by a "great number of the native Mississauga at this place, who were very glad to see us."[48]

Originally the Tyendinaga tract contained about 7000 acres of land. At the behest of the first Lieutenant-Governor of Upper Canada, John Graves Simcoe, and upon urgings from Captain John, this was increased in 1793 to include all of the Tyendinaga Township, a total of 92,700[49] acres. The Simcoe adhesion stipulated that these lands could not be sold, except to the Crown,[50] a condition which was acceptable to the Tyendinaga Mohawks, but not to the Grand River Iroquois who received a similar allotment that same year. From the beginning, however, the Tyendinaga Mohawks pursued a course of action independent of the Grand River Iroquois. They did not engage in the wider affairs of the province or of Indian affairs in general, although it should be said that they professed their loyalty when war appeared possible in 1794 and 1807.[51] Rather they tended to their own reserve which received, in the early years, some considerable assistance from government.[52] In due course, the tract was pressed by White settlement, and consequently, through a series of land surrenders, the major ones occurring in 1820 and 1835, it was reduced to its present 17,448[53] acres. The Tyendinaga Mohawks maintained their village, therefore, in a consistent but unremarkable fashion, and in their own way came to terms with their neighbors and with the government. The one serious study of this reserve, by C. H. Torok,[54] observes that this involved a process of acculturation, but one which still preserved the Indian and Mohawk milieu.

The Grand River Iroquois figured prominently in the provincial and Indian affairs of the late eighteenth and early nineteenth centuries. In the 1780s the white population of Ontario was restricted to small pockets of settlement at Kingston, Niagara and Detroit.[55] In the 1790s York was begun but its population was small. The White population spread slowly from these bases over the next 20 years, to a large extent through immigration from the U.S., but on the eve of the War of 1812 it totalled fewer than 80,000.[56] As early as 1785 the Grand River Indians numbered over 1800, and included members from all six tribes of the Confederacy as well as small groups from allied tribes.[57] Consequently they formed a significant power base in the young colony. The government, particularly the Indian Department, was noticeably anxious about this group for it was led by an energetic and politically astute chief who involved himself in several fields of action, any one of which might have either augmented that base or proven costly or even dangerous to the British in Canada.

It was with considerable anxiety, therefore, that officials observed that the Six Nations of the Grand River were involved in the several councils in 1792 and 1793 which preceded the Anthony Wayne campaign in the Ohio Valley, leading to the Battle of Fallen Timbers. The engagement nearly brought American and British troops to blows in 1794 at Fort Miamis. Canadian officials also were nervous about Brant's continued association with the Iroquois in New York State, and they shuddered at his threats to rejoin them. In the late 1790s Brant was made a chief among the Mississaugas and began to act as their agent in land sales to the crown, thereby forcing up the cost of land to what was considered an outrageous price.[58] It appeared that Brant was attempting to forge a union among the Indians of Canada, and the British feared such a union in the hands of a chief who, despite his Revolutionary War record of loyalty, thought first in terms of Indian interest. The British Indian Department acted to prevent that union, and largely succeeded by 1805. Furthermore throughout this period (1784–1815) Canada was thought to be in danger of attacks by the Spanish and French.[59] The potential role of the Grand River Indians in any of these circumstances, either as friends or enemies, was critical.

The Grand River Iroquois maintained their attachment to the British cause, but the attachment was not automatic. It had to be cultivated. Accordingly, British officials continued the distribution of annual presents and other attentions, such as the issuing of provisions, the use of blacksmiths and interpreters at Indian villages and the support of the Mohawk chapel, etc. These efforts kept the Grand River Six Nations friendly to the British and to the White settlers who gradually came to fill up the colony. Extra efforts and greater generosity also contributed toward winning their active co-operation in the War of 1812. That co-operation, however, was less than wholehearted. Much has been made of their services in such instances as Queenston in 1812, Beaver Dams in 1813 and other engagements.[60] But these had been preceded in the opening weeks of the war by attempts at neutrality; and later in 1814 when the Iroquois of the Grand River learned that they were confronting their

American cousins in combat, as in the Battle of Chippawa, they and their counterparts pulled out of the conflict.[61]

In general, then, the Grand River Iroquois adopted an active stance in the circumstances of the day; and, where possible they pursued their own interest. As long as their numbers and their location made them a significant element in Upper Canada the British had to be rather more circumspect in their treatment of the Iroquois than they might have wished. It was against this background that the highly delicate issue of the lands of the Six Nations on the Grand River must be viewed.

Haldimand's 1784 grant was to include a tract six miles wide on each side of the Grand River from the mouth to the source. It was a portion of the major land cession agreement to the British Crown by the Mississaugas in 1784.[62] Almost immediately thorny questions arose regarding the nature, extent and meaning of the Haldimand grant.

From the beginning Joseph Brant determined that non-Indians would be invited to live on the Grand River. His motives have been examined extensively. It has been argued that he sought White neighbours through sale or lease of Indian lands in order to provide a source of income for his tribesmen beyond the traditional occupations of the chase and rudimentary agriculture. Such neighbours also were expected, by example, to encourage the Six Nations to cultivate their own lands more effectively. Some also have suggested that Brant expected to gain personally from the policy. Regardless of the chief's motives, his determination to follow the policy brought him into conflict with Lieutenant Governor Simcoe, who held the view that Indian lands could legally pass into White hands only through the intermediation of the crown, as stipulated in the 1763 Royal Proclamation. Brant's system of sales and leases, therefore, was invalid. Brant argued that the Royal Proclamation did not apply to the Grand River lands on the grounds that Haldimand's grant had conferred the land in fee simple to the Iroquois.[63] Furthermore, he added that the grant had awarded the Six Nations a national recognition[64] as allies, not subjects, of the crown. And he proceeded to sell or lease some 350,000 acres of Grand River lands to non-Indians. Simcoe denied Brant's interpretation, and in 1793 when he issued the document known as the Simcoe Patent[65] he included the rule that all land transactions of the Six Nations required the crown's approval.

The Simcoe Patent simply confirmed the Grand River lands to the Six Nations. It had been required because the descriptions contained in the original purchase from the Mississaugas and in the Haldimand grand did not conform to the terrain of the region. Brant refused to recognize the Simcoe Patent because of its restrictions on land sales; other Mohawks, then and since, have complained that the Simcoe deed denied them the headwaters of the Grand

River, which lie above the present township of Nichol.[66] The quarrel over the extent and meaning of the Haldimand grant continued for several decades. In the end it was settled, to the satisfaction of no one, not through legal arguments or inquiries, but rather through the interaction of personalities and according to changed circumstances.

While the Indian presence was potentially ominous, Brant was able to exert his will to a large degree. The lands he leased and sold were in fact confirmed by a compromise agreement which Brant virtually forced on Peter Russell, who succeeded Simcoe as the chief executive of Upper Canada. The 350,000 acres in contention were sold to the Crown and then confirmed to their owners according to the arrangements made with Brant. This was "parcelled out in six large but unequal blocks"[67] in 1798. The remaining 200,000 acres were retained by the Indians who spread themselves out over the entire tract. Two developments confused the land situations over the next three decades.

First, despite government disapproval, White squatters continued to move into the valley. The government's Indian Branch simply was too weak, and the general government was too preoccupied, to prevent this movement.[68] Secondly, although there were Indian communities located at the Tuscarora Village and at the Mohawk village,[69] most of the Indians were spread out along the long tract between the growing town of Brantford and the lower river.[70] Families generally worked small farms averaging about twenty acres.[71] And the squatters were mixed among them. Fearing that the white encroachments might combine with the scattering of the Indian farmers to create a situation where the Indians would not control any sizable contiguous block, the government suggested that the Indians sell their 200,000 acres to the Crown. In return they would receive the money from land sales as well as a reserve of 20,000 acres in a single block. They also would retain lands that they were currently cultivating. This was intended to preserve the Indian community and concurrently promote the recently established policy of using reserve communities to promote "civilization."[72] The deal was struck in 1841,[73] but its completion was costly and lengthy. The squatters had to be removed in order to provide the 20,000-acre reserve and the additional 35,000 acres which the Indians claimed they required in order to subsist. The squatters did not go easily, and the Indians had to be convinced to accept the reserve policy. By 1853 most of this had been accomplished, and the government program of consolidating the lands and the Indians was termed successful.[74] Some small surrenders have reduced the main reserve from 55,000 acres to its present 44,914, located on the southwest bank of the Grand River just downstream from Brantford. One of the surrenders was actually a gift of six thousand acres which the Six Nations chiefs made to the Mississaugas in 1848. This forms the present New Credit Mississaugas Reserve in the southeast corner

of the main Six Nations Reserve.[75] The Grand River Iroquois also retain a
small piece of land (about two-hundred acres) within the southeast limits of
the city of Brantford.[76]

Although circumstances prevented the Six Nations of the Grand River
from playing a major role in provincial affairs after about 1820, they remained
a vital link in the Iroquois tribal community. In a way they resembled the
Iroquois enclaves of Oka, St. Regis, Caughnawaga, and Gibson in that they
formed a semi-autonomous community which had been forced to accommodate itself to life within the wider non-Indian society.

But unlike the others the Grand River Iroquois clung more tenaciously
to Iroquois traditions and have asserted a sense of independence rather more
forcefully. They also continued to emphasize their unique relationship of friendship with the British. From the first days on the river, all six tribes of the Confederacy were represented. And shortly after the migration the chiefs of the
Grand River re-established the league[77] by relighting the council fires in the
village of the Onondagas. The American league continued in a weaker form
in New York State. This Canadian organization continued to assert, as Brant
had, that it possessed sovereign status, a claim which is still made by a portion
of the Six Nations.

It was this assertiveness that in part inclined the Oneidas of the Thames
River to seek and obtain membership in the League of Grand River Six Na-
tions. This band of some 436 left New York state under the leadership of
Moses Schuyler and William Taylor Doxtator[78] and moved into the Thames
River valley in Ontario in 1840. With money they brought with them, the
Oneidas purchased 5,400 acres of land on the Thames River near Caradoc.[79]
Their land adjoined a reserve of Chippewas and Munceys, but like the Iroquois at Oka the Oneidas maintained a distance between themselves and their
Indian neighbors. Because they had been pro-American during the American Revolution the Thames River Oneidas were nervous in their new location. To secure their position they hoped to demonstrate their loyalty to their
new monarch by associating with the Grand River League which had a tradition of attachment to Britain.[80] The Oneidas of the Thames are the only
separate Iroquois group to seek and maintain this political tie with the Grand
River.

The Iroquois came to settle permanently in Canada, therefore, in two
distinct movements. Those who settled in Quebec did so at the urgings of
the French, at a time when relations between the Iroquois League and the
French Crown were tense, or even openly hostile. And by the time that the
French regime ended in Canada, these Iroquois had established themselves
in a permanent fashion within the Canadian society of the day. They had
few dealings with the loyalist Iroquois who followed the British flag into Canada after 1783. In the half century after the revolution the Iroquois in On-

tario, after a period of jousting with British authorities, also created a distinct
and permanent community. Although each maintains itself as a local entity,
the several communities at Oka, Caughnawaga, St. Regis, Gibson, Tyendinaga, the Grand River, and the Thames constitute the Iroquois tradition and
history in Canada.

NOTES

1. See Bruce G. Trigger, "Archeological and other Evidence: A Fresh Look at the 'Laurentian Iroquois,'" *American Antiquity* 33, no. 4(1968):429-40.

2. For example, see George T. Hunt, *The Wars of the Iroquois* (Madison: University of
Wisconsin Press, 1940).

3. Ibid., p. 46.

4. G. F. G. Stanley, "The First Indian 'Reserves' in Canada," *Revue d'Histoire de l'Amérique Français* 4(1952-53):196-97.

5. Accounts of the Iroquois invasion of the Huron villages in 1649 can be found in
Hunt, *Wars of the Iroquois*; Bruce G. Trigger, *The Children of Aataentsic*, 2 vols. (Montreal: McGill-
Queens University Press, 1976); and Conrad Heidenreich, *Huronia* (Toronto: McClelland and
Stewart, 1971). Among the Huron groups that fled from Huronia were some 500 who sought
refuge near Quebec in 1650-51. It was among them that the French began the Mission of Notre
Dame de Foye in 1668. The mission was moved to Lorette in 1674 and then to Jeune Lorette
in 1697, on the St. Charles River to the north of Quebec. Stanley, "The First Indian 'Reserves,'"
pp. 191-95.

6. Stanley, "The First Indian 'Reserves,'" p. 197.

7. Ibid., p. 198.

8. William N. Fenton and Elisabeth Tooker, "Mohawk," in *Northeast*, ed. Bruce G. Trigger: vol. 15 of *Handbook of North American Indians*, gen. ed. William C. Sturtevant (Washington,
D.C.: Smithsonian Institution Press, 1978), p. 470.

9. Trigger, ed., *Northeast*, p. 470.

10. Stanley, "The First Indian 'Reserves,'" pp. 199-200.

11. Canada, Geographic Board, *Handbook of Indians of Canada* (Ottawa: King's Printer,
1913), pp. 81-82.

12. Fenton and Tooker, "Mohawk," in *Northeast*, ed. Trigger, p. 470.

13. Ibid., pp. 472-73; Stanley, "The First Indian 'Reserves,'" pp. 205-207.

14. Fenton and Tooker, "Mohawk," in *Northeast*, ed. Trigger, p. 473.

15. Stanley, "The First Indian 'Reserves,'" pp. 203-205.

16. Harold Blau, Jack Campisi, and Elisabeth Tooker, "Onondaga," in *Northeast*, ed.
Trigger, pp. 494-95.

17. Stanley, "The First Indian 'Reserves,'" pp. 200-201.

18. Fenton and Tooker, "Mohawk," in *Northeast*, ed. Trigger, p. 470.

19. Ibid., p. 473.

20. Barbara Graymont, *The Iroquois in the American Revolution* (Syracuse: Syracuse University Press, 1972), p. 87.

21. Ibid., p. 95.

22. Gordon Day and Bruce G. Trigger, "Algonquin," in *Northeast*, ed. Trigger, p. 795.

23. "Return of Indians," 10 December 1786, Simcoe Papers, mss., MU2782, Envelope No. 1, Provincial Archives of Ontario.

24. "Lord Dorchester to the Seven Nations of Lower Canada," in [J. G. Simcoe], *The Correspondence of Lieut. Governor John Graves Simcoe*, ed. E. A. Cruickshank, 5 vols. (Toronto: Ontario Historical Society, 1923-31), 2:149-50.

25. G. F. G. Stanley, "The Significance of the Six Nations Participation in the War of 1812," *Ontario History* 55(1963):225-226.

26. *Report of the Affairs of the Indians of Canada, 1842*, Journals, Legislative Assembly, Canada, 1844-45, Appendix EEE, Section I.

27. Canada, Geographic Board, *Handbook of Indians of Canada*, p. 523.

28. Little is known about the Iroquois who moved west to follow the fur trade. Two recent studies are Jack A. Frisch, "Iroquois in the West," in *Northeast*, ed. Trigger, pp. 544-46; and Trudy Nicks, "The Iroquois and the Fur Trade in Western Canada," in *Old Trails and New Directions*, eds. Carol M. Judd and Arthur J. Ray (Toronto: University of Toronto Press, 1960), pp. 85-101.

29. Stanley, "The First Indian 'Reserves,'" pp. 178-85.

30. D. Claus, "Memorandum of what I can recollect relative to the Settlement of St. Regis from Sault St. Louis," Montreal, 11 March 1784, Haldimand Papers, Manuscript Group 21, B-114:307-308, Public Archives of Canada (PAC), Ottawa.

31. *Report of the Affairs of the Indians . . . 1842*, Section I.

32. *Canada, Indian Treaties and Surrenders, from 1680 to 1890*, 2 vols. (Ottawa: Queen's Printer, 1891), 1:136-38.

33. L. Villeneuve, "The Historical Background of Indian Reserves and Settlements in the Province of Quebec," unpublished paper prepared for the Treaties and Historical Research Centre, Research Branch, Department of Indian and Northern Affairs (Ottawa), p. 41.

34. Ibid., pp. 41-42.

35. *Atlas of Indian Reserves and Settlements, Canada, 1971* (Ottawa: Department of Indian and Northern Affairs, 1971), sheet 2A.

36. Villeneuve, "Historical Background," p. 21.

37. H. C. Langevin, secretary of state and superintendent general of Indian affairs, Report to Privy Council, 9 October 1868, Report No. 40, Record Group 10, vol. 10024, P.A.C.

38. Villeneuve, "Historical Background," p. 27.

39. Villeneuve, "Historical Background," p. 27.

40. *Atlas of Indian Reserves . . . 1971*, sheet 3A.

41. In 1784, the colony of Quebec included all the British possessions south of the Hudson's Bay Company lands (Rupert's Land), from the Gulf of St. Lawrence to Lake Superior. In 1791 this was divided into Upper Canada and Lower Canada, with the division point just east of present day Cornwall. The upper province became Canada West in 1841 and the Province of Ontario in 1867. The lower province was called Canada East from 1841 to 1867, at which time it became the Province of Quebec.

42. C. M. Johnston, "An Outline of Early Settlement in the Grand River Valley," *Ontario History* 54, no. 1(1962):48.

43. *The Valley of the Six Nations*, ed. C. M. Johnston, publications of the Champlain Society, Ontario Series 7 (Toronto, 1964), pp. xxxvi–viii, 49–50.

44. Ibid., p. xxxvii.

45. M. Eleanor Herrington, "Captain John Deserontyou and the Mohawk Settlement at Deseronto," *Queen's Quarterly* 29(1921):170.

46. C. H. Torok, "The Tyendinaga Mohawks," *Ontario History* 57(1965):69–77.

47. E. A. Cruikshank, "The Coming of the Loyalist Mohawks to the Bay of Quinte," *Papers and Records of the Ontario Historical Society* 26(1930):390.

48. Herrington, "Captain John Deserontyou," p. 171; Johnson to Haldimand, 11 August 1783, mss., Haldimand Papers B-115, pp. 138–39, PAC: D. B. Smith, "The Dispossession of the Mississauga," *Ontario History* 73(1981):67–68.

49. Herrington, "Captain John Deserontyou," p. 175.

50. *Canada, Indian Treaties and Surrenders* 1:7–8.

51. Cruikshank, "Coming of the Loyalist Mohawks," p. 402.

52. Herrington, "Captain John Deserontyou," pp. 173–74.

53. *Canada, Indian Treaties and Surrenders* 1:54–58, 100–101.

54. Charles H. Torok, "The Acculturation of the Mohawks of the Bay of Quinte," Ph.D. diss., University of Toronto, 1966.

55. Although Detroit was formally in American territory, it remained physically in British hands until 1796, and until then the British administered the western end of the Ontario peninsula from Detroit.

56. John K. Mahon, *The War of 1812* (Gainesville: University of Florida Press, 1972), p. 15.

57. In 1785 the population of the Grand River was given as follows: Mohawk, 464; Cayuga, 381; Onondaga, 245; Tuscarora, 129; Oneida, 162; Seneca, 78; Delaware, 231; Nanticoke, 11; Tutelo, 74; Other, 68. Total, 1843. See *Valley of the Six Nations*, p. 52.

58. William Dummer Powell, "Memoir on the Refusal of the Messasague Indians to cede their land on Lake Ontario, 1797," mss., Q Series, 284:69–75, PAC.

59. See C. M. Johnston, "Joseph Brant, The Grand River Lands, and the Northwest Crisis," *Ontario History* 55(1963):267–82.

60. For example, "Campaigns of 1812–14: Contemporary Narratives by Captain W. H. Merritt, Colonel William Claus, Lieut. Colonel Mathew Elliott, and Captain John Norton," ed. E. A. Cruikshank, *Niagara Historical Society Paper* 9(1902):4–22.

61. Stanley, "Significance of Six Nations Participation," p. 229.

62. *Canada, Indian Treaties and Surrenders* 1:5–7.

63. Sally Weaver, "Six Nations of the Grand River, Ontario," in *Northeast*, ed. Trigger, p. 525.

64. *Northeast*, ed. Trigger, p. 525.

65. *Canada, Indian Treaties and Surrenders*, 1:7–8.

66. Johnston, "Outline of Early Settlement," p. 51.

67. *Valley of the Six Nations*, p. lv.

68. Weaver, "Six Nations of the Grand River, p. 526.

69. *Report on the Affairs of the Indians . . . 1842*, Section II.

70. The tract north of Brantford had been sold as Blocks 1, 2, 3, and 4 by the Brant sales system. The lower end of the tract consisting of Canborough township (Block 6) and Moulton township (Block 5) had likewise been sold.

71. Weaver, "Six Nations of the Grand River," p. 525.

72. Ibid., p. 526.

73. *Valley of the Six Nations*, p. lxix.

74. Weaver, "Six Nations of the Grand River," p. 526.

75. *Atlas of Indian Reserves . . . 1971*, sheet 3A.

76. This land contains 192 acres according to Sheet 3A of the *Atlas*, but Weaver gives it as 278.09 acres. "Six Nations of the Grand River," p. 527.

77. Weaver, "Six Nations of the Grand River," p. 528.

78. Jack Campisi, "Oneida," in *Northeast*, ed. Trigger, p. 487.

79. *Canada. Report of the Special Commissioners to Investigate Indian Affairs in Canada* (Toronto: Queen's Printer, 1858), p. 44.

80. Campisi, "Oneida," in *Northeast*, ed. Trigger, p. 487.

4

Iroquois Treaties

COMMON FORMS, VARYING INTERPRETATIONS

MARY A. DRUKE

I ROQUOIS TREATIES negotiated in the seventeenth, eighteenth, and nineteenth centuries were international agreements in which Iroquois Indians participated. This essay will discuss varying interpretations of elements of Iroquois treaties and the protocol associated with them.

Significant items used in council negotiations were sometimes weighted differently in relation to one another by people of distinct nations and cultures involved in the transactions. For example, signed and sealed articles of agreement, which were most often considered by Euramericans to be the primary concrete symbols of agreement, were not commonly valued as such by Iroquois people. Similarly, although the presentation and acceptance of wampum belts were principal symbols of agreement to Iroquois people, they were not of such great value to Euramericans. In addition, different elements of council protocol had distinct meanings for various participants. In cross-cultural negotiations, therefore, the presence or absence of wampum, on the one side, or of signed and sealed written articles on the other could make a difference in whether an agreement was considered valid, not by virtue of any intrinsic nature of the forms themselves, but rather because of the meanings of the forms in the context of council procedure.

The various meanings and values attributed to, and different emphases placed upon, elements of treaty protocol are discussed below. Types of documentation that did, and still do, have meaningful roles in council negotiations are explored, and procedures in which these were used are presented in order to demonstrate relative values given to the segments of council transactions.

TYPES OF DOCUMENTS

The phrase "treaty documents" is used here as a blanket term for written records (articles of agreement and minutes or proceedings of councils), wampum belts, and oral tradition, all of which provide evidence of treaty negotiations in the seventeenth, eighteenth, and early nineteenth centuries. In any given instance, the types of treaty documents in evidence must be distinguished and evaluated for interpretation of the agreements presumed to have been made.

Written Records

Values placed on written documents varied well into the eighteenth century at least, because the Iroquois commonly could not read what the colonials wrote. Iroquois negotiators often placed their signatures or their marks (signs of their clans or nations) on papers to show agreement with what they had been told was written down. The document was always written in a European language, and always rendered into an Iroquois language by an interpreter, so the Indian's mark confirmed what the interpreter said rather than the meaningless words on the paper. That there was sometimes much discrepancy between oral and written versions is illustrated by a case in 1698 when two Mohawks claimed that they had not ceded land supposed to have been granted by them to certain individuals. As a signed and sealed deed existed, the Mohawks were asked, "What did they mean when they put their marks and seales to a bill of sale?" if they did not cede the land. They answered that they had been deceived about the contents of the paper; they had been told that it placed their land under the care of the "pretended Purchasers," and that "it should not be in the power of any person to make an Infringement upon their Property, and as long as any of the Maquase [Mohawk] nation lived, the land should be theirs and their Posteritys for ever." The two men asserted that they had been "so deceiv'd, as to sign a Paper contrary to our Intention."[1] They therefore considered the document properly null and void.

Such occurrences were not only characteristic of the seventeenth century. In 1763, a young Iroquois who had signed a document without authority claimed that he did not know the purport of the deed, but had put his mark on the document because he had seen others sign.[2] One statement from an Oneida, also in 1763, indicates that some Iroquois, in return for payment, may have simply added their marks to a document that they considered to be meaningless to accommodate people for whom they nevertheless had little respect. As reported by Sir William Johnson: "Jacobe an Oneidae told me four or five days ago that he was made Drunk by U Klock and Signed it [a disputed deed], and that on being asked lately to Sign some other paper, he told him he would if paid for it, on my asking him why he would sign for Lands he had no right to, He answered that was the reason for his Willingness, Since Klock and Fonda [the men who had obtained the signed document] were Fools or Knaves enough to ask him when they knew it."³ Euramericans, on the other hand, considered signed and sealed articles as concrete evidence that a binding contract had been made.

For English, Dutch, French, and Germans in North America, signed and sealed deeds from Indians were the most important supports for claims to land. Argument over contested claims often centered on whether written documents could be shown and whether they had been obtained under prescribed conditions.⁴ The importance of such written documents to Europeans did not escape Iroquois attention. After some experience, the Indians sometimes requested and preserved duplicate copies of the agreements written by colonial scribes.

While most treaty negotiations were taking place, a clerk or secretary, working with the aid of an interpreter, recorded the official proceedings. These proceedings, as preserved to the present day, are usually lengthy documents that present what are ostensibly verbatim accounts of the negotiations. In actuality, however, the treaty councils involving Iroquois were multilingual events, but the minutes or proceedings and the final articles of agreement were written in one language only; and that language was seldom, if ever, Iroquoian. Much of the evidence provided by these documents, therefore, is but a translation of what was said.

Poor translation was often noted at councils, and sometimes it was thought to be purposefully false. After the death of the Pennsylvania interpreter Conrad Weiser, the Six Nations at Easton in 1761 claimed that Indians and Pennsylvanians could not understand one another as well as they once could.⁵ In 1754, the Iroquois requested interpreters in whom they had the most confidence to be present at land transactions, in order to ensure against deliberate mistranslations.⁶

Although council proceedings are often extensive, they are also necessarily selective. Remarks spoken aside between individuals, no matter how important, were not recorded unless brought to the attention of the clerks. No record of significant nonverbal signs such as facial expressions, posture, and glances between persons usually was written. Scribes chose (often unconsciously) items deemed important enough to warrant inclusion, and their standards of importance were not always the same as the Indians' standards. In Iroquois councils that often lasted for weeks, much of importance was transacted at private meetings off the record. For example, Sir William Johnson wrote, in a letter enclosing a copy of proceedings of a council in August 1770, "They Contain the whole of the Transactions at the publick Conferences, tho' as I have formerly Observed to you, that Is a very small part of the Debates, Arguements and discourses at the private Conferences where the principal Subjects are first Agitated and Determined upon."[7] Given the spread of time over which treaties took place, and the diversity of participants and their interests, even the lengthiest reports of proceedings cannot provide a record of all that may have been significant to the major participants; but Euramericans considered them as the ultimate source for information about their subject negotiations.

Wampum Belts

Iroquois records of treaty negotiations were wampum belts symbolic of words spoken, and exchanged during the transactions. Physically these belts were "cylindrical beads [made principally of quahog, *venus mercenaria*, shells] drilled through from opposite ends,"[8] and strung in rows with sinew, vegetable fiber and/or thread, forming a rectangular belt that is usually longer than wide. The beads are deep purple (black) or white in color. Glass was sometimes substituted for shell. Belts were made of beads of one color or of a combination of black and white beads often strung to form graphic patterns (emblems) of white on black or black on white. White was considered by the Iroquois to symbolize peace and/or life, among other things, while black was said to symbolize war and/or death. Red paint or other pigment was sometimes added to belts to signify war.

Wampum strings, consisting of beads strung on a single sinew, fiber, or thread, were also exchanged, along with wampum belts, at treaties. Strings were commonly considered to represent matters of less importance than issues associated with belts.

For the Iroquois, wampum was the "word" or the "voice" containing messages to be delivered.[9] Wampum played a large role in conveying, accepting, or rejecting messages and proposals at treaties. The presentation of wampum served as confirmation of words spoken. Formal acceptance of wampum was considered by the Iroquois to indicate that a message would be heeded or an agreement upheld. If the wampum's message was acceptable, the receiving party would retain the belt or string and would often reciprocate with their own wampum. Rejection or return of a wampum belt signified that its message or proposal was not acceptable. For example, in 1756 some Delawares would not touch belts offered to them, and they threw their pipes aside as a sign that they refused a message delivered by the Six Nations.[10] In 1694 New France's Governor Frontenac took some wampum and rejected other belts in a council at Montreal, to indicate acceptance of some proposals and rejection of others.[11]

Of course, as long as proposals made without wampum were desired by all parties concerned, items of the proposals were upheld as in any casual, mutually desirable agreement. However, when dissatisfaction arose, a party might turn to the technical point of whether or not wampum had been exchanged in order to escape from an unpleasant predicament, as Mohawks did in February 1757 at a council with Sir William Johnson. The written report quotes an address by the speaker for the Indians of Canajoharie: "We find that the last time you [Johnson] were here, some thing had been said which gave offence and has caused a misunderstanding which we are sorry for and hope to make easy now . . . you may know our words are of no weight unless accompanied with wampum and you know we spoke with none and therefore you will not take notice of what was inconsiderately said by two or three of our People."[12] Because of the possibility of such maneuvering, Euramericans were usually careful to see that wampum was exchanged for matters important to them, in much the same way that the Iroquois often insisted that a written copy of treaty minutes be given to them.

Wampum as a physical substance was not the essential thing in confirming speech or agreement. What mattered most was the *process* of exchange of presents. Numerous records show objects being substituted for wampum at one time or another though wampum was most preferable. In its absence, the confirming presents might be skins, blankets, plates (engraved with figures such as Iroquois clan insignia such as Bear, Wolf, Turtle), guns, flints, or bundles of beads.

In addition to confirming words spoken, wampum also served as a mnemonic device to remind speakers of the symbolized agreements by recalling the speeches associated with the wampum. For this purpose, emblematic designs commonly were woven into the wampum belts. However, to "read" a belt was not primarily to explain the significance of individual emblems, though this sometimes was done, but rather to relate the speeches associated with the belt as a whole. A belt without emblems might therefore represent as rich a record of council proceedings as a belt with figures. Moreover, modern studies suggest that several belts might have been associated at times with a certain agreement, any one of which might have served as sufficient stimulus to recall the entire narrative of transactions.[13]

William M. Beauchamp suggested in a study of wampum published in 1901 that the use of emblems in belts intensified in the mid-eighteenth century.[14] This increase may very well have been a response to the general lack of expertise on the part of the English to remember things precisely without the aid of specific references. As evidence of negotiations, wampum was closely tied as a mnemonic device to what is commonly called oral tradition (to be discussed in the next section). Euramericans never developed a system for transmitting oral tradition associated with wampum belts, so the specific meanings of belts were lost to them. Realizing this, Indians sometimes demanded that a written message explaining their meaning be attached. To guess at the meanings of the emblems themselves may provide a general idea of the topic of agreement, but such speculation gives no indication of what parties were involved, where and when the treaty was made, or the fine points of agreement.

Among the Iroquois, belts were often kept by a specific individual (Keeper of the Wampum) who was particularly adept at reciting speeches associated with them.[15] The meanings of belts were not locked into translation of discrete units of meaning but into the oral tradition associated with them. The word came alive when an association between speeches and belts was made.

Oral Tradition

Oral tradition in the forms of readings of wampum belts and other recitations that conveyed knowledge about historical relationships with people of other nations were common features of Iroquois participation in treaty councils.

Although oral tradition is only truly accessible in oral form, narratives of tradition can be, and were, written down. It should be remembered that such accounts are at least second hand, coming through a transcriber. They offer a valuable record of Iroquois interpretations of the past, however. An example of such a written record of oral tradition is an account of a speech by Red Jacket and Little Billy, two Senecas present at a treaty at Brownstown in September 1810. They recited a précis of relationships between Iroquois and Euramericans at councils that they had attended in the past.[16]

Much research has been done in the last twenty years on oral traditional to illuminate its importance and its nature. One assumption that is incorrectly made in some cases is that there is one original version of oral tradition that is ideally transmitted word for word, but which, through the process of transmission, is changed and varied. It has been demonstrated that in some cultures the transmission of oral tradition is an active narrative or performance. Oral tradition in many cultures, such as Iroquois culture, is often transmitted in public. It is subject, therefore, to criticism by listeners who either were present at the time of a recounted occurrence or who have heard other accounts of the tradition against which to judge a present narrative. The exactitude with which details are transmitted in many cases is not as important, however, as the structure of the narration. As Michael Foster has shown in a 1974 publication about the Iroquois Thanksgiving Address, individual recitals are not verbatim transmissions of a fixed text, but narratives that have a definable structure expressing established interrelationships between beings in the Iroquois universe.[17] In a similar way, many Iroquois oral traditions of treaties are not exact verbatim accounts of council proceedings, but convey an accepted interpretation of relationships based on agreements made in council negotiations. Wampum, of course, served in many cases as an mnemonic device for recall of details of the relationship.

The spoken word was weighted more highly by Iroquois than the written word. For many, oral traditions served as a medium through which accounts of negotiations were preserved in a way parallel to writing—as a record of past transactions. In 1774, an Iroquois speaker, referring to a treaty at Fort Stanwix in 1768, stated plainly: "we hope, that what we have said will not be forgotten, for we remember it still, and you have it all in writing."[18] There is a finer sense of the meanings of documentation, however, in which a distinction between use of writing and oral tradition was made by Indians. Oral tradition is communicated with face-to-face interaction as the written word is not. Samuel Kirkland, a Presbyterian missionary, reported in 1765 that the Seneca Kayenquarachton (Kaienʔkwaahton) told him "that some of the Indians were afraid of *writing* any *letters* because those letters would *speak* for a great many years afterwards."[19] What was being expressed was a realization that it was possible to place undue weight on written words when advantageous, though the person whose words they were was not present. Oneidas in 1771 made what is on the surface an almost contradictory remark to that of words enduring for long periods of time when they inquired about a petition that had been sent to the Governor of New York to request a blacksmith. Samuel Kirkland, who was residing among them at the time, reported: "they begin to think their letter does not speak—that their words are gon to sleep (and say) they fear they will not revive."[20] Both the Seneca and the Oneida observations articulate the Indian belief in the written word's independence from direct personal interaction.

In 1810, at a council at Brownstown, a document purporting to be a deed to John Johnson for "Grand Island" (an island in the Niagara River) was discussed by the Seneca, Little Billy. None of the old men alive remembered selling Grand Island to John Johnson—"no one could tell anything about it." Therefore the agreement was not recognized as valid by the Iroquois.[21] Even when, in rare cases, written documents were lauded by Iroquois in comparison with wampum because the words could not be forgotten, the final determination about what agreement has been made was said to rest beyond the written document. The Onondaga, Tioquanda, in 1765 pointed out that, should written articles of agreement be used to deceive, "the Supreme Being whose worshiper and Servant our Great King and Father is can punish you, because all these promises and engagements have been entered upon before Him and have been ratified in the Face of all your Friends, Brother and Allies."[22] Tioquanda who was praising the durable nature of messages put down on paper at the time concluded that the nature of interaction between "your Friends, Brothers and Allies" was ultimately independent of the written word. In Iroquois culture, the "word," the essence of oral tradition and of wampum, had a life to it by virtue of interaction that paper (written documents) just did not have, regardless of its assumed durability. It was also the case that, for most Iroquois, treaty relationships were not frozen to words written on a page at one point in time, but were active, living relationships, ideally frequently renewed. Continued requests, therefore, were presented for renewal of agreements.

Written documents, wampum belts and oral tradition were elements of cross-cultural interaction that were meaningful in different ways to various participants of treaty councils. Although they were used to mark, identify, and define agreements, they did not determine in and of themselves if a binding agreement had been made. They were meaningful within, and served as evidence of, council protocol, which also contributed toward interpretations of negotiations. We shall now focus on this protocol.

COUNCIL PROTOCOL

Council procedures were segmented affairs which may for the sake of analysis be divided into the following units: (1) invitations; (2) preliminary meetings between delegates of one nation or one party to council negotiations; (3) major council transactions; (4) ratification of a treaty and/or reporting of delegates to the person or group to whom, or for whom, they were responsible in the negotiations.

The elements of treaty protocol were many, including ritual processes such as condolence. All of the elements were not, of course, of equal importance to participants in treaty negotiations. The essay by William N. Fenton in this volume details the many elements of treaty protocol. What will be discussed here are those elements of councils that contributed towards finally determining a binding agreement.

Formal invitations to councils were issued by a party or parties desiring a treaty conference. A message, often accompanied by wampum was sent by a runner to the people invited. The number of days before the council would be held was usually specified. Previous to an international treaty, meetings were held in Iroquois villages to discuss the subjects to be decided upon.[23] Euramericans held preliminary councils among themselves where administrators would draft instructions and authorization for negotiators.

Before a main international council, it was common for hosts to meet with visitors at the "woods edge." This meeting often was held a mile or two outside settlements, especially when councils were held in Iroquois villages. A verbal condolence expressing sorrow for deaths that had occurred since the last council, and refreshing the participants, would be proffered by one side and reciprocated by the other. Generally at least one day passed after the arrival of the visitors before the agenda of the meeting was presented.

The protocol of Iroquois councils in which Euramericans were involved was primarily Indian in form with modifications arising through interaction. Variations in cultural forms were introduced in interaction among Indians as well as in interaction between Indians and Euramericans. The calumet, for example, was gradually introduced to the Iroquois by contact with other Indian people.[24] Dutch, English, and French records of councils with the Iroquois all indicated similar specific forms that are not found in records of exclusively European or colonial councils. This is hardly surprising, given that Europeans came as intruders and/or visitors to a continent inhabited by peoples of hundreds of different nations. Initially, European colonials were very much in a minority dealing as newcomers in other peoples' home territories. They were in no position to dictate their own terms. Success in accomplishing what colonists desired was undoubtedly dependent to some extent on how well the colonials adopted native forms for negotiating with the natives. As late as September 1768, Sir William Johnson wrote to the governor of New York that "whosoever has any affairs to transact with Indians must know their forms and in some measure comply with them."[25]

Main international council meetings were often very lengthy affairs, commonly lasting for a month or more. John Butler, an English deputy agent for Indian Affairs, reported in 1757, that a council meeting he planned to attend at Onondaga would be prolonged because everyone's opinion would have to be heard—that of the warriors as well as that of the sachems.[26] Moreover, as has been mentioned before, treaty negotiations often consisted of many private councils. Delegates of one party or another would commonly withdraw to discuss an issue. Topics of discussion were usually introduced by one party and would be repeated by the other party before an answer to each item was given. Public meetings would often be suspended for socializing and for private meetings for a day or two after proposals were presented.

Wampum was exchanged frequently during formal treaty negotiations as specific propositions were made and answered, and minutes of the councils were written by a clerk, secretary, or interpreter during the meetings. At the end of treaty councils, written articles of agreement were usually signed and sealed by principal delegates in attendance. Then gifts would usually be exchanged. By the mid-eighteenth century, however, the giving of presents other than wampum was often primarily a one-way affair, with presents passing from

Euramericans to Indians (being perceived by English and French to be payment for lands ceded, inducements to provide military aid, etc.).

After main international council meetings, delegates from each party returned to their home base. Iroquois delegates reported about treaty negotiations to confederate, national, or village councils. Whether or not an agreement was valid for the Iroquois depended upon whether or not wampum had been exchanged, and/or delegates had been authorized. In some cases delegates went to a main treaty council with specific instructions, in others they went with general authority to make decisions commensurate with their people's wishes. If consensus on specific issues was not formally articulated before an international negotiation, delegates might be instructed by their people in council to go to the main treaty conference to discuss issues, and to return back to the appropriate home council for consensus before final agreement could be made at main international meetings. Blanket authority was given infrequently. Controls were effective even when authority was deputized, for a leader who made an unfavorable decision seriously risked losing his people's support.[27]

The number of Iroquois attending treaty councils was usually relatively large. Euramericans were constantly trying to encourage Indians to attend in fewer numbers. The large numbers, however, allowed for discussion at meetings and for a sense of support upon which to base decisions, should they be called for. Many of the councils commonly labeled as treaties by Euramericans were probably perceived by Iroquois not to be councils for the making of an agreement, but preliminary meetings to hear and make proposals. The Mohawk Indian, Thayendanegea (Joseph Brant), for example, when first planning to go to a meeting at Fort Stanwix in 1784, wrote to Alexander Fraser, a British deputy for Indian Affairs, that "he wished to apprise the Government that he and the Chiefs that were going along with him were not vested with power from the [Mohawk] Nation to conclude a Peace with the Americans but that they were charged with a message preparatory to that business."[28] Some English were aware of preliminary procedures undertaken by the Iroquois. Sir William Johnson, for example, in 1761, doubted Seneca protestations that they were unaware of a message brought by two Senecas to Wyandots, Potawatomis, Ojibwas, and Ottawas near Detroit. Johnson said that it was the custom to consult before making such a proposition. As he expressed it, "I well know your custom of consulting each other on affairs of much less moment, nay, matters of the smallest importance are never agreed to without the consent of you all."[29] Oneidas, Tuscaroras, Cayugas, Tutelos, and Nanticokes from villages on the Susquehanna River apologized in March 1768 for being late to a meeting at Johnson Hall, saying that the matter of peace to be negotiated between Cherokees and the Six Nations was such a weighty matter that it took a long time to decide upon it at home before delegates could be sent to the treaty council.[30] Tribal council deliberations were prolonged sometimes for years before a consensus could be reached and delegates instructed, as happened when Pennsylvania proposed an alliance in 1732 which Six Nations delegates did not accept until 1736.[31]

For Iroquois, an agreement between them and another party was not valid unless their delegates had received prior instructions on the issues involved, and unless an exchange of wampum had been made for the specific items of agreement at the subsequent treaty negotiations. If a delegate had not received instructions, he could speak only for himself. Euramericans, on the other hand, made treaties through delegates whose agreements were subject to approval by higher authorities. It was usually the process called ratification that determined finally whether a treaty was valid and binding, and ratification required that written documents, signed and sealed, be presented to the proper higher authorities.

Euramerican views on ratification changed somewhat through time, however, becoming more formalized. In the seventeenth and eighteenth centuries, the ultimate right to ratify resided technically with monarchs of European countries. In practice, however, royal ministers or legislative bodies ratified treaties. It was generally considered proper for monarchs to automatically approve agreements made by their commissioners.[32] Nonetheless, the right to make agreements between nations resided with the monarchs. The United States Constitution institutionalized the ratification process in a new way. Treaty-making power was given to the executive branch of government. For a treaty to be ratified, however, it was necessary that the consent of the Senate be obtained as well.

During the colonial period, within the administrative ranking systems of Euramericans, approval of legislative or executive bodies higher in administrative circles than negotiators was required after treaty transactions. In the English colonies for a number of years after the Superintendency for Indian Affairs was created in 1755, there was confusion over whether the superintendency was a military position or a civil one. Whether the Superintendent was responsible directly to the Commander in Chief or to the Secretary of State was uncertain. There was always exhibited, however, a sense that persons in the Indian Department were not independent in and of themselves, but were negotiating in behalf of other parties—for the King, for the Governor, etc. Even when French governors negotiated directly with Indians, they reported to the Minister of Marine. When English governors met directly with Indians, they laid proceedings before legislatures for approval.

The emphasis placed by Euramericans on ratifications is evidenced throughout the historical record. A letter from Timothy Pickering to John Jay, dated 11 March 1797, articulates this emphasis at what is perhaps its most extreme level. Pickering's letter is quoted here at length:

> With a strong desire to enable the State of New York finally to extinguish the remaining claims of the Mohawks to lands within that State, a doubt existed of the President's power to appoint, in the recess of the Senate, a Commissioner to hold a treaty for the purpose . . . I mentioned to the President these facts. That when, in 1794 [at Canandaigua], it was thought of much importance to quiet the claims of the Six Nations and secure their friendship, I was myself appointed to hold a treaty with them, the only evidence of my appointment was a certificate under the hand and seal of the Secretary of State, that I was designated by the President of the United States for that service . . . The subsequent assent of the Senate and ratification of the treaty by the President, cured every defect in its formation.[33]

Whether the consent of the Senate was needed for a legitimate commission or not was open to question at that time. As far as Pickering was concerned, however, it was not the authorization of delegates that was significant in treaty negotiations but whether or not treaty articles were ratified by the President and Senate. According to Pickering, even if delegates were not authorized, if the treaty was authorized, the agreement was valid.

CONCLUSION

It was not simply ratification or authorization to treat that was sufficient for a binding agreement, however. As has been explained a number of elements (exchange of wampum, signed and sealed treaty articles, oral tradition providing an account of negotiations, ratification, and authorization) were significant in various ways to different parties. There was much area for misunderstandings when one or another of these elements was manipulated to make or break agreements, or when unequal emphasis was put on one or more, resulting in different interpretations of the content of agreements. Discussion of the presence or absence of any one feature was often at the center of subsequent determinations of whether or not an agreement had been concluded by due process. Despite these complexities, however, treaties provided a recognized forum in which dialogue to resolve misunderstandings could continue between people of distinct nations and cultures.

NOTES

1. E. B. O'Callaghan and Berthold Fernow, eds., *Documents Relative to the Colonial History of the State of New York*, 15 vol. (Albany, N.Y.: Weed, Parsons, and Co., 1856–87), 4:345–347. Hereafter *N.Y.Col.Docs.*

2. James Sullivan, Alexander C. Flick, et al., eds. *The Papers of Sir William Johnson*, 14 vols. (Albany, N.Y.: SUNY, 1921–65), 4:59; hereafter *Johnson Papers.*

3. Ibid., 10:997.

4. Georgiana C. Nammack, *Fraud, Politics, and the Dispossession of the Indians* (Norman: University of Oklahoma Press, 1969).

5. "Minutes of Conference Held at Easton in August 1761," Bouquet Papers, Additional Manuscripts 21,655, f.132–33. British Library, London.

6. "Plan of a Proposed Union of the Several Colonies . . . ," Newcastle Papers, Add. Mss. 33,030, f.359. British Library, London.

7. *Johnson Papers* 7:852.

8. William N. Fenton, "The New York State Wampum Collection: The Case for the Integrity of Cultural Treasures," *Proceedings of the American Philosophical Society* 115, no. 6 (December 1971):440.

9. Joseph Francois Lafitau, *Customs of the American Indians Compared with the Customs of Primitive Times*, ed. and trans. by William N. Fenton and Elizabeth L. Moore, 2 vols. (Toronto: The Champlain Society, 1974, 1977), 1: 311.

10. Samuel Hazard, ed., *Minutes of the Provincial Council of Pennsylvania*, 16 vols. (Harrisburg and Philadelphia, Pa., 1838–53), 24 February 1756, 7: 49. Vols. 1–3 were reprinted in Philadelphia with different pagination from the original Harrisburg edition; hereafter *Pa. Council Minutes.*

11. Buade de Frontenac and Bochart de Champigny to the Minister of Marine, 4 November 1694, Series C[11]A, Vol. 13, f 4-26. Les Archives Nationales, Paris.

12. *Johnson Papers* 9: 604.

13. Discussions with Jacob E. Thomas, a Cayuga chief of Six Nations Reserve, and Michael K. Foster, Iroquois Ethnologist of the National Museum of Man in Ottawa, led me to make this interpretation of the "reading" of belts.

14. William M. Beauchamp, "Wampum and Shell Articles Used by the New York Indians," *Bulletin of the New York State Museum* 8, no. 41 (February 1901):391–403.

15. E. B. O'Callaghan, ed., *The Documentary History of the State of New York* (Albany: Weed, Parsons and Co., Charles Van Benthuysen, 1849–51), 4:271; hereafter *Doc.Hist.N.Y.*

16. "Cornplanter & Little Billy Review Historical Relationship of Indian and White," September 1810, Erastus Granger Papers, State University of New York College of Arts and Science at Oswego, N.Y.

17. Michael K. Foster, *From the Earth to Beyond the Sky: An Ethnographic Approach to Four Longhouse Speech Events*, National Museum of Man Mercury Series, Paper No. 20 (Ottawa: National Museums of Canada, 1974).

18. *N.Y.Col.Docs.* 8:521.

19. "Journal of the Rev. Samuel Kirkland, November 1764–June 1765," ms., p. 38, Kirkland Papers, Burke Library, Hamilton College, Clinton, N.Y.

20. Letter Samuel Kirkland to Rev. Dr. Rogers, 22 August 1771, ms., Kirkland Papers, Burke Library, Hamilton College, Clinton, N.Y.

21. "Cornplanter and Little Billy Review."

22. N.Y.Col.Docs. 7:757.

23. Johnson Papers 7:1153, 10:555, 12:458; Lafitau, Customs of the American Indians 2:173.

24. William N. Fenton, "The Iroquois Eagle Dance: an Offshoot of the Calumet Dance," Bureau of American Ethnology Bulletin 156 (1953).

25. Johnson Papers, 6: 400.

26. Ibid., 686.

27. Doc.Hist.N.Y. 4:271; Cadwallader Colden, The History of the Five Nations of Canada, 2 vols. (New York: Allerton Book Co., 1922), 1: xvi–vii. An interesting case in which power of attorney was given by Iroquois to a representative who found it necessary to justify his conduct to the Six Nations is evidenced in the letterbook of John Norton, a companion of Joseph Brant; Ayer Manuscripts, Newberry Library, N.A. 654.

28. Alexander Fraser to Mathews, 27 September 1784, Haldimand Papers, Add. Mss. 21,722, British Library.

29. Johnson Papers 3: 464.

30. Ibid., 12: 458.

31. Pa. Council Minutes 3: 451; 4:79.

32. Atherly-Jones, "The Treaty-Making Power of the Crown," Transactions of the Grotius Society 4(1919): 95–109; Fernand Dehousse, La Ratification des Traites (Paris: Librarie du Receuil Sirey, 1935), pp. 7–30; J. Mervyn Jones, Full Powers and Ratification: A Study of the Development of Treaty-Making Procedure (Cambridge: Cambridge University Press, 1946.

33. Timothy Pickering to John Jay, 11 March 1797, mss., Miscellaneous Documents, Pickering Folder, Library of Congress, Washington, D.C.

5

Another Look at the Function of Wampum in Iroquois-White Councils

MICHAEL K. FOSTER

IT IS WELL KNOWN that wampum played an important role in the councils held between the Iroquois and the colonial officials of New France and Great Britain, as well as in the councils held between these groups and other Indian tribes. Indeed, the subject of wampum has become something of a hardy perennial in the ethnohistorical literature.[1] Much of the discussion has revolved around one or another of two general concerns: first, an interest in the history of wampum and the methods of its manufacture, including questions such as whether ground and bored shell wampum was aboriginal, what its role was in Northeastern trade, its use as a form of currency by White men, and so on; second, an interest in the "functions" or "uses" of wampum in the ritual and political practices of the Iroquois and their Algonkian neighbors. With regard to the councils, the point is often made that wampum functioned as a "validating" or "ratifying" device for treaties, serving, as it were, as the Indians' method of signing, sealing and delivering an agreement. This is related to another function, that of record-keeping: along with wooden counters, wampum strings and belts served to mark proposals made and answered. Wampums collected at a council, each with its distinctive emblematic design, could be brought out at a later time as a "mnemonic aid" for recalling details of an agreement.[2]

In this chapter it is not my intention so much to take issue with these observations about wampum functions—all of which find support in the historical record—as to provide some ethnographic depth to the discussion which up to now has been based primarily upon the perceptions of the White participant-observers of the period.[3] I should emphasize at the outset that I do not consider that we are dealing with just another case of culturally biased reporting which must undergo rigorous exegesis if we are to get at the underlying native culture pattern—the sort of thing we must do, say, when we attempt to reconstruct Huron society and culture from the French travel and mission accounts. For while forest diplomacy was undoubtedly the invention of the Indians, probably the Iroquois, it underwent a considerable amount of development during the colonial period, the White participants being responsible for certain innovations even if not the basic pattern itself.[4] In any event, for the period for which the Indian-White councils have been documented (the late seventeenth to the early nineteenth centuries) we are dealing with a phenomenon which was a product *par excellence* of the contact situation. The point of view of the Whites, who formed one "side of the fire" in treaty negotiations, is thus essential in any general anthropological approach to the councils. Just as important, of course, is the Indian point of view. Since most of the discussion about Indian strategies of forest diplomacy has been based on the colonial records, we have not had any firm check on the cultural authenticity of what is attributed to the Indians in council minutes. For instance, with but minor exceptions no transcripts of Indian council speeches survive in the original languages, and when it gets down to fine-grained details it is difficult to know how much the French and English translations faithfully reflect the Indians' point of view, and how much they were influenced by White expectations and motives, including literary fashions of the times.[5]

The same question inevitably arises regarding the use of wampum. White participants were certainly impressed with wampum, both the artifact and its uses, even taking it over as a form of hard currency and becoming heavily involved in its manufacture and distribution. They usually recorded in the minutes the points at which belts and strings crossed the council fire.[6] From these records we can form a pretty good idea of White understanding of Indian understanding of the functions of wampum, but it is difficult to gauge the importance of such notions as wampum as a validating/ratifying or mnemonic device to the Iroquois themselves. For the Whites, whose legal traditions bound them to the use of paper documents, there was the expectation that at some point in treaty negotiations action would be taken to bind an agreement; and they were impressed with Indian speakers' ability to recall past events for which they relied on written accounts. The question is whether there is some means by which we can get closer to the Indians' own understanding of the functions of wampum in the councils.

THE PROBLEM OF THE SURVIVAL
OF THE IROQUOIS-WHITE COUNCIL TRADITION

I believe there is a general impression among Iroquoianists that in the decades following the American Revolution, which had a devastating effect on the Six Nations (among other things, resulting in a permanent division of the Confederacy government), forest diplomacy, which had been the chief method by which Indian affairs were conducted until then, went into a rapid decline, eventually fizzling out altogether with the last land settlements in New York State in the nineteenth century. With the decline in forest diplomacy presumably also went detailed knowledge of the contents and uses of council wampum.

George Snyderman concluded a lengthy discussion of the function question with the following gloomy remark which quite well sums up the prevailing view: "Today, except for the ceremonial purpose associated with Handsome Lake's religion in all the Longhouses, and the clandestine election of chiefs on the Six Nations Reserve, wampum is no longer used by the Iroquois. The wampum belts housed in museums are the ghosts of the golden and glorious era of the League. Few Iroquois in the United States know their former functions and fewer can read the historical messages inscribed in them."[7] From this it might appear that we would never be able to get beyond the observations of White men regarding the uses of wampum. It should be pointed out, however, that most discussions of the function question have overlooked the fact that at irregular intervals in the present century Iroquois leaders have appeared in both North American and European capitals to argue their claims for sovereignty, and that this has been done by reading (i.e., interpreting) some of the old belts.[8] Moreover, as a result of the controversy surrounding the custodianship of the New York State wampum collection at Albany, there has been a considerable revival of interest in wampum among the Iroquois, and this has resulted in renewed interest in the contents of some old belts.[9]

In 1976, intrigued by the possibility that something of the ancient council tradition might still survive, I sought out Chief Jacob E. Thomas at Six Nations Reserve.[10] I knew from local sources that he was regarded as an authority on the political traditions of the League and that he was the son of a leader of his own day, David Thomas, who had been to Ottawa and Washington to plead the chiefs' cause. Still, I was surprised and keenly interested to learn that Chief Thomas was intimately acquainted with the contents of nine wampum belts, as well as the Fifteen Strings of Condolence, and that he would be prepared publicly to interpret them should the appropriate occasion arise. But then in the course of our discussions an even more intriguing fact emerged: it turned out that Chief Thomas not only knew the messages that accompanied various belts, he also had a detailed grasp of the procedures for conducting a council with White government officials. As he himself pointed out, it was not enough just to be able to recall the terms of the ancient agreements: one must be prepared to actually renew these agreements which, as far as the chiefs were concerned, were still in effect and never formally abrogated by the Canadian or American governments. In brief, there

was need for an *active* knowledge of council protocol, not merely passive recall of the way things were once done, as though the matter were now entirely
past history.[11]

Although we originally thought of limiting ourselves to taping, tran-
scribing and translating the speeches accompanying the various belts known
by Chief Thomas, we now enlarged our plans to include the idea of making
a total accounting of his grasp of council protocol. We decided that the best
way to approach this was to imagine a situation in which two of the belts
commonly used in "polishing the covenant chain" (renewing the alliance) would
be read to White officials from Washington, D.C., at Onondaga, New York,
the capital of the League on the U.S. side of the border. We prepared an outline of the entire sequence of events that ideally would occur should a reading be contemplated by the chiefs. This outline served as the basis for staging
the event sequence on tape, namely for Chief Thomas to assume the roles
alternately of the speakers on the two sides of the fire and to talk their speeches
into a microphone.[12] We decided to record the sequence in Cayuga, one of
the Six Nations languages. We justified this on the grounds that even though
protocol entitles each party at a council to speak in its home language, all
speeches are translated into the language of the interlocutors by an interpreter. Hence, speeches by White men would eventually appear in Iroquoian.
Our purpose in any case was to stage an *ideal* council sequence, one which
assumed not only accurate translation but complete facility in the manipulation of council procedures on both sides. If these assumptions seem too san-
guine in terms of White participation in the historic councils where diplomatic gaffes were frequently committed, they are perhaps justified in terms
of the goal of obtaining a purely native account. In such an account the identity of a side as White or Indian is less relevant in determining appropriate
comportment than that side's identity as petitioner vs. respondent on the one
hand, and host vs. visitor on the other.[13] The result was some seven and a
half hours of material recorded entirely in an Iroquoian language.[14]

We cannot here take up the complex problems of interpretation that
arise when we attempt to "upstream" from this extraordinary piece of native
testimony to the historic councils of two and three hundred years ago. ("Upstreaming" is explained in William N. Fenton's Chapter 1, p. 4.) In a more
general treatment we would have to allow for changes in oral tradition over
time: we certainly cannot expect today's native conception of forest diplomacy
precisely to match native conceptions of the colonial period. Nevertheless,
Chief Thomas' version provides a unified perspective expressed in an Iroquoian
language, and this kind of testimony can be of great value in attempting to
piece together past native practice, which we otherwise know only from non-
native records. We can illustrate the point generally before turning to the

question of Iroquoian views regarding the functions of wampum. The procedures for extending invitations to councils and certain other activities preceding what we shall call the "business phase" of a council are seldom described
at any length in the historic accounts, although fortunately there are some
illuminating exceptions.[15] But in the Thomas version, nearly half of the seven
and a half hours of speeches are taken up with these activities. We thus have
a considerable volume of material on a phase of the process which tends to
receive rather short shrift in the historical accounts.

THE IROQUOIAN EMPHASIS
ON THE CHANNEL OF COMMUNICATION

I believe that the modern version of a council reveals in a number of ways
a pronounced emphasis on what I shall call, using a familiar term from information theory, the channel of communication. We associate this term with
the telecommunication engineer's concern for improving the quality of transmissions in electronic media such as radio transmitters, telephones and the
like—i.e., for eliminating interference (noise) from any device conveying a message from a sender to a receiver.

Although one must assume that the concern for establishing, prolong-
ing, and terminating communication is a human universal, there is obviously
room for a great deal of cultural variation in the methods of accomplishing
these things. There is both a qualitative and a quantitative aspect in the
weighting assigned in different societies, or segments of the same society, to
acts such as greeting and leave taking. Longhouse Iroquois, for instance, regard everyday greeting formulas among Whites as being perfunctory compared
to their own practices. Whites, they feel, are too anxious to "get down to business," whereas they like an extended opening in which individuals gradually
establish rapport (or, as they say, allow for a "drawing together of minds")
before taking up business. In this chapter I suggest that a similar concern per-
vades the protocol of Iroquois-White councils. What seems to be involved
is a foregrounding—one might, following Roman Jakobson's line of argument,
call it a *ritualization*—of the contact function in council protocol.[16] There is
an elaboration of a cultural pattern beyond the mere physical or perceptual
requirements of establishing and maintaining contact between two groups.
This cultural pattern is reflected in a number of features of council protocol,
perhaps nowhere more than in the use of wampum and in some of the symbolism of its designs.

WAMPUM AS AN INSTRUMENT FOR ESTABLISHING
AND MAINTAINING CONTACT

The idea that wampum might serve as a device not only for keeping track of council proceedings but for organizing them occurred to me at first from a detail of linguistic structure. The usual term for the invitation string sent out on occasions such as Handsome Lake conventions, the Condolence Ceremony for installing chiefs, and, it turns out, the councils, is enḗtshatiyōtáhkwaʔ which literally means "that which stretches a person's arm."[17] This word contains a morpheme -hkw-, the instrumental suffix, which has the effect of shifting the focus of the action from the agent to an object used to carry out this action. (Without the suffix the word would mean "one's [or her] arm is stretched out.") We might loosely translate the term with the suffix as "the thing that causes one to stretch out one's arm" or "the thing by which invitations are made." In my preliminary analysis of translations of the Thomas version I set out to see in what sense wampum might function as an instrument or tool for making invitations.

Earlier we noted that nearly half of the event sequence staged by Chief Thomas is taken up with the invitation process and certain other activities which precede the "business phase" of a council. Historical accounts of councils tend to pass over the preparatory activities in favor of what the White participants considered to be more substantive matters. One even finds sporadic remarks in the colonial records dismissing the preliminaries as "trifling" and "tedious" Indian ceremonies.[18] For the Indians, on the other hand, the preliminaries were important for establishing what Jakobson calls a "psychological connection between the addresser and the addressee." The role of wampum in the planning of a council is particularly illuminating in this respect.

Although it would be consistent with Iroquoian beliefs about the nature of political alliances for either side of the fire to initiate a council sequence in order to polish the covenant chain, in the Thomas version it is the League chiefs who start things off. The invitation phase begins with a home council at Onondaga held between the tribal divisions of the League: the Elder Brotherhood (the Mohawk, Onondaga, and Seneca) and the Younger Brotherhood (the Cayuga, Oneida, and adopted tribes).[19] The main items of business at this council are, first, the setting of an invitation message in which the time, place and agenda for a scheduled council are specified, and, second, the appointment of two messengers (hatíhnhaʔthraʔ "they [who] are hired").[20] When all has been agreed upon the men selected are summoned to the council and informed of their duties. On instructions from the chiefs, a speaker performs a speech act which roughly translates as "reading the message into the wampum" (tēHatiwēnō:taʔ "they will put the word into it"). In the Iroquois view the wampum is thought literally to *contain* the message; the messengers, on the other hand, are seen as relatively passive bearers of the wampum, which nevertheless is described as being a "heavy burden" which they bear on their backs. To be sure, it is from the mouths of the messengers that the chiefs' invitation ultimately emanates, and the messengers are in fact drilled until the chiefs are satisfied they have the message down cold, but this repetition is believed to increase the "power" of the wampum rather than to improve the messengers' memories. Wampum is regarded as a kind of recording device, somewhat in the way we conceive of the function of a tape recorder. "Reading" a wampum would then be analogous to playing back a taped message. This is one sense in which wampum may appropriately be called a channel device: it is seen as an instrument for conveying messages from a sender to a receiver.

The second stage of the invitation phase begins with the arrival of the messengers in the vicinity of the foreign council fire. Tradition prescribes that this be a point at which the cleared land around the settlement meets the forest (kaHataktá:kyeɂ "along the edge of the forest"). Whatever precautionary purpose this may have served at a time when the sudden arrival of strangers could spell imminent danger, it also bears out the Iroquoian penchant for effecting a gradual rapprochement between alien groups. Protocol requires that a delegation from the host settlement repair to the spot where the visitors are waiting and perform a welcoming ceremony—itself a council in molecular form —called kaēhawahé:tōh, an archaic term of uncertain meaning usually glossed as the "At the Wood's Edge Ceremony," an event borrowed from the Condolence Ceremony. The two groups arrange themselves on opposite sides of a small fire built just for the duration: this arrangement serves to remind all the participants how they will position themselves at the main council later. A speaker for the hosts expresses his side's gratitude that the messengers have arrived safely over the "long forest path" (wathahínɂōthris). There are many things, he says, that could have caused them to stumble and fall. During the colonial period there were physical hardships to contend with (Conrad Weiser, Pennsylvania colony's "ambassador" to the Six Nations for many years, once described a particularly harrowing trip to Onondaga as filled with "misrys and Famine"[21]). Ever present also was the danger of encounters with hostile groups. In the Thomas version these hardships have been delicately transformed into metaphors about vaguely specified things pointing up from the path or hanging overhead.

In any event, a considerable amount of attention is given to the problem of obstructions in the forest path, a problem which parallels the concern of the telecommunications engineer to control interference or noise in the channel. The engineer has technical methods for dealing with the problem of noise; the Iroquoian solution to the problem is to perform a ritual in which the kinds of interference that might result in a distortion of the message contained in the wampum are, as it were, defined out of existence. This ritual

apparently appealed to the White participants in the historic councils, for
it is often alluded to. The Cayuga call it the Rubbing Down of the Body
(aetshiyaʔtotrṓ:koʔ "they rub your bodies down").[22] In words only, the speaker
first "wipes the eyes" of the weary travelers with soft buckskin (their eyes are
full of things they have seen on their journey, things which might have dis-
tracted them from their mission); now, he declares, they will be able to see
normally again. Next he "clears their ears" of all the things they have heard
on their journey, things which might cause them to alter the message; they
now have normal hearing again. Then he "clears the obstructions from their
throats" so that once more they will be able to breathe and speak normally
(their throats were filled with dust from the forest path). Finally, he removes
the briars from their legs and offers them a "walking medicine" (tsyawekahṓʔtēh)
to settle their inner organs which have been dislocated by the rigors of the
journey. Now it is manifestly obvious that the first three "words"—eyes, ears,
and throats—are the physiological organs of speech perception and produc-
tion. They are the primary channels of communication in the human orga-
nism. The successful transfer of a verbal message from a sender to a receiver
depends upon their proper functioning.[23]

Let us summarize the sequence up to this point in terms of the broader
communicative system that is emerging. The senders, here the chiefs, have
encoded a message in wampum which has been conveyed along the forest path
by messengers who, as the eventual decoders of the message, pause before reaching their final destination in order that their bodies, and particularly those
organs involved in the decoding process, may be restored to normal functioning. The sense of being *before* the messengers' final destination has a spatial
as well as a temporal aspect here: the Wood's Edge welcome takes place at the
geographic outskirts of the receivers' village. If we think of the paths linking
settlements during the colonial period as the physical channels by which information was transmitted from one location to another (the analogy to the
telegraph of our own day seems unavoidable), then it is especially appropriate,
within the terms of the communicative framework involved, that attention
be given to the problem of interference at a point in both space and time which
lies between the encoding and decoding phases of the process—in other words,
while the message is still in the channel.

At the completion of the Wood's Edge welcome, the hosts lead the messengers "by the arm" (ēyetshinētshí:neht "they will lead you by the arm") to the
place of council where the greeting sequence continues. The messengers eventually gain the floor, producing the invitation wampum which, they say, has
been leading them by the arm (ōkhninētshinéhtaHneʔ "it has been leading us
by the arm") to the present council fire—phrasing which underscores the perception of their role as relatively passive. They review the events of the council at which they were appointed, mentioning the date, place, and agenda of

the proposed council. They literally speak *for* the chiefs: it is as though the chiefs were directly facing those on the other side of the fire. In a dramatic move they pass the wampum across to the hosts, saying as they do: "they now extend an invitation to you" (*aetshiné:tsha*ʔ "they take you by the arm"). The pronominal reference here is unambiguously to the chiefs; it is they, not the messengers, who effect the invitation.[24] They seem to have reached across the miles and to have taken the hosts directly by the arm to lead them to their council fire.[25] This remarkable feat is made possible because of native beliefs about wampum, i.e., that it is the wampum rather than the messengers that is carrying the message. The council closes out with the hosts' accepting the invitation and commissioning the messengers to convey this information to the chiefs. From the point of view of the sender chiefs, wampum has functioned up to this point in the sequence as an instrument for *establishing* contact or opening a channel of communication.

The third stage of the invitation phase commences with the return of the messengers to their home fire, and the calling of a council to hear the results of their mission. The procedure for greeting the returning messengers is similar to the one described for greeting foreign visitors, except that it is more abbreviated, and the Rubbing Down of the Body ritual takes place within the home settlement rather than at the outskirts. Although the messengers are returning to familiar territory and there is not the same need for a cautious approach as on their outward journey, they have still traveled the "long forest path" with its many natural and human obstacles and are still in need of restoration. Following the welcoming exercises they explain that they have returned *owénoskōh* "[with] the word alone," i.e., without the invitation wampum. This is the news the chiefs are hoping to hear, since a return of the wampum would mean rejection of the invitation.[26] With this the invitation phase of the sequence is complete.

The scheduled council opens with the Wood's Edge welcome as described above. The events at the main council fire (or inside the council house), where the visitors have been escorted "by the arm," are more elaborate, however. Of particular relevance to the present discussion is a formal handshake, the two groups filing past each other with their leaders in front. Here the process of the chiefs' reaching out to take the visitors by the arm literally comes to pass. A speaker for the visitors announces the return of the invitation wampum, whose inherent powers were responsible for leading them to the present council. The string has come full circle, its purpose effected and its power spent. Two opening events revolve around the ritualization of the channel, the recitation of the Thanksgiving Address and the smoking of a pipe, both of which are efforts to catch the attention of the Creator as a hoped-for witness of the proceedings.[27] We will say nothing more about the scheduled council since the rest of it is taken up with the agenda specific to the occasion—the open slot, as it were, in the sequence. Instead, we shall summarize the native view of wampum use as it is revealed in the Thomas version.

We noted earlier that the literature on wampum has tended to emphasize the "validating" or "ratifying" function of wampum on the one hand, and the mnemonic function on the other. The common thread running through the non-native accounts is a focus primarily on the *retrospective* uses of wampum, i.e., as a device for recalling past events. What emerges from the Thomas version is a view of wampum as functioning *prospectively*, i.e., as a device for organizing present and future events. A rule of thumb for the native participant might well be: to know where things stand at any given moment in the event sequence, and where they are going next, "follow the path of the wampum." The retrospective functions are perhaps not so much absent from the native view of wampum uses as they are secondary to the prospective functions.

The prospective function of wampum might be expected to be particularly prominent in the invitation phase of a council sequence: the message it carries concerns a future event. Still, I think the notion of wampum serving as a device for organizing ongoing events applies just as much to the business phase of a council. During this phase in the historic councils wampums were exchanged, sometimes in considerable numbers, between the two sides of the fire. The expectation was that one should give wampum with each major proposal, and that this would be answered with a wampum of like kind. The motive on presenting wampum was thus to elicit a response, and this is a forward-looking rather than a backward-looking activity. Indeed, from a larger communicative perspective, one can view the exchange of wampums across the fire as the principal means for regulating the flow of the council's business and promoting the orderly succession of speakers from the two sides. In brief, while wampum served during the invitation phase of a council to *establish* contact, during the business phase it served to maintain or prolong communication, and, eventually, to terminate it.[28]

WAMPUM DESIGN AND THE CHANNEL FUNCTION

Three metaphors dominate the highly figurative language of Iroquois council oratory: the path, the fire, and the chain. These crop up both in the speeches of Indian and White participants in the historic councils and in the speeches of Chief Thomas's staged version. These metaphors serve to condense and polarize complex ideas and situations, thereby constituting a sort of code by which the participants could evaluate the state of the alliance.

The three metaphors have in common the semantic property that each defines a range of meanings falling between positively valued and negatively valued poles. These poles do not form simple binary oppositions, but rather define vague orders of magnitude on the analog plan – suitable continua, no doubt, for the fine gradations of meaning inherent in the political realities of the colonial period. If a speaker wished to characterize the alliance as being in good shape he spoke of the path as free of "incumbrances." As we have seen, reference to someone's fire meant the principal place of council for that group. But fire also served in another way as a metaphor, i.e., for commenting on the participating groups' sense of commitment to the alliance. The fire might be burning briskly, giving off great warmth to both parties; or it might be burning low or actually be out, so that there was an urgent need for adding "fuel." For its part, the covenant chain, either of iron or silver, might be in a high state of polish, or covered with dust, or even pitted with rust. Restoring the chain to its former luster might require anything from some judicious wiping with a cloth to hard work with a metal file! In the historic accounts one frequently observes a shift during the course of a council from more negative to more positive metaphoric poles. Since the real issues involving disputes over land, terms of trade, and warfare could not be resolved in any lasting way, given the irreconcilable motives of the Indians and the Whites, council oratory furnished a means for presenting a semblance of unity which was in the interests of both parties – the Iroquois and the English – vis-à-vis a common enemy, the French.

Figures representing the path, the fire, and the chain are perhaps the most prevalent designs in eighteenth-century wampum belts.[29] The usual pattern is of two or more abstract figures, often connected or underlain by a single (occasionally a double) line. The figures are slanted lines, diamonds, hexagons (= the Six Nations), squares, human figures, or, in later belts, more realistic figures of houses, animals, or other natural phenomena. These figures stand for the parties to an alliance, or the locations of principal fires, while the line connecting them stands either for the path or the convenant chain. Some belts particularly feature the path by showing a wide row of beads running the length of the belt, with or without figures at the ends, or sometimes two parallel rows of beads signifying the separate jurisdictions of the Indian's and White man's sovereignties. On the other hand, two or more stick-like human figures whose arms are joined by a longitudinal row of beads usually refers to the covenant chain.

The design of many belts reduces to two contrasting components: a set of two or more geometric figures and the line connecting these figures. Against a background of all the possible images that could have been used in the design of belts, this arrangement seems clearly to reflect the special Iroquoian concern for the channel. The designs woven into belts would then be seen as emblems identifying their basic function rather than as complex pictographic devices used for ordering the contents of speeches, as, for instance, in the arrangement of carved figures on the Condolence Cane.

CONCLUSION

In attempting to provide some ethnographic perspective on one aspect of Iroquois-White council protocol, we have taken only the first step in the ethnohistoric method of upstreaming. What is needed now is a testing of these ideas against the colonial records. I hope at least to have brought to light some of the contrasts between native and non-native views of wampum functions and to have underscored the point that both perspectives are needed in any thoroughgoing description of forest diplomacy.

It is important to realize that the Iroquoian emphasis on the process of establishing and maintaining contact goes well beyond the use and design of wampum belts to include the essential meaning of an alliance or covenant itself—a notion to some extent recoverable from the phrase *watrihwiHsʔóhsráʔ tewanētshótaHkōh* "what was agreed upon, it joins their arms." The theme of renewal runs deep in the Iroquoian world view. We see this in the emphasis in council protocol upon clearing obstructions from the path, polishing the covenant chain, building up the council fire, and the procedures at the Wood's Edge. The metaphors of the fire, the path, and the chain reveal a set toward the alliance which recognizes a degree of entropy in the system. In the Iroquoian view the alliance was naturally in a state of constant deterioration and in need of attention. This view contrasts fundamentally with that of the White participants who assumed that once a treaty had been signed it would remain in effect—more-or-less in a steady state—until definite action was taken by one or both sides to change it.

NOTES

1. An early version of this chapter was given at a symposium on the social organization of discourse, at the 1977 annual meeting of the American Anthropological Association in Houston, Texas. I would like to thank Dell Hymes for helpful comments on that version. It was also read, substantially in its present form, at a symposium on ethnohistory during the 1981 annual meeting of the Canadian Ethnology Society in Ottawa.

THE FUNCTION OF WAMPUM

111

2. Only a sampling of the large wampum literature is given here. On questions of origin, manufacture, trade and currency, see William M. Beauchamp, "Wampum Used in Council
and as Currency," *American Antiquarian and Oriental Journal* 20, no. 1 (1898):1–13; idem, "Wampum and Shell Articles Used by the New York Indians," *New York State Museum Bulletin* 41 (Albany, 1901):319–480 (rpt. New York: AMS Press, 1978); Lewis H. Morgan, *League of the Hodé-no-
sau-nee or Iroquois*, ed. Herbert M. Lloyd, 2 vols. (New York: Dodd, Mead, 1901) 2:51–55; J. N. B.
Hewitt, "Wampum," *Handbook of American Indians North of Mexico*, ed. Frederick W. Hodge,
Bureau of American Ethnology Bulletin 30, 2 vols. (Washington, 1910) 2:904–909; William C.
Orchard, *Beads and Beadwork of the American Indians*, Contributions from the Museum of the
American Indian, Heye Foundation, no. 11 (New York, 1929), pp. 61–74; Charles C. Willoughby,
Antiquities of the New England Indians (Cambridge, Mass.: Peabody Museum of American Archae-
ology and Ethnology, 1935), pp. 264–275; J. S. Slotkin and Karl Schmitt, "Studies in Wampum,"
American Anthropologist 51, no. 2 (1949): 223–36; George Snyderman, "The Functions of Wam-
pum," *Proceedings of the American Philosophical Society* 98, no. 6 (1954): 469–94; William N. Fenton,
"The Hiawatha Wampum Belt of the Iroquois League for Peace," *Men and Cultures: Selected Papers
of the Fifth International Congress of Anthropological and Ethnological Sciences, Philadelphia, 1956*
(Philadelphia: University of Pennsylvania Press, 1960), pp. 3–7; idem, "The New York State Wam-
pum Collection: The Case for the Integrity of Cultural Treasures," *Proceedings of the American
Philosophical Society* 115, no. 6 (1971): 437–61; Elisabeth Tooker, "The League of the Iroquois: Its
History, Politics, and Ritual," in *Northeast*, ed. Bruce G. Trigger, *Handbook of North American Indians*, gen. ed. William C. Sturtevant (Washington: Smithsonian Institution, 1978), pp. 418–41.
On the notions of wampum as a validating/ratifying device and a device for keeping records and
aiding memories at councils, see William H. Holmes, "Art in Shell of the Ancient Americas,"
in *Second Annual Report of the Bureau of American Ethnology for the Years 1880–1881* (Washington,
1883), pp. 185–305, esp. 240 ff.; Morgan, *League*, vol. 1, pp. 114–15, 327; Frank G. Speck, "The
Functions of Wampum among the Eastern Algonkian," *Memoirs of the American Anthropological
Association* 6, no. 1 (Lancaster, Penna., 1919): 3–71; Orchard, *Beads and Beadwork*, p. 61; Snyderman, "Functions of Wampum," pp. 478 ff.; Fenton, "New York State Wampum Collection," pp.
455–56.

3. I say primarily because there exist both native language texts and close ethnographic
descriptions of the Condolence Ceremony for the mourning of dead chiefs and the installing
of successors, and this ceremony undoubtedly provided what W. N. Fenton has called the "paradigm" of the forest councils, including the protocol for handling wampum. See Chapter 3.

4. Some of the elements added by the Whites which became a standard part of council protocol were gun salutes, liquor toasts to the sovereigns of the respective sides of the fire,
and the distribution of European goods as presents. According to one Iroquois political leader,
even the notion of the Silver Covenant Chain was strictly an English invention, the Iroquois
preferring to symbolize the alliance bonds as a rope of natural fiber. Regarding the uses of wampum, one of the effects of dealing with White officials over time was that the Iroquois came in-
creasingly to demand copies of signed treaties to protect their interests.

5. See, for instance, Lawrence C. Wroth, "The Indian Treaty as Literature," *Yale Review* 17 (1928): 749–66; Carl Van Doren, "Introduction" in *Indian Treaties Printed by Benjamin Franklin 1736–1762*, ed. Julian P. Boyd (Philadelphia: The Historical Society of Pennsylvania, 1938),
esp. pp. vii–viii; A. M. Drummond and Richard Moody, "Indian Treaties: The First American
Dramas," *Quarterly Journal of Speech* 39 (1953): 15–24. A classic case regarding the authenticity
of a native speech in translation is the controversy that grew up around Logan's celebrated speech
to Lord Dunmore. See D. Seeber, "Critical Views on Logan's Speech," *Journal of American Folklore*
60, no. 236 (1947): 130–46; Roy Harvey Pearce, *Savagism and Civilization: A Study of the Indian
and the American Mind* (Baltimore: Johns Hopkins University Press, 1967), p. 79.

6. We might nevertheless wish that they had kept better records of the distinctive features of the belts and strings changing hands. Only rarely are the wampums described in sufficient detail so that it is possible today to link one of the strings or belts with a particular historic occasion.

7. Snyderman, "The Functions of Wampum," p. 494. Fenton, "The New York State Wampum Collection," pp. 455–56, expresses the view that the ability of the Iroquois to read the charter belts in the State Museum in Albany had disappeared before the present century. Knowledge of the speeches accompanying several such belts (the Hiawatha Belt, the Prophecy [or Remembrance] Belt, the Thadodaho Belt and the Wing [or Evergrowing Tree] Belt at the New York State Museum, as well as the Circlet of the League at the National Museum of Man in Ottawa) continues to the present day at the Six Nations Reserve, however. This statement should not be taken as implying that such knowledge has been lost on the New York Iroquois reservations, only that the matter has not been sufficiently investigated.

8. The latest instance was a reading of the Covenant (or Friendship) Belt and the Two Paths (or Two Rows) Belt before Canadian Governor General Edward Schreyer on 26 February 1981 at Rideau Hall in Ottawa. Other representations by the chiefs have included protesting conscription in Ottawa during World War I and representations in Washington, D.C., one case there having occurred in 1954. There are also records of a delegation going to London from the Six Nations reserve in 1930, and of an individual (Levi General) going to Geneva in 1923–24 to appear before the League of Nations. From the descriptions of these events it seems likely that the same two belts were read on these occasions. An account of Levi General's trip appears in Carl L. Carmer, *Dark Trees to the Wind: A Cycle of York State Years* (New York: W. Sloane Associates, 1949), and in Annemarie Shimony, "Alexander General, 'Deskahe': Cayuga-Oneida, 1889–1965," *American Indian Intellectuals*, ed. Margot Liberty (St. Paul, New York and Los Angeles: West Publishing Co., 1978), p. 167. See Edmund Wilson, *Apologies to the Iroquois* (New York: Vintage Books 1959), p. 258.

9. See the entire issue of *The Indian Historian* 3, no. 2 (spring 1970); Fenton, "New York State Wampum Collection." The Iroquois newspapers *Akwesasne Notes* and *Turtle* have also run stories on the belts. For pictures and historical notes on the belts themselves, see Noah T. Clarke, "The Thacher Wampum Belts of the New York State Museum," *New York State Museum Bulletin* 279 (Albany, 1929): 53–58; Beauchamp, "Wampum and Shell Articles," plate 16; George G. Heye, "Wampum Collection," *Indian Notes* 7, no. 3 (July 1930): 320–24; D. Jenness, "Three Iroquois Wampum Records," *Canada, Department of Mines, National Museum of Canada Bulletin*, no. 70, Annual Report for 1931 (Ottawa, 1932), pp. 25–29; Fenton, "New York State Wampum Collection," pp. 443, 445, Table 1 on p. 458.

10. Chief Thomas has the title Dawenhethon (*teyohōwé:thō:ˀ*), the eighth in the Cayuga roster, and the fortieth in the roster overall; see Tooker, "The League of the Iroquois," p. 425. He is a gifted orator and carver, a widely recognized authority on the traditional culture, an eloquent apologist for the Confederacy, and a fluent speaker of three Iroquoian languages (Cayuga, Onondaga, and Mohawk). He teaches in the Native Studies program at Trent University, Peterborough, Ontario. I wish to acknowledge Chief Thomas as my principal source for the Iroquoian view of forest diplomacy, although he is not responsible for my interpretations.

11. The distinction between knowing *about* a tradition such as the one embodied in the council speeches—as many Longhouse community members do—and knowing how to actually *perform* according to the tradition's norms is obviously of considerable importance in assessing the continuing viability of the tradition. I owe the distinction to Dell Hymes, "Breakthrough into Performance," *Folklore: Performance and Communication*, eds. D. Ben-Amos and K. S. Goldstein (The Hague: Mouton, 1975), pp. 18–20.

12. This facility in switching roles is just what would be expected of speakers in the colonial period when forest councils were held in great numbers. A speaker might at different times represent his group at home as a host, or at a foreign council fire as a visitor, or presenting a petition, or receiving a petition. The ease of switching roles is another indication of the council tradition's vitality.

13. See Michael K. Foster, "On Who Spoke First at Iroquois-White Councils: An Exercise in the Method of Upstreaming," *Extending the Rafters: Interdisciplinary Approaches to Iroquoian Studies*, eds. M. K. Foster, J. Campisi, and M. Mithun (Albany: State University of New York Press, 1984), pp. 183–207.

14. Under the terms of a Translations Grant from the National Endowment for the Humanities (1982–85) this material is being transcribed, analyzed, and translated with the able assistance of Alta Doxtador and Greta Wright of the Six Nations Reserve, Ontario. Grateful acknowledgment is made to the National Endowment and to the National Museum of Man which provided the funds for traveling frequently to the field to conduct the work.

15. For example, the detailed accounts kept by Conrad Weiser, Pennsylvania's "ambassador" to the Iroquois. See the extracts of his letters and journals quoted in Paul A. W. Wallace, *Conrad Weiser, 1696–1760, Friend of Colonist and Mohawk* (Philadelphia: University of Pennsylvania Press, 1945), pp. 66–67, 90–92, 315–16.

16. Roman Jakobson, "Closing Statement: Linguistics and Poetics," *Style in Language*, ed. Thomas A. Sebeok (Cambridge, Mass.: MIT Press, 1960), pp. 353–355. I discuss Iroquois greeting formulas in Michael K. Foster, "Interaction in Historical Perspective," *Native American Interaction Patterns*, ed. Regna Darnell, Canada, National Museum of Man, Mercury Series Paper (Ottawa, National Museum of Canada) (forthcoming).

17. I have briefly characterized Cayuga phonemics in Michael K. Foster, *From the Earth to Beyond the Sky: An Ethnographic Approach to Four Longhouse Iroquois Speech Events*, Canada, National Museum of Man, Mercury Series Paper, no. 20 (Ottawa: National Museum of Canada, 1974), pp. 258–65. In this chapter I write the glottal stop in odd-numbered syllables in its metathesized position (ʔ + vowel) rather than in its pre-metathesized position (vowel + ʔ). The cultural significance of the notion of "stretching arms" will emerge shortly.

18. James Pemberton used the former term in describing the 1762 Treaty of Lancaster, and governor Robert Morris of Pennsylvania used the latter term before the beginning of the 1756 series of Easton conferences. See Boyd, *Indian Treaties Printed by Benjamin Franklin*, p. 319; Wallace, *Weiser*, p. 436.

19. The decision-making procedures for League councils have been described in Morgan, *League*, vol. 1, pp. 105–07, and Parker, "Constitution of the Five Nations," pp. 30–34, 97–100.

20. One messenger is the speaker (*hahthá:haʔ*) and the other is his interpreter (*hatewénaká:tas* "he puts up the word(s)"). The role of the interpreter as a culture broker has perhaps not been sufficiently appreciated. His task consisted of far more than literal translation. As far as can be determined, speeches were not translated line at a time, but rather by major points. The interpreter thus had some latitude in the difficult task of finding equivalences between alien cultural worlds.

21. Wallace, *Weiser*, p. 77.

22. This is sometimes called the Three Rare Words Rite in the ethnographic literature. It forms part of the welcoming sequence borrowed from the Condolence Ceremony.

23. In the historic councils, strings of wampum normally accompanied each of the three words of the Rubbing Down rite, and this is still the practice when the rite is performed in the Condolence Ceremony. In Chief Thomas's version, however, wampum is not used at this stage.

For illustrations of the kinds of string used in the Condolence, see Tooker, "The League of the Iroquois," pp. 438–39.

24. The pronominal segment -etshi- indicates either that a third-person non-singular subject is acting upon a second-person non-singular object ("they to you"), or that a second-person non-singular subject is acting upon a third-person non-singular object ("you to them"); here the context clearly establishes that the first sense is the intended one. In any case, this segment cannot involve a first-person non-singular subject or object (i.e., designate the messengers speaking for themselves). It may be noted that the term aetshinë:tsha:ʔ is grammatically a performative verb, the kind of word whose utterance constitutes an act. It begins with the factual "tense" morpheme a(ʔ)- and ends with the punctual aspect marker -ʔ. As in English, performatives in Iroquoian are essentially first-person present indicative active forms. See Michael K. Foster, "When Words Become Deeds: An Analysis of Three Iroquois Longhouse Speech Events," Explorations in the Ethnography of Speaking, eds. Richard Bauman and Joel Sherzer (Cambridge: At the University Press, 1974), pp. 354–67.

25. Here, speech and gesture unite in a single purposive act. The terms for "invitation," "invitation wampum," and "agreement" all revolve around the notion of extending (or stretching) arms or hands. All of these expressions are verbs incorporating the noun root -nëtsh(a)- "arm, hand." We recall that the invitation wampum is called enëtshatiyötáhkwaʔ "that which stretches a person's arm." When visitors are escorted to the council house they are told: ëyetshinëtshíneht "they [the hosts] will lead you by the arm." An invitation is called ethínëtsha:h "we've got them by the arm," ökhínëtsha:h "they've got us by the arm," etc. One term for the Covenant (or Friendship) Belt referred to earlier (see note 8) is teHonanë:tshö:t "they have joined arms." Such expressions constantly recur in the speeches by Chief Thomas, and they crop up with considerable frequency in the transcripts of translated speeches given at the historical councils. In this case, at least, an important native concept seems to have survived the translation process.

26. This same rule applied historically too, but in the colonial councils a different wampum of comparable type was often sent back with the messengers to confirm the return message.

27. The Thanksgiving Address (Kanóhönyöhk) is routinely given at the beginning of all formal occasions except funerals. It is arranged in sections, each devoted to a "spirit force" in the natural world. First to be mentioned are the things that grow on the earth, then certain beings that dwell in the sky, and finally completely ethereal beings and the Creator himself who dwells "beyond" the sky. The speech thus topically traces an upward course of ascent. In the Iroquois view, the frequent recitation of the speech helps to keep the path from the earth to the Sky World clear. (See Foster, From the Earth to Beyond the Sky, pp. 3 ff.) In terms of our present concerns, we would say that the speech provides a means for establishing contact with the Creator, and again shows the ritualized concern for the channel. Smoking has a similar function, in that rising pipe smoke is thought to open a path to the Sky World. Smoking is also thought to settle the minds of speakers and other key participants who receive the pipe. The taste of tobacco in the mouth, Chief Thomas comments, reminds a speaker of the importance of speaking sincerely and gives him the strength to proceed.

28. Historically, wampum was sometimes used when the council fire was "covered over," i.e., banked in anticipation of future meetings.

29. An extended discussion of the symbolism of wampum belts, with a number of illustrations, is found in Beauchamp, "Wampum and Shell Articles," pp. 390 ff., and plates 13–26.

6

Glossary of
Figures of Speech in Iroquois Political Rhetoric

It is true their speeches are at first very difficult to understand,
on account of an infinity of Metaphors, of various circumlocu-
tions, and other rhetorical methods.—Jean de Brébeuf, S.J., 1636

THE BASIC PRINCIPLE of Iroquois metaphor is the projection of words about
familiar objects and relations into the fields of politics and diplomacy.
This is a common occurrence in languages. Most Iroquois political metaphor
can be deciphered when this principle is applied to a few clusters of concepts
and when the terms are taken as seriously as they were meant.

Certain terms pose special difficulties, especially kinship terms. Family relationships and responsibilities among the Iroquois did not correspond
to those among western Europeans. As translated into French or English,
familial terms are therefore often ambiguous and sometimes misleading. Regrettably, no systematic research has been done by either historians or ethnologists to decipher the precise intent of Iroquois kinship terms in political
contexts; and in any given treaty council the translators may have skewed Iroquois verbal expressions in the process of committing them to paper. Unfortunately, the proceedings of treaty councils were almost never written down
in an Iroquois language so original utterances can no longer be consulted. In
dubious or controversial cases the context and background of recorded state-
ments should be taken into account. A student with knowledge of Iroquois
custom may then be able to guess the words that probably were translated
into the recorded European terms.

It should be noted also that Indian metaphor does not follow the rules
of European rhetoric or logic. Thus it was possible for the Iroquois to address
Delawares in the same sentence as *grandfathers* and *nephews*, and to make other
symbolic combinations that seem strange to non-Indians.

This list refers only to Iroquois metaphor. Figures of speech that have
become familiar through usage by other Indians do not appear here because
they were not in the Iroquois vocabulary.

Antlers

A symbol of peace leaders. A sachem was *crowned with antlers* when he was installed in office. If impeached, he was *dehorned*. While active in office he was *wearing antlers* which were *set aside* when he participated in war or when he became mortally ill. Setting the antlers aside did not carry the opprobrium of dehorning. At the end of a Condolence Council the chiefs' dance was called *rubbing antlers*.

Bushes

Negotiations carried on informally away from the council fire were said to be done *in the bushes*. The phrase might be used for commonly accepted private consultations for expediting the flow of formal business. It could also be used to condemn illegal transactions made without the knowledge or consent of the proper authorities.

Chain

Literally translated from its roots the word for *chain* in Iroquoian language means something like *arms linked together*. Cayuga example: *teHonane:- tosho:t* they have joined hands/arms.

A *chain of friendship* was any bilateral or multilateral alliance.

The *Covenant Chain* was the name of the particular confederacy founded in 1677 at Albany. According to the English, it embraced the Iroquois and their tributaries on the one side, and New York and other English colonies on the other side. Both tributary and colonial memberships varied from time to time.

Records prior to 1677 do not record the term "Covenant Chain," but later Iroquois tradition extrapolated it into the past as a rubric over a long series of treaty relationships that had begun with a *rope* between Mohawks and the Dutch of Fort Orange. The rope apparently signified a nonaggression pact for purposes of trade. It was converted into an *iron chain* connecting the Mohawks with all the Dutch of New Netherland in a bilateral mutual assistance alliance at about 1643. The iron chain was renewed by the English of New York in 1664, at which time it included also the "Senecas," i.e., the non-Mohawk nations of the League. In 1677 the chain became *silver* as a multilateral, bicultural confederation of the Iroquois League and certain English colonies and thus began the Covenant Chain proper. At one point Massachusetts Bay tried to gain primacy in the chain by calling its connection *golden*, but the effort did not succeed.

It was often said that the chain had to be *greased* or *polished* at certain regular intervals because *rust* or *dirt* had accumulated on it. The point was that alliance had to be perpetually renewed and its terms renegotiated. Sometimes the *smell of the bear's grease would last a year*, meaning that renegotiation would be due in one year's time.

Clouds

Trouble or threats that overshadowed interrelationships. To *dispel the clouds* was to remove the cause of trouble.

Covering

In various ways *covering* signified termination.
1. To *cover the fire* was to end a particular council or, alternatively, to end a relationship that centered upon a council site. When the Iroquois nations chose different sides in the war of the American Revolution, they covered the League's fire at Onondaga until such a time as they could come together again.
2. To *cover a death* was to render last honors by eulogizing a dead man.
3. A *death that covered a death* was the vengeance done for a killing.

Cradle board

A symbol of childhood. As applied to a nation it meant that the nation had not achieved full political maturity. Thus the Tuscaroras were received into the Iroquois League as the Sixth Nation *on the cradle board* with the right to speak in League councils but not to vote.

Eating

All sorts of consumption.
1. Used figuratively in sentences such as "Give us muskets to eat."
2. As a symbol of unity: *to eat out of the same dish; to eat with one spoon; to eat across the fire from each other.* Iroquois alliance with the French was often described as a bowl out of which beaver was eaten with one spoon.
3. To *eat someone* was to kill him in war.
4. As a threat: *we shall eat you*, or *we shall put you in the kettle.* In ear-

lier years, when ritual cannibalism was practiced, the threat might be meant literally. Its later significance was more often killing or conquering.

Face, divided

A *divided face* showed distinction as in the 1645 treaty at Three Rivers when the Iroquois negotiator turned the painted side of his face toward the Hurons to show that he "did not see very clearly on that side" while he turned the unpainted side toward the French to show that on that side he could "see clearly, as in broad daylight."

Fire

1. A place of habitation. A family *kept its fire* where it lived. This was also the place where its *smoke* arose.
2. A nation or tribe. For example, the Three Fires were the Potawatomis, Ottawas, and Chippewas.
3. A formally designated location for treaty councils, as Onondaga was where the Iroquois League had its council fire, and Albany was for a long time where the fire burned for treaties between the Iroquois and the English colonies.
4. To *kindle a fire* was to establish the site as proper for councils. To *cover the fire* was to adjourn a council. To extinguish the fire was to terminate the use of a specific place as a council site, at least until the fire was rekindled.
5. As a symbol of unity: *to eat across the fire.*
6. To *cross the fire* was to change sides.

Hatchet or ax

A symbol of war or peace depending on what was metaphorically done with it. *To take up the hatchet* was to go to war. *To bury the hatchet* was to declare peace. *To take the hatchet out of someone's hands* and/or *throw it in the river* was to impose peace or neutrality. A hatchet *tossed to the sky* was more indeterminate because it might be *retrieved by a string.*

House

1. A symbol of the lineage—one extended, continuing family.
2. Hence, the extended house of the Iroquois League: *Kanonghsyonny* or *Kanonsionni* in Horatio Hale, *The Iroquois Book of Rites*, p. 75.

3. The doors to the house had special significance because they provided access and therefore needed to be guarded. The Senecas were *keepers of the western door* and the Mohawks *keepers of the eastern door.* Some contention between Mohawks and Onondagas developed in the mid-seventeenth century when the Mohawks unsuccessfully tried to impose a rule that French negotiators must enter the League by the eastern door, i.e., speak to the Mohawks before going on to the central council at Onondaga. They reproached the French for trying to enter the house improperly by *going down the smoke hole.*

4. *Props* of the house were important allies who defended the League against its enemies.

5. *To knock in the gable* was to raid or destroy a nation's settlement.

I

The first person singular pronoun was used by Indian negotiators to mean the nation for whom each one spoke. When an Onondaga chief said something like, "This is my land," he meant that it was the territory of his nation.

Kettle

An ambiguous symbol. On the one hand it refers to hospitality; on the other hand to hostility.

1. *To hang the kettle* for someone denoted a hospitable reception.

2. To put an enemy *into the kettle* denoted an act of ritual cannibalism. It might also signify torture in the form of burning at the stake.

3. *To make kettle* (to cook together) was to live together in good union.

4. *To break the kettle* was to fall out completely with someone.

5. *To draw a man from the kettle* was to spare him his life.

Kinship

The Iroquois used kinship terms in diplomacy. Nations were referred to and addressed by terms translated as *father, brother, cousin, nephew,* etc. Female terms such as *mother, sister,* and *niece* were not used. Precise meanings in any given situation are often difficult to pin down because the terms in most, if not all, documents of council transactions are translations of Iroquoian terms that meant different things to Europeans than to the Iroquois. Thus Count Frontenac addressed the Iroquois as *children* and required them to call him *father,* intending thereby to establish them as subjects owing him obedience. Since he was rigid on the point, they went along with the terms in order to be able to negotiate with him. But the Iroquois did not have Frontenac's conception of patriarchal authority. In their society, fathers did not have power to command their children; nobody did, although uncles on the mother's side held a greater degree of authority than the father because of lineage relationships reckoned through the mother. New York Governor Sir Edmund Andros tried to emulate Frontenac's example for the same reason, but failed to make the terms stick. His successors addressed Iroquois chiefs as *brethren* and they reciprocated with the same term.

Among the Iroquois themselves, brethren were distingiushed as *elder brothers* and *younger brothers*. Mohawks, Onondagas, and Senecas were the elders. Oneidas, Cayugas, and (later) Tuscaroras were the younger. They were all peers, but the elders might be said to be a little more equal, at least as regarded deference behavior.

Cousin is problematic in translation because the same word in English denotes cousins on both the mother's and the father's side, whereas the Iroquois distinguish. For them, mother's brother's children and father's sister's children are cousins to ego, but mother's sister's children and father's brother's children are brothers and sisters to ego. The meaning of *cousin* in diplomatic discourse, like the meaning of other kinship terms, must be inferred from context. It did not mean a relationship of authority, but it was not identical in equality to *brethren*.

Uncle signified respect and implied an expectation of responsibility for *nephew* on the part of the uncle when they were of the same lineage.

Grandfather was a polite and proper term of ceremonial respect, but it carried no implication of required obedience. It was given especially to the Delawares who had the reputation of being the oldest tribe in the northeast. The grandfather Delawares did not reciprocate by calling the Iroquois grandchildren. Historic treaties show them using the term *uncles*. In response, the Iroquois sometimes called the Delawares *cousins*, sometimes *nephews*, as well as *grandfathers*.

It seems likely that, when kinship terminology is better understood, a student may be able to trace changing statuses by noting changing terms, but caution must be observed. Long after Shawnees and Delawares began acting independently of Iroquois policies and "advice," the *uncle/nephew* terms continued to be used in council. To determine relative statuses, therefore, kinship terms should be regarded as one factor in the whole historical context.

Mat

Symbol of domesticity and hospitality.
1. Siblings *shared one mat.*

2. *To arrive at one's mat* was to arrive at one's home.

3. A *mat stained with blood* denoted a household in which a member had been killed in war. *To wipe clean* a bloodstained mat was to appease the family's grief for their loss.

4. *To prepare a mat* was to make ready to receive a person in the home.

5. *To smoke on one's mat* was to be profoundly at peace.

Path or road

One of the major symbols of diplomatic relations, it included both the idea of communication and that of situation.

1. When the path was *full of brambles* or *fallen logs*, communication was poor and disputes existed.

2. *To sweep the path clean* was to eliminate obstacles to friendship. *To cause great boulders to fall into the path* was a threat to break off relations.

Rope

A symbol of alliance. The strength of the alliance depended on the material of which it was said to be made. After contact with Europeans, a *rope* referred to an alliance that was less strong in some manner than a *chain* (see above definition). In the traditions of alliance between the Iroquois and the Dutch and English jurisdictions of New Netherland and New York, *a rope of bark* preceded an iron chain. It appears to have meant a nonaggression pact for the sake of trade.

Shout

It was customary to show strong approval of particular actions at a treaty council by a conventional cry in unison that is often mentioned in the texts as a shout of approbation and sometimes spelled as "yo-ha."

Smoking

Tobacco had (and has) a sacred quality. As the act of smoking calmed the mind and the smoke ascended to the skies, rapport was established with good spirits. Thus, *smoking together* at a treaty established a basis for peaceful, friendly negotiation. For these reasons the *calumet* or *peace pipe* was a particularly appropriate symbol of peace.

Tree

An important symbol of peace and protection. The celestial tree stood at the center of the earth and extended its branches and roots everywhere.

1. *The everywhere tree of peace*, symbolically shown on a very old wampum belt (see illustration), represented the Iroquois League's extension of authority and internal peace to tributary nations. *The white roots of peace* reached out in every direction from it. Sometimes the roots were made to *bleed* by attacks.

2. *To plant a tree of peace* was to extend protection over some location or people, as New York's governor Edmund Andros planted a tree of peace at Schaghticoke for refugee Indians from New England. To plant the tree of peace *on the highest mountain* was to make a general peace. *To uproot the tree* was to start war.

3. As applied to individuals the tree metaphor was a symbol of peace chiefs. The chief, who was a protector of his people, was *raised up*. He might *fall*, for one reason or another, and possibly be replanted.

Unity

A variety of images were used to express unity.

1. One head, one mind, one heart, one body, one lineage, traveling in one canoe, living in one house.

2. *To smoke from the same calumet* with a nation was to be in perfect union with it.

3. A *bundle of arrows*, one for each nation, was used by Sir William Johnson and afterward by United States commissioners to express unity, but whether this reflected Indian custom or the fasces of ancient Rome is not clear.

Wampum

Wampum had many uses and apparently many kinds of significance; in diplomacy its functions depended on how it was made and how it was handled.

1. A string or belt *carried the words* of a tribal council. These words were *read into it* in the presence of an ambassador or messenger who memorized them and repeated them at his destination, but it was the wampum that carried them. Color and figures in the wampum gave some indication of its general purport, as "black" or red-painted belts proposed war, but there was no code. Every belt's message had to be memorized. A belt's importance was

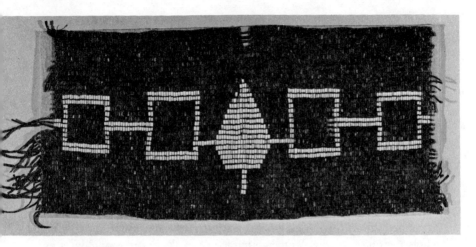

The "Hiawatha" wampum belt of the Iroquois League, symbolizing the League's formation. Four of the five founding nations are represented by rectangles. Onondaga, the central nation, is symbolized by the Tree of Peace. All are linked by paths that extend outward toward other nations. *Photograph courtesy of the New York State Museum.*

suggested by its size. Belts were more important than strings, and large belts more important than small ones.

2. Exchange of wampum represented acceptance of a message or proposal. Refusal to accept a belt represented rejection of the proposal.

3. Wampum without a message was sometimes given as a present in conformity with the general Indian custom that exchange of presents confirmed a treaty's provisions.

4. Wampum might signify a formal relationship as between the Iroquois League and a tributary. Reciprocal presentations of wampum denoted the acceptance by both sides of the responsibilities of that relationship. These varied with time and circumstance.

5. Beauchamp, in *Wampum and Shell Articles* (pp. 395–97), observed that Sir William Johnson was lavish in the use of wampum, that he multiplied the emblems and imparted precision to the symbolisms that were previously indefinite. As the supply of wampum, which had been declining, increased under his regime, Johnson revived usages that evidently had been lapsing. Apparently the supply and usage of wampum reached a peak at mid-seventeenth century, dropped away, and then was revived after Johnson came to power in 1755. Beauchamp stated credibly that most of the belts now extant date from the latter period.

Wood's Edge

Protocol demanded that friendly visitors stop at the wood's edge be-fore entering a village. The concept is so distinct that it is best rendered in English as one word—*woodsedge*. There they shouted to announce themselves, upon which a party came out to escort them into the village. *To be at the wood's edge*, therefore, was a manner of announcing one's readiness to treat.

Woman, women

As applied to tribes or nations, and with some qualification, these terms reflect the sexual division of labor and responsibility in Iroquois culture. Men filled the offices of traditional chiefs and spoke in treaty councils for the whole nation or League. Women attended councils, but in formal meetings their messages were uttered by male speakers. Thus *women* tribes, among whom were the Delawares, were denied the privilege of treating with European col-onies about certain issues. As Delaware chief Sassoonan expressed his under-standing of the status (with Oneida chief Shikellamy looking on), "the Five Nations have often told them [the Delawares] that they were as Women only, and desired them to plant Corn and mind their own private Business, for that they would take Care of what related to Peace and War" (*Pa. Council Minutes*, 10 October 1728, 3:334–35).

In the 1742 treaty at Easton, Pa., Onondaga chief Canastego extended the concept to deny the Delawares' right to sell lands. The resentful Delawares reasserted their independence in the "Ohio country," but the *women* termi-nology continued to be used in certain circumstances.

Words

1. In diplomatic metaphor, *words* were messages or articles of agree-ment that were carried by wampum. The words were confirmed by presenta-tion of the wampum to the person being addressed. Words carried importance according to the size of the wampum belts or according to the value of pres-ents accompanying the words when wampum was not available.

2. The three *rare words* of the Condolence Council metaphorically *cleared the eyes* of a visiting negotiator, *unplugged his ears*, and *cleared his throat* with the host's fingers. Each "word" was accompanied by a string of wampum. Thus the visitor was prepared to enter into formal dialogue.

Some uncertainty exists as to whether this phrase should be "The three Bare Words." It is sometimes written as such.

SECTION II

TREATY EVENTS

7

The Earliest Recorded Description
THE MOHAWK TREATY WITH NEW FRANCE
AT THREE RIVERS, 1645

IROQUOIS TREATIES were made in varied combinations of parties and under widely varying circumstances. Although certain ritual patterns appear in the records repeatedly, they were adapted to changes of situations, issues, and time. No single model accurately reflects the span of historical actuality. This treaty was chosen because it is the earliest for which a full description has survived and is therefore, the best description available of what Iroquois treaty processes were like before being modified by the influence of Europeans.

RITUALS OF PEACE MAKING

The Iroquois, having made their first (unminuted) treaty with the Dutch two years previously, in 1643, needed to expand their beaver hunting territories north of the St. Lawrence and Lake Ontario to satisfy their need of trade goods and the Dutch demand for pelts at Fort Orange (now Albany). For five years they had been acquiring guns there and on the Connecticut River. Peace with the French and their allied Indians, the Algonquin and Huron, offered the possibility of extending trade in that direction and opening the hunting grounds in the Ottawa valley. The Iroquois, Hurons, and Algonquins were taking and burning each other's captives, although a few were spared, and the Iroquois held a Frenchman, Guillaume Couture, who had been taken with missionary Father Jogues three years earlier, as hostage. The French took the initiative, sending an embassy to the Mohawks to return Iroquois captives taken by the Hurons, and request a peace. In July they returned with official deputies from the Mohawk council, including Kiotseaeton, "Le Crochet" (hook), as their speaker. This was a man who proved himself a master of the ritual forms for making alliances which became the protocol for treaty making and which derive from the rich oral literature of the League. Historians like Hunt,[1] who have decried the importance of the League, seem unaware of the importance of ethnological evidence that they cite. Kiotseaeton treated the French to the first recorded performance of the Requickening rite of the Condolence Council, and the report of the proceedings of this 1645 treaty in the *Jesuit Relations* is loaded with metaphors, symbolism, and ethnographic information on Huron-Iroquois culture at a point of transition.[2]

As the mouth of his country, Kiotseaeton stood offshore in the bow of the boat draped in beads, hailing those at the landing as brothers, a kin term of equivalency. After welcome at the landing, he planted two poles, stretched a cord to hang his "words," the wampum strings and belts, and arranged the seventeen items of his message. He then demonstrated considerable operatic talent, pacing to and fro, singing the song of peace, and acting out the episodes of his narrative leading to a climax. The French, too, sensed that it was high drama. Adept at handling wampum, Kiotseaeton tied a belt to the arm of a prisoner, acted out the journey by road and river simulating the burdens and indicating the hazards encountered by his nephew whom he was about to release. He tied a second belt near the first. He added presents to those sent by the Governor and distributed to tribes named. He cast weapons under foot. He cleared the river, smoothed the rapids, and calmed the lake, which amounted to clearing the road between the parties. The ninth burden stressed perpetual fire in all their houses and the light of peace. The tenth would bind the parties arm in arm in a covenant of peace (a great belt). This meant that they would eat with their former enemies. He would restore the Sun, having dispelled the clouds. A thirteenth reminded the Huron of Iroquois good will, that "five days" ago, meaning five years, the Huron had prepared a pouch of wampum to seek peace. He urged the Huron not to be bashful like women, but to speak. The fifteenth would fetch the return of Jesuit missionaries to Iroquoia, and the sixteenth would receive them in Canada. The seventeenth was a belt sent by Jogues' aunt in the Mohawk country commemorative of a name given a captive.

A general euphoria followed the fulfillment of this pattern: The speaker promised to spend the summer dancing and gaming, and a great social dance by all parties followed.

It was the custom for the departing guest to give thanks to his host that the host might continue to see the Sun (to live); the guest would then acknowledge gifts, hail the other party as "brothers," and bid them adieu in these terms from the landing.

The preceding dialogue contains some interesting cultural items. The divided face or split personality concept, that is later encountered in Iroquois masks, was expressed in face-painting. The Iroquois speaker, in replying to a Huron conspirator who sought to alienate him from the French, said his face was painted in this manner, with the dark side toward the Hurons, the clear side toward the French, which affected his vision and views accordingly. The contrast of light and dark, as in sunlight and darkness of night, in life and death, war and peace runs through a symbolic dyad.

A hatchet thrown beyond reach into the sky where no arm is long enough to retrieve it is a reasonable promise of peace. Likewise, a mat suggests both hospitality and brotherhood, since siblings may share a mat. Metaphors of unity extend sharing: to hunt together, roast meat on the same spit, eat across the fire. To hear is to accept a message. It is evidence of a sound heart.

Wampum symbolism and usage abounds. A string of wampum on a stick represents the bonds of a captive led to freedom by the arm. Words of importance are attested by wampum or presents; otherwise, nothing is said or heard.

It is clear that the Hurons understood the same set of symbols. Their speaker speaks of breaking the kettle (of war) in which they (the Iroquois) boiled the Hurons in order to eat them.[3] Although cannibalism is here implied metaphorically, on occasion it was a grisly reality.

In League ritual, the moiety of the Mohawk-Onondaga-Seneca stand as Agadoni, "Sires," Uncles or Elder Brothers to the Oneida-Cayuga moiety who are Kheyahdawen, "Offspring," Nephews, or Younger Brothers to the former; here the Mohawk speaker refers to the Oneida village as a mere "child," which cannot speak for itself.[4] In a later explanatory note we read that the Hurons had exterminated nearly all of the Oneida men, and that the community had to borrow Mohawk men to service their women, this being the reason the Mohawks referred to the Oneida village as their "child."[5]

Of all the surviving Iroquois rites, the Adonwa, or Personal Chant ranks among the four most sacred. It is also pre-Columbian. When the Mohawk speaker took a Frenchman and a Huron on each arm, sang the "peace song" in a loud voice, and marched them the length of the council space and return, to the accompaniment of his native auditors, he was dramatizing their adoption.[6]

The protocol of the return of the Iroquois delegates in September repeats the first conference, but the burden of the message differs. Not having any presents, the speaker simply extends hospitality in Iroquoia, where the voice of Onontio like thunder is heard everywhere. He mentions a soft mat, plenty of firewood against cold nights, and the recorder observes in passing that the natives usually sleep close to the fire. There is food for the kettle, ointment to heal wounds from roots and stones in the path, a guarantee that baggage will be transferred from landing to hearth, and wives for those who wish to marry.[7]

Encouraging the Algonquins and Hurons to speak out, he assures them that Iroquois chiefs only smoke (hold council) in their country, that their calumets (pipes) are always in their mouths, that the souls of Iroquois dead have withdrawn so far into the earth as to mitigate revenge, and that they have passed the summer dancing and feasting. Hatchets are suspended. Shall they continue dancing? In additional remarks concerning return of prisoners, we learn that Algonquin men are invariably killed, but the Huron men and all the women sit waiting on logs and stumps outside the villages, ready to return, being rootless. The gifts to previous ambassadors have been distributed throughout the Confederacy as instructed.[8]

In the reply of Governor Montmagny it is plain that the French in 1645 had learned the required condolence forms,[9] presumably from the Hurons. Their speaker offered the bonds of an Iroquois who had escaped as token that they would have set him free. A second "word" would carry back bones to one's country, and it is explained that it is the Huron custom to strip the bones of their dead and to place them with their relatives wherever they may die. The bond to bind these bones for transport occurs as an element in the modern requickening address.[10] In a moment of genuine antiquarianism, the Huron speaker, knowing the Mohawks had arquebusses, snatches shields (of bark) from their back where they were wont to carry them; but he does not mention slat armor.[11] An Algonquin speaker established their identity as a mobile people transporting wigwams of bark sheets. But they too shared the metaphor of unity: one house, one calumet, one canoe.[12]

Having dispersed the clouds, there was a terminal feast for 400. Despite the drama, peace was only temporary.

WNF

NOTES

1. George T. Hunt, *The Wars of the Iroquois: a Study in Intertribal Trade Relations* (Madison: University of Wisconsin Press, 1940), 75–79.

2. Reuben G. Thwaites, ed., *The Jesuit Relations and Allied Documents* . . . 73 vols. (Cleveland, 1896–1901), 27: 247–53; Marie Guyart, dite Marie de l'Incarnation; *Lettres* à son fils . . . (Paris, 1681), pp. 393–405, 408–10.

3. *Jesuit Relations* 27: 299, 301.

4. Ibid., p. 289.

5. Ibid., p. 297.

6. Ibid., p. 289.

7. Ibid., p. 283.

8. Ibid., pp. 283, 287, 289.

9. Ibid., pp. 294, 303.

10. Ibid., p. 297; J. N. B. Hewitt, "The Requickening Address of the Iroquois Condolence Council," W. N. Fenton, ed., *Journal of the Washington Academy of Sciences* 34, no. 3 (1944): 65–86, Tenth Article, 75.

11. *Jesuit Relations* 27: 299.

12. Ibid., p. 301.

MULTIPLE INTRIGUES

The 1645 treaty between New France and the Mohawks must be understood historically in the context of intertribal and intercolonial competition in trade. Although each constituent tribe and colony pursued its own goals and attempted to serve its own interests, two loosely-knit combinations struggled for dominance. On the one side were New France and its allied Indians, chiefly the Hurons and the Algonquins. On the other were New Netherland and its Mohawk allies.

Crisis began in 1642 when the French founded Montreal and built Fort Richelieu near the junction of the Richelieu River with the St. Lawrence. The effect of these moves was to impede Mohawk trade and raids along the St. Lawrence valley in the country to the north. Recognizing this, the Mohawks unsuccessfully attacked the fort while it was still under construction.[1] At the same time they were involved in war with the Algonquins, one of whose leading warriors, chief Pieskaret, inflicted several humiliating defeats upon them.[2]

Also in the year 1642, Dutch official Arent Van Corlaer journeyed into the Mohawk country and negotiated an agreement for which we have only his report that it was a pact of friendship.[3] According to a later treaty text, the Mohawks made their first treaty with "all" the Dutch (not merely the Dutch of Fort Orange) in 1643.[4] No record survives, but it appears likely that this was their first mutual assistance pact as distinguished from one of simple nonaggression. The reason for thinking so is that the Mohawks subsequently intervened in behalf of the Dutch against hostile Algonquian speaking tribes within New Netherland.[5]

Fairly clearly the Mohawks were trying to get control of the trade going to both the Dutch and the French markets. Even their Onondaga co-members of the Iroquois League chafed under Mohawk controls over access to the Dutch market. The Mohawk treaty with New France is therefore interesting in several respects.

1. It provided access for the Mohawks to French markets and to the hunting territories of tribes formerly at enmity.

2. It was held at Three Rivers, more distant from the Onondagas than Montreal, and the Mohawks later tried to establish Three Rivers as the exclusive location for Iroquois councils with the French.[6]

3. A secret understanding was incorporated into the treaty agreement. Although no formal minutes or written contract exist, a record was made by a Jesuit of governor Montmagny's disclosure of this "clause." To keep the secret, the record was written in Latin instead of the normal French. An English translation is given in the note on p. 315 of the *Journal of the Jesuit Fathers in the Year 1646* (Thwaites' edition). The secret was Montmagny's withdrawal of protection from non-Christian Algonquins in order to secure Mohawk good will for the French and their major trading partners, the Hurons.

4. The peace created by the treaty lasted only a year. It was followed by unreported negotiations between the Mohawks and Canadian tribes, the purport of which is not known, but on 18 October 1646 Jesuit Father Isaac Jogues was killed by Mohawks among whom he had attempted to set up a mission.[7]

5. The full blast of Iroquois renewed warfare was delayed, apparently because of differences between Mohawks and Onondagas within the Iroquois League;[8] but in 1648 the Dutch government sold 400 firearms to the Mohawks,[9] and in 1649 a great war party of Mohawks and Senecas struck a devastating blow at Huronia.[10]

FJ

NOTES

1. *Jesuit Relations* 22:211, 277–79; 21:269–71; Percy J. Robinson, "Introduction" to Francois Du Creux, *The History of Canada or New France*, ed. James B. Conacher, 2 vols. (Toronto: The Champlain Society, 1951–62) 1:xviii–xix.

2. Elsie McLeod Jury, "Pieskaret," in *Dictionary of Canadian Biography* 1:547–48.

3. N.Y. Col. Docs. 13:15.

4. N.Y. Col. Docs. 13:112.

5. N.Y. Col. Docs. 13:18, 191.

6. *Jesuit Relations* 29:53–59.

7. *Jesuit Relations* 31:115–17; Trigger, *Children of Aataentsic* 2:654–56.

8. *Jesuit Relations* 30:175.

9. N.Y. Col. Docs. 1:311–12; 13:23–24, 176.

10. By far the best account of the Iroquois-Huron war is in Trigger, Children of Aataentsic. The 1649 strike is in ch. 11.

UNANSWERED QUESTIONS

The Jesuit Relation of 1644–45, and that of 1645–1646,[1] present valuable evidence of councils of peace held between the Iroquois (Mohawk delegates), French, Hurons, and Algonquins in 1645. According to the Relation of 1644–45, Tokhrahenehiaron, a Mohawk man formerly a prisoner of the Algonquins, had been released by the French and sent to Iroquois country with an invitation to the Iroquois to make peace. In July of 1645, he arrived at the French fort at Three Rivers with two principal men from his country to begin preliminary negotiations. Upon the arrival of the delegates, a brief greeting took place at the bank of the river where they embarked from their canoes.[2] Kiotseaeton, the man who served as speaker, stated that he had come on behalf of all the Iroquois to see if the French, Hurons, and Algonquins were clearly disposed toward peace.

Iroquois relations with French, Hurons, and Algonquins were unsteady in 1645. French constructions of posts on the St. Lawrence and Richelieu rivers had increased in recent years. One, Ville-Marie, was built in May 1642 and another, Fort Richelieu, in August 1642. Iroquois attempted to stop construction at Fort Richelieu by attacking the builders. Ville-Marie was raided in the summer of 1643. Although these attacks were not successful, they created much anxiety among the French.[3] Moreover, the Iroquois were also raiding Huron and Algonquin canoes heading to French posts along the Ottawa and St. Lawrence rivers. This had arrested the transport of furs along these river routes, seriously reducing the number of them arriving at French posts.[4] Therefore, the French, hoping to stop Iroquois attacks, were disposed toward peace in 1645.

The Iroquois undertook the raiding expeditions to divert furs from the French to the Dutch with whom the Mohawks were in alliance. This effort was aided by a supply of firearms that had been provided to the Iroquois by the Dutch. Direct attacks on the French to secure furs and to stop French construction of forts in the St. Lawrence River Valley could never have been sustained by the Iroquois, however, with the few firearms available. Another goal of the raids, therefore, was to weaken the Hurons sufficiently so that they might choose to incorporate with the Iroquois against the French, potentially leading to a halt of French expansion.

By 1645, some efforts had been made by the Iroquois to negotiate directly with the Hurons for alliance with them. The *Relation* of 1644–45 reports that there was a meeting between Iroquois and Hurons five years before July 1645. Although there is no evidence of what transpired, we are told in the *Relation* that the Iroquois were disappointed because the Hurons had not carried through with what was taken by the Iroquois to be an expressed disposition toward peace.[5] Ironically, therefore, the French were enlisted in 1645 by the Iroquois to establish an alliance with the Hurons in order to lead eventually to the demise of the French.[6]

Apparently, Iroquois (primarily, if not exclusively, Mohawk)[7] agreed to negotiate a peace with the French to calm French fears of attack in order to use them as a gateway to negotiations with the Hurons and to convince them to forsake their Algonquin allies so that Mohawk attacks could be concentrated against the latter. They fell into some difficulty, however. They discovered in private councils in July 1645 that the French were not disposed to close their eyes to attacks on the Algonquins, at least not on those who had accepted Christianity.[8]

The three Iroquois men at Three Rivers in July, however, were determined to see that negotiations continued. They returned to their country, therefore, with news of the conference. On 17 September, Iroquois delegates arrived at Three Rivers to meet with French, Hurons, and Algonquins. According to the Jesuit report, all nations agreed to peace at the conference that followed. Delegates of each nation were to go to each other nation to conclude peace, however.[9] The Mohawks had succeeded in setting up independent negotiations with the Hurons.

Unfortunately, historical documentation proves particularly disappointing at this point. Although the *Relation* of 1644–45 provides evidence that two Algonquins, two Hurons, and two Frenchmen left with delegates for Iroquois country,[10] there is little written evidence of the outcome of the meetings, except that Mohawk deputies at Montreal in February and at Three Rivers in May 1646 announced that other Iroquois nations had decided not to make peace. All Iroquois were not of one mind at the time. It was said that the Mohawks, however, were still intent on sending delegates to Huron country. Whether or not this was done is not known.[11] Although Iroquois raiding was greatly relaxed during the winter of 1645–46 and the spring and summer of 1646, by the fall of that year hostilities had broken out again against the French and their Indian allies. Because of the lack of data about possible councils in Huron and Algonquin country to confirm the peace negotiated in September 1645, the councils of 1645 have remained puzzling.

The *Jesuit Relations* of 1644–45, and 1645–46, however, offer much valuable information, despite what they may fail to provide. For one thing, they are a record of Jesuit attitudes toward the treaty proceedings being described. The author of the relation of 1645–46 was clearly impressed with what he described as the dramatic form, and wit, of the speaker, Kiotseaeton. His report of Kiotseaeton's eloquence belies the impression that is conveyed, particularly in the account of the September meetings, that the Indians were akin to wild beasts, their disposition toward peace being miraculous—the result of Frenchmen's prayers and work among them.[12] The Relations were reports of mission activity, published in France. They were designed to convince people of the worthiness of, and need for, the missions in order to stimulate financial support of them. The ambiguity of attitudes expressed in written records should be noted, because it often informs us, at least in a general way, about interaction between persons involved. No matter how much the cultural training of Jesuits disposed them toward viewing the Indians as savage, interaction often led them to observations that did not fit the image, and in some cases, led to refinement of it. The Jesuit, Joseph-Francois Lafitau, for example, wrote an extensive work about the people of America, published in 1724, comparing them with Greeks and Romans of the past.[13] Publication of the Relations resulted in dissemination of mixed observations and impressions.

It is important to note evidence that the councils of 1645 were part of continuing negotiations. Several times the Relations remark that a peace was concluded. The accounts as a whole, however, provide adequate information that the process was ongoing and not yet completed, at least as of 23 September 1645. Iroquois treaty transactions often took place over long periods of time, in various settings.

It can hardly escape one's attention that the Relation of 1644–45 offers a wealth of data on council ritual which not only inform about ceremony and metaphor used in the councils being described, but also provide material for study of ritual through time and space, especially when compared with other accounts of councils held at other times and in other places. The imagery of a multilateral alliance as a linking of parties to one another, for example, is described as having been dramatically portrayed by Kiotseaeton in July when he linked arms with a Frenchman and an Algonquin and held them tightly together—so tightly, he said, that not even lightning could separate them.[14] In September, the Iroquois speaker "took a Frenchman on one side, an Algonquin and a Huron on the other; and holding one another by the arms, they danced in time, and sang in a loud voice a song of peace."[15] This same imagery is found in documents pertaining to treaties from other periods, at other places, and involving other parties. In 1677, a Mohawk at a council at Albany with representatives of several English colonies described the Covenant Chain agreement—the multilateral agreement between the Iroquois, other Indian nations, and several English colonies—as a chain with links bonded together so strongly that not even thunder could break them.[16] Likewise, in August

1776, at a council at German Flats (near present day Herkimer, New York) with American Commissioners for Indian Affairs, an Oneida war leader described the Covenant Chain as follows: "When our ancestors first met, they agreed that they should take each other by the hand, and that no storms, nor even thunder, should be able to break their union."[17]

Every treaty document is unique. Every one has certain strengths and weaknesses. Although the *Relations* of 1644–45 and 1645–46 may leave questions unanswered, they, like most written documents, can be explored for valuable information on various subjects.

MD

NOTES

1. The Relation of 1645–46 is included because it provides information about private councils held in July 1645. The main account discussed here, however, is the Relation of 1644–45.

2. This was equivalent, most likely, to the Woods' Edge ritual so prominent in many Iroquois councils.

3. Gustave Lanctot, *A History of Canada*, 3 vols. (Cambridge, Mass.: Harvard University Press, 1963), 1:169–82.

4. Bruce G. Trigger. *The Children of Aataentsic: A History of the Huron People to 1660*, 2 vols. (Montreal and London: McGill-Queen's University Press, 1976), p. 644.

5. *Jesuit Relations* 27:263.

6. For a discussion of Iroquois strategies, see Trigger, *Children of Aataentsic*, pp. 634–43.

7. Only Mohawk delegates were identified as being at the councils, although they purported to be speaking for all of the Iroquois in the preliminary negotiations. In February and May 1646, however, Mohawks reported that other Iroquois nations were not in favor of the peace.

8. *Jesuit Relations* 28:315.

9. *Jesuit Relations* 27:275, 285.

10. *Jesuit Relations* 27:303.

11. Trigger, *Children of Aataentsic*, p. 654.

12. *Jesuit Relations* 27:275–81.

13. Joseph-Francois Lafitau, *Moeurs des sauvages amériquains comparées aux moeurs des premiers temps* (Paris: Saugin l'aine, 1724); English translation, *Customs of the American Indians Compared with the Customs of Primitive Times*, ed. and trans. by William N. Fenton and Elizabeth L. Moore, 2 vols. (Toronto: Champlain Society, 1974, 1977).

14. *Jesuit Relations* 27:261.

15. *Jesuit Relations* 27:289.

16. Public Record Office, Kew, England, C01/40, folio 82v. Proceedings of council at Albany, 20 July–22 August 1677.

17. *American Archives*, by Peter Force (Washington, D.C.: 1837–53), Series 5, 1:1045.

Herewith, the proceedings recorded by Father Barthelemy Vimont, S.J., of the "Treaty of Peace Between the French, the Iroquois, and other Nations." Originally written in French and Latin, the text was translated into English and published in *The Jesuit Relations and Allied Documents*, edited by Reuben Gold Thwaites, 73 volumes (Cleveland: Burrows Brothers Co., 1896–1901), volumes 27, 28, from which it is here reprinted. The numbers in brackets are the page numbers of the original 1646 edition.

TREATY OF PEACE BETWEEN THE FRENCH, THE IROQUOIS, AND OTHER NATIONS

ON THE FIFTH DAY of July, the Iroquois prisoner who had been set at liberty and sent back to his own country, as I have said in the foregoing Chapter, made his appearance at three Rivers accompanied by two men of note among those people, who had been delegated to negotiate peace with Onontio (thus they name Monsieur the Governor), and all the French, and all the Savages who are our allies.

A young man named Guillaume Cousture who had been taken prisoner with Father Isaac Jogues, and who had since then remained in the Iroquois country, accompanied them. As soon as he was recognized all threw their arms around his neck; he was looked upon as a man risen from the dead, who brought joy to all who thought him dead,—or, at least, that he was in danger of passing the remainder of his days in most bitter and [83] cruel captivity. As soon as he landed, he informed us of the design of the three Savages with whom he had been sent back. When the most important of the three, named Kiotseaeton, saw the French and the Savages hastening to the bank of the river, he stood up in the bow of the Shallop that had brought him from Richelieu to three Rivers. He was almost completely covered with Porcelain beads. Motioning with his hand for silence, he called out: "My Brothers, I have left my country to come and see you. At last I have reached your land. I was told, on my departure, that I was going to seek death, and that I would never again see my country. But I have willingly exposed myself for the good of peace. I come therefore to enter into the designs of the French, of the Hurons, and of the Alguonquins. I come to make known to you the thoughts of all my country." When he had said this, the Shallop fired a shot from a swivel gun, and the Fort replied by a discharge from the cannon, as a sign of rejoicing.

When those Ambassadors had landed, they were conducted into the room of the [84] sieur de Chanflour, who gave them a very cordial reception. They were offered some slight refreshments, and, after they had eaten and smoked, Kiotsaeton, who was always the spokesman, said to all the French who surrounded him, "I find much pleasure in your houses. Since I have set foot in your country, I have observed nothing but rejoicing. I see very well that he who is in the Sky wishes to bring to a conclusion a very important matter. The minds and thoughts of men are too diverse to fall into accord; it is the Sky that will combine all." On the same day, a canoe was sent to Monsieur the Governor to inform him of the arrival of these new guests.

Meanwhile, both they and the prisoners who had not yet been given up had full liberty to wander where they willed. The Alguonquins and Montagnais invited them to their feasts, and they gradually accustomed themselves to converse together. The sieur de Chanflour treated them very well; one day he said to them that they were with us as if in their own country; that they had nothing to fear; [85] that they were in their own house. Kiotsaeton replied to this compliment by a very well-pointed and neat retort. "I beg thee," he said to the Interpreter, "to say to that Captain who speaks to us that he tells a great falsehood with respect to us; at least, it is certain that what he says is not true." And thereupon he paused a little, to let the wonder grow. Then he added: "That Captain tells me that I am here as if in my own country. That is very far from the truth. I would be neither honored nor treated with such consideration in my own country, while here every one honors me and pays me attention. He says that I am as if in my own house; that is a sort of falsehood, for I am maltreated in my house, and here I fare well every day,—I am continually feasting. Therefore I am not as if I were in my own country or in my own house." He indulged in many other repartees which clearly showed that he had wit.

Finally, Monsieur the Governor came from Quebec to three Rivers; and, after having seen the Ambassadors, [86] he gave audience to them on the twelfth of July. This took place in the courtyard of the Fort, over which large sails had been spread to keep off the heat of the Sun. Their places were thus arranged: on one side was Monsieur the Governor, accompanied by his people and by Reverend Father Vimont, Superior of the Mission. The Iroquois sat at his feet, on a great piece of hemlock bark. They had stated before the assembly that they wished to be on his side, as a mark of the affection that they bore to the French.

Opposite them were the Algonquins, the Montagnais, and the Attikamegues; the two other sides were closed in by some French and some Hurons. In the center was a large space, somewhat longer than wide, in which the Iroquois caused two poles to be planted, and a cord to be stretched from one to the other on which to hang and tie the words that they were to bring us,— that is to say, the presents they wished to make us, which consisted of seventeen collars of porcelain beads, a portion of which were on their bodies. The remainder were enclosed [87] in a small pouch placed quite near them. When all had assembled and had taken their places, Kiotsaeton who was high in stature, rose and looked at the Sun, then cast his eyes over the whole Company; he took a collar of procelain beads in his hand and commenced to harangue in a loud voice. "Onontio, lend me ear. I am the mouth for the whole of my country; thou listenest to all the Iroquois, in hearing my words. There is no evil in my heart; I have only good songs in my mouth. We have a multitude of war songs in our country; we have cast them all on the ground; we have no longer anything but songs of rejoicing." Thereupon he began to sing; his countrymen responded; he walked about that great space as if on the stage of a theatre; he made a thousand gestures; he looked up to Heaven; he gazed at the Sun; he rubbed his arms as if he wished to draw from them the strength that moved them in war. After he had sung awhile, he said that the present that he held in his hand thanked Monsieur the Governor for having saved the life of Tokhrahenehiaron, [88] when he drew him last Autumn out of the fire and away from the teeth of the Alguonquins; but he complained gracefully that he had been sent back all alone to his own country. "If his canoe had been upset; if the winds had caused it to be submerged; if he had been drowned, you would have waited long for the return of the poor lost man, and you would have accused us of a fault which you yourselves would have committed." When he had said this, he fastened his collar in the appointed spot.

Drawing out another, he tied it to the arm of Guillaume Cousture, saying aloud: "It is this Collar that brings you back this prisoner. I would not have said to him, while he was still in our country: 'Go, my Nephew; take a Canoe and return to Quebec.' My mind would not have been at rest; I would always have thought over and over again to myself, 'Is he not lost?' In truth, I would have had no sense, had I acted in that way. He whom you have sent back had all the difficulties in the world, on his journey." He began to express them, but in so pathetic a manner that there is no merry-andrew in France so ingenious as that Barbarian. He took a stick, and placed it on [89] his head like a bundle; then he carried it from one end of the square to the other, representing what that prisoner had done in the rapids and in the current of the water,—on arriving at which he had transported his baggage, piece by piece. He went backward and forward, showing the journeys, the windings, and the turnings of the prisoner. He ran against a stone; he receded more than he ad-

vanced in his canoe, because alone he could not maintain it against the current. He lost courage, and then regained his strength. In a word, I have never
seen anything better done than this acting. "Again" (said he), "if you had helped
him to pass the rapids and the bad roads, and then if, while stopping and
smoking, you had looked after him from afar, you would have greatly con-
soled us. But I know not where your thoughts were, to send a man back quite
alone amid so many dangers. I did not do that. 'Come, my nephew,' I said
to him whom you see before your eyes; 'follow me, I wish to bring thee to
thy own country, at the risk of my life.'" That is what was said by the second
collar, which he tied near the first.

The third showed that they had [90] added something of their own
to the presents that Monsieur the Governor had given to the captive whom
he had sent back to their country; and that those presents had been distributed to the Tribes who are their allies to arrest their hatchets, and to cause
the weapons and paddles to fall from the hands of those who were embarking
to go to war. He named all those Tribes.

The 4th present was to assure us that the thought of their people killed in war no longer affected them; that they cast their weapons under their
feet. "I passed," he said, "near the place where the Algonquins massacred us
last Spring. I saw the spot where the fight took place in which they captured
the two prisoners who are here. I passed by quickly; I did not wish to see my
people's blood that had been shed. Their bodies still lie in that place. I turned
away my eyes for fear of exciting my anger; then, striking the earth and listening, I heard the voice of my Forefathers massacred by the Alguonquins. When
they saw that my heart was capable of seeking revenge they called out to me
in a loving voice: 'My grandson, [91] my grandson, be good; do not get angry.
Think no longer of us for there is no means of withdrawing us from death.
Think of the living,—that is of importance; save those who still live from the
sword and fire that pursue them; one living man is better than many dead
ones.' After having heard those voices I passed on, and I came to you, to deliver those whom you still hold."

The fifth was given to clear the river, and to drive away the enemy's
canoes, which might impede navigation. He made use of a thousand gestures,
as if he had collected the waves and had caused a calm, from Quebec to the
Iroquois country.

The sixth was to smooth the rapids and waterfalls, or the strong cur-
rents, that occur in the rivers on which one must sail to reach their country.
"I thought that I would perish," he said, "in those boiling waters. This is to
appease them;" and with his hands and arms he smoothed and arrested the
torrents.

The seventh was to produce a profound calm on the great Lake Saint
[92] Louys that has to be crossed. "Here," he said, "is something to make it

smooth as ice, to appease the winds, and to allay the anger of the waves." Then, after having by his gestures rendered the route easy, he tied a collar of porcelain beads on the arm of a Frenchman, and pulled him straight across the square, to show that our canoes could go to their country without any difficulty.

The eighth performed the whole journey that had to be made on land. You would have said that he felled trees; that he lopped off branches; that he pushed back the bushes; that he put earth in the deepest holes. "There," said he, "is the road, quite smooth and quite straight." He bent toward the ground, looking to see whether there were any more thorns or bushes, and whether there were any mounds over which one might stumble in walking. "It is all finished. We can see the smoke of our villages, from Quebec to the extremity of our country. All obstacles are removed."

The ninth was to tell us that we would find fires all lighted in their houses; that we would not have the trouble of seeking for wood,—that [93] we would find some already cut; and that the fire would never go out, day or night,—that we would see its light, even in our own homes.

The tenth was given to bind us all very closely together. He took hold of a Frenchman, placed his arm within his, and with his other arm he clasped that of an Alguonquin. Having thus joined himself to them, "Here," he said, "is the knot that binds us inseparably; nothing can part us." This collar was extraordinarily beautiful. "Even if the lightning were to fall upon us, it could not separate us; for, if it cuts off the arm that holds you to us, we will at once seize each other by the other arm." And thereupon he turned around, and caught the Frenchman and the Alguonquin by their two other arms,—holding them so closely that he seemed unwilling ever to leave them.

The eleventh invited us to eat with them. "Our country is well stocked with fish, with venison, and with game; it is everywhere full of deer, of Elk, of beaver. Give up," said he, "those stinking hogs that run about among your houses, that eat nothing but filth; and come and eat good meat with us. The road is cleared; [94] there is no longer any danger." He accompanied his discourse with appropriate gestures.

He lifted the twelfth collar, to dispel the clouds in the air, so that all might see quite plainly that our hearts and theirs were not hidden; that the Sun and the truth might light up everything.

The thirteenth was to remind the Hurons of their good will. "It is five days ago," he said,—that is to say, five years,—"since you had a pouch filled with porcelain beads and other presents, all ready to come and seek for peace. What made you change your minds? That pouch will upset, the presents will fall out and break, they will be dispersed; and you will lose courage."

The fourteenth was to urge the Hurons to make haste to speak,—not to be bashful, like women; and, after taking the resolution to go to the Iroquois country, to pass by that of the Alguonquins and of the French.

The fifteenth was to show that they had always desired to bring back Father le Jogues and Father Bressani; that they had thought that Father le Jogues had been stolen from them, and that they had given Father [95] Bressani to the Dutch because he had desired it. "If he had had patience, I would have brought him back. How can I know now where he is? Perhaps he is dead; perhaps he is drowned. It was not our intention to put him to death. If François Marguerie and Thomas Godefroy," he added, "had remained in our country, they would be married by this time; we would be but one Nation, and I would be one of you." When Father le Jogues heard this discourse, he said with a smile: "The stake was all prepared; had not God preserved me, they would have put me to death a hundred times. This good man says whatever pleases him." Father Bressani told us the same thing on his return.

The sixteenth was to receive them in this country when they came to it, and to protect them; to stay the hatchets of the Alguonquins and the cannons of the French. "When we brought back your prisoners, some years ago, we thought that we were your friends, and we heard arquebus and cannon shots whistling on all sides of us. That frightened us; we withdrew; and, as we have courage for war, we took the resolution to give proofs of it the following Spring; [69 i.e., 96] we appeared in your land, and captured Father le Jogues, with some Hurons.

The seventeenth present was the very collar that Honatteniate wore in his country. This young man was one of the two prisoners last captured. His mother, who had been Father Jogues's aunt in the Iroquois country, sent his collar for him who had given her son his life. When the good woman learned that the good Father whom she called her Nephew was in this country, she greatly rejoiced, and her son still more so; for he always seemed sad until Father Jogues came down from Montreal when he commenced to breathe freely and be in good spirits.

When this great Iroquois had said all that is mentioned above, he added: "I am going to spend the remainder of the summer in my country in games, in dances, in rejoicing for the good of peace; but I fear that, while we dance, the Hurons will come to taunt and importune us." That is what occurred at that assembly. Every one admitted that this man was impassioned and eloquent. I gathered only some disconnected fragments, taken from the [97] mouth of the interpreter who spoke only in a desultory manner and did not follow the order observed by the Barbarian.

He sang some songs between his gifts; he danced for joy; in a word, he showed himself to be a very good Actor, for a man who has learned but what nature has taught him, without rule and without precept. The conclusion was that the Iroquois, the French, the Alguonquins, the Hurons, the Montagnais, and the Attikamegues all danced and rejoiced with much gladness.

On the following day, Monsieur the Governor gave a feast to all belonging to those Nations who were at three rivers, to exhort them all together and to banish all distrust that might set them at variance. The Iroquois manifested their satisfaction in every way; they sang and danced according to their custom, and Kiotsaeton strongly urged the Alguonquins and Hurons to obey Onontio, and to follow the intentions and the thoughts of the French.

On the fourteenth of the same month, Monsieur the Governor replied to the presents of the Iroquois by fourteen gifts, all of which had their meanings and [98] which carried their own messages. The Iroquois accepted them all with great marks of satisfaction, which they manifested by three loud cries, uttered at the same time from the depths of their chests, at each word or at each present that was given them. Thus was peace concluded with them, on condition that they should commit no act of hostility against the Hurons, or against the other Nations who are our allies, until the chiefs of those Nations who were not present had treated with them.

When this matter had been brought to a happy conclusion, Pieskaret arose and made a present of some furs to the Ambassadors, exclaiming that it was a rock or a tombstone that he placed on the grave of those who had been killed in the last fight, so that their bones might no longer be disturbed; and that the remembrance of what had happened might be forgotten, and revenge might no longer be thought of.

Then Noël Negabamat arose; he laid down in the middle of the square five great Elk skins. "There," he said to the Iroquois, "is something wherewith to cover your feet and your legs, lest you might hurt them on your return journey, if any stone should remain in the road [99] that you have made smooth." He also gave them five others to serve as shrouds for those who had been killed in the battle, and to allay the grief of their relatives and friends, who could not bear to have them left unburied. He said, moreover, that as he and his people at Sillery were invited in heart with their elder brother Monsieur the Governor, they gave but one present with his. Finally three shots were fired from the cannon, to drive away the foul air of war, and to rejoice at the happy advent of peace.

Some time after this meeting, an ill-disposed Huron accosted the Iroquois Captain who had always been the agent and spokesman, and sought to inspire him with distrust of the French. But the Captain nobly replied to him in these terms: "My face is painted and daubed on one side, while the other is quite clean. I do not see very clearly on the side that is daubed over; on the other side my sight is good. The painted side is toward the Hurons, and I see nothing; the clean side is turned toward the French, and I see clearly, as in broad daylight." Having said this he remained silent; and that evil-minded man was covered with confusion.

[110 i.e., 100] Toward evening, Reverend Father Vimont the Superior of the Mission caused the Iroquois to be brought to our house, where he presented to them some small gifts; he gave them some petun, or tobacco, and to each of them a handsome calumet or pipe wherewith to smoke it. Kiotsae-ton thanked him very wittily: "When I left my country, I gave up my life and exposed myself to death, so that I am indebted to you for being still alive. I thank you that I still see the Sun; I thank you for having received me well; I thank you for having treated me well. I thank you for all the good conclu-sions to which you have come; all your words are very agreeable to us. I thank you for your presents; you have covered us from our feet to our heads. Only our mouth remained free and you have filled it with a fine calumet and have gladdened it with the flavor of a plant that is very pleasing to us. I therefore bid you adieu, but not for long; you will soon hear from us. Even if we are wrecked in the waters, even if we are quite submerged, I [101] think that the Elements will in some way bear witness to our countrymen of your kind deeds; and I am convinced that some good genius has gone before us, and that our countrymen already have a foretaste of the good news that we are going to bring them."

On Saturday, the fifteenth, they started from three Rivers. Monsieur the Governor gave them two young French lads, both to help them to take back their canoes and their presents, and to manifest the confidence that he had in those people.

When the Captain Kiotsaeton saw that his people had embarked, he raised his voice, and said to the French and to the Savages who were on the banks of the great river: "Adieu my brothers; I am one of your relatives. I am going to carry back good news to our country." Then, turning to Monsieur the Governor, "Onontio, thy name shall be great throughout the earth; I did not think that I would take back my head that I had risked,—I did not think that it would go forth from your doors; and I am going back loaded with honor, with gifts, and with kindness. My brothers," speaking to the Savages, "obey [102] Onontio and the French. Their hearts and their thoughts are good; re-main united with them and accommodate yourselves to their customs. You will soon have news from us." The Savages replied by a fine salvo of musketry, and the Fort fired a canon shot. Thus ended their Embassy. May God cause all this to succeed for his greater glory.

CONTINUATION OF THE TREATY OF PEACE

To CONCLUDE and to secure peace in this new world, it was necessary that the delegates of the Iroquois, those of the Hurons, and the principal Captains of three or four Alguonquin tribes, should meet all together at some place with Monsieur the Governor; in order, too, that all these Nations,—who speak three or four different languages, whose dispositions are so distinct one from another, and who for so many years [103] have been eating, devouring, and burning each other like madmen,—should perform an act of the utmost wisdom, and that so many inhuman barbarians should find enough gentleness to agree together. In a word, to make everything sure, it was necessary that each should visit the others in their own country. All this seemed impossible to human skill. But, when God interposes in a matter, it cannot lack direction. The holy and pure souls who support these poor peoples by their prayers and by their vows have accomplished that great work. Never had all these Nations who are accustomed to come and see us every year, come down so late; and, if they had arrived sooner, they could not have gone up again,—for the Iroquois Ambassadors, who held the knot of this matter in their hands, were not here. We expected them every day, speculating from afar upon the reasons that could have caused so extraordinary a delay. Not a single canoe had come down, whether from the Alguonquins, the Nipisiriniens, or the Hurons, to bring us any news of what was going on in the upper country. Each one [104] spoke of it according to his own idea and in accordance with his own inclination. Some said that all the French who had gone up to the Huron country with our Fathers had been massacred; that the Devil had spoken to some Savages, and that consequently we need not expect any news from those countries. Others, who were more inclined to take a favorable view of the matter, conjectured that these tribes would come down in great numbers, and that it required a great deal of time to assemble them. Meanwhile, the season was passing away, and our doubts were about to change to despair, when all of a sudden we saw upon the river saint Lawrence sixty Huron canoes, laden with French, with Savages, and with furs. Father Hierosme Lallemant—whose arrival had been expected and desired for a whole year and more—was in this fine Company, which greatly rejoiced all who had at heart the welfare of the country and the salvation of these peoples. The French soldiers whom the Queen had sent out last year came back in good health, better supplied with virtue and with the knowledge of Christian truths than when they had embarked [105] to leave France. The principal Captains of the Hurons brought back one of the two Iroquois whom they had taken prisoners in the previous year, near Richelieu, with the intention of presenting him to Monsieur the Governor; this they did, as we shall see. These Captains had orders from the whole of their country to enter into full negotiations for peace and to follow the judgment of Onontio. At the same time, the Alguonquins of the upper Tribes arrived, and so opportunely that one would have said that some higher power had sent workmen to make them appear at an appointed spot. All this happened at three Rivers, where only the Iroquois were wanting, who had given their word that they would be there in a short time. Had they delayed but a few days, this great concourse of Savages—Attikamegues, Montagnais, Island Alguonquins and those of the Iroquet Tribe, and others, Hurons—would soon have been dispersed and scattered, without any hope that we could again assemble them together for a long time. But God took pleasure in making them come, one after another, at the most opportune time that could have been chosen. The Montagnais (106) arrived there about the end of August; some Alguonquins came shortly afterward. The Hurons landed on the tenth of September; the Island Savages and other tribes came down two or three days before. Monsieur the Governor came up on the twelfth of the same month. They waited only for the Iroquois delegates. Finally, on the fifteenth, a canoe appeared, bearing five men of that Nation, who assured us that the presents of Onontio had been taken to their country for the confirmation of the peace, and that in a few days we should see some Ambassadors delegated to bring him word to that effect. In fact, on the seventeenth of the same month, we saw four of them,—one of whom delivered a harangue on the bank of the river, according to their custom,—causing joy to all the French and to more than four hundred Savages of various tribes who were then at three Rivers. Monsieur the Governor perceived them from afar, and sent a squad of soldiers to meet them and to prevent disorder. The soldiers formed in two lines and the Iroquois passed through them without being impeded by a large number [107] of persons who gazed at them on all sides. They rested for the remainder of the day, and a council was held on the morrow in the same manner that I have related in the previous Chapter. It is needless for me to repeat so often that words of importance in this country are presents. Suffice it to say that, as he who harangued gave no presents, he spoke in these terms:

"I have no voice; do not listen to me. I speak not; I hold in my hand only a paddle to bring you back a Frenchman in whose mouth is the message from all our country." He spoke of the Frenchman whom I have mentioned above, who had been taken prisoner with Father le Jogues, to whom the Iroquois had confided their presents,—that is to say, their words. This Frenchman drew out eighteen presents, all consisting of porcelain beads, of which he gave this explanation:

The first said that Onontio had a voice of thunder, that he made himself heard everywhere, and that at the sound of his words the whole Iroquois country had thrown away their weapons and their hatchets,—but so far beyond the Sky that there were no arms in the world long enough to draw them back from there.

[108] The second said that, as the arms were beyond the sight of men, they ought to visit each other without fear while they enjoyed the sweets of peace.

At the third present, "Here," he said, representing the Iroquois, "is a mat or bed on which you can lie softly when you come to our country; for, as we are brothers, we would be ashamed if we did not treat you according to your deserts."

At the 4th, "It is not enough to have a good bed; the nights are cold; here is something with which to light a good fire, and to keep yourselves warm." Observe, in passing, that the Savages usually sleep close to the fire.

At the fifth, "Of what use would it be to have a good bed and to lie warmly covered on it if you were not well fed? This present assures you that you will be feasted there, and will find the pot boiling on your arrival." He spoke always to the French.

At the sixth, "Here is a little ointment to heal the wounds which have been inflicted on the feet of the French, while they walked in their country, by stumbling against the stones or the roots that are very often found there."

[109] At the 7th, he said that, from the place where they leave the water to take to the land, there was a distance of fully thirty leagues to be gone over before reaching their villages, and that all the baggage had to be carried on foot; that, as the French had had some difficulty, this present would slightly relieve their shoulders that were chafed by the weight of their packs.

At the 8th, "This is to assure the French that, if they wish to marry in this country, they will find wives here, since we are their friends and allies."

At the 9th, as the Alguonquins had stated, at the first journey of the Iroquois, that they could not say anything positive during the absence of the chief men of their Nation, this present was given that all might speak, and that they might not cast the blame from one to the other, but clearly declare their presents.

At the 10th, "This," said he who explained them, "is to make the Hurons speak, and to draw their sentiments from the depth of their hearts."

The eleventh present said that the Iroquois chiefs did nothing but smoke in their country, and that their calumets were always in their mouths. They wished to say that they awaited the word of the Alguonquins [110] and of the Hurons.

At the 12th, they said that the souls of their relatives who had been killed in war had withdrawn so far into the center of the earth that they could never think of them again, — that is to say, that they had wiped out vengeance from their hearts.

At the 13th, they obeyed the voice of Monsieur the Governor, who had ordered that hostilities be suspended, and that the hatchets be hidden. For that reason, they had passed the summer in dancing and feasting, without thinking of war.

At the 14th, they wished to know as soon as possible if they should continue their dances; and, consequently, they desired that the Alguonquins and the Hurons should hasten to speak,–that is to say, to carry presents to their country,–if they wished for peace.

The 15th was to lessen the fatigues of the French who had been in their country, who had used much diligence and had taken much trouble to bring news from the Iroquois to Onontio.

The 16th begged Onontio to have a woman of the Iroquois country sent back to it, who had been taken in war by the Alguonquins and given to the [111] French. This woman was taken to France some years ago and, after having been instructed and baptized, she died at the Convent of the Carmelites of Paris with evident marks of salvation, as has been stated in the previous Relations.

The 17th begged Onontio to sound the Hurons and Alguonquins, and get them to say clearly what their opinion was respecting peace or war.

The 18th was an excuse for not having brought back a little Frenchman whom they still detain in their country. "He is not a prisoner," he said, "he will return with those who shall bear the word of the Alguonquins and Hurons."

When these presents had been made, the chief man among the Iroquois arose, and, drawing from his pouch some presents of porcelain beads, he spoke in these terms:

At the first present,–which he held in his hands, and showed to the whole assembly, while he walked about the square,–he said that his country was full of Hurons and of Alguonquin women (for, as regards the Alguonquin men, they never spared their lives); that, however, those men and [112] women were seated on logs or on stumps of trees outside of their villages,–that is to say, they were not detained, and were all ready to return to their country like the dried trees on which they sat, which have no roots and can easily be removed.

At the 2nd present, he said that the little Huron girl called Therese– who had been captured just after she had left the Seminary of the Ursulines, while she was being taken to her own country–was quite ready to be delivered up; and that, if the Hurons joined in the peace, she would return with them, if she wished; if not, that they would keep her as a child brought up by the hand of the French, in order to prepare their food when they went to their own country.

The 3rd meant that all the gifts that Monsieur the Governor had given to the first Ambassadors had been carried, according to his orders, to all the Tribes who are allied to them. He named all these.

At the 4th, he said that Onontio had given birth to Ononjote–this is a village that is allied to them–but that, as it was still only a child, it could not speak; that, if Monsieur the Governor took care of it, it would grow and speak. [113] He meant that the present made to that village was a small one for negotiating an important peace, and that it must be increased, in order to get their promise. When this discourse was ended, the Hiroquois began to sing and to dance. He took a Frenchman on one side, an Algonquin and a Huron on the other; and, holding one another by the arms, they danced in time, and sang in a loud voice a song of peace which they uttered from the depths of their chests.

After this dance, a Huron Captain named Jean Baptiste Atironta, a good Christian, arose and harangued loudly and resolutely. "It is done," he said; "we are brothers. The conclusion has been reached; now we all are relatives,—Hiroquois, Hurons, Algonquins, and French; we are now but one and the same people. Betray no one," he said to the Hiroquois. "As for us, know that we have sound hearts." "I hear thee," replied the Hiroquois; "thy word is good; thou wilt find me true." Then, raising the last present, he exclaimed, "All the country that lies between us is full of Bears, of Deer, of Elk, of Beaver, and of numerous other animals. For my part, I am blind; I hunt at haphazard; when I have killed [114] a Beaver, I think that I have secured a great prize. But you," speaking of the Algonquins, "who are clear-sighted, you have but to throw a javelin, and the animal falls. This present invites you to hunt, we shall benefit by your skill; we shall roast the animals on the same spit, and we shall eat on one side, and you on the other."

An Algonquin replied to this: "I can no longer speak; my heart is too full of joy. I have large ears and so many good words crowd in there that they drown me in pleasure. It is true that I am but a child. It is Onontio who has great words in his mouth; he it is who makes the earth, and who rejoices all men."

At the conclusion of this council, Monsieur the Governor caused these three Nations to be thanked for the good words that they had given, exhorting them to remain firm in their purposes, and assuring them that he would always be their friend and faithful relative.

OF THE LAST MEETING HELD FOR THE PEACE

ON THE TWENTIETH of the same month of September, the last meeting was held between the French, the Algonquins,—who comprise several petty Tribes,—the Hurons, and the Hiroquois. Here, in a few words, are all the most remarkable things that occurred.

When Monsieur the Chevalier de Montmagny had received all the presents mentioned in the foregoing Chapter, he had them divided into three portions, in accordance with the usages of these peoples; and, after having made his Interpreter speak, he offered one portion to the Hurons, another portion to the Algonquins, while the third was for the French. Observe, in passing, that it was necessary to speak in four different languages,—in French, in Huron, in Algonquin, and in Hiroquois; we have here Interpreters of all those languages. When these gifts had been presented, Monsieur [116] the Governor gave two others to the Hiroquois,—one to wipe away the tears of the relatives of the Hiroquois woman whom they had asked for, and who had died in France; the other that her bones might be laid to rest in her own country, or that she might be brought back to life, by making some other woman bear her name. Moreover, he also gave two others to the Hurons and to the Algonquins, to invite them to express their thoughts freely with reference to the peace; for it was he, properly speaking, who was the author of it and who procured it for these peoples.

At this speech, a Huron Captain arose and said that, before replying to the words of Onontio, he wished, on behalf of all his country, to make him a present of a Hiroquois prisoner whom he had expressed a desire to have in the previous year. He therefore took this captive with one hand, and with the other he held a branch of Porcelain on a stick;[24] and, walking across the square, he brought the poor Hiroquois to the feet of Monsieur the Governor, with this Procelain, that represented his bonds, the mark of his captivity.

Monsieur the Governor accepted the prisoner, and had him taken at once, with [117] his bond of Porcelain beads, to the quarter where the Hiroquois were seated,—giving him his liberty, and placing him in the hands of his Countrymen. This young warrior showed sufficiently by his countenance that he felt much pleasure at seeing himself gently led toward his Captain, after having escaped the fire and the teeth of his enemies, who had become his friends.

This ceremony over, the Huron Captain replied to the summons of Monsieur the Governor by fourteen presents, which he gave to the Hiroquois, and of which the following is an explanation. These presents consisted of Beaver skins and Porcelain beads.

At the first, "Here," said he, "are the bonds of the prisoner who escaped from our hands last Autumn." You must know, in passing, that the Hurons had taken three Hiroquois near Richelieu; that they had given one of them to the Algonquins, who was afterward handed over to Monsieur the Governor; and had taken the two others to their own country. One of these two captives escaped on the way, but he died in the woods of cold, hunger, and exposure. He belonged to a village called Ononjoté, that was angered to the last degree against the Hurons; [118] for that nation had, in a battle, exterminated nearly all the men of that village, which was compelled to send to the Hiroquois—who are called Agnierronons, and with whom we have made the peace—for men to marry the girls, and the women who were left without

husbands, so that their tribe might not become extinct. That is why the Hiroquois call that village their Child; and, because Monsieur the Governor had
sent them presents, and made peace with those who had repeopled their village, they also called him its Father. Let us return to our subject, if you please.
The Huron Captain therefore offered the bonds of the prisoner who had escaped, as a token that they would not have put him to death, and that they
had intended to set him at liberty.

At the second present, "This," said he, "is to carry back the bones of
your child to his country." It is the custom of the Hurons to remove the flesh
from the bones of their people, and to place them with those of their relatives, in whatever quarter of the world they may die.

At the third, "Here is the bond that will bind those bones together,
and enable you to carry them more easily." In a word, he wished [119] to con-
sole them and to wipe away their tears, according to the fashion of the Barbarians, who give presents to the relatives of their deceased friends.

At the fourth, he said, "This is a token that we are friends; this present
will make a road from your villages to ours."

The fifth opened the gates of their villages and the doors of their
houses.

The sixth invited them to go and see some Hiroquois prisoners whom
the Hurons detained in their country. This was asking them to bring presents
so as to go and claim them in safety.

At the seventh,—as the Hiroquois had said at the previous assembly
that Ononjoté was their child, and the child of Monsieur the Governor and
that it could not yet speak,—"Here," said the Captain, "is something to make
a cradle for it," meaning that the Hurons wished for peace with that village.

The eighth was given to cause all the weapons and all the hatchets
that might still be in the hands of the Iroquois, to drop.

The ninth was to snatch their shields from their backs, where they
generally carry them, moving them backward and forward as [120] they please
in battle.

The tenth was to lower their war Standard.

The eleventh, to stop the reports of their arquebuses.

The twelfth, to wash away the paint from their faces. These Savages
are accustomed, when they go to war, to paint themselves in various colors,
and to oil or grease their heads and faces. "Here," said he, "is something to
remove the stains from your faces and your eyes, so that the day may be quite
fine and serene."

The thirteenth was to break the kettle in which they boiled the Hurons whom they took in war, in order to eat them.

The fourteenth asked that a mat—that is to say, a bed or a lodging—be
prepared for the Hurons who would soon go to the Hiroquois country.

"All these presents," he added, "are nothing; we have many others in our country, which await you."

When the Hurons had replied to the demand of Monsieur the Governor, and had manifested by all these presents that they desired peace, an Algonquin arose and gave [121] some presents, of which the following is the meaning:

At the first, he threw down a bundle of Beaver skins. "This is to show who I am, and to what nation I belong,—I who live in traveling houses built of small pieces of bark." Thus they distinguish the Wandering Algonquins from the Hurons, who are sedentary.

At the second, "This present will stop your complaints; it will subdue your anger, and will cause our rivers and yours to wash away the blood that has been shed by Algonquins and by Hiroquois."

"This third present will give us free entrance to your houses, after breaking down the gates of your villages."

At the fourth, "Here is something wherewith to smoke with one another, both Hiroquois and Algonquins, in the same pipe, as friends do who use tobacco together."

"The fifth will make us sail in the same ship or in the same canoe; so that, as we shall be but one people, but one village, one house, one Calumet, and one canoe will be needed. The remainder of our words, or of our presents, will be carried to your country." Thus he ended his speech.

[122] Monsieur the Governor afterward made the interpreters speak, offering a present that assured the Hiroquois that he would see that those two great nations kept their word.

He also gave another present to be carried to the village of Ononjoté, so as to give news to his child (making use of their own terms), that he desired to make the whole earth beautiful, and to smooth it so that one might walk everywhere without stumbling, and without meeting any misadventure.

When the Hiroquois Captain had received these presents, he arose and, looking at the Sun and then at the entire assembly, he said: "Onontio, thou hast dispersed the clouds; the air is serene, the Sky shows clearly; the Sun is bright. I see no more trouble; peace has made everything Calm; my heart is at rest; I go away very happy."

Onontio caused all these nations to be exhorted to remain constant and faithful; then he broke up the meeting, and on the following day he gave a feast, in the fashion of the Savages, to more than four hundred people.

"Things are going well," said all the guests; "we eat all together, and [123] we have but one dish." Reverend Father Hierosme Lalemant who had started from the Huron country with the fear of meeting Hiroquois, watched them at these assemblies with eyes full of joy. He was delighted to see so miraculous a change, and praised God for it both in public and in private.

Finally, on the 23rd of September, these Hiroquois Ambassadors, accompanied by two Frenchmen, two Algonquins, and two Hurons, returned to their own country, leaving among our Savages, who were now their allies, three men of their nation as hostages, or rather as pledges, of their friendship.

Praised forever be the God of Gods; may his Name be glorified in all the Countries of the Earth. If these Barbarians—who, because they know not God, have hardly any equity or stability—do not disturb this peace,—which is concluded, as far as the French are concerned; and in a very advanced state, as regards the Savages,—it will be possible to go and suffer for *JESUS CHRIST* in a great many nations.

Jesuit Relations 27:247–305

[Ed. Note: A supplemental account of certain secret proceedings of the treaty was inserted into the Journal of the Jesuit Fathers for January 1646. Written in Latin, its report is as follows.]

"Monsieur the Governor . . . himself disclosed to us [Fathers Vimont and de Quen] the whole matter, thus: Last summer, when the Annieronon [Mohawk] envoys came with Cousture to treat for peace, after they had discussed and transacted many things in public, they demanded—their leader being a man named *le crochet*—that Monsieur the Governor would consent to talk with them in a private conference. This man thought that a considerable present should be made to Monsieur the Governor, that, if he desired peace for both himself and the Hurons, he should abandon the Algonquins without shelter. When Onontio [the Governor] was informed of this, he would not even look at any such present, nor would he suffer it to be delivered; and he said that the thing was impossible. Le crochet was chagrined at this repulse, and from that time the peace seemed to be endangered. Monsieur the Governor saw this; and both Father Vimont, the superior, and Father le Jeune thought that the difficulty might be smoothed over. In a 2nd private conference,—at which, as at the former, were present Monsieur the Governor, le Crochet, and Cousture,—Monsieur the Governor said that there were two kinds of Algonquins,—one like ourselves, recognized as Christians; the other, unlike us. Without the former, it is certain, we do not make a peace; as for the latter, they themselves are the masters of their own actions, nor are they united with us like the others. This, as uttered by Monsieur the Governor, was, and perhaps for a worse reason, thus repeated by the envoy to his own people,—which, being understood by all the Annieronons in his country, was made public by such of them as left it, *sed merito*, denied by the french." *Jesuit Relations* 28:315.

SECTION III

REFERENCE MATERIALS

8

Descriptive Treaty Calendar

FOLLOWING is a select list of written proceedings of negotiations involving Iroquois Indians, 1613–1913. It demonstrates that the Iroquois were treating with many different nations on various fronts through long periods of time. The calendar is unique to this volume.

The selection has been dictated to some extent by the availability of documentation. Intertribal treaties were rarely recorded, so the incessant negotiations of the Iroquois with western Indians usually can be inferred only from what was reported back to Albany or Montreal or Philadelphia. Differences in legal outlook between the English and the French caused the former to make treaties for cessions of Indian lands though the latter assumed that "sovereignty" had conferred right to territory and merely negotiated, for the sake of expediency, for permission to occupy and build on it. Such permission, as the French seem to have thought, did not require full-scale treaties. Much negotiation by both the French and the English was conducted within Iroquoia and reported only in brief summaries of the results. The French were especially adept at going into Iroquoia for this purpose, in the persons of missionaries as well as agents appointed by the government; unfortunately, their immense influence over the Iroquois, especially after 1701, was usually exercised directly rather than through formal treaty procedures, and is therefore underrepresented in our list. One must bear in mind also that traders, French and British, frequently acted in semi-official capacities and almost never recorded their intrigues.

This calendar may be regarded therefore as a slightly skewed skeleton outline of Iroquois diplomatic history. Although solemn, fully ritualized treaty proceedings are at its core, other recorded "councils" and "conferences" have been included for their illumination of important negotiations leading up to, and following, the main events. The significance of a "council" or "conference" was often as great as that of a "treaty." Because the formal gradation between such terms may be projections into the past of modern notions, the words have been treated, more or less, as synonyms herein. Difference in importance should be inferred only after careful study of the events.

The calendar is meant to provide points of orientation rather than comprehensive spans of time for each negotiation. To help with orientation, a few events have been noticed that influenced Iroquois history without involving Iroquois participants. For brevity's sake, certain issues that arose constantly in negotiations have been mentioned only occasionally. The presence of French missionaries in Iroquois villages was regularly denounced by the English; the high prices of trade goods were just as regularly denounced by the Indians. These issues may be assumed to have been raised, either formally or in private conversations in almost every one of the councils of the colonial era. Rather than repeat them so often, the editors have chosen to summarize proceedings in such a way as to show the movement of events.

Iroquois treaty-making preceded the earliest documented negotiation with Europeans, and it is said that such intertribal treaties still are being made. The calendar's dates, to repeat, reflect available documentation.

The documents for these and many more treaty events are to be found in the Documentary History of the Iroquois archive at the Newberry Library, Chicago.

1613 A treaty of friendship may have been made between some Iroquois and a Dutch trader at "Tawagonshi." The authenticity of the sole document referring to this event is highly questionable. A photostatic copy is in the New York State Library, manuscripts division.

1624 Treaty of trade between Iroquois and New France.

1624 War between Mohawks and Mahicans who were aided by Fort Orange Dutch.

1628 Mohawk victory over Mahicans and Dutch, probably followed by an unrecorded agreement for Mohawk trading at Fort Orange.

1633 Treaty for trade between Iroquois and French.

1634 Mohawk truce with Canadian tribes.

1635 Council at Oneida pertaining to trade between Mohawks, Oneidas, Onondagas, and Dutch.

1643 Unrecorded treaty of trade and peace held in Mohawk country between Mohawks and Dutch. An "iron chain" of alliance between "all" the Dutch and the Mohawks was forged at this conference, which is substantiated by later references.

1645 July and September. Treaty at Three Rivers between Mohawks, French, Algonquins, and Hurons. See proceedings and analyses herein.

1645 July. Treaty at Fort Orange between Dutch governor Kieft and Mohawks and Mahicans.

1645 August. Treaty terminating war between the Manhattan Dutch and surrounding Algonquian tribes held at Fort Amsterdam in the presence of Mohawk ambassadors who had been asked by the Dutch to act as "mediators."

1649 A decisive attack by Mohawks and Senecas effected destruction of the Huron confederation.

1653 Peace treaty at Montreal between French and Iroquois, each of the Five Nations treating separately.

1657 or **1658** Treaty relations begun between Dutch and "Senecas" i.e., the undifferentiated "upper" Iroquois nations west of the Mohawks.

1659 Conference at the First Mohawk "Castle" (Kahnawakeh) between Mohawks and Dutch, renewing alliance made sixteen years earlier.

1660 Treaty at Esopus between Esopus Indians and Dutch "at the request and intercession of the Maquaas [Mohawks], Minquaas [Susquehannocks], Mohicans, and other chiefs."

1664 September. Surrender of New Netherland to the English. Founding of New York.

1664 September. Treaty of friendship, trade, and mutual aid between Mohawks, "Senecas," and English, at Albany (formerly Fort Orange).

1665 December. Conference at Quebec between the governor of New France and the Iroquois. Peace proposed by Onondaga chief Garakontié.

1666 January. Distrustful French attacked Mohawks.

1666 July. Confirmation by Oneidas and Mohawks (Oneidas speaking for Mohawks) of articles of peace negotiated with the French in 1665.

1666 September. Dutch at Albany forced Mahicans to be at peace with Mohawks.

1667 Council at Montreal between Iroquois and French after Prouville de Tracy's destruction of Mohawk villages. Also discussed was trade in the upper Great Lakes region.

1672 Dutch and English officials at Albany compelled Mahicans to keep peace with Mohawks.

1673 Ottawas and Iroquois negotiated for peace. Count Frontenac, governor general of new France, tried to discourage consummation of the treaty because he feared that it would result in diversion of Ottawa trade from the French.

1673–1674 Dutch reconquered New York and restored New Netherland, but the colony was returned to the English by the treaty of Westminster, February 1674.

1675 Spring. New York's governor Sir Edmund Andros renewed English protection for Mohawks and Mahicans, apparently separately.

1675 August. Andros journeyed to Mohawks' Third "Castle" (Tionondage) to treat with the Five Nations. Iroquois "submitted in an Extraordinary manner, with reiterated promises," according to Andros (no minutes of the proceedings have been found). Iroquois bestowed the title of "Corlaer" upon Andros and subsequent governors of New York.

ca. 1675 Treaty between Iroquois and Ottawas on border of Lake Ontario.

1677 February. Treaty at Shackamaxon [Philadelphia] between Iroquois, Susquehannocks, and Delawares, with participation of English magistrates of Upland [Chester, Pa.]. Most Susquehannocks then went to Iroquoia, some remaining with Delawares.

1677 April and May. First of the "silver" Covenant Chain treaties: multilateral negotiations involving New York and commissioners from Massachusetts and Connecticut on the one hand, and the Five Nations and "River" Indians of the Hudson valley. No minutes have been found; information is derived from references in other sources.

1677 July and August. Second "silver" Covenant Chain treaty. New York's governor and a commissioner representing Maryland and Virginia negotiated at Albany to end the war between the southern colonies and the Five Nations and Susquehannocks. In New York sources the Iroquois were the only Indian parties with formal standing. The Maryland copy of the treaty lists the Delawares also as a party.

1679 Treaty at Albany between the Five Nations and the colonies of New York, Maryland, and Virginia.

1681 New York amputated for the founding of Pennsylvania. Indians in the new colony's territory pass under its protection; it has no treaty relationship with the Iroquois.

1682 August. Peace treaty at Albany between Maryland and the Five Nations.

1682 September. Negotiations at Montreal between the Five Nations and the French.

1683 September. The Iroquois entrusted the Susquehanna valley to the protection of the governor of New York [Thomas Dongan] thereby forestalling William Penn's attempted purchase.

1684 July. Treaty at Albany between the Five Nations and the governors of New York and Virginia. The Iroquois equivocally stated that they were subjects of the English crown, but also a free people allying themselves as they preferred. This statement became the basis for the crown's claim to sovereignty.

1684 September. Treaty at La Famine between French governor La Barre and Onondaga chief Garangula [Otreouati]. La Barre had set out on an expedition of conquest, but after disease disabled his army he was forced to make a humiliating peace. Garangula co-opted New France into the Covenant Chain, but the French crown rejected the membership.

1685 August. Three chiefs of the Piscataway Indians of Maryland journeyed to Albany to make peace and ally themselves to the Covenant Chain.

1685 September. Treaty at Albany between New York's governor Dongan, Virginia's emissary colonel Byrd, and the Five Nations to regulate the passage of Iroquois war parties southward by realigning the Warriors' Path.

1686 May. Governor Dongan renewed the Covenant Chain in a treaty with the Five Nations at Albany.

1686 September. Governor Dongan told the Five Nations that the king of England had taken them as his "children and subjects." Among other business the Iroquois refused Dongan's "desire" for them to interfere with Pennsylvania's trade.

1686 August–September. Governor Dongan sent trading expeditions with Seneca escorts to Michilimackinac. These were captured by the French.

1687 July. French governor Denonville destroyed Seneca villages and proclaimed French sovereignty over the Iroquois.

1687 September. Treaty at Albany between governor Dongan and the Five Nations. Dongan rebuked them for treating with the French, and notified them of a new peace between France and England.

1688 February. Conference at Albany between governor Dongan and the Five Nations.

1688 June. Treaty at Montreal between governor Denonville and three Iroquois nations the Onondagas, Cayugas, and Oneidas. The Indians declared themselves sovereign in their own lands and expressed a desire to be neutral between France and Britain.

1688 September. Edmund Andros, as governor of the Dominion of New England, treated with the Five Nations at Albany. Against their objections, he addressed them as "children," instead of "brethren," and insisted that they call him "father."

1689 May. England declared war on France: The War of the League of Augsburg, known in America as King William's War.

1689 May. Treaty at Albany between Mohawks and Connecticut. Covenant Chain renewed.

1689 June. Overthrow of New York's government by followers of Jacob Leisler.

1689 June. Treaty at Albany of mayor and magistrates with chiefs of Five Nations, Covenant renewed. Iroquois demanded use of "brethren" language. They announced intention of warring against the French.

1689 ca. July. Abenakis treated with Mohawks somewhere in Iroquoia. They proposed an alliance to fight against the English. Events show this was rejected.

1689 July. Iroquois attacked Lachine (near Montreal).

1689 Summer. Senecas made peace with the Ottawas.

1689 September. Agents from Massachusetts Bay, New Plymouth, and Connecticut treated with the Five Nations at Albany. They requested Iroquois alliance in war against the "Eastern Indians." Publicly the chiefs demurred. Privately they assured the colonial agents of their intention to march against Pennacooks and Abenakis.

1690 January. Messengers from Albany treated with the Five Nations at Onondaga. Ottawa peace confirmed by the whole League. Messengers from Canada's governor Frontenac invited the League to treat at Montreal, but were rebuffed. Alliance with the English reconfirmed.

1690 9 February. French troops and Indian allies attacked and destroyed Schenectady. Pursued by Mohawks on their retreat.

1690 25 February. Mohawk chiefs treated with mayor and officers of Albany, condoling losses and exhorting renewed belligerence against the French: "This is butt a beginning of the warr."

1691 June. Conference at Albany between New York and Oneidas, Onondagas, Cayugas, and Senecas.

1691 September. Negotiations at Albany between New York and Senecas and Mohawks.

1692 June. Conference at Albany between the Five Nations and New York's commander in chief, Major Richard Ingoldsby. Mutual exhortations to continue fighting against the French. Iroquois distressed because other colonies had not joined the fight.

1692 September and October. Shawnee emissaries requested permission from

New York to bring their people from the west to settle among the Mini-sinks. Peace treaty with the Iroquois required by New York after Iroquois protests. This done, permission granted. Shawnees joined the Covenant Chain.

1693 February. French attacked and destroyed three Mohawk villages. Pursued by New York's governor Benjamin Fletcher.

1693 25 February. Treaty at Albany between governor Fletcher and the Five Nations. Provision made for the Mohawks. Fletcher given title Cajenquiragoe, meaning Lord of the Great Swift Arrow, in recognition of his speedy pursuit of the French.

1693 June and July. Five Nations chiefs met with governor Fletcher at Albany to renew the Covenant Chain. They informed him of their intention to propose formal peace to the "Dionaondades" [Wyandot/Hurons] allied to the French. Fletcher tried, and failed, to stop informal communication between the Five Nations and New France's governor Frontenac who was trying to woo them away from New York. (During much of the war, Frontenac had been sending messages and wampum belts to the Five Nations in a continuing diplomatic campaign. Many Iroquois were inclined to respond favorably, and the belts were discussed in tribal councils, but information about the discussions is indirect.)

1694 February. Treaty at Albany between the Five Nations and Major Peter Schuyler and the magistrates. Onondaga chief Decanisora [Teganissorens] reported the peace belts received from governor Frontenac. Schuyler tried to forbid further communication with the French, but recognized the impossibility of enforcing the ban. A short truce proposed.

1694 May. Governor Fletcher met the Five Nations chiefs at Albany. Much strain over the issue of correspondence with Frontenac. Fletcher issued an ultimatum for the Iroquois to meet with him in 100 days to determine who was "for" him and who "against," with an apparent implication that he would regard the latter as enemies to be fought.

1694 August. At the term of Fletcher's 100-day ultimatum, the Five Nations chiefs met with him, governor Andrew Hamilton of the Jerseys, and agents from Massachusetts Bay and Connecticut. Fletcher spoke also for Pennsylvania, of which he was then governor as well as New York. Decanisora recited what happened in his negotiations with Frontenac. Much contention. Fletcher refused to treat on Frontenac's terms. Fletcher protected the Delaware Indians in Pennsylvania against Seneca demands for them to send warriors. Iroquois announced that they had made peace with western tribes.

1695 January. Frontenac sent messengers to Onondaga with an invitation for the Five Nations to treat in Canada. This was rejected.

1695 Spring. Renewal of hostilities between Iroquois and western tribes.

1695 August. Inconclusive meeting between governor Fletcher and the Five Nations at Albany.

1696 August. French destroyed Onondaga, but its people escaped.

1696 September–October. Governor Fletcher renewed the Covenant Chain with the Five Nations at Albany and gave them supplies. They complained because other English colonies were not helping. "We are become a small people and much lessened by the warr."

1697 September. Peace treaty of Ryswick between England and France. War continued between Five Nations and New France's Indian allies.

1698 June, July, August. Series of conferences at which the Iroquois proposed peace to the French.

ca. 1698–99 Iroquois abandoned Ontario after heavy defeats by western Indian allies of the French.

1669–1700 Winter. Western Indians proposed peace with free access for themselves to Albany's trade.

1689 February. Onondaga chief Decanisora informed the magistrates of Albany that Oneidas, Onondagas, and Cayugas intended to treat formally and openly with the governor of Canada.

1699 March. Four Iroquois nations, having considered a message from the French, summoned the Mohawks and Col. Peter Schuyler [Quider] and Major Dirk Wessells to a general council in April.

1699 April. New York's government sent emissaries to the general council at Onondaga with instructions to break off Iroquois negotiations with the French.

1699 August. New York's commissioners for Indian affairs rebuked the Iroquois because some of the latter had been to Pennsylvania to treat for trade "in breach of the Covenant Chain" that required them to trade only with New York.

1700 An intense series of negotiations took place involving the Iroquois, the English of New York, the French of Canada, and the Indian allies of the French.

1700 Early June. Delegates from three western tribes of the Ojibwa family came to Onondaga to treat for peace.

1700 28 June. Chiefs of the Christian Indians of Caughnawaga (Canada) came to Albany to negotiate trade.

1700 30 June. Chiefs of the Onondagas, Cayugas, and Senecas complained at Albany of the losses being sustained from attacks by western Indians instigated by the French. Senecas had lost 40 persons during the spring. Speaker Decanisora demanded action to give the Iroquois respite.

1700 18 July. Two Onondagas and four Senecas discussed peace proposals with governor de Calliére at Montreal.

1700 29 July. Sieurs de Maricour and de Joncaire and missionary Father Bruyas came to Onondaga with peace proposals from de Calliére.

1700 31 July. John Baptist van Eps, an emissary from Albany, arrived post haste to forbid negotiations with the French. He was answered equivocally by Decanisora.

1700 27–31 August. New York's governor Bellomont met with chiefs of the Five Nations at Albany, trying once more to prevent negotiations with the French. Failing in this, he obtained permission to build a fort in the Onondaga country.

1700 3 September. Nineteen Iroquois, representing all the Five Nations, accompanied de Maricourt, de Joncaire, and Bruyas to Montreal. Also present at the peace negotiations were chiefs of the Hurons, the Ottawas, the Abenakis, the Montagnais, and the Sault Indians. Preliminary articles of peace signed on the 8th.

1701 April. William Penn treated with the Indians of the lower Susquehanna and upper Potomac valleys to reserve their trade for Pennsylvanians and to confirm the cession to him of the Susquehanna valley by the Susquehannock Indians, made in September 1700. All this was subscribed by Ahookasoongh "brother to the Emperor" of the Five Nations, purportedly representing his brother. A "Chain of Friendship" declared.

1701 June. Emissaries of New France and New York in Onondaga at the same time. Decanisora acted as spokesman for the Five Nations.

1701 July. Newly arrived governor of New York John Nanfan met with chiefs of all Five Nations at Albany. Iroquois confessed inability to hinder the French from building a fort at Tioghsaghrondie or Wawyachtenok [Detroit]. Twenty sachems signed a "deed" to the king of England quitting "for ever" all the Five Nations' "right title and interest" to "all that vast Tract of land or Colony called Canagariarchio" 800 miles in length and 400 in breadth and including Detroit, the Iroquois having become "the true owners of the same by conquest." (The Iroquois understood this as putting the land under protection of the English crown.)

1701 Late summer or early fall. At a council at Onondaga, the Five Nations received an invitation from western Algonquins ["Waganhaes"] to treat for peace at Detroit.

1701 August–September. General peace confirmed at Montreal between the Five Nations and the French and their Indian allies. The treaty stipulated Iroquois neutrality between the French and the English.

1701 4 May. War declared by the European Grand Alliance, including Great Britain, upon France: The War of the Spanish Succession.

1702 July. A grand council at Albany, including Five Nations, Hudson "River Indians," Tightwees [Miamis], and Dionondadies [Wyandot/Hurons] from the region of Detroit, and the newly arrived governor of New York, Lord Cornbury. Five Nations concerned about rumors of Anglo-French war. Western Indians interested in trade. Cornbury renewed the Covenant Chain.

1703 July. A party of Schaghticoke Indians ("River Indians") informed the magistrates of Albany of their intention of settling in the Mohawk country. Opposed by the magistrates, they went anyway "in a Passion."

1703 November. The Five Nations met at Quebec with the new French governor general, the Marquis de Vaudreuil. Agreement on both sides that they should continue neutral between Britain and France.

1704 June. News from Onondaga arrived in Albany that "Far Indians" were warring with Indians in the vicinity of Detroit, and that the latter had come to Onondaga to request aid. Further, that Five Nations Indians who had previously settled near "Cadarachqui" (Fort Frontenac/Kingston, Ontario), had withdrawn to Iroquois country because of fear of the Waganhaes (probably Mississaugas) coming in "who now consist in much greater number than those of the five nations."

1704 ca. October. Onondagas and perhaps others of the Five Nations treated and traded at Philadelphia against the wishes of Yorkers.

1705 August. Four Iroquois nations met at Montreal with governor Vaudreuil. (Only Senecas are identified.) They demanded that he pacify the western Indians who were attacking them, and that they be given restitution for losses sustained in such attacks.

1706 June. Conference at Philadelphia between Pennsylvania council and Conestogas, Shawnees, and Conoys. Conestoga chief spoke also for the Nanticokes who feared danger from the Five Nations. Shawnees also apprehensive.

1706 September. Council at Albany between Lord Cornbury and the Five Nations.

1706 Before November. Governor Vaudreuil met at Montreal with Iroquois representatives, unidentified except Senecas. They complained of Ottawa depredations and demanded that he join with them to punish the Ottawas. According to his report, he persuaded them to "let go the hatchet."

1707 September. Lord Cornbury met the Five Nations at Albany. Iroquois suspected that Virginia, Maryland, and Pennsylvania had withdrawn from the Covenant Chain. Why had they not renewed their alliance in it?

1707 Great numbers of Iroquois warred against the "Flatheads" [Catawbas] in the Carolina back country.

1708 July, August, September. A series of disappointing conferences at Albany. Lord Cornbury waited eleven days in July for the Five Nations chiefs, then returned to New York City, after appointing a new meeting in September. He failed to appear then when the chiefs waited for him. They had news about negotiations with western tribes for trade, among other business, but received no satisfactory answers from the commissioners of Indian affairs. Much disgruntlement.

1709 Spring. A series of informal conferences regarding the expected arrival at Albany of delegates from the "Far Indians," who wanted to treat for trade. These were delayed by Joncaire's assassination of their guide Montour, but chiefs of the Mississaugas and "Nequequents" came to Albany mid-May. Others came early in June.

1709 The English planned an invasion of Canada. New York council ordered the Indians of New York and New Jersey to supply warriors. Minisinks refused: "only Squas and no fighting men." Senecas did not respond. Other four Iroquois nations met with New York's governor Richard Ingoldsby at Albany, 15 July 1709, and promised assistance, but the expedition aborted.

1709 Summer. Senecas treated for peace with the Ottawas.

1710 June. A general council of the Five Nations at Onondaga to ratify the treaty with the Ottawas and negotiate trade. Ottawa chiefs and two invited emissaries from New York present. Ottawas and Senecas journeyed on to Albany where the commissioners of Indian affairs accepted the Ottawas in the Covenant Chain.

1710 June. Tuscarora chiefs met with Senecas, Conestogas, Shawnees, and Pennsylvanians at Conestoga to request refuge and peace for the Tuscaroras in Pennsylvania. Answer referred to Five Nations.

1710 July. Decanisora led chiefs of the Five Nations to Conestoga for a treaty ostensibly with only the Indians resident nearby, but also, by subterfuge, with the governor of Pennsylvania. Tuscaroras were offered a welcome. Subterfuge was necessary because of New York's continued hostility to separate treaties between the Five Nations and other colonies.

1710   July. New York Commissioners of Indian affairs met with Mohawk chiefs at Schenectady to notify of intended settlement at Schoharie. Mohawks protested that land had been acquired fraudulently and the deed voided.

1710   August. New York's governor Robert Hunter renewed the Covenant Chain with the Five Nations at Albany. Unconsummated negotiations with Mohawks for Schoharie lands. Hunter requested end to Iroquois war with Catawbas.

1711   January. Five Nations chiefs came to Albany to inform the commissioners of Indian affairs of their intention to war against "Waganhaes" in revenge for the latters' killing their people. (Term is ambiguous and circumstances murky; these Waganhaes may or may not have been the Ottawas.)

1711   Spring. Charles Le Moyne de Longeuil persuaded the Onondagas to let him build a blockhouse in their country.

1711   May. Colonel Peter Schuyler, at Onondaga, persuaded the Indians to let him tear down Longeuil's blockhouse.

1711   May. Six "Far Indians" from Detroit region came to Albany to renew negotiations begun in 1709.

1711   The English renewed their plan to invade Canada.

1711   June. The Five Nations chiefs met with governor Hunter at Albany. In public they argued for peace between England and France and neutrality for themselves. This because they had given assurances to that effect to French agents at meetings in Onondaga. In private they told Hunter "that the French always dissemble with them and they therefore returned them the same Conduct," and promised to obey his orders. Hunter sent an order to Pennsylvania chiefs to march with their fighting men to join the Five Nations. With Pennsylvania council's tacit approval, these Indians stayed home. Other New York Indians recruited by Hunter and the commissioners for Indian affairs.

1711   August. Iroquois and other Indians marched to Albany to join the Canada campaign, but Decanisora secretly informed Canadian governor Vaudreuil of the campaign plans. As in 1709, the campaign aborted.

1711   October. Five Nations met at Albany with governor Hunter and lieutenant general Francis Nicholson. (In September they had declared themselves so ashamed about the failure of the two Canada expeditions that "we must cover our Faces.") They advised Hunter to fortify his towns.

1711–13 The Tuscarora War in the south. Flight of many Tuscaroras to Pennsylvania.

1712 April. Governor Hunter sent a demand to Onondaga that the Five Nations "interpose their Interest and Authority" with the Tuscaroras to conclude peace with North Carolina, failing which the Five Nations were to join the attack upon the Tuscaroras. Iroquois agreed to try to make peace.

1712 May. Delawares conferred with Pennsylvanians at Whitemarsh while on their way to deliver presents to the Five Nations, as well as a belt entrusted to them eleven years previously by William Penn. ("Presents" lined through in the manuscript report, and "tribute" substituted for it.)

1712 May. Canadian Caughnawagas sent a belt to New York to request an open path between Albany and Canada.

1712 June. Peter Schuyler in Onondaga to assure Five Nations that Queen Anne acknowledged their ownership of land. Covenant Chain renewed. Schuyler reported back that the Iroquois complained of no answer to their offer to mediate the Tuscarora War. They complained also of high prices in trade.

1712 October. Delawares conferred with Pennsylvania council in Philadelphia on return from their negotiations with the Five Nations. They transmitted a message from the Senecas for free trade with Pennsylvania "for they had been ill used by those of Albany." An earlier message from Pennsylvania to the Five Nations had been intercepted by Albany to prevent such a trade.

1712 27 October. News arrived in New York of peace between England and France ending England's participation in War of the Spanish Succession.

1712 Outbreak of war between the Fox Indians at Detroit and the French and allied Indians, especially Potawatomies. Great slaughter of Foxes. About one hundred fled to refuge among the Senecas.

1713 11 April. Treaty of Utrecht signed between English and French. It declared the Five Nations to be "subjects" of Great Britain.

1713 7 May. New York council received a letter from governor of North Carolina reporting defeat of Tuscaroras and requesting that no "succour" be given refugees. Subsequently the council heard that Tuscaroras were coming "daily" among the Five Nations. Council wanted to stop this, but had no money for presents, and governor refused to treat without presents on grounds that this would be worse than no meeting.

1713 13 August. Mohawk chief Hendrick informed New Yorkers secretly that the Five Nations were to have a general council about "making Warr on her Majestys Subjects."

1713 September. Governor Hunter sent a three-man mission to Onondaga to renew the Covenant Chain. They formally announced the peace between England and France. Decanisora responded that the Iroquois expected that "the hatchet will be taken out of our hands in the same manner that it was delivered to us," i.e., by the governor personally, in a formal treaty, with delivery of substantial presents.

1714 February. Nonbelligerent Tuscaroras treated with governor Spotswood of Virginia, agreeing to "submit to such forms of Government, and be obedient to such rules as the Governor of Virginia shall appoint." Correspondence with the Iroquois forbidden.

1714 ca. early June. A general council was held at Onondaga of the Five Nations and "all the Indians bordering upon New Jerseys, Pensilvania, Virginia and Maryland by Deputies." Highly secret; death to informers. Mohawk chief Hendrick reported it to New York's commissioners of Indians affairs, 22 June. The general council agreed to seek closer relations with the French.

1714 20 June. Five Nations chiefs conferred with New York's commissioners of Indian affairs regarding rumors of English intentions to "cut off" the Indians. Commissioners denied, and requested delay of the mission to Canada until after the council with governor Hunter.

1714 September. Treaty council between governor Hunter and the Five Nations chiefs at Albany. Covenant Chain renewed and large present given. Rumors refuted. Iroquois requested a smith and informed that Tuscaroras had been accepted among them. No response by governor to Tuscarora statement which is in draft records but omitted from Robert Livingston's official minutes forwarded to the crown.

1714 1 October. Conestoga Indians informed Pennsylvania council at Philadelphia that Shawnees on the Susquehanna had been without a chief for three years because of their abandonment by chief Opessa. The delegation presented the Shawnees' "new Elected King" who was Carondawana, a chief of the Oneidas. They requested approval of Pennsylvania's government, which was given.

1715 April. Yamasee War broke out in South Carolina.

1715 June. Claud de Ramezay, governor of Montreal and acting governor of Canada, reported to be meeting with the Five Nations at Onondaga. He was campaigning against the Foxes. New York's commissioners of Indian affairs heard that the French had engaged the Senecas to join them against the Foxes.

1715 August. New York's governor Robert Hunter met with the Five Nations chiefs at Albany. Covenant Chain renewed. Hunter recruited the Iroquois to help the Carolinians against their Indian foes, but Decanisora demanded recompense in lower prices for goods and outright gifts of ammunition. Following this treaty, Hunter negotiated with a party of "Far Indians" escorted by Senecas to Albany for trading terms.

1716 No major Five Nations treaty this year. It was marked, however, by much dialogue with New York's commissioners of Indian affairs, involving sharp complaints about the dearness of goods. In January, Oneida chiefs charged that "Far Indians" coming to Albany "found themselves to scandalously imposed on and Cheated by the Traders that it discouraged them from returning." Ca. September the Senecas sent a delegation to Canada independently of the League.

1717 A year of some confusion. Some Senecas killed Catawbas who were negotiating with Virginia's governor Spotswood who then protested to New York in outrage. Frenchmen built a trading post at Irondequoit in Seneca country (Rochester, N.Y.), blocking trade to Albany. Rumors were rife among the Iroquois of English intentions to kill them, and they suspected that an epidemic of smallpox had been caused intentionally.

1717 June. Governor Hunter renewed the Covenant Chain at Albany. He defined it explicitly in terms of a mutual assistance pact. Decanisora blamed Albanians for trading with the French and thus supplying them with the goods that the French traded to the Indians, in turn, at Irondequoit. Decanisora also made the point (omitted from the formal minutes) that "we will be Ready and willing to doe to the utmost of our Power [to aid the English militarily against hostile Indians] but if the English act of Pride or malice should be the agressors and fall upon their Indian neighbours without a Cause we must first Consider of it before we offerd any assistance against those Indians."

1718 September. New York's Governor Hunter scolded some of the Iroquois who were "but messengers," renewing the Covenant Chain and giving presents. He demanded that the ammunition be used only for hunting and self defense, and not for raids upon distant Indians. Response not recorded.

1719 May and June. Indians from various western tribes came to Albany for trade.

1719 New York Commissioners of Indian affairs met with sachems of Mohawks and Oneidas to convey protests of southern governors about Iroquois depredations in their back country.

1719 July. French started building a fort at Niagara to stop traffic from western Indians to Albany.

1719 November. Five Nations chiefs met with Commissioners of Indian affairs at Albany to renew the Covenant Chain. They requested a meeting at Albany with governor of Virginia or his deputies to settle the problem of the southern raids. They insisted also that the best way to hinder French trade with the Indians would be to stop the delivery of English goods from Albany to Montreal "for they get but little Goods themselves from France."

1720 May. Myndert Schuyler and Robert Livingston met with chiefs of the Senecas, Cayugas, and Oneidas "in the Senecas country." Requested that the Iroquois lay down the hatchet and keep at peace with western and southern Indians, and that they expel the French. Iroquois willing, but required that Englishman accompany the party sent to order the French out. This was done, but the French at Niagara stood their ground.

1720 June. Pennsylvania's secretary James Logan met with the Conestogas, Shawnees, Conoys, and some Delawares at Conestoga. They had suffered casualties among their young men who accompanied Iroquois raiding parties southward. Logan advised them to stop the raids. They confessed fear of the Five Nations.

1720 September. Peter Schuyler, as president of New York council, met with Mohawks, Oneidas, Onondagas, and Cayugas in Albany. Senecas arrived later, after Schuyler's departure. Covenant Chain renewed. Iroquois promised not to attack southern Indians allied to the English. Senecas, upon arrival, complained that the French had established themselves at five places in Seneca country. The four nations proposed a joint Iroquois–English party to tear down the French buildings, but Schuyler evaded. They once more complained of Albany merchants selling goods to the French which the French sold later to the Indians.

1720 November. Expansionist policy of British Board of Trade began in New York with new legislation to forbid trade between Yorkers and the French, and plans to build new forts and repair old ones.

1721 June. French marched a hundred men from Irondequoit to Niagara. Met with Senecas. Promised not to strengthen fort.

1721 July. Council at Conestoga between Iroquois party bound southward (Senecas, Onondagas, Cayugas) and Pennsylvanians (governor Sir William Keith and Secretary James Logan). Seneca Chief Ghesaont on his way to negotiate with Virginia's governor about peace with southern Indians; safe conduct provided by Pennsylvanians. Keith forbade use of Susquehanna Valley as warriors' path. Iroquois complained about traders. Inconclusive discussions about competing claims to the valley.

1721 September. New York's Governor William Burnet met with the Five Nations chiefs at Albany. Covenant Chain renewed. Burnet complained about raid into Virginia "last summer" (apparently Ghesaont's party). Discussion of the French threat and trade.

1722 August and September. A grand multi-party treaty at Albany, involving the governors of New York, Pennsylvania, and Virginia in negotiation with the Five Nations chiefs. Governors required Iroquois to be responsible that four other tribes not cross a line in Virginia.

1723 May. A large body of Indians from Michilimackinac and Detroit came to trade at Albany, negotiating with the commissioners of Indian affairs who received the miscellaneous group as the "Seventh Nation." (Six Nations chiefs were present but unrecorded, and subsequent records say nothing of a seventh nation.)

1723 May. Commissioners from Boston treated with the Six Nations at Albany. Covenant Chain renewed. The Bostonians wanted to recruit Iroquois warriors to fight eastern Indians. A St. Francis Indian arrived with a peace message from the eastern nations. Iroquois postponed decision.

1723 August–September. Five Nations chiefs journeyed to Boston. Records say that they agreed to take up the hatchet against the eastern Indians if the latter would not make peace with New Englanders. While there, they agreed also to kindle a new "fire" at Deerfield for treaties with Massachusetts—the first formally proclaimed place besides Albany for negotiations between the Iroquois and English colonials. In a historical narrative, the Iroquois speaker mentioned that Massachusetts had earlier linked to them with a "golden" chain.

1724 The year was marked again by visits to Albany of parties of western Indians as well as some from the vicinity of Montreal. (Peter Wraxall, Secretary of Indian Affairs from 1750 to 1759, suspected the latter of being carriers for Albany merchants engaged in illegal trade with Montreal correspondents.)

1724 Before September. Five Nations chiefs visited Montreal and Caughnawaga to mediate for peace between the eastern Indians and New England.

1724 September. New York's governor Burnet and Massachusetts's commissioner John Stoddard met with chiefs of the Six Nations at Albany. Iroquois denied having promised to war against eastern Indians; asserted only a promise to mediate. Later, in treaty with Burnet, they renewed the Covenant Chain and gave permission for New York to build a trading house at Oswego.

1725 ca. May. At Onondaga, Charles Le Moyne de Longeuil obtained Onondaga permission to convert the French trading house at Niagara (in Seneca country) to a building of masonry which became a fort.

1725 June. Crown's Board of Trade recommended repeal of New York's legislation against trade between Albany and Montreal. This was done by the assembly, but new legislation substituted with much the same effect.

ca. **1726** Iroquois chiefs treated secretly with chiefs of Delawares and Shawnees on the Susquehanna River, demanding that all should join in a war against the English because of the English colonials' encroachments on their lands. The demand was rejected.

1726 July. Council at Niagara. Iroquois demanded cessation of building on fort. Demand rejected by the French.

1726 September. New York's governor Burnet renewed the Covenant Chain with the Six Nations. Chiefs of Senecas, Cayugas, and Onondagas signed a confirmation of the "deed" of 1701. Discussion of raids against the southern Indians. Inconclusive.

ca. **1727** The Iroquois established a new Warriors' Road to the Ohio country by ordering Shawnees in Pennsylvania to relocate their villages westward. "Since you have nott hearkened to us nor Regarded whatt we have said [by rejecting the proposal to war on the English], now wee will put pettycoatts on you, and Look upon you as women for the future, and nott as men." This was said to Delawares as well as Shawnees, but Delawares were not included in the relocation orders.

ca. **1727** Iroquois League sent "orders" to "all the tribes as far as Lake Superior" to attack the French in all their posts simultaneously. The "orders" were disregarded.

1727 July. Chiefs of Five Nations, but mostly Cayugas, met with Pennsylvania's governor Gordon to propose sale of the Susquehanna valley and to request that colonials settle no higher along the river than already located. The governor renewed William Penn's Chain of Friendship; responding, the Iroquois called it the Covenant Chain, after which the governor used the same term. Offer to sell was rejected on grounds that William Penn had already bought the valley twice: from Dongan and the resident Susquehannocks. Iroquois departed discontent.

1727 August. A delegation of eastern Indians arrived in Albany with news of the end of Dummer's War (1722–27) between Massachusetts and the Abenakis, and "to fix a Peace and Friendship" with New York.

1727 August. Two Seneca chiefs informed New York's commissioners of Indian affairs that they had been negotiating with western nations and had won four of them to trade and friendship with New York.

1727 July to end of year. Canada's new governor, the marquis de Beauharnois demanded withdrawal of the Yorkers from Oswego. Much intrigue by English and French with the Iroquois concerning French efforts to dislodge the English.

1728 June. Treaty in Philadelphia between Delaware chief Sassoonan and Pennsylvanians, with Oneida chief Shikellamy present. Shikellamy was identified as supervisor of the Shawnees in behalf of the Six Nations.

1728 October. Delaware chief Sassoonan treated with Pennsylvania's governor Gordon in Philadelphia with Oneida chiefs Shikellamy and Carandowana present. Although Sassoonan remarked that "the five Nations have often told them that they were as Women only" and that the Iroquois "would take Care of what related to Peace and War," he did all the recorded speaking and "in the Name and Behalf" of the Shawnees as well as the Delawares.

1728 October. New York's new governor, John Montgomery, met with chiefs of the Six Nations at Albany to renew the Covenant Chain. He requested their aid in defending Oswego and got an equivocal answer. As customary, he met separately with the Schaghticoke and "River Indians."

1729 June. Chiefs of two nations of "Far Indians" came to Albany to treat for peace, friendship, and trade. Received by commissioners of Indian affairs.

1729 July. Oneida delegation told New York's commissioners of Indian affairs of their nation's loss of fifty-five men in combat with Virginia Indians. Commissioners arranged to condole.

1729 Summer. Shawnee delegation from a community in Pennsylvania met with governor Beauharnois in Montreal to request reception of their people in New France. They were accepted because the French wanted them, privately, "to be a barrier between the Iroquois and us."

1729 November. British Board of Trade recommended repeal by the crown of the acts made since 1725 by New York's assembly forbidding trade with Montreal, on grounds that they were as bad as those repealed in 1725.

1730 February. Governor Gooch of Virginia offered, in a letter to governor John Montgomerie of New York, to mediate peace between the Oneidas and Catawbas, though the latter were considered to be in the jurisdiction of South Carolina.

1730 May. Oneida chiefs met with commissioners of Indian affairs at Albany. They rejected Gooch's proposal for them to treat with the Catawbas in Virginia, demanding that Gooch should bring the Catawbas and their Oneida prisoners to Albany, and threatening otherwise to war against them with the full force of the Six Nations and their allies.

1730 September. Mohawk chiefs met with the commissioners of Indian affairs at Albany to "humbly entreat" New York's governor to forbid future purchases by Christians of the little land remaining to the Mohawks.

1730 October. The Fox Indians, who were at war with New France, sent a request to the Senecas for permission to settle among them. By intervention of Louis-Thomas Chabert de Joncaire, the Senecas referred the request to Canada's governor Beauharnois. Also, Joncaire asked for Seneca permission to build a trading post at Irondequoit.

1730 November. New York's commissioners of Indian affairs protested to the Senecas against their dealing with Joncaire.

1731 May. New York's governor Montgomerie met Five Nations at Albany (Oneidas not there). Covenant Chain renewed. Agreement to forbid colonial settlement south of Lake Ontario.

1731 Summer. Sieur de Joncaire escorted a Shawnee band from the Susquehanna valley to settle west of the Allegheny River.

1731 August. Pennsylvania council sent invitation to the Six Nations for a treaty, the object being for them to use their "absolute authority" to recall the Shawnee emigrants to Pennsylvania.

1731 August. Treaty in Philadelphia between governor Gordon and Delaware chief Sassoonan for cession of Delaware lands. Oneida chief Shikellamy present but silent. Sassoonan granted a tract of land to secretary James Logan; deed witnessed by Shikellamy.

1731 Fall. Iroquois chiefs went to the Allegheny River to forbid the French interpreter "Cahichtodo" from building and trading there (which would have been among the Delaware and Shawnee villages). The chiefs asserted that the land belonged to the Six Nations. The Frenchman rebuffed them. They sent a complaint to Montreal.

1732 February. Mohawks complained to New York's commissioners of Indian affairs against the continuing issuance of licenses to purchase their lands.

1732 April. Mohawk chiefs, at Albany, complained about seizure of a large tract of their lands by Philip Livingston, secretary of Indian affairs.

1732 August. Seneca, Oneida, and Cayuga chiefs (authorized to speak for the whole Iroquois League) met with Pennsylvania's proprietary Thomas Penn and secretary James Logan in Philadelphia. Penn and Logan requested the Six Nations to recall Shawnees and Delawares from the Ohio country, and offered to help in the process. They lit a new fire for the Iroquois in Philadelphia, opened a new road, appointed Shikellamy and Conrad Weiser as go-betweens, and proposed a "League and Chain of Friendship and Brotherhood" between Pennsylvania and the Six Nations—the proposal to be confirmed by the League at Onondaga.

1732 An epidemic of smallpox among the Iroquois and the Mississaugas, perhaps also among other peoples.

1733 September. New York's governor William Cosby met with the Six Nations chiefs at Albany. Covenant Chain renewed. Cosby forbade warring against remote Indians and permitting French to live and build in Iroquoia. Cosby reminded that the Iroquois had put their lands under the king's protection. They acknowledged "having submitted themselves under the protection of the King of Great Brittain." (The minutes omitted the land issue as reported in a later letter of Cosby to the Board of Trade, *N.Y.Col.Docs.* 5:960–62: Mohawks accused Albany corporation of defrauding them of their best lands by converting a deed of trust into an absolute conveyance. Cosby tore the deed up.)

1734 Onondaga chiefs met with Canada's governor Beauharnois to have him patch up a misunderstanding with the Senecas.

1735 August. Caughnawaga chiefs held a solemn treaty with New York's commissioners of Indian affairs to renew peace and friendship with New York and the Six Nations. Commissioners accepted. (Wraxall's comment: the treaty "opened and fixt the Canada trade which I believe was the Chief View our Commissioners had in it.")

1735 New York's governor Cosby met with the Six Nations chiefs at Albany to renew the covenant. They argued a contradiction between his ban on outsiders living among them and his acceptance of the Caughnawaga trade proposals. "The Trade and Peace we take to be one thing."

1736 September–October. Treaty at Philadelphia between Five Iroquois Nations (no Mohawks) and proprietary Thomas Penn and the Pennsylvania Council. Confirmation of 1732 treaty proposals. Iroquois statement: "It is our earnest Desire this Chain [of Friendship] should continue and be strengthened between all the English and all our Nations, and likewise the Delawares, Canayes, and the Indians living on Sasquehanna, and all the Nations, in behalf of all whom . . . we now deliver you this Beaver Coat." The lower Susquehanna Valley was ceded finally to Penn. Negotiations afterward by Conrad Weiser "in the bushes" at Shamokin: Iroquois were recognized by Pennsylvania as having the sole right to sell Indian lands in the province and the sole right to speak formally in treaty for the other Indians there. Iroquois requested intercession by Pennsylvania with Maryland to settle their claims to "conquered" lands there. They signed a deed quitting their claim to lands occupied by other tribes in Pennsylvania, which was so written as to make it a deed of cession of those lands to Pennsylvania.

1737 ca. May. Senecas gave permission to Sieur de Joncaire to build a trading house at Irondequoit.

1737 June–July. Lt. governor George Clarke, of New York, met chiefs of the Six Nations at Albany. Reproved them for permitting French in Irondequoit and made renewal of the Covenant Chain contingent on their rescinding the permission. Iroquois promised "there shall not one French Man setle on our Land," but they reminded Clarke of English inactivity toward Forts Niagara and Crown Point (French Fort St. Frederic). Being told that the Shawnees on the Susquehanna were negotiating to move to Detroit, they denied having sold the land on which the Shawnees lived, and accused Mr. Penn of encroachment on Indian lands. Covenant Chain renewed.

1737 September. Thomas Penn organized the "Walking Purchase" of Delaware Indian lands above Tohickon Creek in Bucks County.

1738–40 No large conferences because of a smallpox epidemic. Struggles by French and English agents among the Iroquois over French efforts to acquire control of Irondequoit and to make a new settlement on the Wood Creek connecting Lake George and Lake Champlain.

1739 August. A Mohawk delegation protested to the French commandant at Fort St. Frederic against settlement on Wood Creek which was in Mohawk territory. Protest referred to higher authority.

1739 October. Canadian governor sent a message to the Mohawks that the king of France claimed Wood Creek, but would allow the Indians (including his non-Mohawk allies) to hunt there. He assured them that no French would settle there and that he would not permit any English to settle there.

1740 August. Lieutenant Governor Clarke met the Six Nations at Albany. Covenant Chain renewed. He "admitted" all the southern and western nations of Indians to the Chain. He asked the Iroquois to be at peace with them all. The Iroquois chiefs "accepted" the other nations (most of which were French allies). They made excuses for some of the Onondaga sachems "who are gone to Canada." Observers from the French mission at Sault St. Louis attended the Albany meeting.

1740 September. Representatives of the Five Nations met with Montreal's Governor Beaucours at Montreal. They rekindled the treaty fire and condoled the death of Louis-Thomas Chabert de Joncaire who had been active as a French agent among them. They requested that his son Philippe-Thomas should be sent to them with a blacksmith. Their message was forwarded to governor general Beauharnois who agreed to their requests and renewed the Tree of Peace. (The text is ambiguous as to whether Onondagas alone were speaking for all the Iroquois.)

1741 March. A deputation of sachems from the Six Nations came to New York's commissioners of Indian affairs in Albany to refute rumors and explain the Onondaga chiefs' Canadian conference in 1740. Their explanation: (1) the Iroquois had been bringing into the Covenant Chain some Indian nations allied to New France; (2) the Onondagas' chief aim had been to secure Iroquois neutrality in case of war between the French and English. (The War of the Austrian Succession had begun in Europe, and rumors of potential Anglo-French hostilities were about.)

1741 June. Famine among the Iroquois.

1741 August. Messages exchanged between governor general Beauharnois, on the one hand, and separate Iroquois parties on the other, including the mission Indians of Sault St. Louis and Lake of Two Mountains; the Onondagas, Cayugas, Oneidas, and Tuscaroras as a group; and the Seneca nation individually. Issues concerning the rival French and English trading posts in Iroquois territories. Professions of friendship. Beauharnois urged continuation of war against southern Indians.

1741 August. Onondaga and Cayuga sachems talked with the New York commissioners of Indian affairs. They reported a general meeting of the Six Nations at Onondaga which resolved to protect the trading house at Oswego against French attack. Reported also peace with the French and their Indian allies unless Iroquois blood should be shed. Urged peace between France and England.

1741 A Caughnawaga delegation invited by the commissioners of Indian affairs arrived in numbers too few to do business. Commissioners thought them evasive about neutrality in case of Anglo-French War.

1742 June. New York's Lieutenant Governor George Clarke met with the sachems of the Six Nations at Albany. He renewed the Covenant Chain and reminded the chiefs of their promise to take other Indian nations into it, especially the southern nations allied to other English colonies; he named particularly the Catawbas, Cherokees, Creeks, Chickasaws, and Choctaws. The chiefs replied that they were willing but wanted to "see the faces of a few of all the Nations you have named to us with whom we are now in alliance." Afterwards the Seneca sachems acknowledged to the commissioners of Indian affairs that they had sold "the land at Irondequoit" to the commissioners' agent acting for New York's government.

1742 July. Some Onondaga and Seneca chiefs conferred with governor Beauharnois. They "repaired the road" between them. The chiefs gave presents to chiefs of the mission Iroquois at Sault St. Louis to ask forgiveness of a murder. Beauharnois urged them to expel the English from Oswego and tried to prevent them from making peace with the southern Catawbas. He sent them a blacksmith as they had been requesting for several years.

1742 July. A treaty was held at Philadelphia in accordance with the alliance forged in 1736. Besides Pennsylvania's lt. governor George Thomas and other officials, those present included chiefs of the Oneidas, Onondagas, Cayugas, Senecas, and Tuscaroras; Delawares, and Shawnees. At the behest of governor Thomas, Onondaga chief Canasatego upheld Pennsylvania's "Walking Purchase" of lands in the upper Delaware valley, harshly castigated the protesting Delaware Indians as "women" without authority to sell land, and ordered them to evacuate the territory immediately. He told them to settle in Iroquois territory on the Ninth Branch of the Susquehanna River. (For several years prior to this affair the Mohawks had played an inconspicuous part in Iroquois League diplomacy. In relation to both New France and Pennsylvania, the Onondagas appear to have had the initiative.)

1742 Late fall or early winter. A party of Iroquois warriors en route to raid southern Indians became involved in conflict with back country Virginians. Both sides suffered fatal casualties.

1743 February. Interpreter Conrad Weiser, as requested by Pennsylvania's governor Thomas, journeyed to Shamokin to initiate settlement of the Virginia-Iroquois conflict by peaceable means.

1743 May. New York's commissioners of Indian affairs reprimanded the Iroquois in a message for their "murders" in Virginia. (The commissioners had earlier shown great alarm because of Pennsylvania's intervention in the affair.) The Six Nations chiefs responded with a message that their men had been victimized by Virginian aggression.

1743 July–August. Conrad Weiser traveled to Onondaga to "take the hatchet out of the head" of the Six Nations in a treaty session described by Weiser and his companion John Bartram with rare attention to council rituals. This council laid the groundwork for the grand treaty of Lancaster in 1755.

1744 January. Britain went to war against France in the complex War of the Austrian Succession. The American phase was called King George's War.

1744 June. Governor George Clinton renewed the Covenant Chain at a council with the Six Nations at Albany. He informed them of the Anglo-French War and asked them to act "offensively and defensively" against the French. They offered to act defensively. They refused to expel the French living among them.

1744 June–July. A great treaty at Lancaster, Pa., between Oneidas, Onondagas, Cayugas, Senecas, and Tuscaroras, and the colonies of Pennsylvania, Maryland, and Virginia. With Pennsylvania acting as mediator, the more southern colonies bought off Iroquois claims to lands within colonial jurisdictions that the Iroquois asserted were rightfully theirs "by conquest." But Virginians wrote the deed to include the Ohio country, and much more, in language that deceived the Iroquois. This treaty and deed prepared the way for expansion to the west by means of the Ohio Company of Virginia. Covenant Chain and Chain of Friendship phrases both used.

1745 May. The Pennsylvania government sent Conrad Weiser to Onondaga to urge the Six Nations to make peace with the Catawbas. Weiser also informed them that Peter Chartier's band of Shawnees had changed sides to ally with the French.

1745 July. Six Nations chiefs met with governor Beauharnois at Montreal. He gave the hatchet to his allied Indians and offered it to the Iroquois. They did not respond, but they brought his war belt of wampum home for consideration, much to the dismay of Englishmen.

1745 October. Chiefs of five Iroquois nations (the Senecas not present) met at Albany with governor Clinton and commissioners from Pennsylvania, Massachusetts, and Connecticut. Renewal of the Covenant Chain. Pennsylvania commissioners (two of whom were Quakers) objected to the proposals of the others and met separately with the Iroquois chiefs to confirm the latter in peace and to urge once more a peace with the Catawbas. New York, Massachusetts, and Connecticut asked the Six Nations to join them militarily against the French and French Indian allies. The reply was evasive: the chiefs accepted the hatchet but only to "keep it in our bosom" until they had con-

sulted further with the French governor. Massachusetts's commissioners were hot to force the issue, but New York's Clinton held back, being unwilling to attract French attacks on his own province.

1746 August–September. Governor Clinton and Massachusetts's commissioners met with the Six Nations at Albany to recruit them for an intended conquest of Canada. New York's record says that they accepted
the war belt, but Conrad Weiser was informed by Oneida chief
Shikellamy, in June 1747, that only the Mohawks had actually declared
war and that the other nations thought this to be rash and were busy
cementing alliances with various Indian allies of the French. At Albany the Covenant Chain was renewed, and the Iroquois announced
that they had taken the Mississauga nation, whose representatives were
present, into their League as the Seventh nation.

1746 September. William Johnson commissioned as "colonel of the forces
to be raised out of the Six Nations of Indians." This marks the beginning of Johnson's ascendancy over Iroquois affairs. Johnson's base was
among the Mohawks who re-emerged thereafter into prominence.

1746 October. New York's commissioners of Indian affairs resigned in a body
and were not replaced.

1747 April. William Johnson met with "the Indians" to spur them to action.
They temporized, saying they were hopeful of winning over the mission Indians of Caughnawaga and Lake of Two Mountains.

1747 June. Conrad Weiser, sent by Pennsylvania to confer with the Iroquois
at Shamokin, met them instead at Paxton, Pa., to renew friendship and
get intelligence. Oneida chief Shikellamy advised the Pennsylvanians
to name a successor to ailing Delaware Chief Olumapies (Sassoonan)
by their own authority. (This was later attempted but frustrated by
Delaware resistance.)

1747 July through September. Onondaga, Oneida, Tuscarora, and Cayuga
deputies, plus Indians of Caughnawaga and Lake of Two Mountains,
met several times at Montreal and Quebec with the French. Indians
warned against intrigues of the Mohawks and English. They requested
the return of Indian prisoners who, according to the deputies, had
joined war parties against the advice of their villages. The Indians af-
firmed neutrality between the English and French, but stated that they
were at variance with the Mohawks in this respect.

1747 October. The Ohio Company of Virginia was formed to colonize the
Ohio country.

1747 November. Ten Iroquois warriors from the Ohio country met with the
provincial council of Pennsylvania in Philadelphia. They informed that

the old men of the Onondaga council still stood neutral as between England and France, but that the warriors on the Ohio had taken up arms against the French. They asked, "How comes it to pass that the English, who brought us into the war, will not fight themselves?" They were given a present and an excuse. Conrad Weiser advised the Pennsylvania council to follow through with further attention to the Ohio Indians.

1747–48   Fall and Spring. Negotiations by the Twightwees [Miamis] with the Six Nations to bring the former into alliance with the Iroquois and the English.

1748   April. New York's representative William Johnson attended a conference at Onondaga. He encouraged the Indians not to go to Canada to negotiate themselves for return of Indian prisoners, promising that the governor of New York would arrange for the captives' return.

1748   July. Governor Clinton treated with the Six Nations and allies at Albany. Covenant Chain brightened and strengthened. Governor William Shirley and commissioners from Massachusetts Bay also present. Much incitement by Clinton and Shirley to keep the Indians belligerent against Canada. Mohawks distressed because of loss of their best men in combat.

1748   July. Lancaster, Pa. Pennsylvania commissioners met with chiefs of the Six Nations, Delawares, Shawnees, Nanticokes, and Twightwees, all of the "Ohio country." (The Allegheny River, now considered a tributary, was then understood to be the upper part of the Ohio River, and its valley was part of the Ohio country.) Twightwees applied for alliance and were admitted to Pennsylvania's Chain of Friendship (Covenant Chain terminology not used). Kakowatchiky's Shawnee band asked forgiveness for straying from the right path and were given probation. (Peter Chartier's Shawnee band not present nor represented, but a number of his people had been won back individually by Iroquois persuasion.)

1748   August. Royal Proclamation of cessation of Anglo-French hostilities received in Philadelphia.

1748   September. Conrad Weiser and Andrew Montour journeyed to Logstown on the Ohio (near Ambridge, Pa.) to make a present to the allied Indians there. They met with Six Nations chiefs, Delawares, Wyandots, Mississaugas, Mahicans, and Shawnees, and opened trade for Pennsylvanians. (Weiser reported that he gave the present in the names of Pennsylvania and Virginia, the Virginians having paid for a share, but they heard later that he had omitted their name.) Covenant Chain language was not used; Chain of Friendship renewed. Weiser recog-

nized the Delawares as "brethren and countrymen." (He later recommended to Pennsylvania that the Six Nations be persuaded to "take
off the petticoat from the Delawares.")

1748 November. Conference between the Onondagas, Oneidas, Tuscaroras,
Cayugas, Senecas, and French at the Chateau St. Louis in Quebec.
The Indians maintained that they were not English subjects, and af-
firmed their position of neutrality.

1749 March. British crown ordered the governor of Virginia to grant the
Ohio Company 500,000 acres of land. Land granted centered upon
the juncture of the Allegheny and Monongahela rivers where they make
the Ohio proper.

1749 June–November. Céloron de Blainville led a large French party 3000
miles down the Ohio valley and back to Montreal to reassert France's
claims to sovereignty. He buried inscribed lead plates and met with
Indian chiefs along the way who gave him an unfriendly reception.
They rejected his demand that they cease to trade or traffic with the
English.

1749 August. Six Nations chiefs met with governor James Hamilton and
council in Philadelphia. They complained about encroachments on
their lands, but received small satisfaction. Pennsylvania paid for
another cession, but it included more than the Iroquois had intended
to offer. Much dissatisfaction. Quarreling between Onondaga chief
Canasatego and Conrad Weiser.

1750 ca. January. Twightwees put themselves under the care of the Six Nations, denoting the Iroquois as Elder Brothers in the Chain of Friendship, and asked for more English traders. Six Nations accepted them.

1750 May. Conference of Cayugas with French governor general La Jon-
quiére. Cayugas assured him of their fidelity to the French.

1750 ca. August or September. Ohio Wyandots complained of having been
left out of peace between England and France, and of being menaced
by the French. Asked Pennsylvania and New York to intercede for them.

1750 September. Pennsylvania's Lieutenant Governor Hamilton observed
that the Iroquois on the Ohio outnumbered those in Iroquoia. Onondaga council as alarmed as the French by this development.

1750 September. Representing Virginia, Conrad Weiser journeyed to Onondaga to invite negotiations for peace with the Catawbas. The invitation was rejected. Weiser found pro-French chiefs in control. Canasatego
was dead, and Weiser suspected a political assassination.

1750–51 September–May. Christopher Gist sent by the Ohio Company to map out the Ohio territory for the proposed colony. He invited the various Ohio Indians to a grand treaty at Logstown to receive a large present from the Crown. (Logstown had become the headquarters for the council of the Ohio Iroquois [Mingos], and also a central depot for Pennsylvania's traders, chief of whom was George Croghan.)

1750 Philippe-Thomas Chabert de Joncaire sent by Canada's governor to the Ohio country to keep the tribes allied to the French and away from English influence. Joncaire also took up headquarters at Logstown, called by the French Chiningué (Ambridge, Pa.).

1751 May. Councils at Logstown. Joncaire's demand for expulsion of the English traders was rejected by Six Nations chiefs. Meeting with the Delawares, Croghan asked them to pick a chief (they being without one) and present him to the Six Nations and Pennsylvania "and he so chosen shall be looked upon by us as your King, with whom Publick Business shall be transacted. (To do so would be to bypass Six Nations chiefs speaking in behalf of the Delawares.) Acting for Pennsylvania, Croghan nevertheless recognized the Six Nations as "Head of al the Nations of Indians," and put the Twightwees and Wyandots in their care. Joncaire was reproached by the Iroquois for French claims to the Ohio country. "Is it not our Land . . . ?"

1751 July. New France's governor general, the marquis de La Jonquière, met with chiefs of the Onondagas, the Iroquois of Sault St. Louis and Lake of Two Mountains, and groups from Michilimackinac. The Onondagas proclaimed their right to the Ohio country and demanded that La Jonquière call back from there his allies of the Sault, the Two Mountains, the Abenakis, and the Ottawas. La Jonquière suggested that the Onondagas do that themselves. He recognized only their right to hunt in the Ohio country.

1751 July. New York's Governor George Clinton, accompanied by commissioners from Massachusetts Bay, Connecticut, and South Carolina, met with the Six Nations at Albany to renew the Covenant Chain. Six chiefs of the Catawbas were with the South Carolinians. Peace negotiations between the Iroquois and the Catawbas got under way at last, conditioned on return of prisoners.

1751 October. Negotiations of French Governor General La Jonquière with the Iroquois of Caughnawaga and Lake of Two Mountains. La Jonquière wished to prevent furs from slipping through the Iroquois of those settlements to Albany.

1751–53 No major treaties between Iroquois and New York because of the prevalence of smallpox.

1752 May–June. Treaty in Mohawk country between Iroquois and Cataw-
      bas. Peace negotiated.

1752 May–June Council at Logstown between Ohio Indians and commis-
      sioners from Virginia and Pennsylvania. Without authority from On-
      ondaga, the Ohio Iroquois confirmed the deed of cession made at
      Lancaster in 1744. Their act was kept secret from the Delawares who
      occupied the land thus ceded. As invited earlier by Pennsylvania, the
      Delawares presented Shingas as their chief. The Iroquois "half king,"
      Seneca chief Tanaghrisson, professed to "give" Shingas to the Delawares
      as their "king."

1752 June. Charles-Michel Mouet de Langlade, synethnic officer in the Ca-
      nadian regular army, led a force of Frenchmen and allied Indians in
      an attack upon the Twightwee town of Pickawillany, killed its chief and
      an English trader, and took prisoner the other English traders present.
      News of this exploit reached Logstown during the treaty council there
      and caused consternation. [Synethnic: descended from mixed ethnic
      stocks.]

1753 February. Advance party left Montreal to prepare the way for a large
      French campaign down the Ohio valley. It began construction of a series
      of forts intended by governor general Duquesne to deny the territory
      to British trade and settlement.

1753 February. Andrew Montour was sent by Virginia to Onondaga with
      an offer to help armed resistance to the French advance. The Six Na-
      tions council kept neutral.

1753 Spring. Pennsylvania's traders were harried out of the Ohio country
      by the French and allied Indians.

1753 June. Canajoharie Mohawks met with New York's governor Clinton
      in New York City. Because of the province's failure to redress Mohawk
      grievances, chief Hendrick declared the Covenant Chain broken and
      walked out with his men. When reported to the Board of Trade in Lon-
      don, this action caused great alarm. The Board ordered a great treaty
      of all colonies allied to the Iroquois which became the Albany Con-
      gress of 1754.

1753 September. Half King Tanaghrisson confronted French Commandant
      Marin at Fort Le Boeuf to demand evacuation by the French of ter-
      ritory claimed by the Iroquois. He was repulsed.

1753 September. A delegation of Ohio Indians led by Oneida chief Scarouady
      journeyed to Winchester, Virginia, to seek aid against the French.
      Scarouady declared that "our Kings [sachems?] have nothing to do with
      our Lands; for We, the Warriors, fought for the Lands, and so the Right

belongs to Us." The term Chain of Friendship was used, rather than Covenant Chain. Scarouady asked the Virginians to desist from making settlements at the Ohio. A present given, but no explicit commitments.

1753   October. Same delegation of Ohio Indians went on to Carlisle, Pa., to meet with Pennsylvania's commissioners (who included Benjamin Franklin). Commissioners responded to Indian requests with a present and promises to take up the issues with the governor. Chain of Friendship language used, but not Covenant Chain.

1754   June–July. The "Albany Congress" treaty between the Six Nations and the English colonies of New York, Pennsylvania, Connecticut, Massachusetts, Maryland, New Jersey, and Rhode Island. Absent Virginia and South Carolina were "represented" by New York Governor James De Lancey. Renewal of alliance expressed in terms of both Covenant Chain and Chain of Friendship. Mohawks acted as spokesmen for the Iroquois and asserted themselves to be "the head of all the other Nations." They complained about land frauds, exhorted the Yorkers to build defense fortifications, and asked that William Johnson be made manager of Indian affairs. De Lancey promised to investigate the fraud charges. A large present given.

In separate sessions among themselves, the colonial delegates adopted Benjamin Franklin's Plan of Union (but this was not ratified by a single province nor ever submitted to Parliament).

"In the bushes," outside the formal councils, Conrad Weiser found "some greedy fellows for money" and got a deed for Pennsylvania of a vast tract of western lands which overlapped the grant made to Virginia at Lancaster in 1744.

Also outside the sessions, and later challenged by the Onondaga council as fraud, John Lydius got an ostensible deed from some Iroquois for Connecticut's Susquehannah Company, granting the Wyoming valley. (This valley is now in Pennsylvania, occupied by Wilkes-Barre and Scranton, but it was then challenged by Connecticut on the basis of that colony's sea-to-sea charter.)

1754   June–July. In the Ohio country, chief Tanaghrisson marched with George Washington and Virginia troops until the Iroquois decided that Washington's refusal to heed advice was leading to certain defeat. Tanaghrisson abandoned him; soon afterward, Washington was surrounded by French troops and forced to surrender Fort Necessity at Great Meadows (4 July). The news arrived at Albany to shock the participants in the Congress there.

1754   October. Conference at Montreal between Cayugas, Oneidas, Tuscaroras, two Senecas, a few Onondagas observing, "domiciliated Indians," and the Marquis de Duquesne, governor general of New France. Oneidas, Cayugas, and Tuscaroras were favorably disposed toward the French. Senecas and Onondagas were uncommitted. Duquesne threatened to punish the Indians if they would not recall warriors fighting against the French.

1754 October. Secret conference at Montreal between deputies of Oneidas, Tuscaroras, Cayugas, Onondagas, Senecas, and Indians of French mission villages. Unity desired. A belt sent to Senecas to cease hostilities against the French had not yet been answered (Duquesne, who wrote the account, apparently got his information from mission Indians.)

1755 January. Meetings at Philadelphia between Mohawks and Pennsylvanians at which the deed of Connecticut's Susquehannah Company for land in the Wyoming Valley was condemned.

1755 April. William Johnson commissioned by general Edward Braddock as sole Superintendent of the affairs of the Six Nations and their allies. Commissioned also by New York's governor De Lancey as major general of New York's forces with instructions to recruit Iroquois.

1755 June–July. Conference at Mount Johnson between William Johnson and the Six Nations and some allied Indians. Johnson renewed the Covenant Chain and preached a recruiting sermon. The Iroquois agreed to war alongside the English, but some Cayuga chiefs privately expressed concern about fighting their kin among the French-allied Caughnawagas. Johnson assured them that the Caughnawagas would be treated as brethren. Protests against land encroachments. Council fire removed from Albany to Johnson's estate. The Iroquois expressed great pleasure at Johnson's mastery of traditional forms of council ritual.

1755 July. Defeat and death of general Edward Braddock in the Battle of the Wilderness before Fort Duquesne. Ignominious retreat of his army to the east coast.

1755 September. Johnson's troops and Indian warriors fought the French near Crown Point inconclusively, but captured baron Dieskau, the French commander in chief in America.

1755 October. Conference between Senecas and the new French governor general the marquis de Vaudreuil [the second by that name]. The Indians requested provisions and complained that Vaudreuil's predecessors had not treated them well. Vaudreuil assured them that they would be treated better if they acted more favorably toward the French.

1755 October. French-allied and -led Indians, now including Delawares and

Shawnees (former Iroquois tributaries), attacked back country settlers in Pennsylvania, Maryland, and Virginia.

1755-56 December–March. Johnson had many meetings with chiefs of the Six Nations to urge them to bring their "cousins" (later "nephews"), the Delawares and Shawnees, under control. The Iroquois said they were trying, by negotiations. Covenant Chain brightened and strengthened.

1756 February. William Johnson commissioned by the crown to have exclusive supervision of the Six Nations and confederates.

1756 April. Conference in Philadelphia between individuals of Six Nations and of the Religious Society of Friends (Quakers). Purpose: to discover why Delawares and Shawnees struck Pennsylvania.

1756 June–July. Treaty conferences at Onondaga and Fort Johnson. Baronetcy conferred on Sir William Johnson. Participants: Johnson, Six Nations, eastern Delawares and Shawnees, Mahicans.

1756 July–August. At a conference with Onondaga and Oneida delegates, on behalf of the Six Nations, Governor Vaudreuil urged the Indians not to engage in hostilities. He denounced the English as deceivers and warned the Indians against them. By a belt he requested that they remove from their villages, but they refused.

1756 July and November. Pennsylvania officials and interested Quakers met with the eastern Delawares led by Teedyuscung who charged that proprietary Thomas Penn had defrauded the Delawares in the "Walking Purchase" of Bucks County lands. Teedyuscung thus challenged Six Nations authority. (See **1742** July.)

1756 August. Oswego was captured by the Marquis de Montcalm.

1756 November–December. Conference at Montreal between Governor Vaudreuil and Cayugas, Onondagas, Oneidas, Tuscaroras, Tutelos, Senecas, Ottawas, Nipissings, Potawatomis, Algonquins. The French attempted to convince the Indians to join them against the English. Iroquois delegates expressed dissatisfaction with the English, and some indicated that they were well disposed toward the French and would offer some support; but neutrality was confirmed for all the Iroquois except the Mohawks, who were fighting strongly alongside the English.

1756 December. Pennsylvania's Lieutenant Governor Robert Hunter Morris declared war on the Delawares and offered scalp bounties, against strenuous objection from Quakers.

1756 December. Founding of the Friendly Association for Regaining and Preserving Peace with the Indians by Pacific Measures.

1757 March. Treaty started at Harris Ferry, Pa. George Croghan, as deputy to Sir William Johnson, met with chiefs of the Six Nations, Nanticokes, eastern Delawares, and Conestogas. Teedyuscung absent. Meeting was inconclusive.

1757 May. Pennsylvania's Lieutenant Governor William Denny and councillors met with deputies of Five Nations "with some Senecas, Nanticokes, and [eastern] Delawares." Croghan also present, and unofficial Quakers. Teedyuscung absent. Much talk about why Delawares became hostile. Chain of Friendship brightened. Preparation for another meeting with elusive Teedyuscung. Quakers in dispute with Croghan. (This dispute broadened into a quarrel with Sir William Johnson who insisted on his exclusive prerogative to administer Indian affairs while Quakers insisted equally firmly on their right and duty to bring about peace by doing justice to Indians with grievances.)

1757 July–August. Pennsylvania's Lieutenant Governor Denny, George Croghan, and others met with eastern Delaware chief Teedyuscung and made peace for the easterners. Much turmoil still about issues of land fraud, Delaware subordination to Iroquois, Quakers' right to attend and speak. Many Senecas present.

1757 July. Negotiations between Five Nations deputies and the French.

1757 September. Sir William Johnson met at Fort Johnson with chiefs of Mohawks, Oneidas, Cayugas, Senecas, River Indians, and some Cherokees. Covenant Chain brightened. Though Onondagas were absent, negotiations began in the name of the entire Six Nations for peace with the Cherokees. Oneida Chief Canaghquiesa told the Cherokees to bring their next delegation to Fort Johnson's "fire of the Six Nations and to no other place," and identified Mohawks and Oneidas as "the heads of the Confederacy."

1758 March. "A number" of Oneidas, Tuscaroras, Cayugas, (eastern) Delawares, Schoharie Mohawks, "etc.," met with Sir William Johnson at Fort Johnson. Absence of Onondagas emphasized by the request of the Indians present that he not attend the impending general meeting of the Six Nations summoned by the Onondagas at their own fire.

1758 Much negotiation in Pennsylvania culminating in the grand treaty at Easton in October. Participants: for the English—governors and councillors of Pennsylvania and New Jersey, and an assembly delegation from Pennsylvania, and Johnson's deputy George Croghan; for the Indians—chiefs of all Six Nations, eastern and western Delawares, Nanticokes and Conoys, Tutelos, Chugnuts, Minisinks, Mahicans, and Pomptons. General peace negotiated. Chain of Friendship brightened. Some territory restored to Iroquois by Thomas Penn. English promised to restrain colonial settlement in Indian territory. Delegations of western Delawares and Iroquois took the agreements back to the Ohio country for approval by councils there, with the result that the Indians withdrew from defense of Fort Duquesne. Western Delawares resumed tributary relationship to Iroquois. (English agreements led to military orders against western settlement and eventually to the reservation of "crown lands" for the Indians by the Royal Proclamation of 1763.)

1758   November. French abandoned Fort Duquesne which was immediately seized by Brigadier John Forbes's expeditionary force and renamed Fort Pitt.

1759   January. Conference at Fort Pitt between colonel Hugh Mercer and chiefs of Six Nations, Delawares and Shawnees. In private the Iroquois warned against unreliability of the others, and plotted to deceive them in the public meeting. In public they demanded evacuation by British troops which Mercer refused as previously agreed privately. Transmitting the minutes, Mercer commented that the Iroquois "are by no means that powerfull and Warlike People they were on our first Settling America: and should the Shawanese and Delawares Join in the Confederacy against them, their ruin would soon be compleated, unless a very powerfull aid is afforded them by the English. This Support from us they come now to Supplicate but are obliged to cover this design."

1759   April. Sir William Johnson met at Canajoharie with chiefs of all Six Nations, Nanticokes, Shawnees, Saponys, and Conoys. Oneida Chief Canaghquieson spoke for Oneidas, Cayugas, and Tuscaroras as well as the tributaries, identifying them as "the younger branch of the confederacy" and referring to "the Onondags and Senecas who are our Fathers." (Cf. treaty of September 1757.) Covenant Chain renewed. Report of French allies wanting to negotiate for English trade. The whole confederacy now "determined to act" with the English in the war.

1759   July. Acting for Sir William Johnson, George Croghan met at Pittsburgh with chiefs of (Ohio) Six Nations, Delawares, Shawnees, and Wyandots, the last named being deputized to speak for eight other nations besides their own. This meeting was sequel to the Easton Treaty of 1758 after which Delaware "King" Beaver crossed the Great Lakes into Canada to invite the French allies into peace and trade with the English. At this meeting the Wyandots responded favorably and promised to recommend confirmation of the peace to their constituents. Beaver was the spokesman for all present, including the Iroquois, who did not speak. Chain of Friendship brightened.

1759 July. Fort Niagara taken by the English, a thousand Iroquois Indians participating in the battle. Johnson negotiated with Indians allied to the French to get them to change sides.

1759 Sometime prior to December, when Delaware chief Teedyuscung reported it to the Pennsylvania council, a great treaty conference of many Indian nations was held at Assinisink on the Chemung River (south central New York). These had responded to Teedyuscung's "halloo," and he brought with him a messenger from eleven western nations who specifically dissociated himself from the Six Nations: "We leave you to Treat with them yourselves." More continuation of the work of peace begun at Easton in 1758.

1759 September. English captured Quebec.

1759 October. Six Nations, Shawnees, Delawares, Twightwees, and Wyandots treated at Pittsburgh with Croghan and general Stanwix to admit the Wyandots to the Chain of Friendship.

1760 February–March. Mohawks complained to Sir William Johnson about encroachments on their lands.

1760 April. Conference at Fort Pitt between Indians of the Ohio region, including Iroquois, and the English. George Croghan, representing Sir William Johnson, requested that English prisoners be returned. The Indians asked that traders bring goods to trade with them. A copy of the boundary line established at the 1758 Easton treaty was delivered.

1760 April. Conference at Canajoharie between the Six Nations and other Indians. The Iroquois declared that they would assist the English against the French.

1760 September. Capitulation of Montreal to general Amherst.

1760 September. Conference at Montreal between the Six Nations, Indians of French mission villages, and the English. Declaration of unity of the Six Nations and the "Eight Nations of Canada." (Previously and subsequently the Eight were known as the Seven Nations of Canada. They became Seven again when the Indians of Oswegatchie merged with those of Akwesasne/St. Regis.)

1760 December. George Croghan and Major Robert Rogers took possession of Detroit for the English, and renewed the ancient Chain of Friendship between the Six Nations and the Wyandots, Ottawas, and Potawatomis. A Wyandot chief responded for all the Indians.

1761 June. Conference at the Wyandot village near Detroit between two Senecas (claiming to be messengers from the Six Nations), Wyandots, Ottawas, Potawatomis, and Ojibwas. The Senecas brought an invitation to Indians around Detroit to meet with Six Nations chiefs to discuss possible military action against the English.

1761 July to October. Sir William Johnson journeyed to Detroit, meeting with Indian tribes along the way, beginning with Mohawks at his own home. Much unrest among the Indians. Johnson accused Senecas of involvement in a conspiracy against the English. September: a great treaty council at Detroit in which Johnson met the Detroit Indians and Six Nations chiefs. General friendship proclaimed, but much intrigue in evidence. Johnson recognized the Hurons as head of the Ottawa confederacy, cautioning them "to keep it in good order, and not to neglect their friends and allies, as the Six Nations have done, notwithstanding all my admonitions." (Johnson later reported that his policy was to provoke jealousy between Six Nations and western Indians.)

1761 August. Treaty at Easton, Pa., between Governor James Hamilton and council members and assembly commissioner and others on the one side, with deputies of the Onondagas, Cayugas, Oneidas, Senecas, Mahicans, Nanticokes, Delawares, Tutelos, and Conoys on the other. Indians expressed much dissatisfaction with Sir William Johnson's trade practices (and prices) and general management of Indian affairs. They requested Pennsylvanians to start a competitive trading post at Tioga (Athens, Pa.). Much worried about their lands, especially those on the Susquehanna. "We, your Brethren of the seven Nations [apparently the Six plus Nanticoke-Conoys] are penned up like Hoggs. There are Forts all around us, and therefore we are apprehensive that Death is coming upon us." Hamilton defended Johnson, held to the Chain of Friendship, protested that the Walking Purchase was valid.

1762 April. Sir William Johnson met the Six Nations at Johnson Hall. Johnson angry about Seneca intrigues. Excuses. Each nation blamed others. Onondagas censured Mohawks for not attending councils at Onondaga. Mohawks retorted they were not invited. Onondagas pointedly replied to Johnson to open the road for "you and the Mohawks." Complaints about trade. All united in anxiety about and opposition to Connecticut's campaign to settle the Wyoming valley (north branch of the Susquehanna). Johnson defended trading practices, promised to try to secure the Wyoming lands. Covenant Chain renewed. Enclosed with Johnson's copy of this treaty is a message of Timothy Woodbridge, in behalf of the Connecticut men, to the Six Nations, demanding that they hold good to the deed some of their men gave to John Lydius in 1754. "Your great men have sold me the Land, and took a great deal of my money for it."

1762 June. At Easton, Pa., Sir William Johnson complied with his instructions from the crown by hearing the complaint of Teedyuscung's Delawares concerning the Walking Purchase of 1737. Thomas Penn's officials and Teedyuscung's Quaker allies did battle. Johnson bore down on the Delawares but solved the problem to his and their satisfaction by persuading Teedyuscung to withdraw the charges of fraud, after which Governor Hamilton gave them a large present on behalf of proprietary Thomas Penn. (Quakers protested a miscarriage of justice. Johnson and Penn became political allies.)

1762 August. Governor James Hamilton treated at Lancaster, Pa., with Ohio Delawares, Tuscaroras, Shawnees, Kickapoos, "Wiwachtanies," and Twightwees. Hamilton brightened and renewed the Covenant Chain. Beaver replied by holding fast to the Chain of Friendship. Western Indians joined by Senecas, Cayugas, Onondagas, Oneidas, Tuscaroras, eastern Delawares, Nanticoke-Conoys, some Saponies, and "a mixture of Shawnees and Munsees." The chief issue was return of colonial prisoners captured during the war. Some returned. Oneida Chief Thomas King brightened old Chain of Friendship. "He added that the Mohawks and Oneidas were the eldest of the Six Nations and both of a Height." He insisted that messages to the Onondaga council must be sent through the door" of either the Mohawks or the Senecas. He protested against encroachment on lands and made a fire for Teedyuscung at Wyoming to guard against settlers. Indians demanded that soldiers be withdrawn from Shamokin (Fort Augustus) as previously promised. No response.

1762 December. Conference at Fort Pitt between Indians of the Ohio region, including Iroquois, and English. Indians complained that English promises to supply Indians with inexpensive trade goods after French defeat had not been fulfilled.

1762 December. Conference at Onondaga. Guy Johnson requested that Senecas living in the primarily Delaware village of Kanestio, who had killed two English traders in November, be surrendered. Indians claimed that the murderers had disappeared.

1763 February. Peace of Paris. France ceded Canada to Great Britain.

1763 May. Outbreak of "Pontiac's War" with participation of many western Indians, including an indeterminate number of Senecas.

1763 May. Conference at Hartford between Connecticut and Mohawks, Onondagas, and Cayugas. Issue: Wyoming Valley deed and lands.

1763 July. Sir William Johnson met with Five Nations (Senecas absent) at the German Flats (Burnetsfield, N.Y.) to rally them against the western Indians.

1763   August. Colonel Henri Bouquet lifted the Indians' siege of Fort Pitt after a technical victory at Bushy Run.

1763   September. Johnson Hall. Sir William Johnson met with chiefs of the Six Nations and the Canadian Caughnawagas. Senecas were reprimanded. Covenant Chain brightened and renewed. Johnson gave the Caughnawagas a "good English Axe" to use "against Covenant breakers."

1763   October. Royal Proclamation issued. Among other matters it forbade the advance of colonial settlement beyond a line to be determined by Indian treaties and colonial surveys. Territory west of the line defined as crown lands reserved for Indians.

1764   March–April. Johnson Hall. Senecas came to seek peace, were introduced by Onondagas. All Six Nations present. Senecas ceded land at Niagara. Return of prisoners arranged. Peace treaty signed. Johnson prevailed on all the Iroquois to take up the hatchet against the enemies of the English.

1764   July–August. Niagara. Sir William Johnson signed a peace treaty with the Hurons of Detroit and the Senecas of Chenussio (Geneseo, N.Y.).

1764   August. Colonel John Bradstreet gave peace terms to western Indians. Bouquet thought them disgraceful and refused to be bound by them; he continued preparations for a march into Indian country.

1764   October. Tuscarawas (near Bolivar, Ohio). Colonel Henri Bouquet met Delawares, Shawnees, and Iroquois of the Ohio region. He threatened to destroy them if they did not give up their prisoners as agreed by their treaty with Colonel Bradstreet.

1764   November. Colonel Henri Bouquet treated with Senecas, Caughnawagas, Delawares, and Shawnees at the forks of the Muskingum River (Coshocton, Ohio).

1765   April–May. Sir William Johnson met with Five Nations (Tuscaroras absent) and the western Delawares at Johnson Hall. He concluded formal peace with the Delawares and negotiated with the Iroquois for the boundary line stipulated by the Royal Proclamation of 1763. (In this and the meetings held previously in 1764, Johnson was noticeably overbearing.) Delawares provisionally taken back into the Covenant Chain of Friendship (an apparent melding of the Covenant Chain and the Chain of Friendship).

1765 May. George Croghan and Major William Murray met at Fort Pitt with chiefs and warriors of the Delawares, Shawnees, Senecas, and "Sandusky Indians." Some prisoners returned. Trade reopened.

1766 February. Because of riots, British commander in chief general Thomas Gage began redeploying British troops from Indian territory to eastern towns. Large regions of the west were soon left without garrisons.

1766 August. George Croghan journeyed to Kaskaskia and Fort Chartres (ca. 30 miles south of St. Louis on the Mississippi River). He mediated between the western and northern confederacies and persuaded the westerners to acknowledge themselves "younger brothers" of the northern confederacy. A peace confirmed. Indians acknowledged right of the French to cede to Britain lands that had previously been purchased, but denied the validity of French cession of all other lands. Indians recognized the "sovereignty" of the British crown.

1766 December. Sir William Johnson reported that 160 Tuscaroras had emigrated from North Carolina to join brethren among the Six Nations.

1767 May. Sir William Johnson met with the Six Nations at the German Flats to notify them of the extension survey of the Mason-Dixon line beyond the Alleghenies into Indian territory, and to secure their consent. He initiated peace proceedings between the Iroquois and the Cherokees, and reassured the Indians of the crown's benevolent intentions toward them.

1767 October. Conference at German Flats between Sir William Johnson and the Six Nations. Discussion of the proposed boundary line between Indians and colonial settlements. Johnson questioned the Indians about "bad belts" circulating among the Oneidas and Senecas.

1768 March. A general congress of the Six Nations "&ca.," Caughnawagas, and the Seven Confederate Nations of Canada, and deputies of the Cherokees, with Sir William Johnson at Johnson Hall. Heavy complaint from the Iroquois of land seizures and murders of Indians. "If you won't keep the people away from the Rivers near Ohio, and keep the Road open making Pennsylvania and Virginia quiet, we must get tired of looking to you, and turn our faces another way." Johnson condoled and compensated for the dead. Peace with the Cherokees who were admitted to the Chain of Friendship.

1768 April–May. George Croghan met at Fort Pitt with chiefs and warriors of the Six Nations, Delawares, Shawnees, Munsees, and Mahicans "residing on the Waters of the Ohio"; Wyandots also. Commissioners from Pennsylvania condoled and compensated for murders of Indians. Much Indian complaint about encroachment on lands. A delegation sent to order eviction of settlements at Redstone Creek in Indian territory (western Pennsylvania). Indians refused to join the delegation for fear of incurring settlers' ill will personally. Chain of Friendship is brightened.

1768   October–November. A treaty at Fort Stanwix (Rome, N.Y.) held by Sir William Johnson with the Six Nations, Shawnees, Delawares, Senecas of Ohio, "and other dependent Tribes." Also present: George Croghan, New Jersey's Governor William Franklin, and Chief Justice Fred Smith, commissioners from Virginia and Pennsylvania, and "sundry Gents: from different Colonies." Boundary between colonies and Indian nations negotiated and deed of cession made. (Map in N.Y. Col. Docs. 8:136) Deed signed only by chiefs of the Six Nations though it obligated all the others. Covenant Chain renewed and strengthened. Large presents given. (Johnson was later reproved by the crown for taking too much territory, and instructed to re-cede some.)

1769   Sir William Johnson toured through Six Nations country, counciling serially with the Onondagas, Cayugas, and Senecas. Great unrest. Johnson later reported much violence and "licentiousness" among both colonials and Indians. He feared the strengthening of a far western confederacy having clandestine French instigation and support. "All we can do, is to divide their Councils and retain a part of them in our Interest. . . . It is highly necessary to prevent a too general Union amongst them . . . we enjoy the most security when they are divided amongst themselves."

1769–70   Winter. Cherokees confirmed peace at Onondaga, but proposed joint war against "several of the Southern and Western Nations who had acted as Enemys to both." Delegation to Johnson to ask summoning of a general congress. He reported to Crown, "we must either agree to permit these people to cut each others throats, or risque their discharging their fury on our Traders and defenceless frontiers."

1770   July. Sir William Johnson met with the following Indians at the German Flats: the Six Nations, their "Dependants"–Canaseragas (Shawnees), Nanticokes and Conoys, Oquagas (mixed, mostly Iroquois), Tuteloes–Indians from Canada–Caughnawagas, St. Regis Indians, Algonquins, "Ganagsadagas," St. Francis Abenakis, Hurons of Loretto, Nipissings, Mississaugas, and a Michilimackinac Ottawa chief–two "River Indians," and seven Cherokee deputies. Total: 2,320 Indians. The chief issue was peace with the Cherokees and their demand that the northern Indians join them in war against western enemies. On instruction from the crown, Johnson maneuvered to keep the war demand off the official agenda so that the crown would not be publicly sanctioning such a conflict (a hint that unofficial agreement may have been reached). Peace with the Cherokees was confirmed. The 1768 cession of the treaty of Fort Stanwix was ratified. Covenant Chain belt given by Johnson to all the nations present and accepted. (No mention by either Johnson or the Iroquois of the Ohio Indians. The western Indians whom the Cherokees wanted alliance against lived in the Illinois country.)

1770 July–August. Sir William Johnson met with the Seven Nations of Canada, the Mississaugas, and the Abenakis of St. Regis at Johnson Hall. He urged them all to work for peace with the western Indians. The Abenakis wanted to stay at St. Regis, but Johnson told them to go back to their own country, the sooner the better, to avoid trouble with the Iroquois there at St. Regis (Akwesasne).

1770–71 Uncertain dates. Chief Guastarax of the Geneseo Senecas circulated a war belt among the western Indians to prepare for an uprising against the British.

1771 July. Sir William Johnson met with the Six Nations at Johnson Hall to demand an explanation of his intelligence about a conspiracy with the Ohio Indians. They laid all the blame on the Geneseo Senecas who "have very often differed from us in Sentiments and Conduct." They reassured him of their continuing fidelity.

1771 November. Conference at Onondaga. The Six Nations had received belts from nations to the south and west inviting them to meet at Scioto (apparently the vicinity of Portsmouth, Ohio). Sir William Johnson recommended that they go to Scioto and manifest their fidelity to the English.

1771–72 Reported by Johnson in February 1772. A Six Nations embassy toured through the south (Cherokees and Creeks) and the Ohio region (Shawnees) to break up an anti-English conspiracy.

1772 July. Sir William Johnson and New York Governor William Tryon met with the Canajoharie Mohawks and the Oneidas at Johnson Hall. Bitter complaint from the Mohawks about being deprived of all their land. "We have seen that those Officers and Soldiers who served in this Country during the late War, have been rewarded with Tracts of Land in return for their services, and as we were aiding and assisting in the same cause, we must deem it a peculiar hardship in case we are not permitted to hold this little Remnant undisturbed." Promises were given to protect their interest. Tryon: "I shall take such measures as are consistent with my authority."

1772 September. British troops evacuated Fort Pitt.

1772 October. Sir William Johnson met with the Six Nations at Johnson Hall. They reported formally upon their embassy to the southern and western Indians and turned over to him the "bad" (anti-English conspiracy) belts they had collected during their tour.

1772 December. The Crown reprimanded New York's Governor William Tryon severely for sanctioning sales of Indian lands to private persons: "unjustifiable collusion. . . . It is the King's pleasure and positive command that you do not, upon any pretence whatever, sign any Grant or Patent for those Lands."

1773 March. Council at Onondaga to discuss reasons for uneasiness among Senecas, who were angered and concerned by Virginians' murder of four of their people in the fall of 1772, among other things. Divided opinions. Most Iroquois wanted to settle the matter peacefully. Others wanted to replace the dead with prisoners or scalps. Report given to Sir William Johnson.

1773 April. Sir William Johnson and retinue met with the Six Nations chiefs at Johnson Hall. They confessed fault in having had too many "foreign alliances," and reported that they had summoned back to Irouoia their people living in the west. Johnson scolded them for delaying punishment of Piankeshaws and Twightwees who had killed some traders. They complained about trade. He overbore the complaint without making concessions. Covenant Chain renewed and brightened. (Since the end of the French regime in Canada, Johnson's behavior toward the Iroquois is conspicuously arrogant in the records.)

1773 November. A council at Johnson Hall about the murder of four Frenchmen by Senecas. Sir William Johnson demanded that the murderers be surrendered to him. Hostages were left by the Indians.

1774 January–October. Virginians occupied the abandoned Fort Pitt and launched Lord Dunmore's War against the Shawnees.

1774 June–July. Sir William Johnson assembled the Six Nations chiefs once more at Johnson Hall to confer about continuing trouble in the Ohio country. Johnson died at the height of the conference.

1774 September, October, November. Six Nations returned to Johnstown to condole the death of Sir William and urge appointment of Guy Johnson in his place. Concern about peace and the Shawnee problem. Covenant Chain held fast.

1774 November. Meeting of the League at Onondaga between chiefs of the Six Nations and the Shawnees. Six Nations determined policy not to support other Indians in Lord Dunmore's War, and the matrons censured the Cayugas for letting their young men aid the Shawnees without council sanction. The warriors were recalled.

1774 December. Representatives of the Six Nations met Guy Johnson, as his uncle's successor, at Guy Park.

1775 August and September. At German Flats the commissioners of the Continental Congress met representatives of the Six Nations "at the woods' edge" and invited them to treat at Albany. The treaty was the last to be held at Albany. The commissioners employed the protocol taught them by Canasatego at Lancaster, appealed to Iroquois metaphors, showed a Union Belt and Path Belt of wampum, and urged neutrality upon the Six Nations in the coming struggle.

1776 March. James Dean, as agent of Congress, attended a League council at Onondaga and found it fractionated in its loyalties.

1776 January, May, and August–September. British representatives held a series of councils with Six Nations chiefs at Niagara to urge loyalty and active support of the Loyalist cause.

1776 July. Congress declared American independence.

1777 January. Reports reached Fort Stanwix that pestilence had struck Onondaga and toppled some principal chiefs. Disheartened and divided in their minds, the remainder "covered" the great council fire. Missionary and congressional agent Samuel Kirkland urged general Schuyler to condole the bereaved nations and win them to the patriot cause, but the ceremony was not performed. (Thereafter during the Revolutionary War, the League ceased to function as a unit, and the individual nations negotiated independently. Most of the Oneidas and Tuscaroras allied to the United States. Most of the other Iroquois held to their alliance with the British.)

1783 September. In the Treaty of Paris, Great Britain ceded sovereignty to the United States over territory east of the Mississippi River. Six Nations omitted from consideration, to their great resentment. (Their postwar political and territorial statuses were determined in negotiations with the governments of Canada and the United States respectively.)

1784 October. Treaty at Fort Stanwix (Rome, N.Y.) between representatives of the Six Nations and United States commissioners for Indian affairs. Agents for both Pennsylvania and New York attended and negotiated concessions in the interests of their states. The U.S. commissioners imposed harsh terms based on an assumption of rights of conquest. They exacted territorial concessions and forced unauthorized Iroquois representatives to sign the treaty and leave hostages in lieu of unreturned prisoners. Division in Iroquois ranks. Mohawk Aaron Hill assumed role of spokesman for the western nations as well as the Six Nations, but Seneca Cornplanter reserved right of the westerners to speak for themselves. (Cornplanter was severely censured by the Seneca council when he returned home, and the League refused to confirm the treaty.)

1784   October. Canadian governor Sir Frederick Haldimand "purchased a tract of land from the Indians situated between the Lakes Ontario, Erie, and Huron" and granted a reserve to the Six Nations in recognition of their service to Britain during the war of the American Revolution. Mohawk Joseph Brant acted as principal spokesman for the Iroquois. (After much attrition, the present Six Nations Reserve on the Grand River in Ontario is the remainder.)

1785   June. Herkimer, N.Y. Under duress, Oneida and Tuscarora Indians ceded to the State of New York the land now comprising the counties of Chenango, Broome, and Tioga, rather than to private parties. (This was the first of a series of New York treaties now considered by some parties to have been held illegally because of the provisions of the Federal non-intercourse act.)

1788   July. Buffalo Creek, N.Y. The Phelps and Gorham purchase from the Senecas of lands east of the Genesee River adjacent to the Massachusetts pre-emption line.

1788   September. Fort Schuyler (formerly Stanwix). At a meeting with New York State commissioners, Onondaga chiefs ceded all the nation's land, but specified a reserve for their people.

1788-89-90   Cayuga. Negotiations for Cayuga lands, culminating in a treaty of June 1790. Chief Fish Carrier rebuked the governor of New York for neglecting ancient usages.

1789   January. Fort Harmar (Marietta, Ohio). General Arthur St. Clair negotiates separate treaties on the same day with the displaced Iroquois and the other western Indians. The Iroquois treaty confirmed terms of the 1784 Fort Stanwix treaty with the Six Nations. It dealt with the adjudication of crimes, but did not return Seneca lands.

1790   October. A confederation of western Indians defeated general Joseph Harmar near present-day Fort Wayne, In.

1790   November. Tioga Point (Athens, Pa.). Colonel Timothy Pickering met chiefs of the Seneca nation to take the hatchet out of their head for the murder of two chiefs at Pine Creek. His purpose was to neutralize the Seneca warriors who were the bulk of Iroquois manpower. Pickering was given lessons in Iroquois protocol from chiefs Red Jacket and Farmer's Brother, and he received the clan matrons.

1790–91   Winter. Philadelphia, Allegheny Seneca chiefs Cornplanter, Half Town, and Big Tree called on President George Washington for relief of grievances arising from the 1784 Treaty of Fort Stanwix. The President enlisted help of Quakers.

1791   July. Newtown Point (near Painted Post, N.Y.). Because of unrest among the Iroquois, and in the hope of recruiting some of their warriors to fight against the western Indians, Washington sent Timothy Pickering to treat. Observing the Indians' disposition—they were mostly Senecas—Pickering violated his instructions by not attempting to recruit, but he did secure a promise of neutrality which his superiors considered a triumph. Among the Senecas, Red Jacket used Pickering as a foil to emerge dominant in his power struggle with Cornplanter. Pickering's efforts to convert Iroquois culture to American-style farming were stalled by Red Jacket's nativist oratory.

1791   August. Quebec. Negotiations between the British and representatives of Six Nations, Ottawas, Ojibwas, Potawatomis, Hurons, Shawnees, Delawares, and Tutelos.

1791   November. Territorial Governor Arthur St. Clair was routed at present-day Fort Recovery, Ohio, by warriors of the western confederation.

1792   March–April. Despite the opposition of Mohawk chief Joseph Brant, Samuel Kirkland recruited and led a delegation of sixty Iroquois to Philadelphia for discussions of programs in agriculture, manual arts, and education. War Secretary Henry Knox aroused strong antagonism by trying to shift the agenda to diplomatic and military issues vis-à-vis the western confederation, as Brant had predicted. Timothy Pickering brought the conference back to its original purpose, Washington addressed the chiefs, and they were urged to explain to their western brethren the limits of United States claims.

1792   Joseph Brant, now ambivalent in loyalties, visited Philadelphia and cooperated with the government, advising that the United States would have to restore some Indian territory.

1793   January. Governor John Graves Simcoe gave a deed to the Six Nations confirming their Grand River lands.

1793   April. Bay of Quinte (at the mouth of the Trent River, Ontario). Canada conceded a tract of land to the Six Nations that became the basis for the present Tyendinaga Reserve.

1793   July. Maumee Rapids (Sandusky, Ohio). An intended treaty between the western confederation, including some Iroquois, and the United States failed because of British interference. Issues were peace, a boundary at the Ohio River, and lands of the Six Nations that had been preempted at Fort Harmar. The failed mission did separate the Six Nations from active participation in the western confederation's war parties. Heavily documented in journals of Quaker observers John Parrish, William Savery, Jacob Lindley, and Joseph Moore.

1793–94 Buffalo Creek (vicinity of Erie County, N.Y.) and Presque Isle (Erie, Pa.). A series of councils culminating in a general peace treaty, postponed from Venango and ultimately held at Canandaigua, N.Y. Attended by Israel Chapin for the U.S., John Butler for the British, and the Six Nations chiefs with Joseph Brant. Issues involved offer by western tribes to help the Six Nations recover lands; and the failure by the United States to honor the boundaries that had been established at Fort Harmar. General Chapin made a dangerous journey to Presque Isle to quiet tensions of the Senecas over settlement of the Erie Triangle. An issue also arose over proper place for council – Buffalo or Canandaigua.

1794 August. General Anthony Wayne defeated warriors of the western confederation at Fallen Timbers (near Maumee, Ohio).

1794 October–November. Canandaigua. Timothy Pickering negotiated a treaty of peace and friendship between the Six Nations and the United States. Though including the Six Nations and all ranks of society it was mainly concerned with the Senecas, the Mohawks being scarcely represented. Provisions: peace and tranquility, neither party to disturb the other, quit claims to lands previously ceded or reserved, an annuity from the United States of $4,500. Word of Wayne's victory at Fallen Timbers permitted the U.S. to demand and secure the Niagara portage.

1794 December. Oneida. Timothy Pickering conferred with Oneidas, Tuscaroras, and Stockbridges to get lands to satisfy land grants to veterans of the War of the Revolution.

1795 August. Greenville, Ohio. Treaty between Anthony Wayne and the western tribes, in sequel to the battle of Fallen Timbers. It tacitly rescinded the conquest theory advanced at Fort Stanwix in 1784, recognized tribal rights to territory, and established a definite boundary line between tribal territory and the lands open to settlement by Americans. The United States did not abjure its sovereignty; it secured preemption right to purchase whenever Indians intended to sell land.

1796 May. New York City. Treaty by the Seven Nations of Canada, including Iroquois of Caughnawaga (Kahnawaka) and St. Regis (Akwesasne), with the United States and New York State. The Seven Nations ceded their land claims in New York State for a lump sum and perpetual annuity.

1797 March. Albany, N.Y. Treaty by Mohawks with the United States and New York State. Conflicting claims of Caughnawaga and Loyalist Mohawks settled in conveyance to New York State.

1797 September. Geneseo, N.Y. Treaty at Big Tree between Robert Morris, representing Massachusetts' interest, and Senecas. It extinguished Indian title to lands west of the preemption line, but reserved ten tracts of which the three present Seneca reservations and the Tuscarora reservation are the only survivors. $100,000 paid in stock of the Bank of the United States, income to be paid as an annuity. (The Bank later failed, and Congress had to appropriate moneys.) Ratified by the United States, this treaty had the effect of establishing reservations.

1798 April. Mohawks of Upper Canada relinquished claims to lands in New York State. Under authority of the United States, New York commissioners met Indian spokesmen Joseph Brant and John Deserontyou.

1798 June. Oneida, N.Y. At a treaty between the Oneidas and New York State, the State purchased part of the reserved lands of Oneida for $500 and an annuity of $700. A United States commissioner was present. (This is but one of about thirty such treaties.)

1802 June. Oneida. Treaty between Oneidas and New York State, with a United States agent present. Several parcels of land previously reserved were ceded.

1802 June. Buffalo Creek. Chiefs and warriors of the Seneca Nation met with O. Phelps, representing the United States, to cede Little Beard's reservation on the Genesee River for a consideration of $1,200.

1802 August. With a U.S. commissioner present, New York's Governor Clinton met with chiefs of the Seneca Nation of Indians. They ceded a mile strip on the Niagara River, from Buffalo Creek to Black Rock to Stedman's farm, reserving fishing and camping rights. Consideration: $200 + a further sum of $5,300 + $500 worth of chintz, calico, and other goods.

1805 May. Buffalo Creek. A council was held between the Six Nations of the Grand River in Canada and the Senecas and other Iroquois of Buffalo Creek. Discussion of relations between the Iroquois in Canada and those in the United States.

1806 Continuation of the foregoing council.

1810 September. Brownstone (near Detroit, Mich.). A conference between Indians, including some Iroquois, and Americans.

1814 July. Greenville, Ohio. Representatives of Wyandot, Delaware, Shawnee, Seneca, and Miami (Twightwee) tribes treated with the United States.

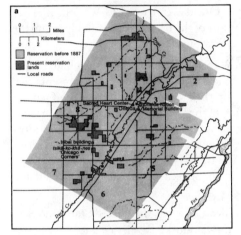

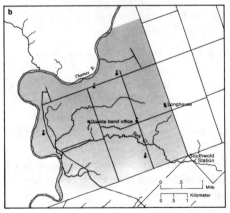

4. Location of modern Oneida lands outside New York: **a**, in Wisconsin; **b**, in Ontario. Numbers in **a** denote neighborhoods: 1. *latihǫlahelaʔa·kâ·* 'gun-laid-on people'; 2. *tekahsokęha·kâ·* 'between-the-lips people'; 3. *talǫʔkowanha·kâ·* 'Duck Creek people'; 4. *tiksęnha·kâ·* 'Dixon people'; 5. *latinatakǫha·kâ·* 'in-the-village people'; 6. *tatsmenha·kâ·* 'Dutchman people'; 7. *ketsyohaleʔkeha·kâ·* 'fish-on-a-pole people'; 8. *simoha·kâ·* 'Seymour people.'

1815   September. Spring Wells (near Detroit, Mich.). A treaty between representative of Wyandot, Delaware, Seneca, Shawnee, Miami, Ojibwa, Ottawa, and Potawatomi tribes and the United States.

1817   September. Maumee Rapids near Lake Erie. A treaty between representatives of the Wyandot, Seneca, Shawnee, and Ottawa tribes, and the United States.

1818–19   A series of treaties between the Six Nations on Grand River and the government of Canada, held at Ancaster and Hamilton in Ontario.

1823   The first party of New York Oneidas emigrated to Wisconsin. They were followed gradually by most of the tribe who eventually set up the Oneida Nation at Oneida, Wisconsin.

1826   August. Buffalo Creek, N.Y. With commissioners from the United States and the Commonwealth of Massachusetts present, the representatives of the Seneca Nation gave up their remaining lands on the Genesee River and sold a large portion of the Buffalo Creek reservation to trustees of the Ogden Land Company. Also all but 12,800 acres of the Tonawanda reservation, and eight square miles of the Cattaraugus reservation. In all, 86,887 acres. The treaty was never ratified by the Senate nor proclaimed by the President. Senecas called the treaty invalid and sued in court, but lost.

1831   February. Washington, D.C. Treaty between the United States and Senecas of the reservation on the Sandusky River in Ohio.

1832   December. Seneca Agency on the Cowskin River in Ohio. Treaty between Senecas, Shawnees, and the United States.

1838   January. Buffalo Creek, N.Y. With a United States commissioner present, Senecas sold to the Ogden Land Company their four remaining reservations: Allegany, Cattaraugus, Tonawanda, and Buffalo Creek. Compensation $202,000. There was much dissension among the Senecas because the intent of the treaty was to bring about emigration of all the Senecas to the trans-Mississippi west, and this was bitterly fought by many of the nation. Asher Wright and the Society of Friends produced evidence of fraud, bribery, and forgery, and objections were raised in Congress; but the transaction occurred during the Jackson administration at the height of the clamor for Indian removal, and the treaty was ratified.

1842   May. Buffalo Creek, N.Y. A treaty of compromise. With the aid of the Society of Friends and other concerned Euramericans, the Senecas regained Allegany and Catteraugus reservations. Buffalo and Tonawanda were lost, and the Ogden land Company retained the pre-emption right to the lands of the Seneca Nation.

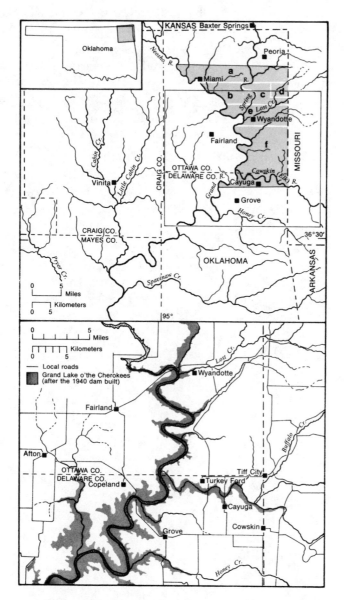

5. Toned area in top map shows bounds of Neosho Reservation in Oklahoma, assigned in 1832 to mixed bands from farther east. Bottom map shows 20th-century Seneca-Cayuga region. Letters in top map identify assignments: **a**, to Peoria, Kaskaskia, Piankashaw, Wea; **b**, to Ottawa; **c**, to Eastern Shawnee; **d**, to Eastern Shawnee and then in 1875 to Modoc; **e**, to Wyandot; **f**, retained by Seneca-Cayuga until allotment, 1888–1903. In 1974, about 1,000 acres of Seneca-Cayuga land remained as tribally owned.

1854 Report in the Vermont House of Representatives of Iroquois land claims presented in 1798, 1800, 1812, and 1826 upon the State of Vermont for their hunting ground.

1855 November. Report to the Vermont State Legislature of the committee appointed by the governor to investigate the Iroquois land claims.

1858 November. Tonawanda, N.Y. Treaty between the Tonawanda Senecas and the United States. The Indians repurchased their reservation land with funds from exchange and sale of Seneca reservation in Kansas.

1861–65 War between the United States and the Confederate States of America.

1861 October. Park Hill in the Cherokee Nation. Treaty between the Confederate States of America and the Senecas and Shawnees.

1867 February. Washington, D.C. Treaty between United States and Senecas, mixed Senecas and Shawnees, and nine other tribal parties.

1913 Treaty between Canada and the Indians of Michel's Band, province of Alberta, many of whom were of Iroquois descent. This supplemented Canadian Treaty Number 6, negotiated in 1876 between Canada and the Indians of western Canada.

9

Gazetteer

THIS GAZETTEER provides brief identifications of place names commonly found in historical documents and scholarly literature pertaining to treaties in which Iroquois Indians were involved. It is designed to be used as a supplement to standard atlases, identifying place names that would otherwise be hard to find. Additional information on place names may be found in some works listed in this volume's Bibliography. Two, upon which this gazetteer has relied heavily, should be noted: William N. Fenton, "Problems Arising from the Historic Northeastern Position of the Iroquois," and Frederick W. Hodge, ed., *Handbook of American Indians North of Mexico*. Notebooks compiled for the *Atlas of Great Lakes Indian History*, edited by Helen H. Tanner, Adele Hast, and Jacqueline Peterson, to be published by the University of Oklahoma Press, 1984, were used as major sources for identification. *Northeast* is also a valuable resource.

Some alternate names and spellings for places are given. Considering the ample imaginations and tin ears of colonial scribes, the variations are far from exhaustive. Identifications are usually presented under one entry only, with a few alternate names and spellings cross-referenced. It is not to be assumed that the names and spellings of the main entry are any more correct than others.

AKWESASNE (Aughquisasne, St. Regis) "Where the ruffed grouse drums" A primarily Mohawk settlement at the confluence of Racquette, St. Regis, and St. Lawrence Rivers. Offshoot from Caughnawaga, q.v. Established about 1754. The modern reservation spans the border between the United States and Canada.

ALLAQUIPPA'S VILLAGE   In the mid-eighteenth century, a village at the mouth of the Youghiogheny River. Home of a prominent woman who was known by the English as "Queen Allaquippa." Her name seems Delaware, but Conrad Weiser identified her as a Seneca.

ALLEGANY RESERVATION (Allegheny)   Seneca reservation that stretches for a number of miles along the Allegheny River and Reservoir, encompassing the town of Salamanca, N.Y.

ALLEGHENY   Thus spelled, the name of a river tributary to the Ohio. The Colonial era "Ohio country" included the Allegheny's valley.

ANDAGORON   Mohawk village south of Lake George in 1642.

ASSERUE   Mohawk village on south side of Mohawk River in 1644. Associated with the Turtle Clan.

ATIGA   See Kittaning.

ATSANINGO   See Otsiningo.

ATTIGUE   See Kittaning.

AUGHWICK (Aucquick, Old Town)   Indian village in the mid-eighteenth century at mouth of Aughwick Creek, near present Shirleysburg, Pennsylvania.

BAY OF QUINTE (Tyendinaga)   Mohawk settlement, 1784 to present. At Deseronto, Ontario.

BIG TREE   Seneca village on west side of Genesee River opposite Geneseo late eighteenth, early nineteenth century.

BRANDT'S TOWN   Present Brantford, Ontario.

BROTHERTON (Brothertown)   Residence of mixed group of Indians (Mohegans, Narragansetts, Mahicans, Pequots, and others) on land provided by Oneidas in 1774. Near present Oriskany, N.Y. The Indians moved to what is now the State of Wisconsin with Oneidas in the early nineteenth century.

BUCKALOONS (Kachinodiagon 'Broken reed', Kasinantiakon, Gachinantiagon, Paille Coupee, 'Cut straw', Poquihhilleu)   Village of mixed Senecas and Delawares on north side of Allegheny River above mouth of Oil Creek. Site near Irvine, nine miles down the Allegheny River from Warren, Pa.

BUFFALO CREEK   Areal location of Cayuga, Onondaga, and Seneca villages, although most commonly associated with Senecas. These villages were established in 1780, after the devastating Sullivan Expedition had destroyed much of Iroquois country. Cayugas settled on banks of Cayuga Creek at the mouth of the Cattaraugus, north of the Onon-

daga and Seneca villages. Onondagas settled near site of present Ebe-
nezer, N.Y., in a village named Onondahgegahgeh. Senecas settled at
village of Dyosyowan (Doshoweh) on Buffalo Creek in present Erie
County, N.Y.

CAHUNGAGE Iroquois village on south side of Oneida Lake in present
State of New York. Existed in the late eighteenth century.

CANADASAGA See Kanatasake.

CANADASEY See Kanatasake.

CANAJOHARIE (Canajohary; Fort Hendrick) Upper Mohawk village during the mid-eighteenth century, near present day Canajoharie, N.Y.
A fort was built at the village in 1755, and named Fort Hendrick, after
the prominent Mohawk leader Hendrick Tyanoga.

CANANDAIGUA (Kanandaigua) Seneca village. Site near present Canandaigua, N.Y.

CANASSERAGA (Ganaserage, Canaseraga, Ganaghsaraga) Tuscarora village of the east bank of Chittenango Creek, south of Oneida Lake.
Site of present Sullivan, N.Y.

CANAWAUGUS (Ganawagus) Seneca village on west side of Genesee River
on site across from present Avon, N.Y.

CANDACHIRAGON Western Seneca village whose site was shifted after
1687 to the Genesee River, where a number of towns sprang up around
present Geneseo, N.Y.

CANEADEA (Karachadeia, Karaghiyadirha) Seneca village on east bank
of Genesee River, across from present Caneadea.

CATARAQUI (Cadarachqui, Kaarachqui, Cataroqui, Catarachqua, Catack-
qui, Fort Frontenac) Present Kingston, Ontario.

CATHERINE'S TOWN (Sheohquago) Seneca village south of Seneca Lake
near present Catherine, N.Y., 1758-79. Home of Catherine Montour.

CATTARAUGUS RESERVATION (Cattaraugus "stinking banks or shore")
Settlement of the Seneca Nation of Iroquois on the main stream of
Cattaraugus Creek in Erie and Cattaraugus counties, between the towns
of Gowanda and Silver Creek on Lake Erie, New York. Name derived
from odor given off by clay banks, like that of old clay chimneys.

CAUGHNAWAGA "AT THE RAPIDS" (Gahnawage, Kahnawake) See
Osseruenen.

CAYADUTTA Mohawk village north of Mohawk River near Sammons-
ville and Cayadutta Creek about 1600. Probably moved south of Mohawk River after 1609.

CAYAGAANHE *See* Cayuga.

CAYUGA (Gayagaanhe, Cayagaanhe, Goigouen) Principal village of the Cayuga near eastern shore of Cayuga Lake. At one time was three or four miles south of present Union Springs, N.Y., at another two miles north. Seat of mission of St. Joseph 1668.

CHEMUNG Seneca village on north side of Susquehanna River on or near present site of Chemung, N.Y. Older village of same name was located about three miles from this site.

CHENANGO *See* Otsiningo.

CHENUSSIO *See* Geneseo.

CHERAGE *See* Chorage.

CHILLICOTHE Name of Shawnee village in the present state of Ohio that was located on at least three different sites from 1773 through 1782.

CHININGUE *See* Logstown.

CHOHARO *See* Thiohero.

CHONODOTE (Chonodok) Cayuga village on east side of Cayuga Lake, at site of present Aurora, N.Y.

CHONOJEHARE *See* Canajoharie.

CHOQUOEN *See* Oswego.

CHORAGE (Cherage) Temporary Seneca settlement from about 1789 to 1796 at site of present Painesville, Ohio.

CHUGNUT (Choconut) Mixed Indian village (Delawares, Shawnees, Conoys, Nanticokes, Mohicans, maybe Munsees as well) on south side of Susquehanna River opposite present Binghamton, N.Y.

CHUKNUT *See* Newtown.

CHURAMUK Iroquois village on east side of Susquehanna River near or in present Tioga County, N.Y.

CONDAWHAW Seneca village at site of present North Hector, N.Y.

CONEWANGO "Below the riffles" Seneca village at the mouth of Cone-wango Creek, near modern Warren, Pa., on the Allegheny River.

CORNPLANTER'S TOWN *See* Jenuchshadego.

CROWS TOWN *See* Mingo Town.

CUYAHOGA FALLS *See* Stigwanish.

DARBY'S TOWN Mingo or Seneca village, probably in existence between 1770 and 1780 near present Leesville, Ohio, on upper Sandusky River.

Moved in 1780 to upper waters of Darby's creek near present Milford Center, Ohio, until 1786.

DAYOITGAO Seneca village on Genessee River, near present day Mount Morris, N.Y.

DEYODIHAKDON (tetyoteha:ʔktonh "bent back upon itself" or "horse-shoe curve)" Old name of Seneca village near Rochester Junction, N.Y. Also the name of Horseshoe Bend of the Allegheny River, east of Salamanca, N.Y., and the name of an extinct Seneca longhouse.

DEYOHNEGANO ("Cold water") A name applicable to two sites: (1) a Seneca village near present day Caledonia, N.Y.; (2) a Seneca village since 1780 on the Allegany Reservation, q.v. This was the site of Cold-spring Longhouse until the Kinzua Dam debacle when the longhouse removed to a site near Steamburg.

DOSHOWEH *See* Buffalo Creek.

DUNOSAHADAHGAH *See* Jenuchshadego.

DUQUESNE French fort on site of Pittsburgh, Pa.

DYONOSONGOHTA (Genesinghuta) Seneca village of the late eighteenth century, on the site of Old Town, near Onoville, N.Y., visited by Quaker missionaries. The name refers to the passage of a ceremony through a house. Now inundated by Kinzua Reservoir.

DYOSYOWAN *See* Buffalo Creek.

EGHSUE *See* Ischua.

FORT ALLEN Present Weissport, Pa. Near the second site of the Moravian mission named Gnadenhütten ("The Huts of Grace").

FORT AUGUSTA *See* Shamokin.

FORT BEDFORD Probably not erected before 1757 on Raystown branch of Juniata River at or near present Bedford, Pa.

FORT BULL English fort in present Oneida County near Rome, N.Y., on Wood Creek. Destroyed by the French in 1756.

FORT CHAMBLY Fort built by the French in 1686 at site of present Chambly, Quebec.

FORT CROWN POINT (Fort Frederic) Located on west bank of Lake Champlain near the southern extremity of the lake. Called Fort Frederic by the French, Fort Crown Point by the English.

FORT DE LA RIVIÈRE AU BOEUF Present Waterford, Pa.

FORT DUNMORE Present Pittsburgh, Pa.

FORT ERIE   On west bank of Niagara River at lower end of Lake Erie. Built 1764.

FORT FRONTENAC   *See* Cataraqui.

FORT GEORGE   Present New York City.

FORT HENDRICK   *See* Canajoharie.

FORT HUNTER   English fort located on the east bank of Schoharie Creek just south of the Mohawk River. Erected 1712.

FORT JOHNSON   First residence of William Johnson at present Fort Johnson, N.Y., near Amsterdam, on north side of Mohawk River. Occupied by him until his move to Johnson Hall, in 1762, at modern Johnstown, N.Y.

FORT LIGONIER (Fort Preservation)   Built in 1777 in present Ligonier, Pa.

FORT LOUDON   Built by the English in 1756, one mile from present town of Loudon, Pa.

FORT MCINTOSH   Built in 1778 on the north bank of the Ohio River where it branches off Beaver River. Is on west bank of Beaver River in present state of Pennsylvania.

FORT MEIGS (Fort Miami)   Built in 1813 on 12 mile square tract at the foot of the Rapids of the Maumee River near present Perrysburg, Ohio, on east bank of the Maumee. Also called Fort Miami.

FORT MIAMI   *See* Fort Meigs.

FORT ONTARIO   Erected in 1755. Located on south bank of Lake Ontario on the east side of the tip of Oswego River, across from Fort Oswego which was erected at the same time on the west side of the river.

FORT ORANGE   Present Albany, N.Y.

FORT PRESERVATION   *See* Fort Ligonier.

FORT PRESQU'ISLE   *See* Presqu'isle.

FORT SCHUYLER   Formerly Fort Stanwix. Site of present Rome, N.Y.

FORT STANWIX   Site of present Rome, N.Y., renamed Fort Schuyler during the American Revolution.

FORT WILLIAM HENRY   English fort at site of present Lake George, N.Y.

FRENCH CREEK (Rivière aux Boeufs)   English name for river or creek named Rivière aux Boeufs by the French. In northwest region of present state of Pennsylvania.

GACHINANTIAGON ("Broken Reed" or "Brokenstraw")   Seneca name for village by its Delaware equivalent Buckaloons (q.v.), which the English adopted. Site at the mouth of Brokenstraw Creek, on right bank of Allegheny River.

GAHATO Indian village (probably primarily Seneca) in present Chemung County, N.Y.

GAHNAWAGE *See* Osseruenen.

GANADAGAN *See* Kanakaro.

GANADOGA Oneida village in present Oneida County, N.Y.

GANAGHSARAGA *See* Canasseraga.

GANARASKE *See* Kanaraske.

GANASTOGUE Seneca village at site of present Youngstown, N.Y., in 1669.

GANATSEKWYAGON *See* Canestiquiaigon.

GANDACHIRAGON (Gannondata) Seneca village that occupied two or more sites during the period for which we have written records. It was first called Gandachiragon. The name was changed to Gannondata after 1672 when the village was moved a mile or so north of where it had been. Both sites were near present Honeoye Falls, N.Y. Gannondata was destroyed in 1687 by French commander Denonville's expedition.

GANDOUGARAE (Ganondagarae, Gandougarse, Cannongarae, Gandagare, St. Michel) Seneca village at or near present East Bloomfield, N.Y., seventeenth century. Location of mission of St. Michel. Huron refugees settled.

GANENTAA (Genentaa) Jesuit mission in Onondaga County, late 1650s. Site at present Liverpool, N.Y.

GANESTIQUIAIGON (Ganatsekwyagon) Seneca village on north shore of Lake Ontario at mouth of Rouge River, c. 1665–87.

GANNEOUS Oneida village on north shore of Lake Ontario. Site of present Napanee, Ontario, c. 1665–87(?).

GANNONDATA *See* Ganadachiragon.

GANONDAGARAE *See* Gandougarae.

GANONDAGOWA ("Great town") *See* Kanakaro.

GAROGA Mohawk village east of present Garoga, N.Y. Probably south of Mohawk River after 1609.

GASKOSADA ("At the falls") The old Seneca name for Rochester at the falls of the Genesee.

GATHTSEGWAROHARE Seneca village on the east side of Canaseraga Creek about two miles from its confluence with the Genesee River.

GAYAGAANHE *See* Cayuga.

GEEVANGE *See* Gewauga.

GENESEO (Genessee Castle, Chenussio, Jenuhsheo, Little Beard's Town) Seneca village on east side of Genesee River, a little below present Geneseo, N.Y., before 1779. Sullivan's Expedition, however, found it moved to the west bank of the river.

GENESINGUHTA *See* Dyonosongohta.

GERMAN FLATS At or near site of present Herkimer, N.Y.

GEWAUGA (Geevauga, Geevange, Gewauge) Cayuga village on site of present Union Springs, N.Y., on east side of Cayuga Lake. When Cayuga reserved land in a cession in 1789, Gewauga was included in the area reserved.

GISTAGUAT (Gistaquat) Seneca village on the Genesee River, south of present Belmont, N.Y.

GLAIZE *See* Grand Glaize.

GOHONTOTO Indian village on site that subsequently became the Munsee, Iroquois village of Wyalusing. At location of present Wyalusing, Pa.

GOIGOUEN *See* Cayuga.

GOUENHO Onondaga village on Lake Oneida.

GRAND CACHE Area in present Alberta, Canada. Residence of some descendants of Iroquois who were involved in the Canadian fur trade.

GRAND GLAIZE (Au Glaize) Ottawa village at juncture of Auglaize and Maumee Rivers in Ohio.

GRAND RIVER *See* Six Nations Reserve.

GREAT MEADOWS Site near present Brownsville, Pa.

HALF KING'S TOWN *See* Upper Sandusky.

HARDIN CITY *See* Seneca Town.

HELL TOWN Delaware and Mingo or Seneca village. Later Delaware and Munsee. Located halfway between present Perrysville and present Butler, Ohio. In 1776 some residents moved to New Hell Town on Sandusky River near present Bucyrus, Ohio. Some remained for a few years at original site.

HISHUE *See* Ischua.

HONEOYE Seneca village on Honeoye Creek, near Honeoye Lake, N.Y. Destroyed by Sullivan's Expedition in 1779.

HONEY CREEK *See* Seneca Reservation community.

HORSEHEAD BOTTOM TOWN Mingo village on Pine Creek, off Little Scioto, in vicinity of present Portsmouth, Ohio.

HOSTAYUNTWA Oneida village on site of present Camden, N.Y.

ISCHUA (Hishue or Eghsue) Iroquois village on upper Allegheny River at or near present Olean, N.Y.

INGAREN (Tuscarora Town) Tuscarora village located in what is now Susquehanna County, Pa.

IRONDEQUOIT Rochester, N.Y.

JENUCHSHADEGO (Dyononhsade:gen?, Jennesedage, Dunosahadahgah, Cornplanter's Town "Burned house") Seneca village on right bank of Allegheny River seventeen miles above Warren, Pa. Now inundated by Kinzua Reservoir. The Seneca chief, Cornplanter, settled on his grant there in 1791 until his death in 1836. Attacked by American expedition against Iroquois villages in 1779.

JENUHSHEO *See* Geneseo.

JOHNSON HALL Home of William Johnson in present Johnstown, N.Y. Occupied by him from the spring of 1762 until his death in 1774.

JUNASTRIYO Tuscarora village after 1785 in the Genesee River valley below present Avon, N.Y.

JUTANEAGA Tuscarora village after 1785 at forks of Chittenango Creek, New York State.

KACHINODIAGON ("Broken reed") *See* Buckaloons.

KADARAGORAS *See* Cattaraugus Reservation.

KAHNAWAKE (Caughnawaga, Cachnawage, Cachanuage, Caghnawaga, Cagnewage, Caughnawagah, Cognahwaghah, Cognawagah, Cannawaghe, Kaghnuwage, Gannawaghe, Sault St. Louis) Iroquois village (primarily Mohawk) established as a Jesuit mission in 1676. Present Caughnawaga/Kahnawake Reserve. Near Montreal, Quebec. *See also* Osseruenen.

KAHONGORONTON Potomac River.

KANAGHSAWS Seneca village one mile northwest of present Conesus Center, N.Y. Attacked by Sullivan's Expedition in 1779.

KANAKARO (Kanagaro, Ganadagan, Kanakao, Ganondagowa "Great town") Principal Seneca village one mile south of present Victor, N.Y. Location of mission St. Jacques. After 1687, the site was moved to present Canandaigua.

KANARASKE (Ganaraske)   Cayuga village on north shore of Lake Ontario 1665–87. Site of present Port Hope, Ontario.

KANATASAKE (Canadasaga, Canadasegy, Kanadesaga, Kanadasege, New Castle)   Seneca village near present Geneva, N.Y.

KANESTIO (Canisteo, Canestio, Kanestia)   Mixed village, primarily Delaware or Munsee, on upper Susquehanna River. Site of present Canisteo, N.Y.

KANHATO   Tuscarora village after 1785.

KANOWALOHALE (Kanawalohale, Kannawalohalla, Kanawalahalla, Conowaroghere, Kanowalohare)   Oneida village on site of present Vernon, N.Y.

KANYENGO   Ticonderoga, N.Y.

KARAGHIYADIRHA   *See* Caneadea.

KASHONG   Seneca village on Kashong Creek at its entrance to Seneca Lake, south of present Geneva, N.Y. Destroyed by Sullivan's Expedition in 1779.

KAUNEHSUNTAHKEH   Tuscarora village south of Oneida Lake.

KENDAIA   Cayuga and Seneca settlement at or near site of present Kendaia, N.Y.

KENTE   *See* Quinte.

KENTSIO   *See* Quintio.

KIOHERA   *See* Thiohero.

KITTANING (Kittanning, Kittannin, Atiga, Attigue)   Reference to two or three mixed Delaware and Iroquois villages about fifty miles above Pittsburgh on the banks of the Allegheny River. Called Atiga (Attigue) by the Six Nations. Site of present Kittanning, Pa.

KONENTCHENAKE   Roanoke River.

KUSKUSKI (Cushcushkee)   Delaware village at or near present Newcastle, Pa. Seneca also lived there during mid-eighteenth century.

LAC DES DEUX MONTAGNES (Oka, Scawendadey, Lake of Two Mountains)   Former mission village (Iroquois, Algonquins, Nipissings) near present Montreal, Quebec. Now an Indian reserve.

LACHINE (La Chine)   Iroquois village near site of present Lachine area of the City of Montreal, Quebec, around 1541.

LA CONCEPTION   *See* Deyodihakdon.

LAKE OF TWO MOUNTAINS   *See* Lac des Deux Montagnes.

LA PRAIRIE Iroquois (primarily Mohawk and Oneida) settlement near present Montreal, Quebec, on south shore of the St. Lawrence River, opposite the island of Montreal. In 1676, the settlement was moved upstream to Sault St. Louis.

LA PRESENTATION *See* Oswegatchie.

LEWISTON (Lewistown) Shawnee village in 1800. After 1805 mixed, Shawnee and Seneca. Present Lewistown, Ohio.

LICK TOWN (Shawanese Salt Licks) Mingo village on Scioto River at or near present Columbus, Ohio.

LITTLE BEARD'S TOWN *See* Geneseo.

LOGAN'S TOWN Mingo, Seneca village just south of present Kenton, Ohio.

LOGSTOWN (Loggstown, Chiningué, Shenango) Delaware, Shawnee, and Iroquois settlement on the north bank of the Ohio River at site of present Ambridge, Pa. In the early 1750s, it was an important English trading post. Called Chiningué by the French.

LOWER MOHAWK CASTLE Name applied to a number of different sites through time. May have been village east of Schoharie Creek, about fifty miles from Albany, that was abandoned in 1626 warfare of Mohawks with Mahicans. Moved on north side of river in 1677. After 1693, it was located on south of Mohawk River on flats just west of Schoharie Creek. It remained in this general location during most of the eighteenth century.

LOWER TUSCARORA VILLAGE Tuscarora village three miles down Susquehanna river from present Windsor, N.Y.

LOYAL CONFEDERATE VILLAGE Temporary Iroquois village about eight miles south of Youngstown, N.Y. British General H. Watson Power named the village upon an invitation to do so by Joseph Brant. In 1784, Iroquois who had settled there moved to land on the Grand River in the province of Ontario.

MAHUSQUECHIKOKEN (Maghinquechahocking) Seneca and Munsee village on the Allegheny River about twenty miles above present Franklin, Pa. Fox refugees (Mesquakies) among the Seneca also inhabited this village. It was destroyed by an American expedition led by Colonel Daniel Brodhead in 1779.

MIAMI RAPIDS *See* Rapids of the Miami.

MIDDLETOWN At or near present Chemung, N.Y. Same site as the later Indian village of Chemung.

MINDEN   See Otstungo.

MINGO TOWN   Mingo village, probably on or near Mill Creek in the present State of Ohio. Companion to village of Darby near site of present Milford Center, Ohio. (2) Mingo, Delaware, Ottawa, Ojibwa, Wyandot, Mahican, and Abenaki village at site of present Cleveland, Ohio. Regional occupancy, 1747, Six Nations living on borders of Lake Erie on or near the Cuyahoga River. (3) Temporary Mingo settlement at site of present Mingo, Ohio, 1795–1805. (4) (Crows Town, Wiishto) Mingo Delaware village at mouth of Cross Creek at site of present Mingo Junction, Ohio. (5) (Wyandot Town) Wyandot, Mingo village, also called Wyandot Town, near site of present Zanesville, Ohio.

MOHAWK TOWN   Village on Honey Creek three-quarters of a mile from the Sandusky River and three or four miles south of present Tiffin, Ohio. Established about 1818.

NEW CANANDAIGUA   Seneca settlement near present Canandaigua, N.Y.

NEW CASTLE   See Kanatasake.

NEW STOCKBRIDGE (Stockbridge)   Settlement of various Indians from New England on land provided to them in Oneida country, about fourteen miles south of present Utica, N.Y., in 1785. Many, if not most, of the Indians originally settling there came from the village of Stockbridge in the present State of Massachusetts. The Indians of New Stockbridge moved to the present State of Wisconsin with Oneidas in the early nineteenth century.

NEWTON (Chuknut)   Probably a Seneca village on the north bank of the Chemung River, five miles below present Elmira, N.Y.

NIAGARA (Oniagara, Onyagaro, Onnyagara, Onyagara, Onyagre, Onyegere)   Area around the Niagara River in present western New York State and the eastern tip of the Georgian Peninsula of the Province of Ontario.

NICHOL'S POND   Formerly thought to be the site of Oneida or Onondaga town attacked by Champlain and the Hurons in 1615. Site proved to be prehistoric. In Town of Fenner, Madison County, N.Y.

NOWADAGA   Mohawk settlement on south bank of Mohawk River in present Herkimer County, N.Y.

OHIO REGION   General term used in colonial times to include both the Allegheny and the Ohio River Valleys.

OIL SPRINGS VILLAGE   See Tecarnohs.

OKA   See Lac des Deux Montagnes.

ONEIDA (Onneiout)   Oneida village whose location shifted at different periods of time. In 1757, it was near present Oneida, N.Y.

ONEIDA AND ONONDAGA ENCAMPMENT   Site at present Deerfield, Ohio.

ONEIDA RESERVE ON RIVER THAMES   Oneida settlement 1833 to present.

ONENGO   See Venango.

ONEOCQUAGO   See Oquaga.

ONEWYIURE   Mohawk village, reached by floating down the Hudson River past Fort Orange (presently Albany, N.Y.) in 1646.

ONINGO   See Venango.

ONNEIOUT   See Oneida.

ONNONTARE   See Onontare.

ONOGHQUAGA   See Oquaga.

ONONDAGA   Village whose location shifted some at different periods of time. Iroquois capital. In 1600, about two miles west of present Cazenovia, N.Y., and east of West Limestone Creek. From 1609 to 1615, it was moved southwest to hilltops around Pompey. Next moved north along east bank of West Limestone Creek, where it was identified with two sites, one of which was about two and one-half miles southwest, and the other one mile south, of Delphi. In 1630, it was one-half mile northwest of Delphi. In 1640, it was located about two miles south of present Manlius, N.Y. In 1720, moved to Onondaga Creek. Present reservation is in the valley of Onondaga Creek, a few miles south of Onondaga Lake, near present Nedrow, N.Y.

ONONDAGA AND ONEIDA ENCAMPMENT   Site at present Deerfield, Ohio.

ONONDAGA SETTLEMENT   Site near mouth of Portage River at present Port Clinton, Ohio. Small band of Onondagas that chose to live with Wyandots.

ONONDAGHARA   Onondaga village, three miles east of present Onondaga Hollow, N.Y., in 1829.

ONONDAHGEHAHGEH   See Buffalo Creek.

ONONDARKA   Seneca village on the Genesee River.

ONONTARE (Onnontare, St. Réné)   Cayuga village whose location shifted some at different times. Mission of St. Joseph to Cayugas included the mission station of St. Réné located at Onontare. May have been located in the vicinity of present Savannah, N.Y.

ONYAGARA　*See* Niagara.

OQUAGA (Oghquaga, Onoghquaga, Oquago, Oneocquago)　Village inhabited primarily by Oneidas and Tuscaroras on the east branch of the Susquehanna River, on both sides of the river, at the site of present Windsor, N.Y.

OPOLOPONG　Mixed village under the auspices of the Oneidas, on east bank of Susquehanna River's north branch in present Luzerne County, Pa., about thirty miles above Sunbury, Pa., and ten miles below Wilkes-Barre.

OSSERUENEN (Ossernenon)　Mohawk village in locality called Teatontaloga "two mountains apart." In 1634, it was south of the Mohawk River. Moved downstream about 1640 to a hilltop west of Schoharie Creek, one-quarter mile south of the Mohawk River, southeast of present Auriesville, N.Y. In 1659, it moved less than a mile to hilltop west of Auries Creek, at which time its name was changed to Caughnawaga ("at the rapids"). In 1666, Caughnawaga moved west, to the north side of the Mohawk River, northwest of present Fonda, N.Y. The name Caughnawaga (Gahnawage) was also given to the mission village near present Montreal, Quebec, where Mohawks and Oneidas settled in 1676. Here the name referred to the Lachine rapids in the St. Lawrence River.

OSSEWINGO　Mixed Indian village. Site a few miles from present Chenango, N.Y.

OSTANGAES ("Long Rock")　A prominent rock on the Susquehanna River, opposite an Indian village which took its name from the rock.

OSTOGERON　Oneida village on east bank of north branch of the Susquehanna River, or on east bank of Chenango River in the present State of New York.

OSWEGATCHIE (Fort Oswegatchie, Oswegatchy, Osweegachie, Swegatsy, Swagassie, Oswegoshaa, La Presentation)　Village inhabited by Onondagas, Oneidas, and Cayugas. Established as Sulpicion mission village of La Presentation in 1749. Site of present Ogdensburg, N.Y.

OSWEGO (Fort Oswego, Choquoen, Techouguen)　Site at present Oswego, N.Y.

OTSININGO (Chenango, Shenango, Otseningo, Otsaningo, Atsaningo, Otsineke, Otsineange, Otsininky)　Mixed Indian village (Conoys, Six Nations, Nanticokes, Mahicans, Shawnees). Near present Binghamton, N.Y., on east branch of Susquehanna River.

OTSTUNGO (Minden) Mohawk village south of the Mohawk River about 1600. Site four miles northwest of present Fort Plain, N.Y.

OWEGO Mixed Indian village under the auspices of the Cayugas on right bank of Owego Creek about two miles from the Susquehanna River in present Tioga, N.Y.

OYONWAYEA Tuscarora settlement. Site four miles east of the outlet of the Niagara River. Tuscarora moved to this location in 1780 after their villages south of Oneida Lake were destroyed during the American Revolution.

PAILLE COUPEE ("Cut Straw") See Buckaloons.

PAINTED POST At or near present Painted Post, N.Y.

PLUGGY'S TOWN Mingo village at site of present Delaware, Ohio.

POQUIHHILLEU Delaware name for Seneca village called Buckaloons by English speakers. See Buckaloons.

PRESQU'ISLE (Fort Presqu'isle, Rique) Site of present Erie, Pa. French fort built in 1753, on site of seventeenth-century Erie village called Rique.

QUINOUATOUA (Tinawatawa) Iroquois settlement on northern shore of Lake Ontario near present Westover, Ontario. Visited by Joliet in 1669.

QUINTIO (Kentsio) Cayuga village on north shore of Lake Ontario, on Rice Lake, 1665–87.

RAPIDS OF THE MIAMI (Miami Rapids) Rapids of the Maumee River in the present State of Ohio. Approximately eighteen miles from the mouth of the Maumee River. Delaware and Munsee towns were located in the vicinity in 1792.

RIQUE See Presqu'isle.

RIVIÈRE AUX BOEUFS See French Creek.

ROYAL BLOCK HOUSE Site of present Vienna, N.Y.

RUNONVEA Iroquois village near present Big Flats, N.Y.

ST. JACQUES See Seneca.

ST. MARY'S Present St. Mary's, Ohio.

ST. MICHEL See Gandougarae.

ST. REGIS See Akwesasne.

ST. RENÉ See Onontare.

ST. SACREMENT   Lake George, N.Y.

ST. STEPHEN   *See* Thiohero.

SALT SPRINGS   Indian settlement. Site at present Weathersfield, Ohio. Delaware, and possibly Seneca, residents.

SANDUSKY RIVER   Mohawk settlement about fourteen to sixteen miles above the mouth of the Sandusky River in present State of Ohio at the beginning of the nineteenth century. In 1819, moved to Honey Creek. Three or four miles south of present Tiffin, Ohio.

SAULT ST. LOUIS   *See* Kahnawake.

SAYENGAROGHTA   Seneca village established on Buffalo Creek in the spring of 1780, about four miles above the mouth of the creek. Associated with the Seneca chief, Kaien kwaahton.

SCAWENDADEY   *See* Lac des Deux Montagnes.

SCHANATISSE   Mohawk village on south side of Mohawk River about 1655.

SCHENECTADY (Shanegtade, Shinnochtady, Scharnactida, Schennectady, Schoneghtedy, Schonegtedy)   Present Schenectady, N.Y.

SCHOHANDAWANA   *See* Wyoming.

SCHOHARIE (Eskahere, Skohere)   Mixed Indian village, primarily Mahicans and Mohawks. Site on west bank of Schoharie Creek, opposite present town of Schoharie, mid-eighteenth century.

SCHOHERAGE   Oneida village on west bank of each branch of Susquehanna River (maybe Chenango River) a short distance above present Windsor, N.Y.

SCHOYERRE   Seneca village on west side of Seneca Lake, probably in present Ontario or Yates County, N.Y.

SCIOTO   Scioto River in present State of Ohio.

SENECA (Sonontoen, Sonnotouan, St. Jacques)   Seneca village located in the mid-seventeenth century a mile south of site of present Victor, N.Y. Jesuit mission of St. Jacques was in this village.

SENECA AT CUYAHOGA FALLS   *See* Stigwanish.

SENECA CASTLE   Site near present Geneva, N.Y.

SENECA RESERVATION COMMUNITY (Honey Creek)   Indian village on east side of Sandusky River, in township of present Clinton, Ohio. On or near Honey Creek. Created by treaty of 1817. Ceded in 1831, although some lands were reserved for Indians at that time.

SENECA TOWN (Fort Seneca)   Indian village on the west bank of the Sandusky River, seven to eight miles north of site of present Tiffin, Ohio. Location of Fort Seneca.

SENECA TOWN (Hardin City)   Seneca, or Mingo, village near site of present Hepburn, Ohio. Late eighteenth century.

SEVEGE   Oneida village, a short distance above present Tioga, N.Y., on west side of east branch of Susquehanna River.

SHATAKARONHIES ("Skies of equal height or length; level skies or level heavens")   Title of Seneca sachem in Iroquois league. Also name of his town. *See* Deyodihakdon.

SHAMOKIN (Fort Augusta)   Indian village of Delawares, Shawnees, and Iroquois on the confluence of the north and west branches of the Susquehanna River at site of present Sunbury, Pa. Probably settled about 1718. Site of English Fort Augusta, built in 1756.

SHANEGTADE   *See* Schenectady.

SHATEKARONHIES   *See* Deyodihakdon.

SHAWANESE SALT LICKS   *See* Lick Town.

SHAWIANGTO   Tuscarora village on the west side of the Susquehanna River not far from site of present Windsor, N.Y.

SHENANGO   *See* Logstown.

SHEOHQUAGO   *See* Catherine's Town.

SHESHEQUIN   Seneca, Delaware, Munsee village on east side of Susquehanna River on site of present Ulster, Pa. Moravian mission on site, 1769–72.

SIX NATIONS RESERVE (Grand River)   Iroquois settlement 1784 to present. On the Grand River, encompassing Ohsweken, southeast of Brantford, Ontario.

SKANNAYUTENATE (Skanneyut)   Cayuga village on the west end of Cayuga Lake, northeast of the site of present Canoga, N.Y., and nearly opposite present Cayuga, N.Y. Village was on land reserved by Cayugas in 1789.

SKOIYASE   Seneca village on south side of the Seneca River at present site of Waterloo, N.Y.

SOGHNUYADIE   *See* Susquehanna River.

SOLOCKA   Mixed Indian village under the auspices of the Oneidas, in the present State of Pennsylvania.

SOLOMON'S TOWN   Mingo Indian village under the auspices of the Oneidas, in the present State of Pennsylvania.

SONNOTOUAN   *See* Seneca.

SQUAKIE HILL (from Meskwaki)   Place at Mt. Morris on Genesee River where Fox refugees from the west lived.

STANDING STONE   *See* Stigwanish.

STIGWANISH (Standing Stone, Seneca at Cuyahoga Falls)   Seneca village at site of present Cuyahoga Falls, Ohio. *Stigwanish* means "Standing Stone."

STOCKBRIDGE   *See* New Stockbridge.

SWAGASSIE   *See* Oswegatchie.

SWAHYAWANAH   Cayuga village of northeast corner of site of present Romulus, N.Y.

SWEGATSY   *See* Oswegatchie.

TAGORONDIES   *See* Deyodihakdon.

TAWAGONSHI (Tawaqunshe)   Mouth of Normans Kill Creek near Albany, N.Y.

TEAGON   *See* Tioga.

TECARNOHS (Oil Springs Village)   Seneca village, commonly known as Oil Springs Village on Oil Creek, near site of present Cuba, N.Y.

TECHIROGUEN   Fishing station on river down from present Oswego, N.Y.

TECHOUGUEN   *See* Oswego.

TETYOTIHAKDON   *See* Deyodihakdon.

TEUSHANUSHSONGOTHA (Genesinghuta)   "Old Town" of the Senecas of Allegany, upriver from Cornplanter's Town, and some twenty miles southwest of Salamanca, N.Y., near Onoville, on right bank of Allegheny River. *See* Jenuchshadego, Dyonosongohta.

TEWANONDADON   Mohawk village situated in peninsula formed by outlet of Otsego Lake and Senivas Creek in the present State of New York.

TEYAIAGON (Teiaiagon)   Iroquois village on north shore of Lake Ontario at present day Oakville, Ontario. It was the most important village on the north shore during the 1680s.

THIOHERO (Kiohera, Choharo, St. Stephen)   Cayuga village, named for rushes bordering Seneca River, "river of rushes." Location of Jesuit mission of St. Stephen. About twelve miles north of site of present Union Springs, N.Y.

TINAWATAWA   *See* Quinouatoua.

TIOCHSAGHRONDIE (Tiochsagrodie, Tiughsaghrondie, Tuchsagrondie) Detroit, Mich.

TIOCHTIAGE (Mont Royal, Mont Royall, Montreal) Present Montreal.

TIOGA (Tiahogo, Teagon, Diaogo, Deahoga) Mixed Indian village (Iroquois, Saponis, Tutelos, Nanticokes, Munsees, Mahicans, and others) on site of present Athens, Pa., on right bank of Susquehanna River near its junction with the Chemung. Shawnees settled there for short time, 1756–60.

TIONONGARUNTE Seneca village on the north side of the Allegheny River at site of present Ischua, N.Y., before 1767.

TONAWANDA (Tonawanta "Along the riffles") Seneca village on Tonawanda Creek. Present Tonawanda Reservation near Basom, N.Y.

TOTIAKTON *See* Deyodihakdon.

TUSCARORA Tuscarora settlement about eight miles south of site of present Youngstown, N.Y., 1793. Present Tuscarora Reservation at or near Lewiston, N.Y.

TUSCARORA TOWN *See* Ingaren.

TUSCARORA VILLAGE Tuscarora settlement, for a number of years c. 1766. Two miles west of present Tamaqua, Pa.

TUTONAGUY Iroquois village above rapids of St. Mary in the present Province of Quebec, around 1541.

TYENDINAGA *See* Bay of Quinte.

UPPER CAYUGA Cayuga village in vicinity of present Union Springs, N.Y., about one mile south of its contemporary, Cayuga (Goigouen).

UPPER MOHAWK VILLAGE *See* Canajoharie.

UPPER SANDUSKY (Half King's Town) Wyandot, Mingo village on the Sandusky River about forty-four miles south of Sandusky Bay.

VENANGO (Onengo, Oningo, Oninge, Wynango, Wenango, Weningo) Primarily Delaware village in the 1740s and 1750s. Primarily Seneca in the 1760s and 1770s. Also residence of Shawnees, Wyandots, and Ottawas. At mouth of French Creek at site of present Franklin, Pa.

WASP'S TOWN Seneca/Mingo village. Site about eight miles from present Tiffin, Ohio.

WENANGO *See* Venango.

WIISHTO *See* Mingo Town.

WIOMING *See* Wyoming.

WYALUSING   Munsee, Iroquois village. Moravian mission, 1763–72. Formerly Indian village of Gohontoto. Site of present town of same name in State of Pennsylvania.

WYANDOT TOWN   *See* Mingo Town (5)

WYANDOT VILLAGE   Wyandot village, with possibly some Seneca and Ottawa residents, at or near site of present Sandusky, Ohio.

WYANGO   *See* Venango.

WYOMING (Wiomink, Wioming, Schohandawana)   Mixed Indian village (Munsees, Delawares, Iroquois, and Mahicans) at site of present Wilkes-Barre, Pa. Mainly Shawnees there in 1742, but primarily Delawares by 1756.

YORKJOUGH   Seneca village in vicinity of present Honeoye Falls, N.Y. (probably in Livingston County).

10

Persons Participating in Iroquois Treaties

This select list has been compiled from a variety of sources, shortened and adapted for the purpose of identification rather than biography. The editors wish to acknowledge especially their indebtedness to the *Dictionary of Canadian Biography* which is exceptional in its attention to the lives of Indians. The Smithsonian's *Northeast* volume 15 in the *Handbook of North American Indians* is also a valuable resource. While few Indian lives are in the *Dictionary of American Biography*, 21 vols. and supplements, edited by Allen Johnson et al. (New York: Charles Scribner's Sons, 1928–), it is useful, for colonials active in Indian affairs.

Achiendasse *See* Lalemant, Jerome

Agwerondongwas (Agwelontongwas) *See* Good Peter

Ahookasoongh An Onondaga chief who signed the 1701 treaty between William Penn and the Susquehannock/Conestogas. Identified as "Brother to the Emperor."

Andros, Sir Edmund, 1637–1714 Architect of the Covenant Chain. Colonial governor successively of New York, the Dominion of New England, and Virginia. Called "Corlaer" by the Iroquois as a mark of esteem. Intervened decisively in "King Philip's War" by inciting and arming the Mohawks to attack the hostile tribes of New England; and, in the war of Virginia and Maryland against the Susquehannocks, by strenuous efforts to make peace. In both instances he offered protection to the defeated tribes which all became tributary links in the Covenant Chain in 1677. Andros presided over the first multi-colonial treaties with the Iroquois League at Albany in 1677 when the "iron" chain of friendship became the "silver" Covenant Chain.

Annenraes, d. 1654   Onondaga chief involved in the intertribal negotiations preceding the Seneca and Mohawk onslaught against Huronia in 1649. Later he was captured and killed by the Eries.

Aouenano (Awenano, Awanano), fl. 1699–1701   Seneca civil chief played a leading role in the negotiations with the French that led to the peace treaty of 1701.

Aradgi, fl. 1700–1702   Onondaga sachem played a leading role in the negotiations with the French that led to the peace treaty of 1701.

Assaryquoa (Sword or Big Knife)   Iroquois title for governors of Virginia after 1684 when Lord Howard of Effingham, then governor, presented them with a cutlass.

Atarhea   *See* Tareha

Athasata   *See* Togouiroui

Atoyataghroughta   *See* Cook, Lewis

Atterwana   *See* Ottrowana

Atytoghhanongwea   *See* Cook, Lewis

Awenano   *See* Aouenano

Bacqueville de La Potherie, Claude-Charles Le Roy   *See* Le Roy de La Potherie

Batard, Flammand   *See* Flemish Bastard

Beauharnois de la Boische, Charles de, Marquis de Beauharnois   Governor general of New France, 1727–47. Frequent negotiator with the Iroquois. A critic of the mission at Caughnawaga and of the trade with Albany merchants carried on by the Indians and other people associated with that mission.

Belknap, Jeremy, 1744–98   Harvard Class 1762; congregational minister Boston; wrote journal of investigating tour with Jedidiah Morse into conditions among the Oneida in 1796, MHS *Proc.* 14 (1881–82): 409.

The Belt of Wampum   *See* Tohaswuchdioony (Onondaga) and Kaghswaghtaniunt (Seneca)

Berry, Gilbert R., d. 1796 or 1797   First settler (1789) in Avon, N.Y., married daughter of Wemple, the Indian trader, and himself supplied rum for the treaty at Canandaigha. Berry's tavern was a notable institution on the frontier, serving travelers and the Senecas of nearby Canawagus village. Afterward "Widow Berry's Tavern."

Bigot, Jacques, S.J., 1651–1711   Missionary to the Abenakis. In the autumn of 1691, went to France, taking with him the Abenaki vow to Our Lady of Chartres and a large wampum belt for the canons of the cathedral. The belt was still extant in the summer of 1967 and subsequently restored at the Musee de l'Homme.

Bigtree *See* Karontowanen

Blawbek (or Blewbeck) *See* Cagenquarichten

Bouquet, Henry, 1719–65 Swiss mercenary in British military service. Active in the Ohio region, 1762–65, he was involved in extensive negotiations with the Delawares, Shawnees, and Iroquois in 1764 and 1765 to settle a peace between them and the British. His *Papers* are a valuable source for the period.

Bradstreet, John, 1714–74 Acadian-born professional soldier in the British army. Commanded a campaign from Niagara to Detroit in 1764, during which he negotiated a controversial peace treaty with the hostile Delawares and Shawnees.

Brant, Joseph (Thayendanegea), 1742–1807 Mohawk war chief, protégé of Sir William Johnson, secretary to Guy Johnson, leader in the war out of Niagara against the Mohawk Valley settlers; obtained Haldimand Grant to lands along the Grand River in Canada, afterward the Six Nations Reserve; translated Anglican Book of Common Prayer and Gospel of Mark into Mohawk; built two chapels at Indian Castle, N.Y., and Brantford, Ont.

    Biographies: William L. Stone, *Life of Joseph Brant-Thayendanegea,* 2 vols. (New York: G. Dearborn and Co., 1838); Louis Aubrey Wood, *The War Chief of the Six Nations* (Toronto: Brook and Co., 1920); Isabel Thompson Kelsay, *Joseph Brant* (Syracuse, N.Y.: Syracuse University Press, 1984).

Brisay de Denonville, Jacques-René, 1637–1710 Military man, governor of New France (1685–89); invaded Seneca country (1687), which precipitated retaliation at La Chine (1689); his peace negotiations with Iroquois failed.

Bruyas, Jacques, S.J., 1635–1712 Missionary to Iroquois tribes, especially the Oneidas; grammarian; interpreter, and deputy to the governor general of New France in negotiations with the Iroquois and English.

Buade de Frontenac et de Palluau, Louis de, 1622–98 Soldier, governor general of New France; architect of French expansion in North America; defended New France against attacks of the Iroquois. Participant in numerous conferences and treaty negotiations with Iroquois, Huron, and Far Indians.

    Biography: William J. Eccles, *Frontenac: The Courtier Governor* (Toronto: McClelland and Steward, 1959).

Butler, John, Baptized 1728, d. 1796   British agent and interpreter among the Indians. Attended many Indian councils and organized Iroquois hostilities against the United States during the War of the American Revolution.

The Bunt   *See* Hotsinonhyahta?

Cachointioni   *See* Kakienthiony

Cagenquarichten (Kajnquiratiton, Kanakarighton, etc.) also called Blawbek (Blewbeck), fl. 1699–1726   Leading sachem of the Senecas, apparently the chief who signed the 1726 treaty placing Seneca lands under the British crown.

Caghswoughtiooni   *See* Kakouenthiony

Calliére, Louis-Hector de, 1648–1703   Governor of Montreal and successor to Frontenac as governor general of New France. With Frontenac in the French campaign against Onondaga in 1696. Negotiated the grand treaty with the Iroquois in 1701.

Canaghquieson, d. ca. 1777   Protégé of Sir William Johnson, he rose to prominence as an Oneida chief, often serving as speaker at Iroquois treaties and as ritualist for condolence ceremonies. Allied most commonly with the British, he often manipulated his alliance to benefit his nation.

Canasatego, fl. 1742–d. 6 September 1750   Onondaga chief. Spokesman at the Easton Treaty (1742) where he acted at the request of Pennsylvania's governor to condemn the Delawares as "women" and to forbid them to sell land thereafter. He was Iroquois spokesman again at the Treaty of Lancaster (1744) with Virginia, Maryland, and Pennsylvania. He is recorded at two treaties in 1745: with Conrad Weiser at Onondaga, and with Weiser and New York's governor Clinton at Albany. Canasatego came to Philadelphia in 1749 to make a cession of land, and was disappointed in his reception. His policies were repudiated by a new, pro-French leadership in the Iroquois League. Weiser hinted that his death may have been a political execution.

Cannehouet   *See* Tekanoet

Carheil, Etienne, S.J., 1633–1726   Missionary to the Cayugas (1668–83); made few converts; afterward among Ottawas where he persuaded them not to form an anti-French alliance with the Iroquois. Active with Kondiaronk and Calliére in peace of 1701. Spoke Iroquois with ease of native. Author of *Racines Hurones*.

Carondawana ("Big Tree" aka Robert Hunter), fl. 1714–29   Oneida chief. Appointed by Indians living at Conestoga to be "king" of the Shawnee band nearby (1714).

Cassiowea *See* Newcastle

Casswettune *See* Kakouenthiony

Cavelier de La Salle, René-Robert, 1643–87 Trader, explorer, agent of Canadian expansion in the Great Lakes and Mississippi valley regions. He was much opposed by the Five Nations because he extended French trade and protection to their enemies further westward. A close associate of Buade de Frontenac.

Cayenquirago ("Swift Arrow") See Fletcher, Benjamin.

Céloron de Blainville, Pierre-Joseph, 1693–1759 French Canadian professional soldier. He commanded an expedition through the Ohio country in 1749 to proclaim France's sovereignty and to warn the Indians of the region against trading or treating with the English.

Chabert de Joncaire, Daniel-Marie, ca. 1714–71 French agent and interpreter among Indians in the Ohio region. Son of Louis-Thomas Chabert de Joncaire, q.v., and brother of Philippe-Thomas, q.v., he replaced his brother in 1748 as principal agent. He had close contacts with Senecas and encouraged the Iroquois to remain neutral or join the French in controversies with the English. He was fluent in several Indian languages.

Chabert de Joncaire, Louis-Thomas, *dit Sononchiez* by the Iroquois, ca. 1670–1739 Soldier, agent, and interpreter for New France among the Iroquois. Learned Seneca as a captive. Active in negotiations in Iroquoia. He contrived the building of Fort Niagara.

Chabert de Joncaire, Philippe-Thomas (Nitachinon), 1707–c. 1766 Soldier, trader, Indian agent, and interpreter. In 1735 he succeeded his father, Louis-Thomas Chabert de Joncaire, q.v., as principal French agent among the Iroquois. Extremely active and influential in the western New York, Pennsylvania, and Ohio region. His principal base was among the Senecas.

Champlain, Samuel de, c. 1570–1635 Geographer, explorer, cartographer, and founder of Quebec. Expeditions to Huronia, against the Iroquois (1609, 1615), and ethnographer of their customs and politics. For his writings see the *Works*, edited by H. P. Biggar, 7 vols. (Toronto: The Champlain Society, 1922–36).

 Most recent biography: Samuel Eliot Morison, *Samuel de Champlain, Father of New France* (Boston: Little, Brown, 1972).

Chapin, Capt. Israel, Jr., 1764–1833 Son of General Israel Chapin. On his father's death, named to succeed him as superintendent of the Six Nations, which office he held during the administrations of Washington and Adams. Active in the Canandaigua and Oneida treaties of 1794, and subsequent negotiations with the State of New York.

Chaudiére Noire (Black Cauldron), d. 1697   Onondaga chief. A firm enemy of French Canada, active in war and negotiations.

Chenughiyata   *See* Hotsinonhyahta?

Chew, Joseph, 1720s–1798   The transcriber of proceedings of many Indian councils. Chew was appointed secretary to the British northern department of Indian affairs in July 1774. His duties were suspended during the American Revolution, but resumed in the 1780s under the superintendency of John Johnson. He then remained in office until his death.

Claus, Daniel, 1727–87   Born in Germany, he became involved in British Indian affairs after a trip to Onondaga with Pennsylvania interpreter Conrad Weiser in 1750. He learned Mohawk from Hendrick Theyanoguin of Canajoharie, q.v. From 1760 to 1775 he was based in Montreal as British Indian deputy in Canada. During the American Revolution he was stationed at Lachine. In 1778 he became deputy agent for the refugee Mohawks in Canada and held the position until his death. His papers at the Public Archives of Canada contain some material written in the Mohawk and Oneida languages.

Claus, William, 1763–1826   Son of Daniel. Executive councillor of Upper Canada where he settled after the American Revolution. Appointed deputy superintendent of Indian affairs, 1799. He encouraged Senecas, Cayugas, and other Indians of Buffalo Creek, N.Y., to migrate to the Six Nations Reserve at Grand River in the early nineteenth century, much to the consternation of Joseph Brant and many of Brant's followers.

Clinton, George, ca. 1686–1761   Colonial governor of New York, 1741–53. A British imperialist who opposed the clandestine Albany-Montreal trade. He negotiated with the Iroquois to solicit military aid against the French, and was a patron of William Johnson.

Clinton, George, 1739–1812   First Governor of New York, extinguished Indian land titles in State of New York, 1784–91.

Connessoa   *See* Teganissorens

Cook, Lewis ("Col. Louis Cook," or Atoyataghroughta, Atyatoghhanongwea), ca. 1740–1814   alleged Negro-Mohawk admixture, born at Saratoga, mother from Caughnawaga. Served both French and the Colonies after 1775; commissioned lieutenant colonel (1779); resided at Oneida after war, then St. Regis until War of 1812, when re-entered service.

Corlaer (The Governor of the province of New York) This name was bestowed by the Iroquois upon Governor Edmund Andros, ca. 1675, as a title of friendship, and continued in use for following governors except Benjamin Fletcher, q.v., who was given a special personal title. The name recalled Arent van Curler (or Corlaer) who had negotiated the first treaty of mutual assistance between the Mohawks and "all the Dutch" in 1643.

Cornplanter (Kayentwahkeh Gyantwaia, KaiutwaKu), ca. 173?–1836 Seneca chief on Allegheny river, also known as John O'Bail, after his father Abeel, an Albany Dutch trader. He participated in the Treaty of Ft. Stanwix (1784), also Ft. Harmer (1789), and in 1790 with Halftown visited President Washington in Philadelphia for redress of grievances. Present at Canandaigua (1794), and at Big Tree (1797). Received a personal grant of land from the governor of Pennsylvania (now flooded by Kinzua Dam reservoir).

Coswentannea *See* Kaghswaghtaniunt

Coursey, Henry, fl. 1675–83 Maryland official. As agent for Maryland and Virginia, Coursey negotiated one of the founding treaties of the Covenant Chain in 1677 at Albany, and returned for another treaty in 1682.

Croghan, George, d. 1782 Trader and land speculator. Participant in Logstown Treaty of 1752. French raids destroyed his trade in 1753 after which he became spokesman for "the suffering traders" in their land claims. Sir William Johnson, q.v., commissioned him in 1756 as Deputy Agent. As such for fifteen years he traveled constantly to negotiate with many tribes. His journals and letters are important historical sources.

Biographies: Nicholas B. Wainwright, *George Croghan: Wilderness Diplomat* (Chapel Hill: University of North Carolina Press, 1959); Albert T. Volwiler, *George Croghan and the Westward Movement, 1741–1782* (Cleveland: Arthur H. Clark and Co., 1926).

Cryn *See* Togouiroui

Cusick, Nicholas, fl. late 18th cent. Tuscarora. Active as an ally of the Americans in the American Revolution, during which he was commissioned in the United States army.

Dean, James, 1748–1823 Learned Oneida as a boy, graduate of Dartmouth College (1773), interpreter, judge, active in Oneida land questions. Agent to Oneidas during Revolution. Afterward Judge.

Deanaghrison *See* Tanaghrisson

Dearborn, Henry, 1751–1829 American Revolutionary General, led a regi-

236   REFERENCE MATERIALS

ment in Sullivan's campaign (1779), Secretary of War (1801–1809), active on Niagara frontier in War of 1812.

Decanesora *See* Teganissorens

Degawehe *See* Gawehe

Deiaquande *See* Teyoqueande

Denonville *See* Brisay de Denonville

De Tracy *See* Prouville de Tracy

Deyohninhohhakarawenh *See* Theyanoguin

Dollier de Casson, Francois, 1636–1701 Military man, Sulpician Priest, Superior (1671–74, 1678–1701). Expedition against the Mohawks (1666); explored the lower Great Lakes; important as first historian of Montreal and of contemporary events.

Dominie Peter *See* Good Peter

Dongan, Thomas, 1634–1715 New York governor, 1682–99. An aggressive expansionist, Dongan tried to use the Five Nations to penetrate the Canadian protectorate and trading system, but was rebuffed by the French. He blocked William Penn from acquiring an Iroquois cession of the Susquehanna valley, and initiated the myth of an Iroquois conquest of the Susquehannocks. The Iroquois rejected his proposal to destroy Pennsylvania's trade in order to benefit Albany.

Donnacona, d.c. 1539 Chief of the "Laurentian Iroquois" at Stadacona (Quebec). Kidnapped by Jacques Cartier in 1536. Donnacona had tried to prevent Cartier from going up the St. Lawrence to Hochelaga (Montreal). Donnacona was presented to King Francis I, and died in France.

Douw, Volckert Petrus, 1720–1801 Indian Commissioner, appointed 1774 by Congress. Present at treaty at Albany (1775) and German Flats.

Dutch Bastard *See* Flemish Bastard

Dyaderowane *See* Ottrowana

Emlen, James, 1760–98 Quaker of Chester County, Pa., attended Canandaigua Treaty (1794) with David Bacon, John Parrish, and William Savery, as observers in a concern for the Indians.

Enjalran, Jean, S.J., 1639–1718 Missionary; accompanied de la Barre to Hungry Bay 1684; envoy to Far Indians in French alliance.

Farmer's Brother, d. 1815, aged 90 Seneca chief of Buffalo Creek (Ogh-ne-wi-ge-was, properly *Honanyawas*); present at treaties during federal period; made celebrated speech at council at Genesee river in 1798; signed Treaty at Big Tree (1797), Buffalo (1801); fought with U.S. in War of 1812.

Fish Carrier (Hojiagede, Ojagaghte, etc.)   Cayuga Chief during the federal period. Signed various treaties, including Canadaigua (1794).

Flemish Bastard (Batard Flammand, Dutch Bastard, Jan Smits, John Smiths, Canaqueese fl. 1650–87)   Mohawk chief, son of Mohawk mother and a Dutch father, broke between French, Dutch, and English; famous for his advice on the structure of the Iroquois Longhouse at Quebec (1654).

Fletcher, Benjamin (Cayenquirago, Swift Arrow) 1640–1703   Governor of New York 1692–98. Simultaneously Governor of Pennsylvania, 1692–95.

Franklin, Benjamin 17 Jan. 1706–17 Apr. 1790   Printer, statesman, philosopher, scientist. One of the commissioners who treated with a delegation of Ohio Indians at Carlisle (1753). In 1754 he was a delegate to the Albany Congress convened by the crown to formulate a united colonial policy for Indian affairs, and he there proposed his Plan of Union. It was adopted by the Congress but not ratified by the crown or any colony. The printing firm of Franklin and Hall published a series of Pennsylvania's Indian treaties in splendid folio volumes that have been reprinted by the Historical Society of Pennsylvania. Most of Franklin's papers are in the American Philosophical Society and Yale University. They are being published in a comprehensive edition by Yale University Press.

    Biography: Carl Van Doren, *Benjamin Franklin* (New York: Viking, 1938).

Frontenac, Count   *See* Buade de Frontenac

Gage, Thomas 1721–1787   British general in North America (1754–74) and governor of Massachusetts Bay (1774–75). Sir William Johnson and Guy Johnson reported to him. His *Correspondence*, 2 vols., edited by Clarence E. Carter (New Haven: Yale University Press, 1931–1933). His papers are in the William L. Clements Library, University of Michigan, Ann Arbor.

Gaghsaweda   *See* Lodweek X Gaghsaweda

Gaghswaghtaniunt   *See* Kaghswaghtaniunt

Gaiachoton   *See* Kayahosota?

Garakontie (Garakonke, Harakontie   Baptized Daniel; most probably the *sagochiendagehte* ("name bearer" an official term for the Onondagas) of the *Jesuit Relation* of 1654; Onondaga chief and leading negotiator with the French until his death in 1677–78.

Garangula (Grangula)   *See* Otreouti

Garnier, Julian, S.J., 1643–1730   Missionary to the Iroquois, mastered languages, tutored Lafitau; Superior of mission of New France. Greatest exposure to Iroquois culture of any of the Jesuits.

Gaspar Soiaga   *See* Kondiaronk

Gatrowani   *See* Ottrowana

Gawehe (Degawehe, Gawickie, Goweaaey, Goweah, Koe, Kouee, Koweahe), fl. 1756–66   Oneida councillor. Active in the Seven Years War, he treated with both the French and the British, passing intelligence to both. He gave Sir William Johnson intelligence about the western Indians during Pontiac's War.

Gawickie   *See* Gawehe

Gayahgwaahdoh   *See* Kaienʔkwaahton

Geyesutha   *See* Kayahsotaʔ

Giengwahton   *See* Kaienʔkwaahton

Good Peter (Dominie Peter, Gwedelhes, Agwerondongwas, Agwelontongwas), fl. early 18th cent.–d. 1792   Oneida warrior, chief of Eel clan, and friend of Samuel Kirkland. Gifted orator. Spokesman at treaties with New York commissioners, particularly with Cayugas at Albany (1788–89).

Gorham, Nathaniel, 1738–96   Associated with Oliver Phelps in Phelps and Gorham Purchase (1788).

Goweaaey   *See* Gawehe

Goweah   *See* Gawehe

Granger, Erastus, d. 1823   Indian Agent (1804–19); citizen of Canandaigua, Judge; later, Buffalo (1803). Superintendent of the Six Nations (1804); held council with them (1811) on eve of war with Britain.

Grasshopper, d. 1788   Oneida chief sachem

Guyart, Marie (dite Marie de l'Incarnation), 1599–1672   Founded Ursuline order in New France; chronicler of Indian events in New France, of the education of Indian maidens, their skills in crafts; voluminous writer and correspondent.

Guyasuta   *See* Kayahsotaʔ

Gwedelhes   *See* Good Peter

Gwuiyahgwaahdoh   *See* Kaineʔkwaahton

Gyantwaia   *See* Cornplanter

Haldimand, Sir Frederick, 1718–91   Swiss-born professional soldier who became a British officer in America in 1756. Rising steadily in rank, he was appointed governor general of Quebec in 1777, holding the commission of lieutenant general. He organized Indian raids into the back settlements of New York and Pennsylvania, and provided lands for refugee Iroquois as well as colonial Loyalists, after the American Revolution. His papers at the British Library hold much valuable information about Indian diplomacy. Microfilm publication distributed by Clearwater Press, N.Y.

Half King *See* Tanaghrisson. This title was also given to Tanaghrisson's successor Scarouady, q.v.

Harakontie *See* Garakontie

Harmar, Josiah, 1753–1813   An officer of patriot troops during the American Revolution. As commander in Ohio after the war, he participated in the treaty of Fort McIntosh (1785) and attempted afterwards to expel the Indians from territory ceded by that treaty. A poor organizer and disciplinarian, he was badly defeated by Shawnees and other Indians in the Maumee Valley, 22 October 1790.

Hateouati *See* Otreouti

Hendrick or Hendrick Peters *See* Theyanoguin

Hill, David (Kanonghyontye, Karonyonte), d. 1790   Mohawk leader allied with the British during the American Revolution. He was present at the treaty of Fort Stanwix (1784) and reported it to Daniel Claus in a letter written in the Mohawk language. Later associated with Joseph Brant (Thayendanegea) in the Six Nations settlement on the Grand River in Ontario.

Hodatchehte *See* Millet, Pierre

Hojiagede *See* Fish Carrier

Honanyawas *See* Farmer's Brother

Honatteniate (dit "le Berger" shepherd)   Mohawk friend of the French and protector of Isaac Jogues, S.J. (d. 1650 in Paris). Hostage in crucial peace negotiations of 1645. *See* Kiotseaeton.

Horehouasse *See* Ourehouare

Hoteouate (Hotrehouati, etc.) *See* Otreouti

Hotsinonhyahta? (Chenughiyata, Chinoniata, Kotsinoghyata, Otsinughyada, Otsinoghiyata, Rozinoghyaya, aka The Bunt), fl. 1748–74.   Onondaga chief. Although his career paralleled Sir William Johnson's, he was a proponent of Iroquois neutrality and did not join British fighting forces until Johnson's capture of Fort Niagara in 1759.

Huault de Montmagny, Charles, c. 1583–c. 1653 First governor and lieutenant general of New France from 1636 to 1648. Negotiator of the peace of 1645 with the Five Nations who translated his name into "Onontio," their term meaning "Big Mountain," and thereafter used it as the title of the governor of New France, whatever his given name.

Jemison, Mary, 1743–1833 White Woman of the Genesee, captured (1758) by Delawares and taken to Ohio; then adopted by two Seneca women at Ft. Duquesne; eight children by two husbands (Delaware and Seneca); refused to leave the Senecas after the Revolution; commented on Ft. Stanwix treaty (1784) and its aftermath.

Johnson, Guy, c. 1749–88 Nephew of Sir William, Deputy for the Six Nations (1762), became Superintendent on Sir William's death (1774), a crucial year in Indian negotiations. Portrait by Benjamin West in National Gallery of Art, Washington, D.C.

Johnson, John, 1743–1830 British superintendent of Indian affairs in Canada from 1782 until his death.

Johnson, Sir William, 1715–74 Merchant, planter, soldier, provincial and crown agent for Indian affairs, baronet. He came to America from Ireland in 1738 and quickly established a plantation in the Mohawk Valley where he traded with the Indians, and gained the trust of the Iroquois, especially the Mohawks. He rose to great power and wealth after being commissioned royal superintendent of Indian affairs in the beginning of the Seven Years War, a post he kept the rest of his life. Johnson's basic policy was simple: to increase his own influence over the Mohawks, the Mohawks' influence within the Iroquois League, and the League's influence over other Indians; but he also followed the rule of divide and conquer. His published *Papers* are the most important single source of information about Iroquois politics and diplomacy in his time. *See* Bibliography.

    Most recent biography: Milton W. Hamilton, *Sir William Johnson, Colonial American, 1715–1763* (Port Washington, N.Y.: Kennikat Press, 1976).

Johonerissa *See* Tanaghrisson

Joncaire *See* Chabert de Joncaire

Jones, Horatio, 1763–92 Hoc-sa-gowwa, "Handsome boy"; captive among the Senecas (1781) when in service as a ranger; adopted in Seneca family; attended treaty councils in 1788–97; U.S. Interpreter with Jasper Parrish. Known as Captain Jones.

Kaghswaghtaniunt (Coswentannea, Gaghswaghtaniunt, Kachshwuchdanionty, Tohaswuchdoniunty, aka Belt of Wampum, Old Belt, Le Collier Pendu, White Thunder), f. 1750–62 Mingo Seneca chief closely associated with Tanaghrisson, later (after 1759) with Sir William Johnson.

Kaghswoughtioony *See* Kakouenthiony

Kachshwuchdanionty *See* Kaghswaghtaniunt

Kaienʔkwaahton (Sayenqueraghta or Siongorochti, in Mohawk; Gayahgwaahdoh, Giengwahtoh, Gwuiyahgwaahdoh, Kayenquarachton, Old Smoke, Old King, the Seneca King, the King of Kanadesaga), fl. 1751–d. 1786 Seneca war chief whose home village was Ganundasaga (Geneva, N.Y.) A noted warrior, he participated in treaty councils in Philadelphia (1754), Easton, Pa. (1758), Johnson Hall (1764), and Fort Stanwix (1768). Pro-British, he helped capture Fort Niagara (1759) and was conspicuous during the American Revolution in the Battle of Oriskany and the Iroquois-British raids into the Susquehanna valley.

Biography: George S. Conover, *Sayenqueraghta, King of the Senecas* (Waterloo, N.Y., 1885).

Kajnquiratiton *See* Cagenquarichten

Kakouenthiony (Cachointioni, Caghswoughtiooni, Casswettune, Kaghswoughtioony, Kaghswughtioni, aka Red Head), fl. 1748–56 Onondaga council member and speaker. His son Ononwarogo, q.v., came to be known as Red Head after the father's death.

Kalondowea *See* Karontowanen

Kanaghkwase *See* Karaghtadie

Kanakarighton *See* Cagenquarichten

Kanuksusy *See* Newcastle

Karaghtadie (Karaghiagdatie, Kanaghkwase, Kuriahtaaty, Nicholas, Nickus, Nickus Hance), c. 1700–59 Mohawk sachem important as ally of the British. A daughter married George Croghan, and Croghan's daughter Catherine married Thayandanegea (Joseph Brant) whose sister Mary was "housekeeper" to Sir William Johnson.

Karontowanen or **Kalondowea** Seneca chief during the federal period. Accompanied Cornplanter to Philadelphia (1790), where he died from too much hospitality.

Kayahsotaʔ (Gaiachoton, Geyesutha, Guyasuta, Kayashoton, Kiyasuta, Kiashuta, Quiasutha), c. 1725–c. 1794 Seneca chief. Although he was one of George Washington's escorts in 1753, he helped defend Fort Duquesne against Edward Braddock in 1755. So important in Pontiac's War that it has sometimes been called the Kiyasuta and Pontiac War.

Afterward he served as an intermediary between the British and the western tribes. A neutral at first during the American Revolution, he finally fought on the British side, but he stayed in the United States after the war.

Kayenquarachton   *See* Kaien?kwaahton

Kayentwahkeh   *See* Cornplanter

Kiashuta   *See* Kayahsota?

King, Thomas, d. 1774   Oneida chief who resided at Oquaga. Speaker for Oneidas, Tuscaroras, Conoys, and Nanticokes of villages on the Susquehanna River, he was prominent in the Easton treaty of 1758 when he spoke also for the Cayugas and Tutelos. Sir William Johnson considered him to be prominent and important, but he was characterized by one of the Onondaga council as a "straggling Indian" when his name was associated with the controversial deed to the Susquehannah Company. He died in 1774 while escorting a Cherokee embassy from Iroquoia to Charleston, S.C.

King Hendrick   *See* Theyanoguin

King of Kanadesaga   *See* Kaien?kwaahton

Kiotseaeton (Kioutsaeton, dit "Le Crochet" The Hook)   Mohawk chief, orator, and envoy to the French at Three Rivers in 1645. First recorded performance of Condolence protocol by an Iroquois. See chapter 7 herein.

Kirkland, Samuel, 1741–1808   18th-century missionary to the Oneida Iroquois, Revolutionary chaplain, government interpreter and agent, and founder of Hamilton College. His published journals are a valuable historical source. *See* Bibliography. His strong influence probably kept the Six Nations from participating in Lord Dunmore's War with the Shawnees, and was decisive in keeping the Oneidas attached to the United States during the American Revolution.

Knox, Henry, 1750–1806   Secretary of War under Washington (1785–94). Established federal Indian policy.

Koe or Kouee   *See* Gawehe

Kondiaronk (dit *Le Rat*, also Gaspar Soiaga, Souoias, Sastaretsi), c. 1649–1701   Tionontati or Petun Huron chief at Michilimackinac; negotiator with Iroquois and French; key figure in events leading up to and during Grand Settlement of 1701, during which he died and received honors of both French and Indians present at Montreal. Full Condolence Ceremony was conducted.

Kotsinoghyata *See* Hotsinonhyahta⹀

Koweahe *See* Gawehe

Kryn *See* Togouiroui

Kuriahtaaty *See* Karaghtadie

La Barre *See* Le Febvre de la Barre

La Grande Geule ("Big Mouth") See Otreouti

La Grande Terre *See* Ohonsiowanne

Lahontan, Louis-Armand de Lom D'Arce de, 1666–1716 Officer of colonial regular troops, author of philosophical dialogues, voyages, satirist of l'ancien regime. Learned Algonkian; observed and recorded de la Barre's humiliation; served under Denonville; met Le Rat (Kondiaronk) and made him hero of his dialogues. Disgraced in France, wandered European capitals. Some of his Iroquois observations are quite apt, but he must be read with caution. *See* Bibliography.

Lalemant, Charles, 1587–1674 Jesuit missionary and first superior of the Jesuits in Quebec (1634–39). Brother of Jerome.

Lalemant, Jerome, 1593–1673 Called *Achiendasse* by the Hurons, Jesuit priest and superior of the Huron mission (1638–45), superior of the Jesuits in Canada (1645–50, 1659–65); brother of Charles and Gabriel. Spiritual advisor to Marie de l'Incarnation, her informant on Indian ceremonies; advisor to Bishop Laval. In the background of secular affairs in the period.

Lamberville, Jean de, S.J., 1633–1714 Missionary to the Onondagas, diplomat, elder brother of Jacques, S.J. (also missionary to Onondagas, q.v.), warned La Barre of futility of trying to divide Iroquois Confederacy; correspondent of Dongan; work ruined by Kondiaronk, q.v.

La Potherie *See* Le Roy de La Potherie

La Salle *See* Cavelier de La Salle

Le Berger ("The Shepherd") *See* Honatteniate

Le Collier Pendu *See* Kaghswaghtaniunt

Le Crochet ("The Hook") *See* Kiotseaeton

Le Febvre de La Barre, Joseph-Antoine, 1622–88 Governor-general of New France (1682–85); recalled for disgrace by the Iroquois (1684). Replaced by Louis XIV with Denonville.

Le Grand Agnier ("The Great Mohawk") *See* Togouiroui

Le Moyne de Maricourt, Paul, 1663–1704   Officer, interpreter, negotiator with the Indians; officer of Denonville's expedition; had traveled as youth with brothers and mastered Indian dialects; enjoyed high prestige among the Onondagas, derived partly from that of his father, Charles Le Moyne de Longueuil; had a gift for symbolic oratory.

Le Rat   See Kondiaronk

Le Roy de La Potherie, Claude-Charles (dit Bacqueville de La Potherie, Claud-Charles), 1663–1736   Historian of events leading up to the Grand Settlement of 1701; one volume of letters on Iroquois customs and metaphors. Of the 4 vols., 1, 3, and 4 are in form of letters; 3 and 4 are devoted to the Iroquois wars and peace parleys up to 1701. Summarizes speeches of Calliére; account of funeral and burial of Kondiaronk, q.v.

Lincoln, Gen. Benjamin, 1733–1810   Revolutionary veteran, appointed by President Washington chairman of the three U.S. Commissioners (T. Pickering and Beverley Randolph) to treat with the Indian tribes of the northwest of Ohio (1793).

Little Abraham   See Teiorhenhsere?

Little Billy, fl. late 18th and early 19th centuries   Seneca chief; received special annuity after Treaty at Big Tree (1797). At a council in 1816, he summarized English-Iroquois relations in a speech with Red Jacket.

Livingston, Robert, 1654–1728   Merchant, manor lord, imperialist politician. He was the first secretary of Indian affairs in New York province and held the post for life. Most of the records of New York's Iroquois treaties were minuted by him or his agents. Ever an advocate of western expansion, he allied with governors of the same persuasion and opposed accommodation with New France.
    Biography: Lawrence H. Leder, *Robert Livingston, 1654–1728, and the Politics of Colonial New York* (Chapel Hill: University of North Carolina Press, 1961).

Lodweek X Gaghsaweda   Lodowick, alias Gaghsaweda, Oneida chief of federal period.

Logan, James, 1674–1751   Pennsylvania merchant and official. Logan became William Penn's secretary in 1699 and sailed with him to Pennsylvania. As treaty negotiator, merchant, and land speculator, he was heavily involved in Indian affairs. With Shikellamy, q.v., and Conrad Weiser, q.v., he contrived Pennsylvania's 1736 alliance with all the Iroquois nations except the Mohawks, by means of which the province's client tribes were reduced under Iroquois domination and a new Iroquois treaty "fire" was lit at Philadelphia. Logan also conceived a plan (for which credit was stolen by Sir William Keith) for enforting the frontiers of the British colonies; for this he has been called a "Quaker imperialist." The plan was adopted by the Board of Trade (1722) as part of a policy of aggressive expansion into Indian territory.

Biography: Frederick B. Tolles, *James Logan and the Culture of Provincial America* (Boston: Little, Brown, 1957).

Lydius, John Henry ("Baron de Quade"), 1694?–1791 Trader, interpreter, adventurer, land speculator. Active in the smuggling trade between Albany and Montreal, he eventually lost the trust of both the French and the English. He acquired reputedly spurious deeds from Iroquois chiefs for lands in the Wyoming valley of the upper Susquehanna River. As he was agent in this matter for the Connecticut Susquehannah Company, which intended to settle the lands immediately, both the Iroquois and the Pennsylvania government opposed strongly.

McKee, Alexander, c. 1735–99 Indian agent, fur trader, and local official. As assistant to George Croghan after 1760, he acquired much influence among tribes north of the Ohio River, which he strengthened by marrying a Shawnee woman. A Loyalist in the American Revolution, he fled to Canada and was promoted by 1794 to be deputy superintendent and deputy inspector general of Indian affairs in Upper Canada. He was "the most important official organizing Indian resistance to American advance across the Ohio River."

Mercer, Hugh, c. 1725–12 Jan. 1777 Physician and soldier. B. Aberdeenshire, Scotland. Landed Philadelphia, 1746 or 1747, and settled near present day Mercersburg, Pa. He was an officer in the Seven Years War and the American Revolution. After Forbes's victory at Fort Duquesne in 1758, Mercer became commandant of the new Fort Pitt where he negotiated with the Six Nations.

Mercer, John, d. 1768 Lawyer and land speculator. Of Scottish ancestry, he emigrated from Dublin in 1720. Settled at "Marlborough," Stafford County, Va. Became secretary and shareholder in the Ohio Company of Virginia. Compiled *The Case of the Ohio Company Extracted from Original Papers* (1762). Sons James and George also active in the Company's affairs. *See George Mercer Papers* in Bibliography.

Millet, Pierre, S.J., 1635–1708 Missionary and captive, adopted among Oneidas and endowed with title of leading Oneida sachem in the League— Hodatchehte (Quiver Bearer). Sat in councils of Oneida tribe and League.

Monacatoocha *See* Scarouady

Morgan, George, 1742–1810 Trader and business man who was made Indian agent at Fort Pitt in 1776 and commissioned colonel in the Continental Army in 1777. Very prominent in Indian negotiations in the Ohio region from 1774 to 1783. He exploited his Indian contacts to become a large-scale land speculator.

Newcastle (Kanuksusy, Cassiowea), d. 1756 Seneca war chief, son of "Queen Allaquippa." Active as messenger for Pennsylvania in negotiations with hostile Delawares and Shawnees early in the Seven Years War. He accused the Delawares of bewitching him to bring about his death, but he died of smallpox. In his final illess he called himself a Quaker, and he was buried at his request in a Quaker graveyard.

Nicholas *See* Karaghtadie

Nitachinon *See* Chabert de Joncaire, Philippe-Thomas

Norton, John (Teyoninhokarawen, Te-yo-nin-ho Kalawen), ca. 1760–1826 or 1831 Synethnic son of Cherokee father and Scottish mother, Norton was adopted by the Mohawks of Six Nations Reserve on Grand River. He had a knockabout career as trader and British military officer. He became a protégé of Joseph Brant and Brant's amanuensis, sometimes speaking himself for the Six Nations in Canada. Notable for translating the Gospel of St. John into the Mohawk language, 1805, and for his historical *Journal* (1816). *See* Bibliography.

Ogden, Samuel, 1746–1810 Iron founder and real estate promoter. He negotiated persistently with Senecas for land near Tonawanda, N.Y., early in the nineteenth century.

Ogh-ne-wi-ge-was *See* Farmer's Brother

Ohonsiowanne (*La Grande Terre*, Tohonsionwanne, Ouhensiouan, etc.), fl. 1699–1704 Onondaga sachem, chief of the Old Men and Warriors. Delegate to Montreal (1699) to persuade Calliére to end war; again in 1700; at Quebec with Teganissorens (1703).

Ojagaghte *See* Fish Carrier

Old Belt *See* Kaghswaghtaniunt

Old King *See* Kaineʔkwaahton

Old Smoke *See* Kaienʔkwaahton

Onas ("Feather") Iroquois title for governors of Pennsylvania. A translation of the name of William Penn, q.v.

Ondaaiondiont, Charles, fl. 1645–49 Huron Christian convert; headed embassy to Susquehannocks.

Oneyanha (Oneyanhagh, Oneyangha) *See* Beech Tree

Onkiswathetami (Swatana, Ungquaterughiathe, Shikellamy), fl. 1728–48 Born French, he was captured by Indians and adopted by the Oneidas. Important as an architect of the Pennsylvania-Six Nations alliance formed in 1736. Until then he had been supervisor for the Iroquois of the Shawnees in Pennsylvania. By terms of the alliance the Iroquois became responsible for all the province's client Indians and Shikellamy, as he was known to the Pennsylvanians, collaborated closely with James Logan and Conrad Weiser.

Onontio ("Great Mountain") Iroquois title for governors of New France. A translation of the name of Governor Huault de Montmagny, q.v.

Ononwarogo (Red Head), fl. 1751–64 Onondaga chief warrior. Active in the French interest at the mission of La Presentation until the outbreak of the Seven Years War after which he became a strong follower of Sir William Johnson.

Orehaoue *See* Ourehouare

Otetiani *See* Red Jacket

Otreouti (Hateouati, Hoteouate, Hotrehouati, etc., dit La Grande Geule "Big Mouth," "Garangula"), fl. 1659–88 Onondaga chief and orator, often deputy in peace negotiations between Iroquois and French. Lahontan made him famous for humiliating Governor La Barre at Hungry Bay (1684).

Otsinughyada *See* Hotsinonhyata?

Ottrowana (Adrawanah, Atterwana, Dyaderowane, Gatrowani), fl. 1746–74 Cayuga chief and war leader. Frequently supplied Sir William Johnson with intelligence from Canada, including information on Iroquois-French conferences such as that at Montreal, November–December, 1756. He described the way in which Iroquois war leaders formed war parties by throwing down a war belt and waiting for it to be picked up.

Ouhensiouan *See* Ohonsiowanne

Ourehouare (Orehaoue, Horehouasse), c. 1650–98 Cayuga chief. Seized and sent to France to labor as a galley slave in 1687, he was returned to Canada as a conciliatory gesture in 1689. He was much courted by Count Frontenac who used him as an ambassador in attempts to reconcile the Iroquois.

Parrish, Jasper, 1767–1836 Captured as a boy of eleven in 1778 by Delawares, removed to Niagara in 1779, when sold to David Hill, a Mohawk, for £2, and lived with him five years. First learned Mohawk and then the other Five Nations dialects. Returning to Goshen, N.Y., was employed as interpreter for Pickering in negotiations from 1790 through 1794, and then as U.S. interpreter by General Chapin at Canandaigua, becoming agent in 1803.

Pemberton, Israel, 1715–79   Philadelphia merchant and leader of the Pennsylvania Quakers. Opponent of Sir William Johnson. He formed the Friendly Association for Regaining and Preserving Peace with the Indians by Pacific Measures, active in the Easton treaties from 1756 to 1758 and in 1762. He organized emergency trade with the Indians of Ohio after the fall of Fort Duquesne. The Pemberton Papers at the Historical Society of Pennsylvania, Philadelphia, have valuable background material on Indian affairs.

> Biography: Theodore Thayer, *Israel Pemberton: King of the Quakers* (Philadelphia: Historical Society of Pennsylvania, 1943)

Penet, Peter   Merchant adventurer of Nantes, France. After the American Revolution he became closely associated with the French faction at Oneida. Acquired large properties by dubious means.

Peter, the Quarter Master   *See* Beech Tree

Peters, Richard, c. 1704–76   Anglican clergyman, provincial secretary and councilor. From about 1742, Peters wielded much influence in Pennsylvania's Indian affairs, usually behind the scenes. He was correctly accused by anti-proprietary supporters of the Delawares of writing misleading minutes in the series of Easton treaties (1756–58), and he participated actively in the proprietary legal defense against charges of fraud. His chatty, confidential reports to Thomas Penn are full of information about political intrigues. *See* the Peters Papers at Historical Society of Pennsylvania.

> Biography: Hubertis Cummings, *Richard Peters, Provincial Secretary and Cleric, 1704–1776* (Philadelphia: University of Pennsylvania Press, 1944).

Phelps, Oliver, 1750–1809   Associated in 1788 with Nathaniel Gorham in the purchase of the so-called Massachusetts land in western New York. Settled at Canandaigua 1789.

Pickering, Timothy, 1745–1829   American Revolutionary General, Secretary of War and Secretary of State, U.S. Commissioner in treaties with the Six Nations: Newtown (1791), Maumee Rapids (1793), Canandaigua (1794), Oneida (1794). His instructions to General Anthony Wayne for the terms of the Treaty of Greenville (1795) established firmly the principles of native territorial right, a precisely demarcated boundary between tribal and American jurisdictions (without conceding U.S. ultimate sovereignty), and an exclusive pre-emptive right for the United States government to obtain cession of Indian lands as the tribes should become willing to sell. For Pickering's papers see the index and directory in *Collections of the Massachusetts Historical Society*, 6th ser., 8 (1896). Biography: Gerard H. Clarfield, *Timothy Pickering*, 2 vols. (Columbia: University of Missouri Press, 1969; Pittsburgh: University of Pittsburgh Press, 1980).

Proctor, Thomas Colonel after American Revolution, made mission to Six Nations at Buffalo Creek and Cornplanter on behalf of Secretary Henry Knox to persuade them not to join the western coalition of Indians in Ohio.

Prouville de Tracy, Alexandre de, 1596–1670 General of the French Army, commander in America, sent to New France when the king decided to have done with the Iroquois; invaded Mohawk country and destroyed towns and crops (1666); impatient with peace negotiations.

Quiasutha *See* Kayahsota?

Quider *See* Peter Schuyler

Radisson, Pierre-Esprit, c. 1640–1710 Coureur de bois, explorer, captive of Iroquois (ca. 1651), escaped via Ft. Orange; served as interpreter for Dutch; later returned to Three Rivers. Accompanied Jesuits to Onondaga (1657); left account of episode, including escape. Learned Iroquois; vied in dream contest. Later explored the Far Great Lakes and left vivid account of Feast of the Dead among Chippewas, Ottawas, and Potawatomis. In 1662, he and Médard Chouart Des Groseilliers turned against France because of abuse, and joined the English, becoming cofounders of the Hudson's Bay Company in 1670.
  Biography: Grace Lee Nute, *Caesars of the Wilderness* (New York: D. Appleton-Century Co., 1943).

Randolph, Beverly, 1755–97) Governor of Virginia, U.S. Commissioner to treaty at Maumee Rapids (1793).

Red Head A name given to two Onondaga chiefs, father and son. *See* Kakouenthiony and Ononwarogo.

Red Jacket, c. 1758–1830 Chief and orator of the Senecas, first named *Otetiani*, "always ready," and then *Sagoyewatha*, "keeps them awake," principal in Canandaigua treaty (1794) and at Big Tree in 1797. Visited President Washington and received medal (1792). Opposed Christian missionaries at Buffalo Creek, and upheld "pagan" or traditional way of life.
  Biography: William L. Stone, *The Life and Times of Sa-go-ye-wat-ha, or Red Jacket* (Albany: J. Munsell, 1866).

Rémy de Courcelle, Daniel de, 1626–98   Governor of New France (1665–72), collaborated with de Tracy in subduing the Iroquois. Succeeded in getting Iroquois raiders off the backs of the habitants. Left New France in peace.

Rigaud de Vaudreuil, Philippe de, 1643–1725   Chevalier and marquis, military man, governor of Montreal, and of New France (1703–1725); sought to preserve peace of 1701, dreaded nothing more than a third Iroquois war; period of the black market trade with Albany; problem of Albany competition in trade with Far Indians.

Robert Hunter   *See* Carondawana

Rozinoghyata   *See* Hotsinonhyahta?

Sagochiendagehte   *See* Garakontie

Sagoyewatha   *See* Red Jacket

Sagwayeangualaghton   *See* Kaien?kwaahton

Sastaretsi   See Kondiaronk

Savery, William   One of the Friends of Philadelphia who accompanied the U.S. Commissioners to the Maumee Rapids (1793); also attended Canandaigua treaty (1794) in the same capacity as observer.

Sayenqueraghta   *See* Kaine?kwaahton

Scarouady (Skaroyady, Monacatoocha), fl. 1751–56   Oneida chief, successor to Seneca Tanaghrisson as "half king" of "Mingo" Iroquois and allied tribes in the Ohio region. He led a mixed delegation in 1753 to Winchester, Va., and Carlisle, Pa., to solicit help against the advancing French. He acted equivocally toward the Onondaga council, consulting sometimes and acting independently at other times.

Schuyler, Peter, 1657–1724   Soldier, government official, and the most influential Indian expert in the New York province during his day. Called "Quider" by the Mohawks, there being no labials in Iroquoian. In 1690 he led an English delegation to Onondaga to frustrate or head off a French delegation to the grand League council. He served as an Indian Commissioner throughout his adult life, and as acting governor of New York (1719–20). Schuyler's journals are important historical sources. Many have been printed or extracted in *N.Y.Col.Docs.* and the *Calendar of State Papers, Colonial Series, America and West Indies.*

Schuyler, Philip, 1733–1804   Politician and soldier; served on the United States Board of Indian Commissioners during the American Revolution.
  Biography: Don R. Gerlach, *Philip Schuyler and the American*

Revolution in New York, 1733–1777 (Lincoln: University of Nebraska Press, 1964).

Seneca King *See* Kaien?kwaahton

Shikellamy (Shikellimy or Shickellamy) *See* Onkiswathetami

Simcoe, John Graves, 1752–1806 First British governor of Upper Canada (Ontario) (1791–96). During his tenure, he negotiated with the Iroquois of Canada–Oka, St. Regis, Caughnawaga, Bay of Quinte, and the Six Nations reserve–especially concerning land grants and cessions.

Siongorochti *See* Kaien?kwaahton

Skenandon, John, d. 1816 Oneida chief, a convert of the Reverend Samuel Kirkland, who influenced the Oneida declaration of neutrality between Britain and its colonies in 1775. Later he aided the Americans against invasion from Canada. Captured by the British in 1780, he gained release by promising to serve as a British scout. He was a participant in treaties and agreements with the State of New York between 1790 and 1811, and in the treaty with the United States, December 1794.

Sononchiez *See* Chabert de Joncaire, Louis-Thomas

Sose *See* Togouiroui

Souoias *See* Kondiaronk

Stedman, Philip, d. 1798 He and brothers were carters carrying goods around Niagara Falls; in 1795, the Indians gave him a grant of some 94,000 acres on the Grand River. Agent at times for Joseph Brant.

Swatana *See* Onkiswathetami

Taddyuscung *See* Teedyuscung

Tagancout *See* Tekanoet

Tanaghrisson (Deanaghrison, Johonerissa, Tanacharison, Thanayieson), fl. 1747–d. 4 Oct. 1745 The "Half King" of the Ohio Indians. A Catawba who had been captured young and adopted by the Senecas, he was a chief of the Mingo Indians at Logstown (Ambridge, Pa.) when he was recognized as "Half King" spokesman for all the English-allied Ohio Indians by Conrad Weiser in 1748. George Croghan (1751) and commissioners from Virginia (1752) treated with him in the same capacity. In 1753 he tried futilely to get the French to withdraw from the Ohio County and later accompanied George Washington on an equally futile mission for the same purpose. In 1754 he helped a Virginia party building a fort at the juncture of the Allegheny and Monongahela rivers. After this was seized by the French, Tanaghrisson joined Washington's Virginia troops to attack a French party. They killed the French commander Joseph Coulon de Villiers de Jumonville in an episode that became a cause célèbre in Canada. But when Washington built Fort Necessity at Great Meadows (near Brownsville, Pa.), Tanaghrisson correctly judged it indefensible and withdrew his warriors. He counseled again at Aughwick, fell ill, and went on to John Harris's where he died.

Tareha (Atarhea, etc.), fl. 1691–95   Oneida chief, peace emissary to Frontenac, intermediary with Father Millet, and instrumental in his liberation. Settled at Caughnawaga.

Tayorheasere   *See* Teiorhenhsere?

Teedyuscung (Taddyuscung), 1700–63   Delaware pine tree chief. Emerged to leadership of the eastern Delawares during the Seven Years War, working closely with the Pennsylvania Quakers. His charges of fraud in the Walking Purchase of Bucks County lands created a great scandal.

   Biography: Anthony F. C. Wallace, *King of the Delawares: Teedyuscung, 1700–1763* (Philadelphia: University of Pennsylvania Press, 1949).

Tee Yee Ho Ga Row   *See* Theyanoguin

Teganissorens (Decanesora, Connessoa), fl. 1675–1725   Onondaga chief, orator, diplomat, played leading role in Iroquois-French-English relations; Colden likened him to Cicero; commanding personality and great dignity. Spokesman of Iroquois policy and supporter of Covenant Chain. Architect of the policies by which the Iroquois rebuilt their strength after disastrous defeats in the seventeenth century.

Tegannehout   *See* Tekanoet

Tehastakout   *See* Tonatakout

Teiorhenhsere? (Tayorheasere, Teyarhasere, Tigoransera, Tiyerhasere, Tyorhansera, aka Little Abraham), d. 1780   Son of Old Abraham. A prominent warrior during the Seven Years War, and a noted orator, he tried to save Mohawk lands from encroaching speculators. Neutral during the American Revolution, he stayed behind when most of his people went to Canada after the war.

Tekanoet (Tegannehout, Cannehouet, Cannehoot, Tegancouti, Tagancout, Tegancout, Teganeout), fl. 1680–1701   Seneca war chief. Leader of Iroquois war parties against the western nations. Present at the great treaty in Montreal in 1701.

Tekarihoken (Tegarihogen, etc.)   Title of the leading sachem of the Mohawk roster on the Roll Call of Iroquois Chiefs; acted as both military and civil leader, contrary to theory; a chief of this title (1653); there was also a chief in this title living at Caughnawaga (1726).

Teoniahigarawe   *See* Theyanoguin

Teyarhasere   *See* Teiorhenhsere?

Teyohaqueande (Deiaquande, Diaquande, Teiyoquande, Tiahogwando, Tuya-guande), fl. 1756–83   Onondaga sachem. A close ally and favorite of Sir William Johnson, he took part in many treaties. At the time of the American Revolution he remained loyal to the British.

Teyoninhokarawen (Te-yo-nin-ho Kalawan)   *See* Norton, John

Thanayieson   *See* Tanaghrisson

Thayandanegea   *See* Joseph Brant

Theyanoguin (Teoniahigarawe, Tiyanoga, Tee Yee Ho Ga Row, Deyohnin-hohhakarawenh, aka White Head, Hendrick, King Hendrick, Hendrick Peters), c. 1680–1755   Mahican by birth, adopted by Mohawks, con-verted to Protestantism. A strong supporter of the English against New France. Presented at the court of Queen Anne (1710). Led many Mo-hawk war parties. Died at the Battle of Lake George (1755).

Tiahogwando   *See* Teyoqueande

Tigoransera   *See* Teiorhenhsere?

Tiwatacout   *See* Tonatakout

Tiyanoga   *See* Theyanoguin

Tiyerhasere   *See* Teiorhenhsere?

Togouiroui (Togoniron, *Kryn*, etc., Joseph — Sose — dit le Grand Agnier), d. 1690   A Mohawk war leader who lifted Mahican siege of Gandaougue (Fonda, N.Y.) in 1669, and in 1672 departed to ultimately settle at Caughna-waga, where known as the Great Mohawk. Marched on Schenectady 1690 when Frontenac declared war. Had opposed his countrymen in LaChine massacre the year previous.

Tohaswuchdioony (The Belt of Wampum), fl. 1750,   A Roman Catholic, pro-French Onondaga chief who succeeded Canasatego in leadership. Noticed by Conrad Weiser at the council in Onondaga in 1750. See P. A. W. Wallace, *Conrad Weiser, 1696–1760, Friend of Colonist and Mo-hawk* (Philadelphia: University of Pennsylvania Press, 1945), pp. 310 ff.

Tohaswuchdoniunty   *See* Kaghswaghtaniunt

Tohonsiowanne   *See* Ohonsiowanne

Tonatakout (Tiwatacout, Tehastakout), fl. 1700–34   Seneca chief. Played a leading role in the negotiations with the French that led to the peace treaty of 1701.

Trent, William, Jr. ca. 1715–1787   Pennsylvania Indian trader and land speculator. He attended Indian treaty councils at Logstown (1752); Easton (1757); and Fort Pitt (1759). At Fort Pitt he traded for the firm of Simon, Trent, Levy, and Franks. At the Treaty of Fort Stanwix, 1768, he obtained a grant from the Six Nations of vast acreage that became part of the projected colony of "Indiana," later incorporated in "Vandalia." Author of several journals important as source materials.

     Biography: Sewell E. Slick, *William Trent and the West* (Harrisburg, Pa.: Archives Publishing Co., 1947).

Tyorhansera   *See* Teiorhenhsere?

Tuaguande   *See* Teyohaqueande

Ungquaterughiathe   *See* Onkiswathetami

Vaudreuil   *See* Rigaud de Vaudreuil

Viele, Arnout Cornelissen, 1604–c. 1704   "Buschloper," interpreter and negotiator. For about twenty years he served as interpreter of the province of New York, coming into the records in 1682. Viele spent much time living in Onondaga, but he also traveled widely in the Great Lakes region.

Wadsworth, Jeremiah, 1743–1804   After Revolution settled at Geneseo, and acted as U.S. Commissioner for the Treaty at Big Tree (1797).

Washington, George, 1732–1799   Surveyor, planter, land speculator, soldier, statesman. Related to principal partners in the Ohio Company of Virginia, Washington was commissioned in 1753 by Virginia Governor Dinwiddie (also a partner) to warn the French out of the Ohio country where the Company proposed to plant settlements. After French rejection of the ultimatum, Washington returned in command of troops and attacked a French party. His Iroquois allies withdrew in disgust over his strategy, and he had to surrender to the French (1754). He served under generals Braddock and Forbes in campaigns against Fort Duquesne, was commander in chief of patriot forces in the American Revolution, and served two terms as President of the United States. Throughout, he maintained interest and investments in western Indian territory.

     Washington's mostly hagiographical biographers rarely report accurately his transactions with Indians or Indian lands. Papers: *The Writings of George Washington . . . 1745–1799,* edited by John C. Fitzpatrick. 39 vols. (Washington, D.C.: USGPO, 1931–44).

     Biography: Douglas Southall Freeman, *George Washington,* 7 vols. (New York: C. Scribner's Sons, 1948–57).

Wayne, Anthony, 1 Jan. 1745–15 Dec. 1796   Soldier. A prominent officer in the war of the American Revolution, he is known in Indian affairs for two campaigns. (1) He defeated the Creeks and Cherokees (1782–83) and negotiated their submission in treaties. (2) He defeated the Western Confederation at Fallen Timbers on the Maumee River (near Toledo, Ohio, 20 Aug. 1794). The Treaty of Greenville that he negotiated with the western tribes in 1795 tacitly rescinded the conquest theory on which the 1784 Treaty of Fort Stanwix had been based and re-established the principle of recognition of tribal territorial rights.

> Biography: Thomas Boyd, *Mad Anthony Wayne* (New York: Charles Scribners Sons, 1929).

> Documents: *Anthony Wayne, A Name in Arms . . . The Wayne-Knox-Pickering-McHenry Correspondence,* trans. and edited by Richard C. Knopf. (Pittsburgh: University of Pittsburgh Press, 1960).

Weiser, Conrad, 1696–1760   Interpreter, soldier, local official. A Palatine German immigrant to Pennsylvania from New York, Weiser had lived with the Mohawks as a youth and learned the language. He was an important go-between for the Six Nations and Pennsylvania's government, trusted by both and an architect of their alliance along with James Logan and Onkiswathetami.

> Biography: Paul A. W. Wallace, *Conrad Weiser, 1696–1760: Friend of Colonist and Mohawk* (Philadelphia: University of Pennsylvania Press, 1945).

White Head   *See* Theyanoguin

White Thunder   *See* Kaghswaghtaniunt

Wright, Asher, 1803–1875   protestant missionary to the Senecas at Buffalo Creek (1831–45), then at Cattaraugus until his death. Published *Mental Elevator,* Seneca spelling book, and other works on Mission Press; protested first Treaty at Buffalo Creek as fraudulent and secured compromise treaty.

BIBLIOGRAPHY

T HIS LIST is selective by necessity. A fully comprehensive bibliography would require a large book exclusively for itself. Full publication data for the titles mentioned in these introductory remarks will be found in the list below.

Because of the widely scattered condition of the source materials, research on the Iroquois can be compared to putting a jigsaw puzzle together after assembling the pieces from places hundreds, sometimes thousands, of miles distant from each other. It is not to be wondered at that parts of the puzzle are still missing. No one book contains a comprehensive history of the Iroquois Six Nations. For early history consult Bruce G. Trigger, *The Children of Aataentsic* and Allen W. Trelease, *Indian Affairs in Colonial New York*. Both are concerned exclusively with the seventeenth century. Richard Aquila, *The Iroquois Restoration* and Francis Jennings, *Ambiguous Iroquois Empire* carry the history forward to mid-eighteenth century, with emphasis on the formation and development of the Covenant Chain. Chronologically this is followed by Randolph C. Downes, *Council Fires on the Upper Ohio* and Howard H. Peckham, *Pontiac and the Indian Uprising*. The title of Barbara Graymont, *The Iroquois in the American Revolution* explains its contents. Nineteenth-century official reports, administrative decisions, and legislation are accessible in *The American Indian and the United States: A Documentary History*, edited by Wilcomb E. Washburn; Iroquois affairs can be traced through the tribal entries in the index. A superior ethnohistory of the early nineteenth century is Anthony F.C. Wallace, *The Death and Rebirth of the Seneca*.

For Iroquois culture the student should read first the relevant essays in *Northeast* and *Extending the Rafters*. Some historical development is also contained in these two volumes, but they give major attention to the concerns of ethnologists, archaeologists, and linguists. W. N. Fenton's articles, listed below, are the findings of "the dean of Iroquois studies." All the aforementioned books contain extensive bibliographies.

A handy separate bibliography, with a critical review essay, is Elisabeth Tooker, *The Indians of the Northeast*. Readers with access to a major research library will find useful Henry F. De Puy, *A Bibliography of the English Colonial Treaties with the American Indians*, but should note that it lists only treaties printed in separate publications, and not all of those now known. Treaties included in collections of colonial, state, and national archives number in the thousands. These are scattered, hit-or-miss, among other kinds of papers so that a student must search them out. Sometimes they are indexed, sometimes not.

A comprehensive archive of Iroquois treaties and associated documents has been created at the Newberry Library, Chicago, Illinois, and is published in microfilm by Research Publications, Inc.

This Bibliography is supplemented by some writings noted under their authors' names in the foregoing chapter, "Persons Participating in Indian Treaties."

Among the many museums with displays of Iroquois artifacts and studies of Iroquois culture, the following are outstanding.

The Smithsonian Institution, Washington, D.C.

The National Museum of Man, Ottawa, Ontario.

The New York State Museum, Albany, N.Y.

Two outstanding museums operated by Iroquois organizations are: The Seneca-Iroquois National Museum, Salamanca, N.Y., and The Turtle, Niagara Falls, N.Y.

Research in Iroquois studies has increased greatly in recent years. The editors of this book know of many doctoral dissertations under way or already completed that give promise of being published in the near future. Most scholars in the field are in touch with the Conference on Iroquois Research which can be reached through the Anthropology Department, State University of New York, Albany, 12222. Another clearing house is the D'Arcy McNickle Center for the History of the American Indian, Newberry Library, 60 West Walton Street, Chicago, Illinois 60610.

Abernethy, Thomas Perkins. *Western Lands and the American Revolution*. University of Virginia Institute for Research in the Social Science Monograph 25. London and New York, 1937. Reprinted New York: Russell and Russell, 1959.

Anthony Wayne, A Name in Arms: Soldier, Diplomat, Defender of Expansion Westward of a Nation. Comp. and ed. Richard C. Knopf. Pittsburgh: University of Pittsburgh Press, 1960. A documentary biography.

American Archives: Consisting of a Collection of Authentic Records, State Papers, Debates, and Letters and Other Notices of Publick Affairs . . . Ed. Peter Force. 4th series, 7 March 1774 to 4 July 1776. 6 vols. Washington, D.C., 1837–1846; 5th series, 4 July 1776 to 3 September 1783. 3 vols. Washington, D.C., 1848–1853.

The American Indian and the United States: A Documentary History. Ed. Wilcomb E. Washburn. 4 vols. New York: Random House, 1973. Nineteenth-century sources.

Aquila, Richard. *The Iroquois Restoration: Iroquois Diplomacy on the Colonial Frontier, 1701–1754*. Detroit: Wayne State University Press, 1983.

Archives of Maryland. Eds. William Hand Browne, et al. Baltimore, Md.: Maryland Historical Society, 1883– . Contains much Iroquois material, often misunderstood, in the latter eighteenth century especially.

Atlas of Great Lakes Indian History. Eds. Helen H. Tanner, Adele Hast, and Jacqueline Peterson. Published for the Newberry Library. Norman: University of Oklahoma Press, 1984. The first of its kind, this atlas maps location and movement of tribal villages, including the Iroquois, from the 16th century to the 20th.

Atlas of Indian Reserves and Settlements, Canada, 1971. Ottawa: Dept. of Indian and Northern Affairs, 1971.

Bacqueville de La Potherie. *See* Le Roy de Bacqueville de La Potherie.

Bartram, John. *Observations on the Inhabitants, Climate, Soil, Rivers, Productions, Animals, and other matters worthy of Notice. Made by Mr. John Bartram In his Travels from Pennsylvania to Onondago, Oswego and the Lake Ontario, In Canada.* London: J. Whiston and B. White, 1751. Bartram was a botanist with an interest in Indians. He accompanied interpreter Conrad Weiser on a trip to Onondaga and reported the experience carefully. However, his general observations on tribal politics were heavily influenced by Cadwallader Colden's thesis of the Iroquois as imperialists.

Beauchamp, William M. "Civil, Religious and Mourning Councils and Ceremonies of Adoption of the New York Indians." *New York State Museum Bulletin* 113. Albany, 1907. Reprinted Albany: State Education Department, 1975; pp. 341–451.

———. "An Iroquois Condolence." *Journal of American Folk-Lore* 8, no. 31 (1895): 313–16.

[Bouquet, Henry.] *The Papers of Henry Bouquet.* Eds. S. K. Stevens, Donald H. Kent, and Autumn L. Leonard. 4 vols. to date. Harrisburg: Pennsylvania Historical and Museum Commission, 1951– . Records formal and informal conferences with Indians. Well indexed and annotated.

Boyce, Douglas W. "A Glimpse of Iroquois Culture History Through the Eyes of Joseph Brant and John Norton." *Proceedings of the American Philosophical Society* 117, no. 4 (1973): 286–94.

Brodhead, John Romeyn. *History of the State of New York.* 2 vols. New York: Harper and Brothers, 1853–71. Detailed paraphrasing of documents in chronological order, valuable especially for contents of manuscripts that have been burned since its publication.

Calendar of Historical Manuscripts in the Office of the Secretary of State, Albany, New York. Vol. 1, *Dutch Manuscripts, 1630–1664.* Vol. 2, *English Manuscripts, 1664–1776.* Ed. Edmund B. O'Callaghan. Albany, N.Y.: Weed, Parsons, and Co., 1866.

Calendar of the Sir William Johnson Manuscripts in the New York State Library. Comp. Richard E. Day. Albany: University of the State of New York, 1909. Itemizes many documents that later were destroyed in the Albany fire of 1911.

Calendar of State Papers, Colonial Series, America and West Indies. Eds. W. Noel Sainsbury et al. London: Her Majesty's Stationary Office, 1860– . Paraphrases of selected documents in England's official archives. A basic set of prime sources, it includes much miscellaneous material that was enclosed in the reports of governors and other colonial offices. However, many texts are merely listed, not extracted, and the exact text of any document can only be had in the original manuscript. These extracts and paraphrases represent the judgments of editors, and reflect changing historiographical interests. The calendar is unfinished; it stops at 1737. *See also Documents of the American Revolution.*

Canada. Geographic Board. *Handbook of Indians of Canada.* Ottawa, King's Printer, 1913.

Canada. *Indian Treaties and Surrenders, from 1680 to 1890.* 2 vols. Ottawa: Queen's Printer, 1891. Vol. III, supplement to 1902. Ottawa: King's Printer, 1912. 3 vols. facsimile reprint, Toronto: Coles Publishing Co., 1971. Exclusively official texts and drafts of tracts of land. No editorial apparatus.

Canada. Legislative Assembly. *Report on the Affairs of the Indians of Canada, 1842.* Legislative Assembly Journals, 1844–45. Appendix EEE, Section I.

Canada. *Report of the Special Commissioners to Investigate Indian Affairs in Canada.* Toronto: Queen's Printer, 1858.

Chafe, Wallace L. *Seneca Morphology and Dictionary. Smithsonian Contributions to Anthropology* 4. Washington, D.C., USGPO, 1967.

Clarke, Noah T. "The Thacher Wampum Belts of the New York State Museum." *New York State Museum Bulletin* 279 (1929): 53–58.

Clarke, Noah T. "The Wampum Belt Collection of the New York State Museum." *New York State Museum Bulletin* 288 (1931): 85–121.

Cohen, Felix S. *Handbook of Federal Indian Law.* Washington, D.C.: USGPO, 1945. The standard guide as of its date of publication and not yet superseded in comprehensive treatment of basic principles, but subsequent court decisions must be consulted in specific cases.

Colden, Cadwallader. *The History of the Five Indian Nations Depending on the Province of New-York in America.* New York, 1727. Paperback reprint by Great Seal Books, Ithaca, N.Y.: Cornell University Press, 1958. A highly influential book that propagandized the British diplomatic argument that the Iroquois had conquered an empire over other tribes and that therefore the territories and persons of these tribes were under British sovereignty. Useful nevertheless for accounts of some treaties taken from New York's records.

Costo, Rupert, and Jeannette Henry Costo. *Indian Treaties: Two Centuries of Dishonor.* San Francisco: Indian Historical Press, 1977. Expresses views common among contemporary Indians.

De Puy, Henry F. *A Bibliography of the English Colonial Treaties with the American Indians, Including a Synopsis of Each Treaty.* New York: The Lenox Club, 1917.

Desrosiers, Leo-Paul. *Iroquoisie.* Montreal: Institut d'Histoire de l'Amerique francaise, 1947. Detailed treatment of the earliest period of recorded Iroquois history.

Dictionary of Canadian Biography/Dictionnaire Biographique du Canada. Eds. George W. Brown, et al. Toronto: University of Toronto Press and Les Presses de l'université Laval, 1966– . Includes a large number of Indian biographies and extensive lives of French Canadians active in Indian affairs. Of the volumes published so far, 1–4 have become essential for Iroquois studies.

Doc. Hist. N.Y. = Documentary History of the State of New York. Ed. E. B. O'Callaghan. 4 vols. Albany: Weed, Parsons and Co., 1849–1851. Source materials.

Documents of the American Revolution, 1770–1783 (Colonial Office Series). Ed. K. G. Davies. 21 vols. Shannon: Irish Universities Press, 1972–81. An extension of the *Calendar of State Papers, Colonial Series, America and West Indians,* q.v. This is a selection of documents useful as a guide to official information gathering and policy making. Texts are given in very generous paraphrase that usually amounts to quotation, but Indian treaties are only cited.

Documents Relative to the Colonial History of the State of New York. Ed. E. B. O'Callaghan. 15 vols. Albany: Weed, Parsons, and Co., 1853–87. A basic set, but somewhat selective in spite of its appearance of comprehensiveness. Its translations of French and Dutch documents have been criticized adversely. Vol. 11 is an index to the preceding vols. Short ref. = *N.Y. Col. Docs.*

Documents Relating to the Constitutional History of Canada, 1759–1791. Ed. Adam Shortt and Arthur G. Doughty. Ottawa, 1907. Includes materials that show the process of policy making as well as the formal declarations of policy.

Downes, Randolph C. *Council Fires on the Upper Ohio: A Narrative of Indian Affairs in the Upper Ohio Valley until 1795.* Pittsburgh: University of Pittsburgh Press, 1940. Effectively a study of tribal politics and diplomacy from about 1745 to 1795. Sympathetic to Indian difficulties.

Druke, Mary A. "Structure and Meanings of Leadership Among the Oneida Indians During the Mid-Eighteenth Century." Ph.D. diss., University of Chicago, 1982.

Drummond, A. M., and Richard Moody. "Indian Treaties: The First American Dramas." *Quarterly Journal of Speech* 39 (1953): 15–24.

Du Creux, Francois, S.J. *The History of Canada or New France* (1664). Trans. with intro. by Percy J. Robinson. Ed. James B. Conacher. 2 vols. Publications of the Champlain Society 30, 31. Toronto, 1951–52.

Early American Indian Documents, Treaties, and Laws, 1607–1789. Gen. ed. Alden T. Vaughan. Vol. 1: *Pennsylvania and Delaware Treaties, 1629–1737.* Ed. Donald H. Kent. Washington, D.C.: University Publications of America, 1979.

Eccles, William J. *The Canadian Frontier, 1534–1760.* New York: Holt, Rinehart and Winston, 1969. Eccles is the senior Canadian historian of New France's Indian relations. Requisite reading.

———. *France in America.* New York: Harper and Row, 1972.

———. *Frontenac: the Courtier Governor.* Toronto: McClelland and Stewart, 1959. Reprinted Carleton Library No. 24, same publisher, 1965.

Eid, Leroy V. "The Ojibwa-Iroquois War: The War The Five Nations Did Not Win." *Ethnohistory* 26, no. 4 (fall 1979): 279–324. An iconoclastic article debunking the idea of Iroquois conquests.

Emlen, James. "The Journal of James Emlen, Kept on a Trip to Canandaigua, New York." Ed. William N. Fenton. *Ethnohistory* 12 (1965), pp. 279–334.

Extending the Rafters: Interdisciplinary Approaches to Iroquoian Studies. Eds. Michael K. Foster, Jack Campisi, and Marianne Mithun. Published for the Newberry Library. Albany: State University of New York Press, 1984. Together with *Northeast,* q.v., these essays represent the state of the art in Iroquoian cultural studies.

Fenton, William N. *American Indian and White Relations to 1830: Needs and Opportunities for Study*. Published for the Institute of Early American History and Culture. Chapel Hill: University of North Carolina Press, 1957.

―――. "Collecting Materials for a Political History of the Six Nations." *Proceedings of the American Philosophical Society* 93, no. 3 (1949): 233–38.

―――. "The Hiawatha Wampum Belt of the Iroquois League for Peace: A Symbol for the International Congress of Anthropology," in *Men and Cultures: Selected Papers of the Fifth International Congress of Anthropological and Ethnological Sciences, Philadelphia, 1956.* Philadelphia: University of Pennsylvania Press, 1960, pp. 3–7.

―――. "Iroquoian Culture History; A General Evaluation," in *Symposium on Cherokee and Iroquois Culture.* Eds. William N. Fenton and John Gulick. *Bureau of American Ethnology Bulletin* 180. Washington, D.C., 1961, pp. 253–77.

―――. "An Iroquois Condolence Council for Installing Cayuga Chiefs in 1945." *Journal of the Washington Academy of Sciences* 36, no. 4 (1946): 110–27.

―――. "The Iroquois Eagle Dance: an Offshoot of the Calumet Dance." *Bulletin of American Ethnology Bulletin* 156 (1953).

―――. "The Lore of the Longhouse: Myth, Ritual, and Red Power." *Anthropological Quarterly* 48 (1975): 131–47.

―――. "The New York State Wampum Collection: The Case for the Integrity of Cultural Treasures." *Proceedings of the American Philosophical Society* 115, no. 6 (1971): 437–61.

―――. "Northern Iroquoian Culture Patterns." *Northeast*, q.v., pp. 296–321.

―――. "Problems Arising from the Historic Northeastern Position of the Iroquois." *Smithsonian Miscellaneous Collections* 100 (1940): 159–252. Detailed study of locations of Iroquois settlements through time.

―――. "The Roll Call of the Iroquois Chiefs: A Study of a Mnemonic Cane from the Six Nations Reserve." *Smithsonian Miscellaneous Collections* 111, no. 15 (1950): 1–73.

―――. "Seth Newhouse's Traditional History and Constitution of the Iroquois Confederacy." *Proceedings of the American Philosophical Society* 93, no. 2 (1949): 141–58.

―――. "Toward the Gradual Civilization of the Indian Natives: the Missionary and Linguistic Work of Asher Wright (1803–1875) Among the Senecas of Western New York." *Proceedings of the American Philosophical Society* 100, no. 6 (1956): 567–81.

Foster, Michael K. "From the Earth to Beyond the Sky: An Ethnographic Approach to Four Longhouse Iroquois Speech Events." *National Museum of Man, Ethnology Division, Mercury Series Paper* 20 (1974).

―――. "The Recovery and Translation of Native Speeches Accompanying Ancient Iroquois-White Treaties." *National Museum of Man, Canadian Ethnology Service, Canadian Studies Report* 5e (1978).

———. "When Words Become Deeds: An Analysis of Three Iroquois Longhouse Speech Events." *Explorations in the Ethnography of Speaking*. Eds. Richard Bauman and Joel Sherzer. Cambridge: Cambridge University Press, 1974, pp. 354–67.

George Mercer Papers Relating to the Ohio Company of Virginia. Ed. Lois Mulkearn. Pittsburgh: University of Pittsburgh Press, 1954. Heavily annotated.

Gipson, Lawrence Henry. *The British Empire Before the American Revolution*. 15 vols. New York: Alfred A. Knopf, 1939–70. The most sweeping survey of Britain's worldwide empire and conflicts from 1748 to the American Revolution. Useful for large perspective (definitely pro-British) and for the bibliographies in vols. 14 and 15, but marred by ethnic bias, especially lack of knowledge of American Indian cultures and diplomacy.

Goldenweiser, Alexander A. "On Iroquois Work 1912." In *Summary Report of the Geological Survey Branch of the Canadian Department of Mines for the Calendar Year 1912* (Ottawa, 1914), pp. 464–75.

———. [Review of] "*The Constitution of the Five Nations*, by Arthur C. Parker." *American Anthropologist* 18, no. 3 (1916): 431–36.

Graymont, Barbara. *The Iroquois in the American Revolution*. Syracuse: Syracuse University Press, 1972. The standard work.

The Great Law of Peace [Kaianerekowa] of the Longhouse People [Hotinonsionne]. Drawings by John Fadden [Kahonhes]. Mohawk Nation at Akwesasne: White Roots of Peace, 1971. With minor differences of word or phrase, this follows the text of Arthur C. Parker's section on "The Great Binding Law, Gayanashagowa: in *The Constitution of the Five Nations*, q.v., pp. 30–60. It comments: "There may be some quarrels over order of articles, interpretations, omissions. But this pamphlet is offered as a starting point for discussion until a sanctioned translation is available" (last, unnumbered page).

Haan, Richard L. "The Problem of Iroquois Neutrality: Suggestions for Revision." *Ethnohistory* 27, no. 4 (Fall 1980): 317–30.

Hale, Horatio. *The Iroquois Book of Rites*. Brinton's Library of Aboriginal American Literature 2. Philadelphia: D. G. Brinton, 1883. Reprinted with introduction by W. N. Fenton, Toronto: University of Toronto Press, 1963. A pioneer work on Iroquois council rituals. Hale's historical understanding was much influenced by Cadwallader Colden.

———. "An Iroquois Condoling Council." *Transactions of the Royal Society of Canada*, 2d. ser., 1, no. 2 (1895): 45–65.

Hamilton, Milton W. *Sir William Johnson: Colonial American, 1715–1763*. Port Washington, N.Y.: Kennikat Press, 1976. The most recent and most comprehensive biography. Highly admiring of Johnson.

Handbook of American Indians North of Mexico. Ed. Frederick W. Hodge. 2 vols. *Bureau of American Ethnology Bulletin* 30. Washington, D.C., 1907. Organized dictionary-fashion as short articles in alphabetical order, it is still a valuable reference despite its age and the supersession of much of its information by later works.

Heckewelder, John. *An Account of the History, Manners, and Customs of the Indian Nations Who Once Inhabited Pennsylvania and the Neighbouring States.* Philadelphia: Abraham Small, 1819. Rev. ed., ed. William C. Reichel. Issued as Memoirs of the Historical Society of Pennsylvania 12. Philadelphia, 1876. Sympathetic reporting by a Moravian missionary of Delaware and Mahican traditions and customs, and the relationships of these tribes with the Iroquois. Critical of the Iroquois.

Hewitt, J. N. B. "Legend of the Founding of the Iroquois League." *American Anthropologist* 5, no. 2 (1892): 131–48. Hewitt (1859–1937) was a Tuscarora Indian employed as an ethnologist on the staff of the Bureau of American Ethnology.

————. [Review of] "*The Constitution of the Five Nations,* by Arthur C. Parker; *Traditional History of the Confederacy of the Six Nations,* by Duncan C. Scott; and *Civil, Religious and Mourning Councils and Ceremonies of Adoption of the New York Indians,* by William Beauchamp." *American Anthropologist* 19, no. 3 (1917): 429–38.

————, and William N. Fenton. "The Requickening Address of the Iroquois Condolence Council." *Journal of the Washington Academy of Sciences* 34, no. 3 (1944): 65–85.

————, and William N. Fenton. "Some Mnemonic Pictographs Relating to the Iroquois Condolence Council." *Journal of the Washington Academy of Sciences* 35, no. 10 (1945): 301–15.

Heye, George G. "Wampum Collection." *Museum of the American Indian/Heye Foundation Indian Notes* 7, no. 3 (July 1930): 320–24.

Hunt, George T. *The Wars of the Iroquois.* Madison: University of Wisconsin Press, 1940. Hunt attacked the Parkmanesque thesis of the Iroquois being savages who delighted in war irrationally. He advanced the counter thesis of commercial motivation for Iroquois wars. Hunt has been criticized severely for too narrow an outlook and much factual error, but his book marks a turning point in historical studies of the Iroquois.

Indian Affairs, Laws and Treaties. Comp. and ed. Charles J. Kappler. 2 vols. Washington, D.C.: Government Printing Office, 1903–1904. Official texts in a handy format.

Indian Treaties Printed by Benjamin Franklin, 1736–1762. Ed. with intro. by Julian P. Boyd. Philadelphia: Historical Society of Pennsylvania, 1938. Facsimile reproduction of Franklin's handsome volumes. The editor's Introduction leans heavily on the printed materials produced by Proprietary Thomas Penn's lawyers in his contest with Franklin and the Assembly over Indian affairs. The treaty texts themselves are very important.

The Indian Tribes of the Upper Mississippi Valley and Region of the Great Lakes as Described by Nicolas Perrot . . . Bacqueville de la Potherie . . . Morrell Marston . . . and Thomas Forsyth. Ed. Emma H. Blair. 2 vols. Cleveland, O.: Arthur H. Clark Co., 1911.

Iroquois Indians: A Documentary History of the Diplomacy of the Six Nations and Their

League. Eds. Francis Jennings, William N. Fenton, Mary A. Druke, and David R. Miller. Woodbridge, Conn.: Research Publications, 1984. Microfilm publication of the Iroquois treaty archive at the Newberry Library.

Jacobs, Wilbur. *Diplomacy and Indian Gifts: Anglo-French Rivalry Along the Ohio and Northwest Frontiers, 1748-1763*. Stanford, Calif.: Stanford University Press, 1950. Discusses importance of the ritual of giving presents at treaties.

————. "Wampum, the Protocol of Indian Diplomacy." *William and Mary Quarterly* 6 (1949): 596-604.

Jenness, Diamond. "Three Iroquois Wampum Records." *National Museum of Canada Bulletin* 70 (1932): 25-29. Description and traditions of belts acquired by the National Museum of Canada from Chief William D. Loft, a Mohawk Indian of Caledonia.

Jennings, Francis. *The Ambiguous Iroquois Empire: The Covenant Chain Confederation of Indian Tribes with English Colonies from its beginnings to the Lancaster Treaty of 1744*. New York: Norton, 1984. The most extensive historical treatment of its subject thus far.

————. "The Delaware Interregnum." *Pennsylvania Magazine of History and Biography* 89, no. 2 (1965): 174-98.

————. "Glory, Death, and Transfiguration: The Susquehannock Indians in the Seventeenth Century." *Proceedings of the American Philosophical Society* 112, no. 1 (Jan 1968): 15-53.

————. "The Indian Trade of the Susquehanna Valley." *Proceedings of the American Philosophical Society* 110, no. 6 (1966): 406-24.

————. *The Invasion of America: Indians, Colonialism, and the Cant of Conquest*. Chapel Hill: University of North Carolina Press, for the Institute of Early American History and Culture, 1975. Paperback ed., New York: W.W. Norton and Co., 1976.

————. "Miquon's Passing: Indian-European Relations in Colonial Pennsylvania, 1674 to 1755." Ph.D. diss., University of Pennsylvania, 1965.

————. "A Vanishing Indian: Francis Parkman Versus His Sources." *Pennsylvania Magazine of History and Biography* 87, no. 3 (July 1963): 306-23.

The Jesuit Relations and Allied Documents: Travels and Explorations of the Jesuit Missionaries in New France, 1610-1791; the Original French, Latin, and Italian Texts, with English Translations and Notes. Ed. Reuben Gold Thwaites. 73 vols. Cleveland: Burrows Brothers, 1896-1901. Reprinted, New York: Pageant Book Co., 1959. Thoroughly indexed in vols. 72-73. See especially the long entry "Iroquois," 72:362-371, and its outline, 72:24. Essential to Iroquois studies after allowance for ethnocentrism. The Jesuits were keen observers and they lived among the tribes.

Johnson, Sir William. *The Papers of Sir William Johnson*. Eds. James Sullivan, et. al. 14 vols. Albany: University of the State of New York, 1921-65. Thoroughly indexed in vol. 14. Essential reference for Johnson's period, but must be used as a complement to other sets whose documents it notices but does not reprint. Organized chronologically within sub-groups of volumes. Index must be consulted.

Johnston, Charles M. "An Outline of Early Settlement in the Grand River Valley." *Ontario History* 54, no. 1 (1962): 43–67.

———. "Joseph Brant, the Grand River Lands, and the Northwest Crises." *Ontario History* 55, no. 4 (1963): 267–82.

Jones, Dorothy V. *License for Empire: Colonialism by Treaty in Early America*. Chicago: University of Chicago Press, 1982.

Journals of the Continental Congress, 1774–1789. Ed. Worthington Chauncey Ford. 6 vols. Washington, D.C.: USGPO, 1906. Contains background information on Iroquois treaties, including legislative resolutions pertaining to treaty making.

Kelsay, Isabel Thompson. *Joseph Brant*. Syracuse, N.Y.: Syracuse University Press, 1984.

Kent, Donald H. "Historical Report on Pennsylvania's Purchases from the Indians in 1784, 1785 and 1789 and on Indian Occupancy of the Areas Purchased;" and "Historical Report on the Niagara River and the Niagara River Strip to 1759." *Iroquois Indians* I–II. American Indian Ethnohistory Series. Ed. David Agee Horr. New York: Garland Publishing Co., 1974.

Kirkland, Samuel. *The Journals of Samuel Kirkland: 18th-century Missionary to the Iroquois, Government Agent, Father of Hamilton College*. Ed. Walter Pilkington. Clinton, N.Y.: Hamilton College, 1980. Kirkland was a Congregationalist missionary employed by the Society in Scotland for the Propagation of Christian Knowledge to work among the Iroquois. He is credited with swaying the Oneidas to the side of the United States during the American Revolution.

Lafitau, Joseph-Francois, S.J. *Customs of the American Indians Compared with the Customs of Primitive Times* (1724). Ed. and trans. by William N. Fenton and Elizabeth L. Moore. 2 vols. Publications of the Champlain Society 48, 49. Toronto, 1974–77. An ethnological classic.

Lahontan, Louis Armand de Lom D'Arce de. *New Voyages to North-America*. London, 1703. Reprinted ed. Reuben Gold Thwaites. 2 vols. Chicago: A.C. McClurg and Co., 1905. Volume 1 is more reliable than volume 2 in which Lahontan fabricated some material. A rather cynical nobleman, Lahontan went into exile in England after becoming hostile to the Jesuits and antagonistic to the government of New France. Useful as a corrective to official self-praise.

Lanctot, Gustave. *A History of Canada*. Trans. Josephine Hambleton and Margaret M. Cameron. 3 vols. Cambridge, Mass.: Harvard University Press, 1963–65. Based on manuscript research by the former Archivist of the Dominion of Canada, this set is highly detailed but also highly ethnocentric. In it, Indians are mere savages in the most pejorative sense.

Leder, Lawrence H. *Robert Livingston, 1654–1728, and the Politics of Colonial New York*. Chapel Hill: University of North Carolina Press, for the Institute of Early American History and Culture, 1961. Biography of New York's first Secretary of Indian Affairs.

Le Roy de Bacqueville de la Potherie, Claude-Charles. *Histoire de l'Amérique septemtrionale.* 4 vols. Paris, 1722. Reprinted Rouen, 1722; Paris, 1753. A long extract translated into English in *The Indian Tribes of the Upper Mississippi Valley . . .* q.v., entitled "History of the Savage Peoples who are Allies of New France."

The Livingston Indian Records, 1666–1723. Ed. Lawrence H. Leder, with historical introduction by Paul A. W. Wallace. *Pennsylvania History* 23, no. 1 (Jan 1956), entire issue. Reprinted facsimile, Gettysburg, Pa.: Pennsylvania Historical Association, 1956. An assemblage of file copies of New York's first Secretary of Indian Affairs Robert Livingston. Does not duplicate documents in *N.Y.Col. Docs.* Mss. now in Franklin D. Roosevelt Library, Hyde Park, N.Y. Leder's preface notes: "It can be safely assumed that the Livingston Indian Records contain the bulk of the two missing volumes" of records of New York's Commissioners of Indian Affairs.

Logstown, Treaty of, 1752. Complementary, and sometimes contradictory, documents appear in the following:
1. "The Treaty of Logg's Town, 1752: Commission, Instructions, Etc,; Journal of Virginia Commissioners and Text of Treaty." *Virginia Magazine of History and Biography* 31 (1905–1906): 143–74.
2. *George Mercer Papers,* q.v., pp. 54–66 et passim; see index.

Lounsbury, Floyd G. "Iroquois Place-names in the Champlain Valley." *Report of the New York-Vermont Interstate Commission on the Lake Champlain Basin* 9 (1960): 23–66. Reprinted separately, Albany: University of the State of New York, 1960.

Mahon, John K. *The War of 1812.* Gainesville: University of Florida Press, 1972.

Manley, Henry Sackett. *The Treaty of Fort Stanwix, 1784 – First Attempt to Collect Facts Surrounding the Peace Negotiations by U.S. Congress and Six Nations after Britain Acknowledged the Freedom of Her Colonies.* Rome, N.Y.: Rome Sentinel Company, 1932.

Marshall, Peter. "Sir William Johnson and the Treaty of Fort Stanwix, 1768." [British] *Journal of American Studies* 1, no. 2 (1967): 149–79.

Marshe, Witham. "Journal of the Treaty . . . at Lancaster in Pennsylvania, June, 1744." In *Collections of the Massachusetts Historical Society,* 1st ser., 7:171–201. Reprinted as *Lancaster in 1744.* Ed. William H. Egle. Lancaster, Pa.: New Era Steam Book and Job Print, 1884. Valuable supplement to the official minutes; this journal described the circumstances of the treaty council. The original manuscript has disappeared.

Milliken, Charles. "The Kon-on-daigua Peace Congress." *New York State Archeological Association Research and Transactions* 2, no. 3 (1920): 67–79.

Minutes of the Provincial Council of Pennsylvania (spine title Colonial Records). Ed. Samuel Hazard. 16 vols. Vols. 1–3 published, Harrisburg: Theophilus Fenn, 1838–40. Reprinted, different pagination, Philadelphia: Jo. Severns and Co., 1852. Vols. 4–16 published, Harrisburg: Theo. Fenn, 1851–53. Essential sources for Pennsylvania's Indian affairs.

Morgan, Lewis H. *League of the Ho-dé-no-sau-nee, Iroquois.* Rochester: Sage and Brother, 1851. Reprinted, 2 vols. ed. Herbert M. Lloyd, New York: Dodd, Mead, 1901. Reprinted New Haven, Ct.: Human Relations Area Files, 1954. Facsimile reprint of 1st ed., intro. William N. Fenton, New York: Corinth Books, 1962. An anthropological classic. Morgan's description of kinship structures and political organization in the Iroquois League is still respected today. Morgan is called the Founder of American anthropology. As a cultural evolutionist, he is also regarded as authoritative by Marxist philosophers although his outlook was capitalistic.

Nammack, Georgiana C. *Fraud, Politics, and the Dispossession of the Indians: The Iroquois Land Frontier in the Colonial Period.* Norman: University of Oklahoma Press, 1969. Except for an introductory chapter, deals with the eighteenth century.

Narratives of New Netherland, 1609–1664. Ed. J. Franklin Jameson. Original Narratives of Early American History series. New York: Charles Scribner's Sons, 1909. Rpt. New York; Barnes and Noble, 1959.

Nash, Gary B. "The Quest for the Susquehanna Valley: New York, Pennsylvania, and the Seventeenth-Century Fur Trade." *New York History* 48 (1967): 3–27.

New York (State) Legislature. Assembly. *Report of Special Committee to Investigate the Indian Problem of the State of New York, Appointed by the Assembly of 1888.* Albany: Troy Press Co., 1889.

Nicks, Trudy. "The Iroquois and the Fur Trade in Western Canada." in *Old Trails and New Directions: Papers of the Third North American Fur Trade Conference.* Eds. Carol M. Judd and Arthur J. Ray. Toronto: University of Toronto Press, 1980, pp. 85–101.

N.Y.Col.Docs. = *Documents Relative to the Colonial History of the State of New York,* q.v.

Northeast. Ed. Bruce G. Trigger. Vol. 15 of *Handbook of North American Indians.* Gen. ed. William C. Sturtevant. Washington, D.C.: Smithsonian Institution Press, 1978. A collection of authoritative essays grouped on regional and tribal topics. Nearly all the contributors are ethnologists, archaeologists, or linguists, with a small minority of historians. Viewpoints and interests vary. Handsomely and authoritatively illustrated, and has many maps.

Norton, John. *The Journal of Major John Norton, 1816.* Ed. with introductions and notes by Carl F. Klinck and James J. Talman. Publications of the Champlain Society 46. Toronto, 1970. Norton (d. 1831?) was a synethnic son of a Scottish mother and a Cherokee father. As an adult he was adopted by the Mohawks on Grand River Reserve where he learned their language and traditions. He became an officer in the Indian Department of the British army.

Norton, Thomas Elliot. *The Fur Trade in Colonial New York, 1686–1776.* Madison: University of Wisconsin Press, 1974.

The Olden Time. Ed. Neville B. Craig. 2 vols. (1846–48). Rpt. Cincinnati: Robert Clarke and Co., 1876. A collection of sources, rare at the time, made by an antiquarian and first published in periodical format.

Pa. Council Minutes. = *Minutes of the Provincial Council of Pennsylvania,* q.v.

Parker, Arthur C. *The Life of General Ely S. Parker, Last Grand Sachem of the Iroquois and General Grant's Military Secretary*. Buffalo Historical Society Publications 23. Buffalo, N.Y., 1919. Arthur C. Parker was a Seneca Indian, nephew to the renowned Ely S. Parker. He became an anthropologist and museum curator and wrote several highly respected monographs on Iroquois culture. His *Constitution*, however, is controversial. See Fenton's Introduction to *Parker on the Iroquois*.

Parker, Arthur C. *Parker on the Iroquois*. Ed. William N. Fenton. Syracuse, N.Y.: Syracuse University Press, 1968. Includes Editor's Introduction and three studies by Arthur C. Parker: *Iroquois Uses of Maize and Other Food Plants; The Code of Handsome Lake, the Seneca Prophet; The Constitution of the Five Nations*.

Pearce, Roy Harvey. *The Savages of America: A Study of the Indian and the Idea of Civilization*. Baltimore: Johns Hopkins University Press, 1953. Rev. ed. 1965, rpt. as *Savagism and Civilization: A Study of the Indian and the American Mind*. Baltimore: Johns Hopkins University Press, 1967.

Peckham, Howard H. *Pontiac and the Indian Uprising*. Chicago: University of Chicago Press, 1947. Rpt. Phoenix paperback, 1961. Corrects and supersedes Francis Parkman's *Conspiracy of Pontiac*.

Pennsylvania Archives. 9 series, 138 vols. Philadelphia and Harrisburg, 1852–1949. Papers on the colonial and Revolutionary period of Pennsylvania supplemental to the *Minutes of the Provincial Council*. 8th series is the *Votes and Proceedings of the House of Representatives* (Assembly).

Pennsylvania Historical Survey, Work Projects Administration. *Wilderness Chronicles of Northwestern Pennsylvania*. Eds. Sylvester K. Stevens and Donald H. Kent. Harrisburg: Pennsylvania Historical Commission, 1941. An assemblage of French and English sources relevant to the region.

Prevost, Augustine. Diary, in "Turmoil at Pittsburgh," ed. Nicholas Wainwright *Pennsylvania Magazine of History and Biography* 85 (1961): 129–48.

Proceedings of the Commissioners of Indian Affairs Appointed by Law for the Extinguishment of Indian Tribes in the State of New York. Ed. Franklin B. Hough. Published from the original manuscript in the library of the Albany Institute of History and Art. 2 vols. Albany: Joel Munsell, 1861. Covers the period 1784–90. Includes texts of several treaties between the Iroquois and New York State.

Richter, Daniel K. "Rediscovered Links in the Covenant Chain: Previously Unpublished Transcripts of New York Indian Treaty Minutes, 1677–1691." *Proceedings of the American Antiquarian Society* 92, pt.1 (April 1982): 45–85.

———. "War and Culture: The Iroquois Experience." *William and Mary Quarterly* 3d ser., 40(1983), 528–59.

Ritzenthaler, Robert. *The Oneida Indians of Wisconsin*. Bulletin of the Public Museum of the City of Milwaukee 19, no. 1 (1950).

Seeber, Edward D. "Critical Views of Logan's Speech." *Journal of American Folklore* 60, no. 236 (1947): 130–46.

Shea, John Gilmary. *History of the Catholic Missions Among the Indian Tribes of the United States, 1529–1854.* New York: P.J. Kenedy, 1883.

Simcoe, J. G. *The Correspondence of Lieut. Governor John Graves Simcoe.* Ed. E. A. Cruikshank. 5 vols. Toronto: Ontario Historical Society, 1923–31. Negotiations with the Iroquois dispersed from New York into Canada after the American Revolution.

Smith, Donald B. "Who are the Mississauga?" *Ontario History* 17, no. 4 (Dec 1975): 211–22.

Synderman, George S. "Behind the Tree of Peace: A Sociological Analysis of Iroquois Warfare." *Pennsylvania Archaeologist* 18 (Fall 1948), entire issue.

——. "The Function of Wampum in Iroquois Religion." *Proceedings of the American Philosophical Society* 105, no. 6 (1961): 571–608.

Sosin, Jack M. "The British Indian Department and Dunmore's War." *Virginia Magazine of History and Biography* 74 (1966): 34–50.

——. *The Revolutionary Frontier, 1763–1783.* New York: Holt, Rinehart and Winston, 1967. The perspective is generally that of the frontiersman.

——. *Whitehall and the Wilderness: The Middle West in British Colonial Policy, 1760–1775.* Lincoln: University of Nebraska Press, 1961. Research based heavily on British mss. sources.

Spotswood, Alexander. *The Official Letters of Alexander Spotswood, Lieutenant Governor of the Colony of Virginia, 1710–1722.* Ed. Robert A. Brock. 2 vols. Collections of the Virginia Historical Society, New Series. Richmond, 1882, 1885. Spotswood was active in Indian affairs, often frustrated by the Iroquois.

Stagg, Jack. *Anglo-Indian Relations In North America To 1763 And An Analysis of The Royal Proclamation of 7 October 1763.* Ottawa: Research Branch, Indian and Northern Affairs Canada, 1981. A highly documented policy study of the period 1748 to 1763.

Stanley, G. F. G. "The First Indian 'Reserves' in Canada." *Revue d'Histoire de l'Amerique Francais* 4, no. 2 (Sept 1950): 178–210.

——. "The Significance of the Six Nations Participation in the War of 1812." *Ontario History* 55, no. 4 (1963): 215–32.

Surtees, Robert J. *Canadian Indian Policy: A Critical Bibliography.* Bloomington, Ind.: Indiana University Press for The Newberry Library, 1982.

——. *Indian Land Surrenders in Ontario, 1763–1867.* Ottawa: Indian and Northern Affairs Canada, 1984.

Sutton, Imre. *Indian Land Tenure: Bibliographical Essays and a Guide to the Literature.* New York: Clearwater Publishing Co., 1975. The standard work.

The Statutes at Large of the Provisional Government of the Confederate States of America from the Institution of the Government, February 8, 1861, to its Termination, February 18, 1862, Inclure. Arranged in Chronological Order, Together with the Constitution for Provisional Government, and the Permanent Constitution of the Con-

federate States, and the Treaties Concluded by the Confederate States with the Indian Tribes. Ed. James M. Matthews. Richmond: R.M. Smith, 1864.

Tehanetorens (Aren Akweks). *Wampum Belts.* Onchiota, N.Y.: Six Nations Indian Museum, 1947. A handy pamphlet of wampum pictures and their significance.

Tilghman, Tench. *Memoir of Lt. Colonel Tench Tilghman, Secretary and Aid to Washington, Together with an Appendix, Containing Revolutionary Journals and Letters Hitherto Unpublished.* Ed. Samuel Alexander Hanison. Albany: J. Munsell, 1876. Tilghman was Secretary of the Indian Commissioners from the 13 United Colonies at the treaty with the Six Nations at German Flats, New York. His memoir includes an account of the treaty.

Tooker, Elisabeth. *The Indians of the Northeast: A Critical Bibliography.* Bloomington: Indiana University Press, 1978.

————. *The Iroquois Ceremonial of Midwinter.* Syracuse, N.Y.: Syracuse University Press, 1970.

Torok, Charles H. "The Tyendinaga Mohawks: The Village as a Basic Factor in Mohawk Social Structure." *Ontario History* 57, no. 2 (1965): 69–77.

Treaties, Land Cessions, and Other U.S. Congressional Documents Relative to American Indian Tribes. Greeley: University of Northern Colorado, 1970– . Multivolume set still in process of publication.

Trelease, Allen W. *Indian Affairs in Colonial New York: The Seventeenth Century.* Ithaca, N.Y.: Cornell University Press, 1960. An important and readable scholarly synthesis.

Trigger, Bruce G. "Archeological and Other Evidence: A Fresh Look at the 'Laurentian Iroquois.'" *American Antiquity* 33, no. 4 (1968): 429–40.

Trigger, Bruce G. *The Children of Aataentsic: A History of the Huron People to 1660.* 2 vols. Montreal: McGill-Queens University Press, 1976. A classic of ethnohistory written by an anthropologist/archaeologist. Authoritative on the Hurons and now the standard work on the Iroquoian "Beaver Wars" of the mid-17th century.

————. "Hochelaga: History and Ethnohistory." In *Cartier's Hochelaga and the Dawson Site.* Eds. James F. Pendergast and Bruce C. Trigger. Montreal: McGill-Queen's University Press, 1972, pp. 1–93. Evidence and argument concerning the Laurentian Iroquois.

Trudel, Marcel. *The Beginnings of New France, 1524–1662.* Toronto: McClelland and Stewart, 1973.

Tuck, James A. *Onondaga Iroquois Prehistory: A Study in Settlement Archaeology.* Syracuse, N.Y.: Syracuse University Press, 1971. Argues that Iroquois culture developed *in situ.*

Upton, Helen M. *The Everett Report in Historical Perspective: The Indians of New York.* Albany: New York State American Revolution Bicentennial Commission, 1980. Investigation of controversial report by the Everett Commission to the New York State Legislature about relations between the Iroquois and New York State.

The legislature refused to accept the report which disappeared for many years after it was made.

The Valley of the Six Nations. Ed. C. M. Johnston. Publications of the Champlain Society, Ontario Series 7. Toronto, 1964.

Van den Bogaert, Hermen Meyndertsz. "Narratives of a Journey into Mohawk and Oneida County, 1634–1635." *Narratives of New Netherland*, q.v., pp. 135–62. Original Dutch mss. is in Henry E. Huntington Library, San Marino, California, MS. 819.

Van der Donck, Adriaen. *A Description of the New Netherlands* (1655). Tr., 1841 by Jeremiah Johnson for *Collections of the New York Historical Society*, 2d ser., Vol. 1. Reprint ed. ed. Thomas F. O'Donnell. Syracuse, N.Y.: Syracuse University Press, 1968. The section "Of Manners and Peculiar Customs of the Natives of the New Netherlands" is one of the most valuable early sources.

Wallace, Anthony F. C. *The Death and Rebirth of the Seneca.* New York: Alfred A. Knopf, 1970. Ethnohistorical study focusing on the revitalization movement of Handsome Lake.

———. *King of the Delawares: Teedyuscung, 1700–1763.* Philadelphia: University of Pennsylvania Press, 1949. Required reading on the Delaware land tenure system and the Walking Purchase.

———. "Origins of Iroquois Neutrality: The Grand Settlement of 1701." *Pennsylvania History* 24 (1957): 223–35. A disputed interpretation.

Wallace, Paul A. W. *Conrad Weiser, 1696–1760, Friend of Colonist and Mohawk.* Philadelphia: University of Pennsylvania Press, 1945. An exemplary biography of a provincial interpreter in Indian affairs. Contains many long extracts from unpublished manuscripts.

———. *Indians in Pennsylvania.* Harrisburg: Pennsylvania Historical and Museum Commission, 1961. A popular and reliable short account. Excellent introduction to the subject.

———. *The White Roots of Peace.* Philadelphia: University of Pennsylvania Press, 1946. The constitution legend of the Iroquois as given in the Gibson-Hewitt mss. translated by W. N. Fenton.

Wampum. A sampling of wampum literature is given in note 2 of Michael K. Foster's chapter 5 herein.

Washington, George. *The Diaries of George Washington, 1748–1799.* Ed. John C. Fitzpatrick. 4 vols. Boston: Houghton Mifflin Co., 1925.

Webb, Stephen Saunders. *1676: The End of American Independence.* New York: Knopf, 1984. Argues that the Covenant Chain was an "Anglo-Iroquois empire."

Wilson, Edmund. *Apologies to the Iroquois.* New York: Farrar, Straus and Cudahy, 1960.

Wraxall, Peter. *An Abridgment of the Indian Affairs Contained in Four Folio Volumes, Transacted in the Colony of New York, from the Year 1678 to the Year 1751.* Ed. with intro. by Charles Howard McIlwain. Harvard Historical Studies 21. Cambridge, Mass.: Harvard University Press, 1915. Rpt. New York: Benjamin Blom, 1968.

The selection and extracting are tendentious in support of the policies of Sir William Johnson whom Wraxall served as secretary. Nevertheless, the book contains much material unavailable elsewhere. McIlwain's introduction has been highly influential though not unchallenged.

Wright, Asher. "Seneca Indians" (1859). Ed. W. N. Fenton. *Ethnohistory* 4, no. 3 (1957): 302–21.

Worth, Lawrence C. "The Indian Treaty as Literature." *Yale Review* 17 (1928): 749–66.

INDEX

Abenaquis, 70
Ahookasoongh, 40
Algonquians, 17, 25, 41, 68, 70, 99
American Revolution: 57–58; change in treaty practices following, 25; Iroquois confederacy and, 30–31, 57–59, 69–70, 100–101, 117
American Society for Ethnohistory, xvii
Amherst, Lord, 55, 69
Andros, Gov. Edmund, 120, 122

Beauchamp, William M., 89, 123
Beaver Wars, 39
Boyd, Julian B., 6
Braddock, Gen. Edward, 52–53
Brant, Joseph, 13, 15, 30, 73–79, 94
Brant, Molly, 56
Bruyas, Father, 67
Buffalo Creek, 31
Butler, John, 93

Canadian Indian Act (1924), 31
Canaqueese, 25
Canasatego, 27, 46, 49, 124
Canondondawe, 20
Captain John. See John Deseronto
Cartier, Jacques, 67
Catawbas, 40
Caughnawaga Iroquois, 58, 68–73, 75, 79–80
Cayugas: 7, 11, 15, 30–31, 40–42, 58, 69, 94, 102, 104, 106, 116, 120; current government, 71; multiple chiefships, 9
Champlain, Samuel de, 39
Chaumont, Father, 67
Cherokees, 58, 94
Chickasaws, 58

Chippewas, 58, 79, 118
Choctaws, 58
Clans. See Iroquois social structure
Clinton, Dewitt, 26
Colden, Cadwallader, 4–5
Communication barriers: interpretation, 4–5, 26, 87; non-verbal, 26; verbal, 25–26
Communication patterns: Iroquois-European differences, 103
Condolence Council: 3–5, 17–22, 124; first recorded performance, 20; foundation of, 18; program of events, 18–21; treaty protocol and, 6, 18–22, 30, 101–108
Condolence Council moieties: 10–11; Elder brothers–Younger brothers principle, 11, 104; four brothers–female principle, 11; three brothers–male principle, 11
Conestogas, 39–43
Cornplanter. See Captain O'Bail
Covenant Chain: 20–24, 37–44; dissolving, 42, 45; evolution, 116, 121; formation (1677), 116; sites of treaty negotiations, 43
Creeks, 58
Croghan, George, 49, 54

Dablon, Father, 67
Decanisora, 40–41
Deganawidah, 14–15, 60
Deganawidah epic: 9, 14–18; Iroquois constitution, 15
Delawares: 9–10, 25–26, 41–43, 48, 50, 58, 88, 115, 120; eastern, 53–55; loss of land rights, 45–47, 124; Ohio, 48–49, 51, 53–55, 124
Deseronto, John, 73–75
Diadorus, 21
Dinwiddie, Gov. Robert, 50–51

275

THE HISTORY AND CULTURE OF IROQUOIS DIPLOMACY

was composed in 10-point Digital Compugraphic Goudy Old Style and leaded 2 points
by Metricomp Studios,
with display type in Goudy Handtooled by Dix Typesetting Co., Inc.;
printed by sheet-fed offset on 50-pound, acid-free, Glatfelter Antique Cream,
Smythe-sewn and bound over 80-point binder's boards in Joanna Arrestox B,
by Maple-Vail Book Manufacturing Group, Inc.;
and published by

SYRACUSE UNIVERSITY PRESS
SYRACUSE, NEW YORK 13210